LIFE AFTER NUCLEAR WAR

LIFE AFTER NUCLEAR WAR
The Economic and Social Impacts of Nuclear Attacks on the United States

ARTHUR M. KATZ

BALLINGER PUBLISHING COMPANY
Cambridge, Massachusetts
A Subsidiary of Harper & Row, Publishers, Inc.

International Standard Book Number: 0-88410-096-0 (H.B.)
0-88410-907-0 (P.B.)
Library of Congress Catalog Card Number: 81-1300

Printed in the United States of America

Second printing, February, 1982

Library of Congress Cataloging in Publication Data

Katz, Arthur, 1942–
   Life after nuclear war.

   Includes index.
   1. Atomic warfare – Economic aspects – United States.
   2. Atomic warfare and society – United States.   I.   Title.
UF767.K34   355′.0217   81-1300
ISBN 0-88410-096-0 (H.B.)   AACR2
      0-88410-907-0 (P.B.)

DEDICATION

To Dara and Margaret, with love

CONTENTS

About the Author

LIST OF FIGURES

LIST OF TABLES

FOREWORD

As the bomb fell over Hiroshima and exploded, we saw an entire city disappear. I wrote in my log the words: "My God, what have we done?"

Robert C. Lewis
American Aviator

A developer in Utah puts the finishing touches on a community of disaster-proof condominiums sunk under three feet of earth and eight inches of concrete. The units come complete with air and water filtration systems, independent utilities, and a decontamination chamber. Other "survivalists," perhaps numbering a thousand, are scattered across the country with C–rations and Geiger counters stockpiled in basements.

Their vigil is looked upon with amusement by some as an anachronism from the Cold War 50s and 60s. Nevertheless, the survivalists sit and wait, for the odds continue to mount that they may end up among the living who will pick through the rubble to bury, or worse, envy the dead.

The facts speak for themselves. Six nations now belong to the nuclear club. Another 30 stand in the wings with either the capability or desire to go nuclear. More than 30,000 warheads are now stockpiled throughout the world, equal to the force of over 1 million Hiroshima-sized bombs. Another 10,000 will likely come off the assembly lines by the end of the decade—all this, despite evidence

that the United States and the Soviet Union would be destroyed in
an hour with a few hundred. Yet strategic war gamers on both sides
talk of a winnable nuclear war through limited attacks with pinpoint
targeting.

The atomic bomb, which George F. Kennan described as "the
most useless weapon ever invented," has become the dominant
weapon of our time. The defense of America, a subject largely dor-
mant since the painful days of Vietnam, is now on everyone's minds,
from Main Street to the Pentagon, from the think tanks to the halls
of Congress. Fearful that the military edge has slipped to the Soviets,
the United States has launched the largest defense buildup since
World War II—a staggering $1.5 trillion worth over the next five
years.

The debate over how much we should spend has been settled. We
have decided to spend more. The remaining issue is how to spend this
military largess—a decision that pits the fantasies of the strategist
with the reality of the battlefield. "Human kind cannot bear very
much reality," wrote T.S. Eliot. Strategic military and civil defense
planners suffer from the same affliction.

The defense of America is premised on the retaliatory attack—
that is, the ability of the United States to launch enough of its 9,000-
odd strategic warheads to destroy the Soviet Union should it decide
to strike first. This doctrine of mutually assured destruction, however, has relegated the notion of survival to a back seat. Or, to put it
another way, we have become so preoccupied with arming for Armageddon, we have largely ignored the fact that the nation that wins a
nuclear war may not survive it.

A nuclear conflict between the United States and the Soviet Union
will incinerate life as the two societies now know it, but it will not
destroy mankind. There will be people left on this planet after the
silos are emptied—the occupants of those Utah condominiums possibly, the survivalists with their C–rations and Geiger counters, and
millions more.

What will life be like after the bombs have fallen? Perceptions have
stopped far short of reality. Civil defense analysts have displayed a
surprising degree of tunnel vision in forecasting the effects of nuclear
war by studying only the number of casualties and the amount of
physical damage. To be sure, casualty and damage figures are valuable pieces of information that by themselves paint a picture beyond

comprehension. (Can anyone really imagine *90 million* Americans perishing in a full-scale nuclear war?) But dwelling on body and building counts creates a serious misapprehension in our analyses of life after the bombs have dropped. It assumes that when the radioactive dust settles, the remaining population and industry will comprise a viable nation, albeit one with 40 percent fewer people and 80 percent less productive capacity.

Dr. Arthur M. Katz's book, *Life After Nuclear War*, offers a much needed dose of reality to this subject. A thorough debate of the effects of nuclear war, reports Dr. Katz, should include not only a discussion of who or what is left standing, but also a consideration of the social, economic, institutional, political, and psychological traumas faced by the survivors.

Dr. Katz first explored this issue in a study he prepared for Congress's Joint Committee on Defense Production, which I chaired. *Life After Nuclear War* is an updated and expanded version of that 1979 study.

Dr. Katz's conclusions: The casualty figures from a nuclear attack would be gruesome, the physical damage would be devastating; but equally ominous would be the dismemberment of the social, economic, and institutional relationships that hold a nation together.

Banks would fold from evacuees drawing out accounts. Farms not contaminated would have no transportation system to haul their goods to market. Areas not struck would become clogged with evacuees. Millions of managers, supervisors, technicians, and administrators—the people needed to organize a recovery—would be dead. Distrust of government and its leaders, already prevalent, would increase. Uncontaminated survivors would be suspicious of the survivors nearer the explosions, fearing they might spread the radiation. The problems are endless.

Even in a limited nuclear war, in which 20 million persons die as a result of an attack on our land-based missiles, the damage might be more extensive than the strategic planners envision. The industrial bottlenecks alone would be enough to create economic chaos here and abroad. Furthermore, public pressure and outrage might prevent the political leadership from keeping a limited war limited.

New relocation concepts are being considered by civil defense experts to reduce the damage and death toll. Evacuation studies indicate that in small and medium sized cities, many lives could be saved with an orderly dispersal program. Even so, Dr. Katz's findings should offer fair warning that the aftermath will be far more nightmarish than we have heretofore imagined.

Strategic decisions should be based on both an accurate assessment of our military posture and an accurate projection of our losses once the guns have fired. If this is done, we may finally come to the realization that the only answer to survival is the reduction of the nuclear armaments that have brought us to this precipice. SALT I and SALT II merely place limits on the expansion of our arsenals. It is time to move vigorously forward with negotiations that actually *reduce* the number of nuclear weapons on each side, before Dr. Katz's post-holocaust projection becomes reality.

William Proxmire
United States Senator

PREFACE

This book evolved out of a decade-long exploration of the meaning of nuclear war for society. In the early 1970s I was a staff member to a modest effort by the Arms Control Seminar at MIT to examine the effects of nuclear war on Massachusetts. Our work there grew into a broader examination of the national effects of urban, economically oriented nuclear war. One result of these efforts was a report, *Economic and Social Effects of Nuclear War on the United States*, which I wrote for the Joint Committee on Defense Production of the U.S. Congress; this report was published in 1979 by the Senate Committee on Banking, Housing and Urban Affairs after the Joint Committee's dissolution. Part III and to a lesser degree Part I of this book are based on that report.

Because of its growing appeal during the mid-1970s I began to examine the issue of limited nuclear war—that is, military oriented attacks. Ironically, within the normal definition of full-scale urban attacks, even the economically oriented attacks discussed in this book are limited in size. My hope in combining all of these variations of nuclear war is that the reader will carry away a respect for the meaning of nuclear war in all its guises and an ability to cut through the strategic planning rhetoric to ask some fundamental and demanding questions of military planners.

This book is not a product of my personal efforts alone, and I gratefully acknowledge the assistance of many people. I would like to express my profound thanks to a thoughtful critic and supportive and gracious human being, Professor Bernard Feld. It was he who guided me through the early stages of my studies while I was working for him on the MIT Arms Control Seminar. I also extend my deepest appreciation for their help and support to other members of the Seminar: Francis Low, Viktor Teplitz, Leo Sartori, Steven Weinberg, and particularly, Henry Kendall and James MacKenzie. Over the years Geoffrey Kemp, Ted Greenwood, Kosta Tsipis, George Rathjens, and Newell Mack read innumerable drafts; I am indebted to all of them for their incisive criticism and generous support.

My admiration and thanks go to Peter Scharfman of the Office of Technology Assessment, whose understanding and patient communication of the subtleties of strategic issues enhanced substantially my understanding and, I hope, the quality of my discussion of these issues. I would also like to thank Marshall Goldman for his thoughtful review of Chapter 10.

My largest debt of gratitude is owed to William Kincade, who as staff director of the Joint Committee on Defense Production saw the potential of my work and helped to shape it intellectually and editorially into the committee study. After the Joint Committee was dissolved, he continued to work with me at considerable sacrifice to time spent on his own doctoral thesis and with his family. Even after this truly demanding effort he made the time to review and criticize constructively drafts of this book. He is a true friend. Whatever value this book is deemed to have, he deserves recognition as a substantial contributor to creating it.

I would like to thank sincerely Senator William Proxmire for his support of the original report and for his later assistance in making possible the publication of this book. Ron Tammen and Leon Reed were always ready to help in times of trouble, for which I am deeply grateful. The person who deserves the award for valor in the face of trying circumstances and congressional reorganization is Martha Braddock; she managed to oversee the painful progress of my congressional report. Also deserving recognition for extraordinary efforts are Lory Breneman and Sharon Carter who turned illegible scrawl into typed copy, and Ed Mallon who worked wonders in getting the final committee report into print.

I am very grateful to Michael Connolly, president, and Carol Franco, editor, of Ballinger Publishing Company, who believed enough in this book to support its publication. Carol and Ruth Chasek, copyeditor, are gratefully acknowledged for helping to edit and organize this book. My sincere appreciation also goes to Steven Cramer, assistant editor at Ballinger, who was always helpful and tolerant as he struggled to bring this book to fruition. To a good friend, Sarah Andrew, who applied her considerable editorial talents under severe time pressures and shaped this book as best she could into its final form, I want to express my deepest appreciation and affection. Bonnie Jones was efficient in typing the revised version of this book, and Linda Heffner always found a way to assure that help was available when I most needed it. Finally, I want to thank my wife, Sima Osdoby, who endured the demands of this book while providing her usual forthright and constructive comments. Of course, any errors and shortcomings are entirely my own.

Arthur M. Katz
Rockville, Maryland

LIFE AFTER NUCLEAR WAR

UNDERSTANDING DISASTER

Turning and turning in the widening gyre
The falcon cannot hear the falconer;
Things fall apart; the centre cannot hold;
Mere anarchy is loosed upon the world,
The blood-dimmed tide is loosed, and everywhere
The ceremony of innocence is drowned;
The best lack all conviction, while the worst
Are full of passionate intensity.

—William Butler Yeats, "The Second Coming"

1 OVERVIEW

And we are here as on a darkling plain
Swept with confused alarms of struggle and flight,
Where ignorant armies clash by night.

                Matthew Arnold, "Dover Beach"

Nuclear war conjures up images of mass destruction and mutilation—images so overwhelming that they normally represent the end, not the beginning, of a dialogue. Yet in the 1950s and early 1960s a great deal of energy was devoted to thinking and arguing publicly about the "unthinkable"—nuclear war and its effects. Could the United States survive and win a nuclear war? The cold war atmosphere and recent experiences at Hiroshima and Nagasaki imbued this question with a frightening reality.

However, in the 1960s strategic thinking moved away from a strategy of fighting a nuclear war to making it genuinely unthinkable. The concept of deterrence or MAD (Mutually Assured Destruction) evolved. MAD sought to assure that both adversaries retained enough nuclear weapons, even after a surprise attack (first strike), to inflict totally unacceptable damage on the other. An adversary, therefore, would be deterred from initiating a nuclear war because the outcome would be inevitable and devastating. The concept became embedded in U.S. policy and negotiation strategy. The effect of accepting the MAD doctrine as the basis of nuclear policy was that over the next

3

decade, while nuclear technology advanced, the reality of nuclear war faded. It appeared remote and unbelievable—a possibility that could not happen.

However, rapid improvements in technology—embodied particularly in the proliferation of nuclear warheads (multiple independent reentry vehicles or MIRVs), increased accuracy, and targeting flexibility[1] —made possible a change from a "blunderbuss" urban retaliation to a capability to destroy selectively critical military as well as civilian targets. These changes provided a new impetus for the emergence of proposals that spoke of a "controlled" nuclear war—a more subtle, benign, and surgically accurate nuclear war; a possible extension of conventional war.

The influence of technology and its ability to enhance the credibility of nuclear "war fighting" was evident in the change in U.S. strategic policy represented by Presidential Directive 59 issued in 1980.[2] Although characterized as extending deterrence to blunt the impacts of sophisticated small scale nuclear attacks, it nevertheless reflects a changed technological reality that brings us closer to a model of low level nuclear war. The result of these changes is that the debate about nuclear strategy in the 1980s and 1990s is likely to intensify as technology provides a Pandora's box of possibilities.

Paralleling these policy and technology changes is the re-emergence of interest in nuclear war and its effects as part of the serious discussion and controversy over the direction of U.S. strategic nuclear policy. A realistic understanding of the effects of nuclear war is needed so that the implicit assumptions upon which nuclear policy alternatives are based may be understood. This is essential since some strategies are based on particularly precarious assumptions about our ability to foresee the effects and control the response to nuclear war.

This book attempts to provide a level of understanding of nuclear war effects that can be used by those involved in trying to formulate strategic policy in the executive, Congress and most importantly the general public. It is designed to build a framework, a basis to evaluate whether the many proposed technological and strategic policy alternatives make any real sense. This will be accomplished by examining in detail the effects and underlying assumptions of various types of nuclear war. The book will also develop a frame of reference (criteria) to judge the credibility of nuclear strategies.

Chapter 1 will construct the framework for the rest of the book. It will define the problem, present an approach, and identify the larger domestic and international context needed to determine accurately the effects of nuclear strategies. This chapter attempts to create a larger canvas within which to examine nuclear strategies. The second chapter in Part I provides a discussion of the physical effects of nuclear weapons.

THE QUESTION

Despite the discussion of options created by sophisticated technology, the plausibility of any strategic policy depends on the projection of the implications—political, military, economic, and social—of the effects of nuclear war.

The previous estimates of damage to society have seriously understated the true extent of these effects because of their narrow focus. They are often based upon crude physical measures of destruction, such as human fatalities and casualties, number of cities destroyed, or damage to overall economic capacity. These indicators alone do not exhaust the direct and indirect effects of nuclear weapons on society. Particularly, they do not identify the "interactive effects," effects of one part of society upon another—for example, the impact of damage to one industry on the productive capacity of other industries. In addition, they underemphasize the impact of social and political reactions to nuclear war. Thus, previous studies do not give a complete picture of the potential vulnerabilities and strengths of complex industrial societies. Nor, except in the crudest terms, do they speak to the issue of the "acceptability" or "unacceptability" of nuclear attack damage.

These deficiencies have created serious misconceptions about the survival of national power and political flexibility after a variety of nuclear war situations. These misconceptions in turn can lead, and in some cases have led, to dangerously flawed strategic policies. They have created inflated nuclear weapons requirements, emboldened advocates of war-fighting strategies, and exaggerated the possible flexibility available to political leaders during a nuclear conflict.

To correct these deficiencies and create a more accurate picture of the effects of nuclear war, several pivotal questions will be addressed: How damaging are nuclear attacks to society? What level of weapon capability is needed to insure that "unacceptable" damage is a reality? Or put more simply: How much is enough?

UNACCEPTABLE DAMAGE

The meaning of "unacceptable" damage is a key concept in the process of understanding nuclear war. This concept acts as a bridge between two types of apparently different but fundamentally similar issues.

The first use of the term has to do with the traditional concept of unacceptable damage — the ability (weapons required to survive) to wreak massive destruction on the urban centers and economic capability of a hostile society. What has changed in recent years is the potential sophistication of the paralyzing attack. The vast increase in numbers and accuracy of warheads implies the capability to develop a comprehensive but highly selective targeting strategy aimed at key economic and social structures. Thus this capability has created the possibility of minimizing the actual number of nuclear weapons needed to carry out a successful counterattack, while insuring that maximum damage could be inflicted on the highly integrated economic and social structure of a modern industrial society. This issue is encompassed in the question: How much is enough?

The second, more subtle, use of the term "unacceptable" revolves around the question of the validity of the concepts of military oriented ("limited") nuclear war and low-level nuclear conflict. These concepts assume that a high degree of rational political control can be exerted even during the most chaotic part of the crisis period. Unacceptable damage in this context defines at what level of destruction or disruption *political control* is lost and the goal of a limited or controllable nuclear war cannot be achieved.

For example, as conceived, limited nuclear war is a massive attack on U.S. (or Soviet) land-based ICBMs (intercontinental ballistic missiles) and, possibly on the air bases where nuclear-weapons-carrying bombers (strategic air command or SAC) are stationed and the few nuclear submarine support (maintenance) facilities (SSBNs). It was formulated on the assumption that because of increasing accuracy and remote siting (at least for ICBM bases), critically large numbers of ICBMs, bombers, and support bases could be destroyed without the attacked nation suffering extensive economic damage and massive civilian casualties. This, however, creates a dilemma for the attacked nation. The United States, for example, could only retaliate or "pull the trigger" effectively against urban targets, because the large losses of its most accurate missiles, the ICBMs, would make any attack against the Soviet Union's remaining land-based missiles ineffective. "Pulling the trigger," however, would turn the proposed minimal U.S. economic and population losses into a nightmare of massive destruction, since the Soviet Union in turn could then retaliate against U.S. urban areas. Under these circumstances to retaliate or not to retaliate becomes the ultimate political and psychological question—a political, not a military, question because despite its losses the United States, if it chose not to retaliate, would still retain a MAD capability, that is, its remaining submarines, ICBMs, and bombers would be sufficient to assure destruction of the Soviet Union.

What are the factors that would really shape the decision whether to retaliate? Under these circumstances, the United States would have to examine domestic and international damage. For example, if the United States chose not to retaliate, the most devastating international result of losses from a limited nuclear war would be a perceived inferiority and impotence in the eyes of other nations and, thus, potentially limited strength and flexibility on the world stage. Is this loss of status in the eyes of the world sufficiently damaging to initiate a more destructive nuclear exchange?

As noted above, one of the basic assumptions in any concept of limited nuclear exchanges is that the events following a nuclear exchange are subject to rational calculation by political leaders; that is, they are controllable. The success of rational calculation, however, is highly dependent on the type of damage absorbed in the attack and on how it is perceived by the population. If the public perception is one of vulnerability and danger in a chaotic postattack situation, the emotions generated by these reactions are likely to create a driving force for "pulling the trigger," especially in a prolonged conflict. As a consequence, political leadership wishing to retain power would be constrained to take actions appropriate to its citizens' expectations.[3] Thus, understanding the effects on society becomes an important part of determining the acceptability of limited nuclear war.

Both aspects of acceptability will be explored in the book, over a wide range of nuclear war scenarios.

ACCEPTABILITY: A BROADER VIEW

To judge the acceptability of a particular attack or strategy requires more than a description of the societal effects; a set of criteria for comparison is needed. These criteria are discussed below in terms of damage levels.

These levels of survival define the range of possible outcomes from nuclear war. In decreasing order of damage, they are:

1. *Biological Survival of Individuals.*   Individuals or groups of individuals survive, but not necessarily within the organized political, social, and economic structure of a modern society.

2. *Regional Survival of Political Structures.*   Some subnational political units survive as viable entities but without a functioning central government.

3. *Survival of a Central Government.*   Some form of viable, central control over all preattack national territory survives, but the effectiveness of this control may vary over an extremely wide range, depending on the specific nature and pattern of the attack(s). The ability to act independently on world affairs may also be restricted or eliminated.

4. *Survival Intact of Basic Societal Structure.*   Damage to the nation is characterized as relatively limited socially, politically, and economically. It remains viable, and while weakened, potentially capable of international independence. This last concept forms the basis of the notion of limited or controlled nuclear war.

These levels are qualitative because much of what will be identified as important has no numerical measure. In fact, except at the upper boundary of extreme damage, quantification is inevitably a misleading measure of the seriousness of a problem.

Sorting Out Survival.   The first two levels of survival, although often found in public discussion, make little sense in terms of the normal expectations of an organized society. Simple biological survival of some members of the species or survival at a subnational level could not be an acceptable outcome for a nation as a whole and still less for its government.

Levels 3 and 4 represent a more meaningful basis for discussion of the acceptability of nuclear attack damage, since they include the maintenance of a functioning national entity as well as some significant portion of the economic structure that supports a modern society.

Within the third level, however, there is considerable room for differing judgments as to what might constitute an acceptable or an unacceptable outcome of a nuclear exchange. One test of acceptability would be the maintenance of the minimum economic, political, and social capacity required for full recovery of the nation within a reasonable period of time. A higher standard would be the continued ability to play an effective independent global role, politically, economically, diplomatically, and militarily. This ability would be measured in relation to the analogous surviving capability of the attacking nation(s) and in relation to the capability of undamaged or less damaged nations that did not participate directly in the nuclear exchange. (The willingness and ability of either attacker or attacked to renew the nuclear war after an initial attack also has a bearing on these judgments.) The question becomes not *whether* the nation survives, but *what kind* of entity remains to fend for itself in the postattack world. This may not be an easy question to answer since it is conceivable that on a superficial level, substantial military and strategic capability equal to or more potent than other nations may remain. However, military power alone is not sufficient or necessarily effective if the social structure is in disarray or on the verge of collapse. In terms of acceptability, the issue is what constitutes an acceptable postattack national status, in relation to both domestic aspirations and international standing. This last point would also be true, but in a more subtle sense, for Level 4.

An extreme form of changed status for either the United States or the Soviet Union would be that of a client state, implying that foreign policy and/or internal institutions are controlled to some degree by other nations. This was the status of Japan and Germany after World War II. It continues to be the status, in differing degrees, of Eastern European countries.

The criteria used to judge vulnerability may differ sharply from nation to nation. It depends on each nation's current world status, on its aspirations, and on its perceived as well as real vulnerabilities. For example, the Soviet Union lies near a hostile China, a potentially unstable Eastern Europe, and a potentially unfriendly Western Europe and Japan. All of these bordering states have or could have nuclear weapons. Under these conditions, it is legitimate to ask whether the Soviet leadership's concept of acceptable economic and societal damage will require lower levels of destruction than the more isolated United States, which has a history of reasonably cordial relations with its neighbors. Expressed another way, will a nation, perceiving itself surrounded by potentially hostile powers, be willing to absorb much damage and still call it acceptable if it runs the risk of falling prey to the traditional enmity of its neighbors or to the latent ethnic aspirations of populations within its borders? This would also be true in a somewhat different vein for a country such as the United States, whose vulnerability to manipulation of key resources (e.g., petroleum) by hostile or unstable foreign nations is an established experience.

An additional and important question not often addressed in crude estimates of postattack physical damage relates to the more general postattack international situation. A nuclear exchange of the magnitude addressed in Part III of this book implies serious damage in the Soviet Union, the United States, and probably Europe, Japan, and China. Major political upheavals and contests for hegemony in various regions of the world are possible consequences of large-scale nuclear attacks and may significantly affect responses to requests for immediate or long-term recovery assistance. This would occur apart from the basic limitations on the ability of less advanced regions to provide such assistance.

Upheavals of this magnitude would be triggered for the limited damage described by Level 4. Under these circumstances of conflict and uncertainty, the world financial markets, and world trade, particularly the exchange of valuable commodities such as petroleum and food, would fluctuate wildly in this atmosphere leading to a pervasive and desperate period of world instability. Limited nuclear war is a prime example of the type of attack that would induce international reactions of this type, particularly in a period of prolonged stalemate. In this case, the reactions would be related more to perceived weakness or disorganization in the attacked nation and the strength and intentions of the attacker than simply to the extent of physical damage.

This discussion does not exhaust the list of variables that have a significant bearing on how national survival is defined by different nations. It is sufficient here to point out that in the aftermath of a nuclear exchange, all of the preexisting political, economic, and military relationships that define the preattack international environment will not remain the same. No judgments on national survival that exclude consideration of potential changes in the international scene will be complete or adequate.

A FLAWED APPROACH

Strategic decisions are essentially political decisions. In contrast with the necessarily narrower perspective of military or civil defense planners, the officials who must make strategic decisions, as well as the public that have to support them, need to understand the full range of possible consequences of nuclear war and to appreciate its complexity.

To understand fully the consequences of nuclear war for society, it is necessary to examine some of the possible effects of nuclear war on the complex relationships among the economic, social, and political elements that define a modern industrial state. To satisfy that need, this book attempts to evaluate some of the "secondary effects" of these nuclear attacks on the American economy and society—for example, on the quality of medical care after a nuclear attack—and their impact on social relationships and reconstruction efforts. As mentioned before, this is in contrast to many studies of nuclear war effects which examine destruction quantitatively, focusing on physical measures such as human fatalities and casualties, number of cities destroyed, damage to overall economic capacity, or radiation damage to food crops. Social effects have been studied separately. The result of this approach is a significant degree of isolation and fragmentation in the assessment of nuclear war effects, limiting the ability to see the operation of the economic, social, and political systems as a whole under post-attack conditions. In part, the limitations of these studies reflect the fact that most of the effects literature is produced for civil defense purposes, rather than for strategic policymaking. Their orientation is necessarily the identification and, most importantly, the "solution" of the post-attack management problems of civil defense. The analytical approach is shaped by these requirements, tending to examine quantifiable, analyzable, and, in a sense, solvable pieces of the problem. Therefore, these studies should be used only with great caution in developing strategic policy, because they do not tell a public official that problems are insoluble or intractable, or that the projected damage would be unacceptable from the perspective of a political decisionmaker.

Significantly, the civil defense approach leads to quite different weapons requirements than that of the strategic planners. For deterrence purposes, the strategic planner assumes the worst case—that the enemy is always highly effective in its attacks while the United States is inefficient. The strategic planner emphasizes enlarged U.S. weapons needs and minimizes Soviet weapons requirements. In contrast, civil defense literature, emphasizing the solubility of problems created by nuclear war effects, makes it appear that the United States could endure a massive nuclear attack. This creates the opposite scenario, enlarging the apparent Soviet weapons requirements for an effective attack. If these approaches remained separated and their biases recognized, they would represent information that could be used cautiously in a public policy debate.

The problem arises when the implicitly optimistic approach of civil defense analysis, which projects minimum U.S. damage (that is, effective U.S. war survival), is linked to a projection of a highly effective attack by the United States on the Soviet Union. The latter assumes a degree of success for the U.S. attack against the Soviet Union, similar to that projected for a Soviet nuclear attack on the United States. In their extreme formulations, optimistic versions of both U.S. survival and weapons effectiveness are combined, deterrence is discarded, and war "winning" becomes a seemingly attainable goal.

The consequence of using the civil defense approach inappropriately, therefore, is to force the public dialogue, and ultimately the judgments of policymakers and the public itself, away from a realistic discussion of nuclear war effects and policy. The debate is focused on casualty and aggregate physical damage issues while treating the critical, complex societal questions cursorily or not at all, especially those that require judgments about political, social, and psychological effects. This limited vision does not provide a complete picture of the potential vulnerabilities and strengths of complex industrial societies. Nor, except in the crudest terms, does it speak to the issue of the acceptability or unacceptability of nuclear attack damage. Therefore it creates the mistaken impression that a certain level of biological and physical resource survival is equivalent to a functioning nation and, in turn, an international power. It fails to take into account that a society is not defined merely by population or productive capacity, but includes the multiplicity of values, institutions, and social and economic relationships that create its sense of national wholeness and effectiveness.

While indeed some of the social and economic areas such as medical care, food production, and energy supply lend themselves to quantification—doctor–patient ratios, food-processing and energy facility losses—even in these categories key findings reflect a combination of quantitative losses and organizational and human changes. For example, it is quite possible that in a gross sense, food supply and surviving population will balance, but because of social disintegration and chaos, there may be no adequate organizational mechanism to distribute the food. This interdependence of the social and physical parts of the system is a pivotal problem requiring careful attention—which it rarely receives. In addition, interactions between specific physical parts of the system (e.g., the effect of the loss of a product from one key industry on the productive capacity of many others) also lead to serious problems and thus need scrutiny.

The introduction of broader societal effects, including these interactive effects, creates a more accurate and complete picture of the potential strengths and vulnerabilities of complex industrial societies. Without this type of approach, the national injury created by a nuclear war could be seriously understated and distorted.

By examining nuclear war from this perspective, critical areas and critical questions should be revealed. In a sense, learning the questions that need to be asked and answered may in some ways be as important as the specific results of the analysis itself. By identifying these questions, we can clarify what we do know, what we are likely to know, and what will essentially be speculative and subject to change. By addressing the full range of impacts we will expose the importance of the huge uncertainties confronting the public and its elected officials in making these critical decisions. The approach of this book, therefore, is geared to assist the reader to rethink the problem and, to develop a framework to evaluate critically the implication of new technical or policy decisions. By combining quantitative and qualitative elements, a framework can be developed for understanding the implications of various nuclear war scenarios.

The book is designed to provide benchmarks for measuring technical weapon strategies against the critical criteria of nuclear war—controllability and unacceptable damage. Therefore, the book should

be viewed not as an effort to make definitive statements about nuclear attack effects. Rather, it is an attempt to define at least some of
the societal boundaries within which a postattack nation will have to
struggle—indicating the dangers and range of uncertainties as well as
identifying how various effects might change as the character and
size of the proposed nuclear attack changes.

To say that nuclear war is bad is to repeat a homily that by itself
is of little value when confronted by sophisticated political and technical discussion. However, to say that a new policy fails or succeeds
in meeting the two criteria mentioned above (and certainly others) is
to join the debate in a manner that will force the process of decisionmaking away from abstract numbers into a set of meaningful political and societal choices.

FOCUS OF THE BOOK

A national attack is defined as one aimed at crippling the economic
capacity of a nation and injuring or killing a substantial portion of its
population. A limited attack is defined as one that seeks to eliminate
significant military or military-related facilities; chief among such
targets would be bases for the launching or deployment of strategic
nuclear weapons. This book will examine both types of attack.

As mentioned above, while this chapter develops a framework, the
next is designed as a reference for basic nuclear weapons effects.

Part II will examine limited nuclear attacks on the United States.
National and local (Massachusetts) impacts will be analyzed, and a
variety of social and economic issues will be addressed, including
those that lend themselves to a certain degree of quantification. In
this case, the object is to provide a basis for determining whether the
damage described is limited enough to be acceptable in a political
sense, thus creating a controllable political situation.

Part III will define and examine a series of national attacks of increasing size directed against U.S. economic and population centers.
These attacks have the goal of undermining and destroying the U.S.
economy. To complement this broad analysis, the book will again
turn to a specific area, Massachusetts, and attempt to clarify the
effects these larger attacks might have on a local level, creating significant subnational problems. Part III will also examine the demands
of pre-attack evacuation as an effective political and civil defense

tool, and finally discuss the vulnerability of the Soviet Union to nuclear attack.

Addressed in both the cases of military and civilian targets will be the complex political, social, economic, and psychological factors, and particularly their interrelationships, which constitute the basic determinants of the strength and viability of the postattack society. The major categories evaluated are:

1. *Economic Damage.* The ability of the economy to meet national needs in terms of general industrial production and in such specific areas as food, fuel, and electric power.

2. *Institutional and Social Damage.* The ability of surviving or emergency political, economic, and social institutions and authorities to maintain their credibility with the populace, to provide basic services (such as medical care, education, or emergency and occupational training), and to provide an appropriate environment for recovery of the economic infrastructure and preattack political and social values.

3. *Psychological Damage.* The ability of individuals and groups to cope effectively with the emotional disorientation and apathy that have typically marked people and societies under severe stress or suffering from some measure of social disintegration. Those stresses are especially severe for a society that is inadequately prepared.

NOTES TO CHAPTER 1

1. Targeting flexibility is the ability to change the targeting of individual missiles quickly. Currently U.S. land-based intercontinental ballistic missiles (ICBMs) can be retargeted in about 30 minutes.
2. The Directive calls for less emphasis on retaliation against Soviet cities in the event of an attack and more emphasis than in the past on knocking out Soviet military forces and political and military leadership centers in the initial phase of conflict. Getler, M., "Changes in U.S. Nuclear Strategy," *The Washington Post*, August 14, 1980, p. A3.
3. This should be true despite the fact that immediate decisions by surviving leadership would be insulated initially from strong direct public or political pressure. Nevertheless, this leadership must evaluate and incorporate in its decisions the effect of damage on national viability.

2 THE PHYSICAL EFFECTS OF NUCLEAR WEAPONS

In this chapter, some of the more precise physical effects of nuclear weapons are reviewed to provide a basis for the discussion in subsequent chapters of the social and economic effects.

Nuclear weapons differ from conventional weapons in the variety and intensity of their physical effects. The predominant effect of conventional weapons is their blast damage accompanied by some effects from heat (burns and fire). In contrast, nuclear weapons, depending on how they are exploded, produce heat (burns and fire), blast, and radiation effects of significant but varying intensity. However, the prime characteristic of nuclear weapons is the enormous physical areas engulfed by the effects of a detonation. Even a small nuclear weapon produces damage on an unimaginable scale. Instead of affecting city blocks as the large conventional weapon does, the nuclear weapon's damage is comparable to the scale of cities. Thus, when we talk about putting these bombs together in a national attack, the terminology "small" versus "large" is deceptive. Even small national attacks (using limited numbers of weapons) mean enshrouding whole or major portions of cities in a blanket of devastation. Thus, the following discussion of physical effects should be seen from this broader perspective.

DESCRIPTION

The physical effects of detonating a single nuclear device are fairly well known due to extensive tests in the 1950s and 1960s with nuclear explosives of varying yields. From the data gathered in these tests, a range of possible effects from multiple detonations can be projected.[1] Actual effects would depend on particular circumstances, many of which are unknown but can be assumed or predicted, such as height of burst, predominant type of construction, weapon yields, population density, prevailing wind direction, weather patterns, and so forth. Most studies of nuclear weapons rely on the standard base of testing data, but vary in their assumptions about these particular conditions.

The thermal, blast, and radiation effects of a 1 megaton (Mt) and a 100 kiloton (Kt) weapon detonated substantially above the surface of the earth (air burst)[2] are depicted in Figure 2–1, and those for a 1 megaton weapon only, Table 2–1.[3] For perspective, approximately the entire central city of the following metropolitan regions would be within the area of virtually total destruction from a 1 megaton weapon: Wichita, Kansas; Boston, Massachusetts; Tulsa, Oklahoma; Salt Lake City, Utah; Colorado Springs, Colorado; Akron, Ohio; Baton Rouge, Louisiana; Fresno, California; and Columbia, South Carolina. The 100 kiloton weapon would enclose cities such as Aberdeen, South Dakota; Abilene, Kansas; and Camden, New Jersey. The indicators for these effects are given in pounds per square inch (psi) for blast damage; calories per square centimeter (cal/cm^2) for thermal (heat) damage; and roentgen equivalent man (rem) for radiation effects.[4]

Blast and Thermal Damage

A surface burst[5] (a weapon detonated on or near the ground) has a range three-quarters as far for blast damage and four-fifths as far for second degree burns as the distances indicated for an air burst. To provide a better feeling for the distances involved, Figure 8–4, p. 249 shows 1 megaton air bursts on three Massachusetts metropolitan areas.

Figure 2-1. Comparison of Blast, Thermal, and Radiation Effects for 100 KT and 1 MT Weapons.

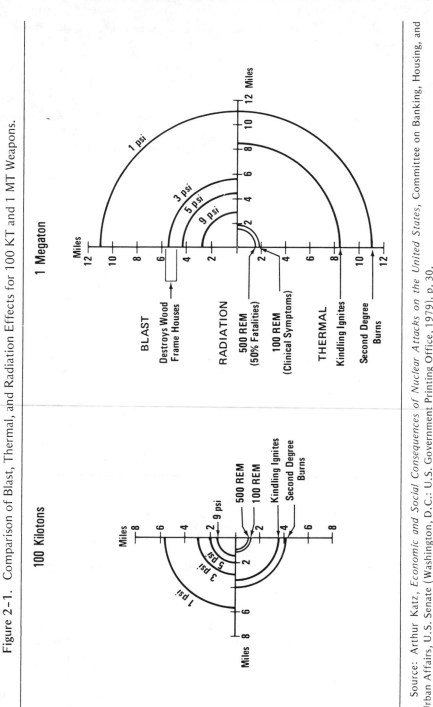

Source: Arthur Katz, *Economic and Social Consequences of Nuclear Attacks on the United States*, Committee on Banking, Housing, and Urban Affairs, U.S. Senate (Washington, D.C.: U.S. Government Printing Office, 1979). p. 30.

Table 2-1. Damage Ranges for One Megaton Typical Air Burst at Height of about 2,000 Meters.

Peak Wind Velocity (mph)	Peak Over-Pressure (psi)	Range from Ground Zero	Miles	Description
		11		Light Damage to Window Frames and Doors, Moderate Plaster Damage out to about 15 Miles; Glass Breakage Possible out to 30 Miles.
44	1.2			
		10		Second Degree Burns
		9		
51				Fine Kindling Fuels: Ignited.
		8		
60				
		7		
72	2.1			Smokestacks: Slight Damage.
				30% of Trees Blown Down.
		6		Wood-Frame Buildings: Moderate Damage.
98				Radio and TV Transmitting Towers: Moderate Damage.
		5		Wood-Frame Buildings: Severe Damage.
117	3.5			Telephone and Power Lines: Limit of Significant Damage.
				Wall-Bearing, Brick Buildings (Apartment House Type): Severe Damage.
		4		
177	5.5			Standard Building Materials Ignite.
				Light Steel-Frame, Industrial Building: Severe Damage.
		3		Multistory, Wall-Bearing Buildings (Monumental Type): Severe Damage.
278	9.4			
				Highway and RR Truss Bridges: Moderate Damage.
		2		Transportation Vehicles: Moderate Damage.
464	18.0			Multistory, Reinforced-Concrete Frame Buildings (Office Type): Severe Damage.
		1		
307	27.0			
			Miles	All (Above Ground) Structures: Severely Damaged or Destroyed.
		0		Ground Zero for 1 MT Air Burst.

Source: Samuel Glasstone, ed. *The Effects of Nuclear Weapons*, rev. ed. Washington, D.C. Government Printing Office, February 1964, Atomic Energy Commission, p. 640.

In general, the area receiving blast damage at 5 psi or above is usually considered completely destroyed or unusable (see Figure 2-2).[6] Rehabilitating even repairable facilities will often not be worth the expenditure of manpower and resources because of the extent of substantial damage to urban infrastructure, for example, utilities, the added burden of clearing away wreckage, and the comparative advantage of building anew from the ground up. At Hiroshima, for example, within the 5 psi blast area, two-thirds of all buildings were destroyed, and casualties were approximately 50 percent dead and 30 percent injured. Moreover, the area within the 1 to 5 psi range or "contour" would also absorb substantial damage and high casualties. Between the 5 psi and 3 psi contours most common residential wooden frame buildings would be destroyed. At 1 psi light damage will occur, mostly broken windows and minor structural damage. Even outside of 1 psi (for example, 0.5 psi), for a 1 megaton weapon, glass breakage could continue for thirty miles or more. A combination of blast and thermal effects determines the extent of initial destruction. Unless the weapon is small (10 Kt) nuclear radiation plays an important role only if substantial fallout occurs.

For some of the attacks described in this book, several weapons fall within the same area. Under these circumstances their thermal and blast effects can overlap. In the case of multiple weapons, a single structure would be struck by several blast waves, each from a different direction. While one blast wave by itself might leave the building salvageable, the combination would ensure its destruction. The potential for fire will also increase because debris and other damage (such as broken gas lines) caused by the first blast will provide abundant combustible material for the thermal radiation of the subsequent blast. The overlap of blast and thermal effects from multiple detonations will insure, in many situations, almost complete destruction of wide areas (see Figure 2-3).

An additional consequence of simultaneous ignition over a wide area can be a fire storm. A fire storm is a coalescing of many small fires into one huge conflagration. Initially, the nuclear blast wave creates massive quantities of flammable debris, and the fires cause a violent updraft by heating the air. This updraft results in strong air movements inward from the fire perimeter to replace the heated air and thus helps form and coalesce the fires into a holocaust, completely destroying the area within the fire perimeter. In Hiroshima, after a 12.5 kiloton explosion, 4.4 square miles of the center of the

Figure 2-2. Examples of Damage Produced by 5 psi.

Source: Reprinted from Samuel Glasstone, ed., *The Effects of Nuclear Weapons,* rev. ed. (U.S. Atomic Energy Commission, February 1964).

Figure 2-3. Thermal and Blast Effects of Three 1-Mt Weapons on a Single Target.

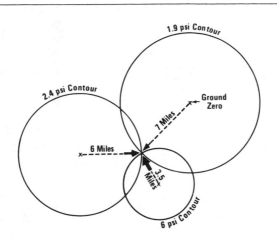

The Blast Impacts of Three One-Megaton Weapons on a Single Point. The X's Are Ground Zero, and the Arrows the Relative Magnitude (1.9 psi, 2.4 psi, 6.0 psi) and Direction of the Blast Waves

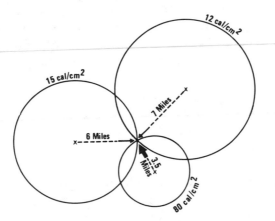

The Thermal Impacts of Three One-Megaton Weapons on a Single Point. The Arrows Represent Direction and Relative Magnitude of Thermal Radiation. (The 12 to 15 cal/cm² Contours Are within the Thermal Range for Ignition of a Number of Materials.)

Source: Arther Katz, *Economic and Social Consequences of Nuclear Attacks on the United States*, Committee on Banking, Housing, and Urban Affairs, U.S. Senate (Washington, D.C.: Government Printing Office, 1979). p. 34.

city were completely destroyed, corresponding to a circle with a radius of approximately 1.2 miles or about a 4.0 to 4.5 psi contour line. An illustration of the extent of the damage at Hiroshima is shown in Figure 2-4.

Electromagnetic Pulse

Also produced in a nuclear detonation is Electromagnetic Pulse (EMP). EMP is a large pulse of energy produced by a nuclear blast that takes the form of radiowaves—that is, electromagnetic energy which has similar frequencies to those used in radio or television communication. This phenomenon is of concern because it can damage communication equipment and electronic power systems, seriously disrupting critical elements needed to maintain a functioning society.[7,8]

EMP creates this problem because of two factors. The first is that the energy produced by a weapon is delivered in very large quantities. For example, the energy received by a radio antenna would be thousands of times greater than a normal radio signal. Second, the energy burst (change in voltage) received by the antenna is at a rate a hundred times faster than a lighting bolt. Thus all normal protection against the effects of lighting are useless against EMP. Not only can large radio antennae receive and conduct this energy, but also power lines and piping; in fact, any long wire can absorb and conduct this energy pulse to electrical equipment.

The energy burst can physically damage the equipment, shorting out capacitors or burning out transistors (which are particularly vulnerable). It can also cause temporary operational disruption such as instabilities in electric power lines, resulting in a power grid shut down, similar to what happened in the Northeast United States in 1965.

Finally, while ground and low level air bursts do cause local EMP damage and disruption, it is the use of high altitude nuclear blasts that are of greatest concern. One or two blasts strategically exploded over the United States between 12.5 and 25 miles above the earth can literally blanket most of the United States with a brief but powerful EMP. Thus, in this case, undamaged or lightly damaged regions would not escape at least some direct disruptive effects of a nuclear attack.

Figure 2-4. A Part of Hiroshima After the Atomic Blast.

Source: U.S. Air Force.

Nuclear Radiation

An intense burst of various types of nuclear radiation is produced by the initial explosion. The resulting exposure to radiation occurs in three phases: (1) initial radiation directly from the explosion; (2) immediate radioactive fallout (deposited in the first twenty-four hours); and (3) long-term fallout (months and years).

The detonation of the fission-fusion reaction (hydrogen bomb) produces an intense burst of neutron and gamma rays. This initial radiation burst causes immediate radiation exposure. The extent of the exposure area is related to the yield of the bomb. The larger the bomb, however, the less significant the initial exposure may be, since as weapon size increases, blast and thermal effects become dominant. These effects are devastating at distances where direct radiation is not lethal. As noted, only with weapons smaller than 10 Kt (Figure 2–5) will the distance at which individuals are exposed to a 500 rem dose of initial radiation (causing many casualties) exceed the distance of severe blast and thermal destruction (see the 5 psi contour in Figure 2–5).

If the warhead is detonated as a surface burst, material in particle form from the earth is drawn into the fireball. The radioactive material from the warhead detonation is deposited on these particles, which are of varying size. The heavier, larger particles fall to the surrounding area; moderate and smaller sized particles, however, can drift hundreds of miles. These are normally deposited within twenty four hours. The remaining radioactive material is injected into the stratosphere, where it stays for months or years. The seriousness of the health effects of exposure to initial radiation or immediate fall-out varies considerably. In general, for radiation received in a relatively short period of time (seconds to a week) the acute lethal dose (usually described as the dose from which 50 percent of those exposed will die) is taken as the dose range from 400 to 500 rems.[9] In addition to the deaths expected within the group exposed to 400–500 rems, the 50 percent who survive will require extensive care during long periods of immobilization. However, other survivors will suffer and be disabled. Acute radiation doses above 100 rems will bring on symptoms of varying seriousness. These symptoms are related to a variety of hematological changes (changes in the blood system), specifically, depression of white blood cell levels and dimin-

Figure 2-5. Comparison of Effects of Nuclear Weapons by Yield.

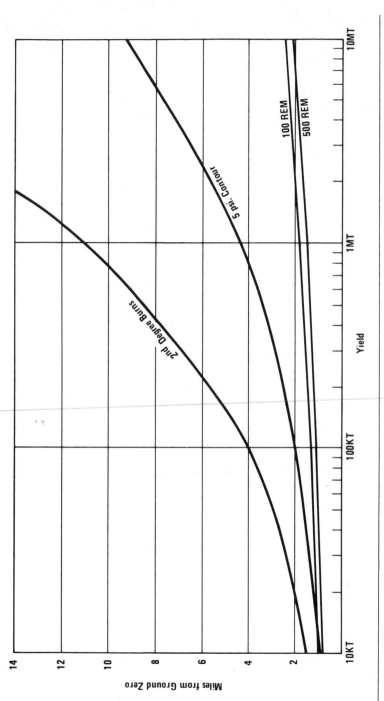

Source: Arther Katz, *Economic and Social Consequences of Nuclear Attacks on the United States*, Committee on Banking, Housing, and Urban Affairs, U.S. Senate (Washington, D.C.: U.S. Government Printing Office, 1979). p. 36.

ishing of immunological capabilities. These weakened victims would be vulnerable to infection, especially if they suffered from other blast and burn injuries, thereby seriously complicating the prognosis for their eventual recovery or significantly increasing the length of their convalescence.

Even at 25 rems, immediate observation of clinical symptoms may be possible for acute doses. However, since these are standards for a healthy adult population, the old, young, or chronically ill will be even more vulnerable. The effects of longer term exposure (a week to a month), such as received from fallout, is shown in Table 2-2. As the radiation dose absorbed by an individual is spread over longer periods of time, the dose necessary to produce radiation illness increases. It should be clear that even modest radiation exposure of the population will result in massive social service demands (hospitals, home care, child care) and psychological debilitation (radiation fears) powerfully shaping society's ability to function.

With regard to both low-level exposures and long-term fallout problems, the elevation of immediate radiation levels and the presence of short- or long-lived radioactive I^{131} (iodine), Cs^{137} (cesium), or Sr^{90} (strontium) in the survivors' bodies present additional problems; strontium-90 presents the most serious, long-term internal problem. Long-term increases in genetic damage and various cancers are well documented [10] and could increase the demands on the medical care system. For example, if 1 million persons survive doses of 200 rems, then we would expect to see 1,300 to 4,000 cases of can-

Table 2-2. Biological Effects of Radiation.

	Dose (rems)	
Effect	If Delivered Over One Week	If Delivered Over One Month
Threshold for radiation illness	150	200
5 percent may die	250	350
50 percent may die	450	600

Note: Biological effects of nuclear radiation vary with the rate at which a dose is delivered. The dose unit, the rem, takes into account the relative effectiveness of the type of radiation.

Source: S.D. Drell and F. Von Hippel, "Limited Nuclear War," Scientific American, 235, no. 5 (November 1976): 27.

cer per year beginning four to five years later and continuing for at least twenty-five years after exposure, resulting in a total of 33,400 to 100,200 deaths in excess of the current rate. This would be a lifetime increase of 20 to 60 percent over the approximately 164,000 lifetime cancer deaths per million of population expected from the present cancer death rate.[11]

In reviewing the physical effects of nuclear weapons some important observations need emphasis:

1. The destructive effects of nuclear weapons are of such physical magnitude that they are comparable to the geographical scale of cities, including surrounding urban regions. Moreover, while massive physical destruction does not extend everywhere even those far from the detonation of the weapons (thirty miles for 1 megaton weapons) will become psychological if not physical victims. The accident at Three Mile Island (discussed in Appendix A) indicated that this type of reaction is quite possible particularly since the extent of radiation exposure to fallout may be uncertain.

2. The accumulated impact of weapons in urban areas, where boundaries for significant damage produced by one weapon overlap and intrude into the area of damage of others is not normally discussed. Thus, the potential devastation from this type of attack is significantly understated. No serious modeling or analysis of this type of problem is associated with discussions in the open literature.

3. Radiation exposure both immediately and from fallout has a massive social dimension that a purely physical description of effects portrays inadequately. While radiation deaths and temporary land denial are almost the exclusive focus of most discussions of effects, the extreme demands on human services (hospitals, home care, and family support) and serious psychological impacts (radiation fears) are at least as significant for the recovery and well being of society. These effects are seriously neglected, if addressed at all. Moreover, the impact of substantial radiation exposure on the development, or ultimate outcome, of other major diseases is ill-defined and needs serious consideration. The competition for medical supplies between radiation victims and those ill with normal serious illnesses could easily become the basis for a wrenching social trauma—victim against victim.

In conclusion, it is a sense of the overwhelming, almost incomprehensible, intensity and physical scale of destruction that the reader should carry into the later discussion of nuclear war effects.

NOTES TO CHAPTER 2

1. Much of this information is contained in Samuel Glasstone, ed., *The Effects of Nuclear Weapons*, rev. ed., U.S. Atomic Energy Commission, (Washington, D.C.: Government Printing Office, February 1964) and the third edition, Samuel Glasstone and Phillip J. Dolan, eds., U.S. Department of Defense and U.S. Department of Energy (Washington, D.C.: Government Printing Office, 1977).

2. Technically, an air burst is the explosion of a weapon at such a height that the expanding fireball does not touch the earth's surface when the luminosity (brightness) is at maximum.

3. A megaton is equivalent in force and destructive power to 1 million tons of TNT; a kiloton is equal to 1,000 tons of TNT.

4. These indicator quantities are used instead of distances since, no matter how large the nuclear weapon, similar (though not identical) effects will be found for the same indicator size.

5. A surface burst (or ground burst) is the explosion of a nuclear (or atomic) weapon at the surface of the land or water at a height above the surface less than the radius of the fireball at maximum luminosity.

6. *Blast effect* is measured in pounds per square inch (psi) of *overpressure* — that is, the pressure in pounds per square inch greater than normal atmospheric pressure (14.7 psi) experienced at a particular point and caused by a blast wave from a nuclear explosion.
    Thermal or heat radiation (as opposed to nuclear radiation) is measured in calories per square centimeter (cal/cm^2). Its effects vary for different weapon yields because the maximum thermal intensity is delivered at different rates. Thus 7 cal/cm^2 may be delivered in one-half of a second for a 100 kiloton bomb and in two seconds for a 1 megaton bomb. The longer the exposure time (1 megaton), the more efficient the transfer of energy, and in general, the larger the impact.

7. Office of Technology Assessment, *The Effects of Nuclear War*, Congress of the United States (Washington, D.C.: Government Printing Office, May 1979), p. 22.

8. Defense Civil Preparedness Agency, DCPA Attack Environment Manual, Chapter 4, CPG 2-1A4, (Washington, D.C.: Department of Defense, June 1973).

9. Radiation dose to the population is measured in roentgen equivalent man (rem), a combined measure that includes the radiation absorbed dose (rad)

and the radiation biological effectiveness (rbe)—that is, the varying biological effectiveness of different types of radiation (gamma, alpha, beta, x-rays,
etc.). The rem is calculated by the formula: rem = rad × rbe. Roentgen (R),
is a physical measure of radiation exposure and is sometimes used in place
of rads. The rem is equivalent to the rad for x-rays but differs significantly
for alpha radiation.

10. The rate of increase for all cancers is about 167 to 501 cases per million
persons exposed per rem over twenty-five or more years. This corresponds
to a rate of 6.7 to 20 cases per year per million people exposed per rem per
year after five years. Committee on the Biological Effects of Ionizing Radiation (BEIR), "The Effect on Populations of Exposure to Low Levels of
Ionizing Radiation," Report of the Advisory Committee on the Biological
Effects of Ionizing Radiations, National Academy of Sciences/National Research Council, Washington, D.C. (1980): 263.

11. Ibid., p. 263.

▌▌ LIMITED NUCLEAR WAR
Military Targets

The term "controlled" nuclear war encompasses a variety of nuclear war strategies, each contending that they will limit the damage and control the progress of further escalation so that a full-scale nuclear attack will not be inevitable. Control implies an ability of political and military leaders to impose a rational direction on events occurring after a nuclear exchange. Under these circumstances, the post-attack response of a nation is assumed to be calculated, one chosen carefully from various options. Strategies purporting to satisfy these requirements range from targeting strictly strategic nuclear forces, to attacking selected key conventional forces and those institutions and individuals that are crucial elements of a nation's political and economic life. In this section, one strategy of controlled nuclear war, counterforce or "limited" nuclear war, will be examined.

The importance of understanding the implications of a controlled attack stems from the likelihood that it will be the pivotal action between a rising international confrontation or an initial conventional war (e.g., in Europe) and a full-scale economic/urban nuclear exchange. If successful, it implies a genuine assertion of political control in a chaotic military situation. Therefore, if controlled nuclear war can be seen as credible, a direct major military confrontation between the United States and the Soviet Union could become less fearful, and the incorporation of nuclear weapons into a broader range of military strategy could be viewed as less potentially catastrophic.

3 NATIONAL CONSEQUENCES

THE CONCEPT

In 1974, U.S. Secretary of Defense James Schlesinger formally acknowledged the adoption of limited nuclear war as a part of the strategic doctrine of the United States.[1] Although the concept of limited or controlled nuclear conflict had long been discussed by military planners and strategists and had, for a brief time, formed part of the strategic doctrine espoused by one of Secretary Schlesinger's predecessors, Robert McNamara,[2] it had been relegated to a minor role in nuclear attack planning in preference to the concept of deterrence through mutual assured destruction (MAD).[3] Advances in technology, particularly in terms of missile accuracy, warhead size, and retargeting flexibility, however, made it possible to integrate "counterforce targeting" (as limited nuclear war is technically defined) into the declared strategic policy of the United States.[4]

Limited nuclear war is conceived of as a nuclear attack on one or more elements of a nation's land-based strategic arsenal: intercontinental ballistic missiles (ICBMs), strategic bombers, or nuclear-powered ballistic missile submarine support bases (see Figure 3-1). Variations on the concept include possible attacks on other critical military, industrial, or command and control centers. Individually, or in combination, these options could be used either as a means of

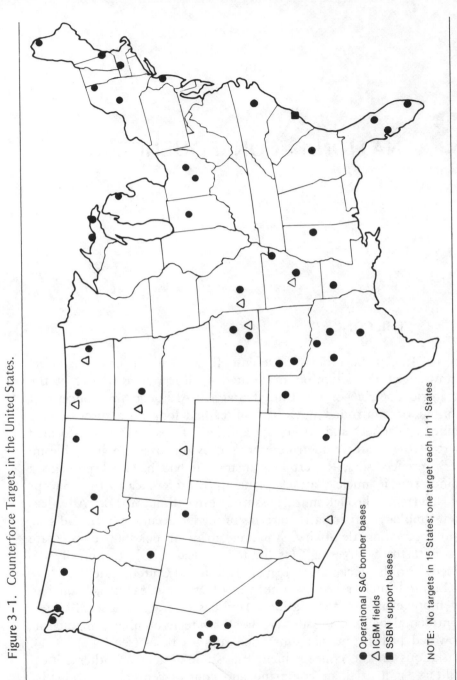

Figure 3-1. Counterforce Targets in the United States.

● Operational SAC bomber bases
△ ICBM fields
■ SSBN support bases

NOTE: No targets in 15 States; one target each in 11 States

Source: Office of Technology Assessment (OTA), *The Effects of Nuclear War*, Congress of the United States (Washington, D.C.: Government Printing Office, May 1979), p. 82.

paralyzing effective military response or to demonstrate the attacker's resolve and ability to employ the ultimate weapon in furtherance of its interests. For example, the Department of Defense has hypothesized a scenario in which, during a conventional conflict in Europe, the Soviet Union might employ nuclear weapons to destroy the five major heavy airlift bases in the United States (Dover, Maguire, Travis, Charleston, and McChord Air Force Bases)[5] in an effort to halt American efforts to resupply forces in Europe and to signal its determination.

The adoption of this counterforce strategy rests on two postulates. The first is that it is possible to limit and structure a nuclear attack in such a way that serious damage could be inflicted on ICBM silos or other strategic targets without also inflicting substantial damage, either directly or indirectly, on the civilian population or the society as a whole. This assumes a military-oriented attack can be launched that would be so benign in its societal (and thus political) impacts that it would be acceptable to the nation attacked, not automatically triggering escalation toward a full-scale nuclear response in reprisal.

The second, and inextricably related postulate is that after a limited nuclear attack an effective political mechanism will exist to constrain and terminate the nuclear exchange — preventing a slow or rapid escalation to a full-scale nuclear conflict. This mechanism could be used either to negotiate a settlement after, perhaps, a highly circumscribed nuclear response to "even the score" politically, or to express tacit acceptance of the postattack status quo by inaction (no response). However, no one has put forth a credible description of this termination process nor have the "final results," that is, the nature of the international and domestic world after an attack, been analyzed with any clarity.

Whatever the purported mechanism for termination, the success of this strategy requires, explicitly or implicitly, the continuing credibility and legitimacy of a central authority. This central authority must retain confidence based on the public's judgment of its effectiveness in preventing the attack from occurring at all, the extent of the destructiveness of the attack, and its ability to cope with the attack's effects.

Therefore, in the context of limited nuclear war, the first issue to be considered is not national survival but the political acceptability, in domestic and international terms, of the damage inflicted by a counterforce nuclear attack. The political acceptability of this assault is paramount because, as noted, it bears directly on the government's ability to explore policy or response options that avoid nuclear escalation. The avoidance of escalation is crucial because a broadened nuclear exchange undermines the entire concept of controllability, that is, the ability to avoid wholesale damage. Escalation again makes national survival the paramount issue, and limited nuclear war becomes a prelude to destruction rather than a preventative—a disastrous exercise in self deception.

Political control may slip away in limited nuclear war because, while actual physical damage may be quantitatively limited, there is no guarantee that the limited attack will be perceived as benign. If the leadership and/or the general public believe they have been the victims of the equivalent of a large-scale nuclear attack, with all its apocalyptic implications, then the political consequences would be grave: severely limiting the maneuverability and even the viability of the existing leadership. Thus, one of the critical issues determining political acceptability is the public perception of the effects of the attack—the degree to which they feel endangered or threatened.

Complicating this problem further is the possibility that the nation as a whole or its leadership may decide that a limited attack is highly destructive to its international standing. Under these circumstances it may believe that accepting an even implied subservient postattack status would jeopardize national survival. Such a decline in status could precipitate a loss of faith on the part of its allies and their withdrawal to a less dependent or friendly relationship. In turn, this could result in an accelerated international realignment, eventual isolation, and, thus, greater future vulnerability. Therefore, to redeem this potential prestige loss, a more extensive level of retaliation may be seen as needed.

Given this array of potential consequences, the result of a limited nuclear attack may not create a set of flexible options but instead may result in a nation very resistant to a negotiated resolution of the crisis that triggered the attack. The subtle differentiation made by military strategists between counterforce (military) and countervalue (economic/human) attacks may be lost or negated in real political terms. Though this may not be a consideration for military planners, since for planning purposes they assume everything goes well for the adversary (minimum nonmilitary damage), it will definitely be an important factor in the decisions of political leaders.

Therefore, central to the analysis of a limited nuclear war and its consequences, and controlled nuclear war in general, is the distinction between the customary discussion of national survival, and the extremely restrictive requirement that the nuclear attack be perceived as societally benign.

AN ATTACK SCENARIO

To evaluate the consequences of limited nuclear war, a specific attack scenario is examined. The proposed basic Department of Defense (DOD) "counterforce" attack by the Soviet Union is focused on various combinations of 1,054 ICBM silos,[6] 46 Strategic Air Command (SAC) bases, and 2 nuclear-powered ballistic missile submarine bases (SSBN) in the United States, shown in Figure 3–1. This attack is equivalent to about one quarter of the Soviet strategic warheads and megaton equivalents in 1985. However, only a portion of the Soviet Union's strategic forces will have the accuracy and size (yield) to accomplish this type of attack. The actual number of surviving missiles of the 1,000 in land-based silos will depend on Soviet capabilities. While this scenario is used to determine the effects, it is not a prediction. The attack options examined by DOD generally include the ICBMs, but in some cases exclude SAC and SSBN bases. Moreover, there are substantial variations in potential impacts depending on different estimates of shelter utilization and effectiveness, meteorological conditions (such as winds, rain, and terrain), numbers and yield of weapons, and targeting options (such as ground bursts or air bursts). For example, Figure 3–2 depicts the variation in numbers of casualties as a function of monthly winds for a 1 megaton (Mt) ground burst on each ICBM silo and SAC and SSBN bases.

The Defense Department initially presented an analysis that projected anywhere from 800,000 to 6 million fatalities, depending on the attack strategy used (i.e., the combination of air and ground burst and the inclusion or exclusion of SAC bases and ICBM silos). After new attacks were introduced these figures were later revised upward (see p. 41). The nuclear attack DOD used for reference employs air bursts to attack ICBM silos and the other targets.

An alternative set of scenarios was developed by Congressional consultants with extensive use of ground bursts (explosions) against ICBM silos; specifically, the reference attack reported to the Senate

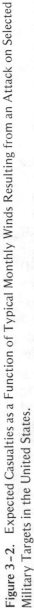
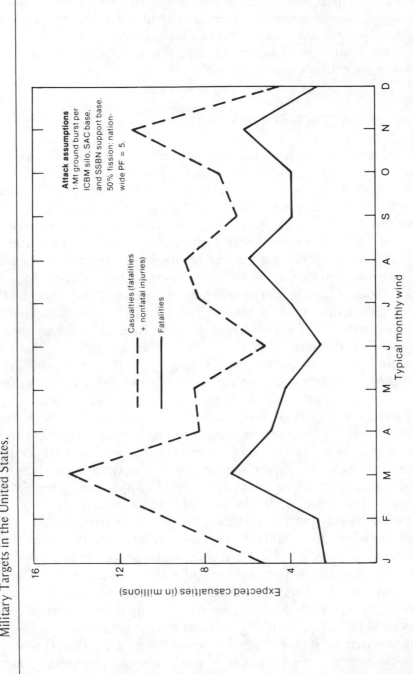

Figure 3-2. Expected Casualties as a Function of Typical Monthly Winds Resulting from an Attack on Selected Military Targets in the United States.

Source: Office of Technology Assessment (OTA), *The Effects of Nuclear War*, Congress of the United States (Washington, D.C.: Government Printing Office). p. 85.

Committee on Foreign Relations and discussed in this book targets simultaneously 1,054 ICBM silos, 54 SAC bases, and the 2 SSBN bases.[7] The weapons used include two 1 megaton ground bursts per each ICBM silo, three 1 megaton air bursts targeted against each SAC base, and one weapon against each of the SSBN bases. They argued that a technical consideration such as fratricide (the disruption of one incoming warhead by the prior explosion of another) makes the DOD strategy of optimum height of burst (HoB)—detonating a weapon efficiently in the air—less desirable than ground bursts in assuring the destruction of ICBM silos. They pointed out it would be pointless to embark on a limited nuclear attack without assuring a high level of destruction of an adversary's missiles. Otherwise the number of missiles "wasted" may leave the attacker with no strategic advantage.

Congressional estimates of fallout patterns were used as the reference case to analyze some broader societal effects of the limited nuclear war attack. The areas of radioactive contamination combined with DOD casualty estimates for these fallout patterns provide a reasonable basis for projecting impacts associated with this type of attack.

The fallout patterns for two 1 megaton ground bursts on each of the 1,054 ICBM silos are shown in Figures 3–3 and 3–4 for both a typical winter and spring (March) day.

CASUALTIES

A re-evaluation of casualty estimates by DOD produced a different range of fatalities. The changes were based on the use of air and surface bursts, number of arriving weapons, March and winter instead of August wind patterns, and different levels of fallout protection based on shelter effectiveness. The DOD estimates for some scenarios (cases I to III) are shown in Figure 3–5. Case III is the counterforce attack used as our reference. It includes two 1 megaton surface bursts per silo, all SAC bases were pattern attacked (that is, three 1 megaton weapons per base), 1 megaton bursts on the two SSBNs, as well as a 25 percent degradation of the DOD estimates of fallout protection.[8] The result is 16.3 million deaths.[9] The attack in Case III would produce the destruction of somewhat more than half (57 percent) of the U.S. land based ICBM force and heavy damage to SAC and submarine facilities.

Figure 3-3. Fallout Patterns for a Typical Winter Day.

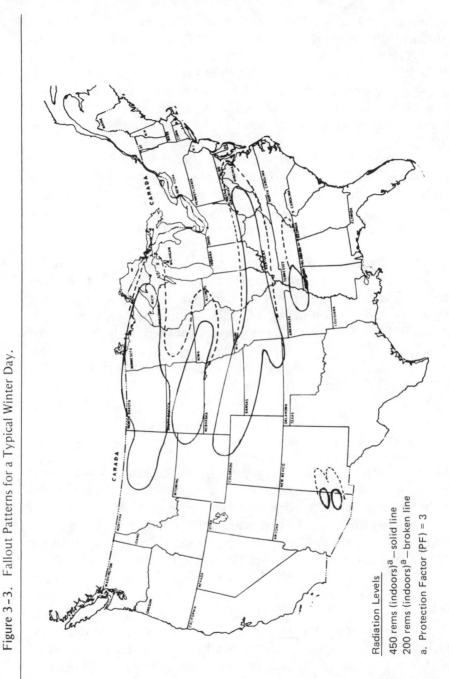

Radiation Levels

450 rems (indoors)[a] —solid line
200 rems (indoors)[a] —broken line

a. Protection Factor (PF) = 3

Source: Subcommittee on Arms Control, International Organizations and Security Agreements, *Analyses of Effects of Limited Nuclear War*, Committee on Foreign Relations, United States Senate (Washington, D.C.: Government Printing Office, September 1975). p. 52.

Figure 3-4.   Fallout Pattern for a Typical March Day.

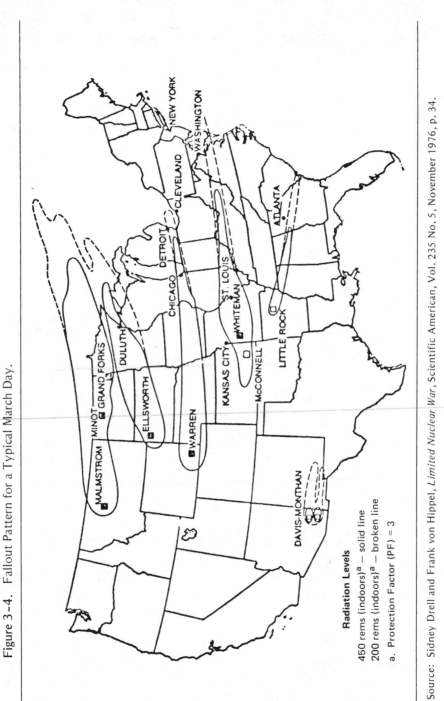

Radiation Levels

450 rems (indoors)[a] — solid line
200 rems (indoors)[a] — broken line

a. Protection Factor (PF) = 3

Source: Sidney Drell and Frank von Hippel, *Limited Nuclear War*, Scientific American, Vol. 235 No. 5, November 1976, p. 34.

Figure 3-5. Sensitivity of Expected Fatalities and Attack Assumptions.

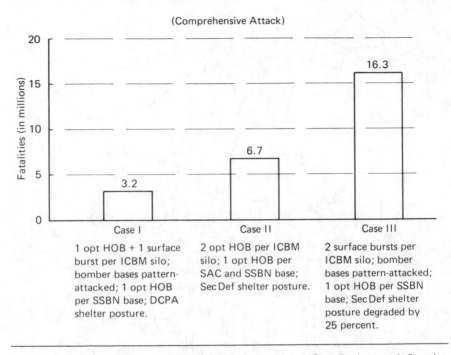

(Comprehensive Attack)

	Case I	Case II	Case III

Case I: 1 opt HOB + 1 surface burst per ICBM silo; bomber bases pattern-attacked; 1 opt HOB per SSBN base; DCPA shelter posture.

Case II: 2 opt HOB per ICBM silo; 1 opt HOB per SAC and SSBN base; SecDef shelter posture.

Case III: 2 surface bursts per ICBM silo; bomber bases pattern-attacked; 1 opt HOB per SSBN base; SecDef shelter posture degraded by 25 percent.

Source: Subcommittee on Arms Control, International Organizations and Security Agreements, *Analysis of Effects of Limited Nuclear Warfare*, Committee on Foreign Relations, United States Senate, (Washington, D.C.: Government Printing Office, September, 1975). p. 18.

The Office of Technology Assessment (OTA)[10] reviewed all available counterforce impact casualty estimates. It found, depending on the assumptions, a range of between 2 and 22 million deaths (1 to 11 percent of the population) in the United States during the first thirty days after an attack on all silos, and SAC and SSBN bases. Attacking silos alone produced only a slightly more limited range of 2 to 20 million fatalities. The upper part of this range assumed the use of weapons larger than 1 megaton—the largest are 3 megatons, probably an extreme upper bound. Most deaths, especially high estimates, are attributed to fallout impacts. The OTA study appeared to conclude that the middle of this range, 8 to 14 million fatalities, was most reasonable. Another recent report[11] concluded that with the current

U.S. civil defense preparations 8 to 12 million people would be killed without warning, and 5 to 8 million with warning. Since the estimates for fatalities are limited to the first thirty days after the attack, we would expect to see hundreds of thousands, more likely millions, of cancer and other radiation-related deaths over the next two to three succeeding decades. A specific estimate for a counterforce attack developed by OTA is shown in Table 3–1. The effects would be understated because fallout is reduced when only one instead of two 1 megaton weapons used against each ICBM silo are ground burst. It should be noted that while there are a large number of thyroid effects for humans shown in Table 3–1, many will not be fatal.

Injury Projections

Fatalities alone do not accurately reflect the true impact of radioactive fallout on society. Focusing exclusively on estimates of fatalities and not fatalities *plus injured* seriously understates the short- and long-term problems that will develop.

To remedy this new estimates of casualties are presented here. An abitrary but reasonable rule of thumb was used—that one to two times as many injured are produced as fatalities. Thus, the range of 6 to 16 million fatalities (Cases II and III above) would be equivalent to 6 to 32 million injured. OTA[12] estimated that the injured would equal fatalities. Accepting this estimate would give on the order of 14 to 30 million casualties (7 to 15 million dead plus 7 to 15 million injured) as a possible middle case. A modified range of 10 to 20 million initial injuries will be used in this book. However, as noted, millions of genetic abnormalities and other deleterious health effects such as thyroid nodules and thyroid cancer (both of which can be successfully treated) will be delayed, appearing in succeeding decades.

The burden of the 10 to 20 million initially injured would represent a massive, complex, and threatening disruption of society. The implications of this injury level are seen most clearly in the overwhelming demands on the medical care system. On the other hand, the effect of millions of delayed injuries would be more insidious. Their appearance would be less likely to create medical catastrophies, but their demoralizing psychological impacts—a continuing sense of

Table 3-1. Long-Term Radiation Effects from Nuclear Attacks.

Estimated total effects of an attack on U.S. ICBM silos, using one air burst and one surface burst (each 1 Mt) against 1,054 silos. A case in which bomber and submarine bases are also attacked with air bursts gives similar results. Fallout sheltering is treated parametrically:

Counterforce Attacks (Mixed air and surface bursts)

	$PF = 5$[a]	$PF = 10$	$PF = 40$
Somatic Effects			
Cancer deaths	1,000,000–6,000,000	700,000–5,000,000	500,000–4,500,000
Thyroid cancers	about 2,000,000	about 2,000,000	about 1,500,000
Thyroid nodules	about 3,000,000	about 3,000,000	about 2,500,000
Genetic Effects			
Abortions due to chromosomal damage	300,000–3,000,000	250,000–2,500,000	200,000–2,000,000
Other genetic effects	900,000–9,000,000	750,000–7,500,000	650,000–6,500,000

Estimated effects outside the United States from this attack:

Somatic Effects			
Cancer deaths			400,000–3,800,000
Thyroid cancers			about 1,400,000
Thyroid nodules			about 2,000,000
Genetic Effects			
Abortions due to chromosomal damage			170,000–1,700,000
Other genetic effects			600,000–6,000,000

Estimated total effects of an attack on Soviet ICBM silos, using one air burst and one surface burst (each 100 kt) against 1,477 silos. The overwhelming bulk of deaths are from "worldwide" (between 30° and 60° north latitude) fallout, and hence fallout sheltering in the Soviet Union makes little difference:

Somatic Effects

Cancer deaths	300,000–3,300,000
Thyroid cancers	about 2,500,000
Thyroid nodules	about 3,600,000

Genetic Effects

Abortions due to chromosomal damage	120,000–2,500,000
Other genetic effects	400,000–4,000,000

a. *PF* = Protection Factor.

Source: Office of Technology Assessment, *The Effects of Nuclear War*, Congress of the United States (Washington, D.C.: Government Printing Office, May 1979), p. 113.

individual fear, helplessness, and vulnerability—would have corrosive effects on the society.

ECONOMIC IMPACTS

Table 3-2 puts the potential extent of disruption from fallout (winter or March) into perspective. Approximately one-third of the United States's manufacturing capacity, as measured by manufacturing value added (MVA)[13] in 1977,[14] was within contaminated states for either the winter or March fallout patterns. Furthermore, examining a limited number of the individual industries also reveals a similar pattern. However, the very general two digit standard industrial category (SIC) codes include in any one category very diverse manufacturing groups, and the results should therefore be interpreted carefully. Nevertheless, as Table 3-2 shows, the affected states contained approximately 30 to 40 percent of MVA in these industrial categories. The results support the potential for substantial disruption of economic activity, despite the limited destruction of physical plants, in these affected areas. Thus in most instances,

Table 3-2. National Economic Activity Potentially Disrupted by Fallout.[a]

SIC	Economic Categories Affected	March	Winter
28	Chemicals and allied products[c]	25	30
283	Drugs[c]	30	25
33	Primary metal industries[c]	30	35
331	Blast furnaces, steel works, and killing and finishing mills[c]	35	45
34	Fabricated metal products[c]	40	40
346	Metal forgings and stampings[c]	50	40
361	Electrical distribution products[c]	20	40
Total MVA (1977)[b] for Affected States		30	30

a. Rounded to nearest 5 percent.

b. Bureau of Census, 1977 Census of Manufacturing, Department of Commerce, (Washington, D.C.:, Government Printing Office).

c. Bureau of Census, 1972 Census of Manufacturers, Department of Commerce, (Washington, D.C.: Government Printing Office).

while the entire state will not be contaminated, the general social disorganization, the impact of the enormous casualty load, and the initial drive to evacuate should make the full utilization of even the industrial capabilities of uncontaminated areas very uncertain.

The reaction of other surviving workers to the magnitude of casualties and fallout threat, is likely to be similar to those of Japanese workers in W.W. II:

> ... After the big raids (from March on) the ... majority of workers in (the bombed) areas disengaged themselves from production and became very interested in their own self-preservation.[15]

In addition to the potential disruptions from social disorganization, radioactive contamination, and casualties on specific regional economic capacity, the losses that will affect industrial production in other geographical areas must also be counted. The problem of greatest concern is industrial bottlenecking. Bottlenecking is the disruptive effect losses in a key industry (e.g., steel) have on other dependent economic activities (e.g., automobiles and machine tool production). Even modest reductions in capacity in basic pivotal industries can have severe widespread effects on the economy (this is discussed further in Chapter 5). Despite the possibility of product substitution (e.g., plastics for steel), the short- and even midterm ramifications of a disruption of 25 to 50 percent of regional economic activities (equivalent to 8 to 15 percent of national economic activities) would be serious to the national economy. This disruption could easily last several months and would increase if a postattack stalemate resulted in further urban evacuation throughout the nation.

While the effects described would be severe for the regional and national economy, other less obvious changes would occur. The banking system would be faced with a particularly severe burden, such as potential bankruptcies; defaults on basic time payments, such as mortgages; and major shifts of monies by individuals during evacuation. These problems would be just a sample of the difficulties. In contaminated areas individuals or businesses would be unable to gain access to money, especially in local banks, for long periods. In general, it would be virtually impossible for banks to either regionally or nationally pursue "normal" lending and borrowing policies.

Moreover, business insurance will not cover this type of catastrophe. The requirement of the federal government to provide regional disaster loans to prevent bankruptcy and help resettle workers and their families from severely contaminated areas would be on a scale unknown in U.S. experience. A parallel issue will be the decisions about which industries and plants to decontaminate first. These decisions will be politically explosive. Exacerbating this atmosphere of conflict is the fact that production in many dependent industries in safe areas throughout the nation will be affected by decontamination and aid decisions. Thus, the pattern of reemployment and industrial survival will be determined by these federal choices. The potential for national political conflict is obvious.

Prices and the distribution of goods would have to be controlled in a manner unknown in peacetime, and probably in our recent wartime experience, to assure some sense of equity and stability. This too will be politically explosive. Of equal concern, is that these decisions will relate directly to the United States's competitiveness and balance of trade with other nations.

A stalemate or prolonged conflict could only exacerbate the financial and economic problems identified, since the disruptive and disorienting effects of large-scale urban evacuation are almost certain to occur.[16] Under these circumstances attempting to keep workers at factories; social services for those in need; and business, especially retail commercial outlets, afloat will be a monumental organizational task.

In the area of foreign trade, there will be a serious question of whether other trading nations would sell to or invest in the United States in a period of frightening instability. The effects on the prices and supply of goods, particularly oil, could be devastating.

The image of a physically undamaged, functioning economy, particularly during a prolonged low-level or stalemated war, thus has no relation to the reality that will confront government and industrial leaders.

FOOD SUPPLY AND DISTRIBUTION

On a national scale, the most serious aspect of a counterforce or limited nuclear attack, even one restricted to ICBM silos, is its potentially severe consequences for short- and midterm food production. If the U.S. food production and distribution system is significantly disrupted (not necessarily destroyed), the attack creates the potential to unleash tremendous political pressure for retaliation.

The basis for this concern is the concentration of production capabilities in areas vulnerable to heavy fallout effects, and the United States's severe geographical imbalance between food production capabilities and population. Regions I, II, III, and VII of Figure 3-6 account for more than half the population (about 64 percent), but only about one fifth of food production capabilities. On the other hand, Regions IV, V, VI, and VIII have 80 percent of the food production capabilities and only 40 percent of the population. Region VI produces almost 40 percent of the food energy of the United States alone (Table 3-3). Moreover, two-thirds of the livestock requirements and three-fourths of the feed crops are produced in IV, V, and VI; Regions IV and VI are responsible for more than half of the nation's production in these two food sectors alone.[17]

Figures 3-7 and 3-8 display the fallout patterns for a typical winter and March counterforce attack, respectively, on a map of the distribution of U.S. grain production. Figure 3-9 compares the March fallout pattern and United States cattle distribution. In all cases, heavy radioactive contamination exists in a significant part of the major food-producing areas of the United States. This includes Region VI and substantial parts of Region IV; in addition, Region V is affected. The result of this contamination is that many farmers will die because they will be subjected to 450 rems or more (lethal to 50 percent of an exposed population). Even if radiation protection is effective, individuals exposed to doses of 100 to 200 rems or more will show varying clinical symptoms—many requiring extensive care and long convalescence. Skilled human resources would be severely depleted. Despite U.S. agriculture's present level of mechanization, the loss of many skilled individuals would lead to immediate crop losses. However, the longer term effects are poor (reduced) crop yields rather than total failures. This problem will diminish in subsequent years as new farmers are trained. High levels of contamination from radioactive elements cesium-137 and strontium-90 above United States's population standards for radiation will also exist in much of this area, in some cases for years, particularly in "hot spots" (areas of high intensity radiation). This contamination will prevent or limit access to land for food production. Land denial or direct radiation damage to crops (in the late spring or early summer) will be particularly effective in reducing yields if the attacks occur in the first six months of the year or during or just prior to the harvest period.[18]

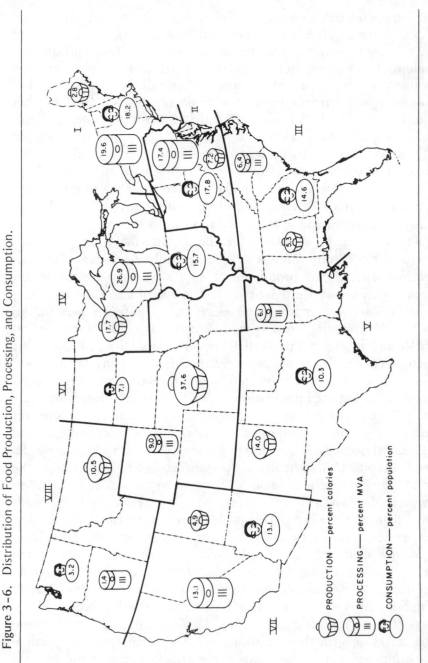

Figure 3-6. Distribution of Food Production, Processing, and Consumption.

Source: Stephen L. Brown and Ulrich F. Pilz, "U.S. Agriculture: Potential Vulnerabilities." (Menlo Park, California: Stanford Research Institute, 1969). p. 60.

Table 3-3. Impacts of Counterforce on Food Production Capabilities.

| | Percent Contained in Region | | |
	Most Serious[a] Area	Region VI	Region IV	Total IV & VI
Food value (energy)	b	37.6	17.7	55.3
Feed crops	b	38.6	30.7	69.3
Livestock requirements	b	34.2	22.8	57.0
Grains				
Wheat	62	51	9	60
Rye	69	55	19	74
Corn (grain)	79	41	42	83
Sorghum	44	44	3	47
Oats	69	41	38	79
Barley	55	31	10	41
Silage Corn	45	32	27	59
Soybeans	70	30	37	67
Dairy				
Milk	28	12	33	45
Eggs	22	9	15	24
Meat				
Poultry—broilers	4	1	1	2
—chickens	16	6	11	17
Hogs	63	38	28	56
Cattle—production	42	33	11	44
—slaughter	49	45	14	59
—on farm	43	32	12	44
—calved				
beef	42	32	6	38
cow	29	13	32	45
—feed lot				
Jan. 1	49	46	12	58
July 1		37		

a. North Dakota, South Dakota, Nebraska, Wyoming, Kansas, Missouri, Illinois, Indiana, Kentucky, Tennessee, Minnesota, Montana.

b. Not available from data.

Source: United States Department of Agriculture, *Agricultural Statistics, 1974* (Washington, D.C.: Government Printing Office, 1974).

Figure 3-7.   Fallout Pattern (Winter) on Grain Production by County (*Tons for 1974*).

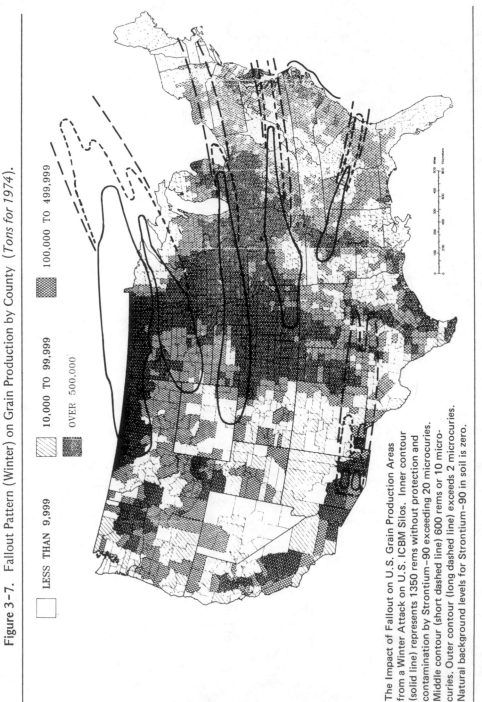

LESS THAN 9,999

10,000 TO 99,999

100,000 TO 499,999

OVER 500,000

The Impact of Fallout on U.S. Grain Production Areas from a Winter Attack on U.S. ICBM Silos. Inner contour (solid line) represents 1350 rems without protection and contamination by Strontium–90 exceeding 20 microcuries. Middle contour (short dashed line) 600 rems or 10 microcuries. Outer contour (long dashed line) exceeds 2 microcuries. Natural background levels for Strontium–90 in soil is zero.

Source: Analyses of Effects of Limited Nuclear War, Committee on Foreign Relations, U.S. Senate, 1975.

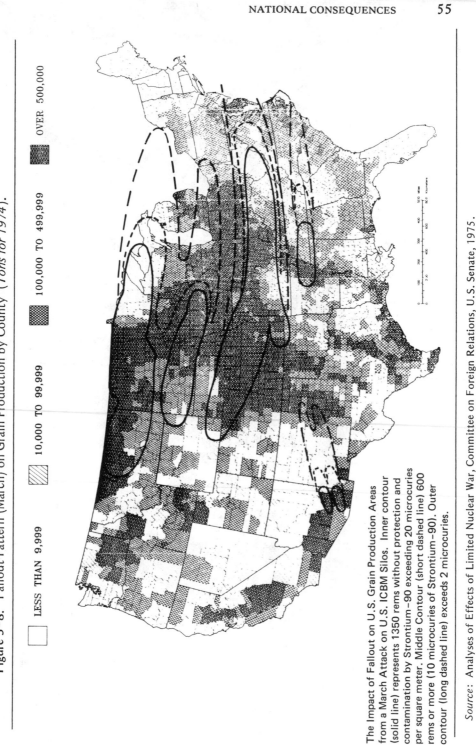

Figure 3-8. Fallout Pattern (March) on Grain Production by County (*Tons for 1974*).

LESS THAN 9,999

10,000 TO 99,999

100,000 TO 499,999

OVER 500,000

The Impact of Fallout on U.S. Grain Production Areas from a March Attack on U.S. ICBM Silos. Inner contour (solid line) represents 1350 rems without protection and contamination by Strontium-90 exceeding 20 microcuries per square meter. Middle Contour (short dashed line) 600 rems or more (10 microcuries of Strontium-90). Outer contour (long dashed line) exceeds 2 microcuries.

Source: Analyses of Effects of Limited Nuclear War, Committee on Foreign Relations, U.S. Senate, 1975.

Figure 3-9.   Fallout Pattern on Cattle Distribution by County (1974).

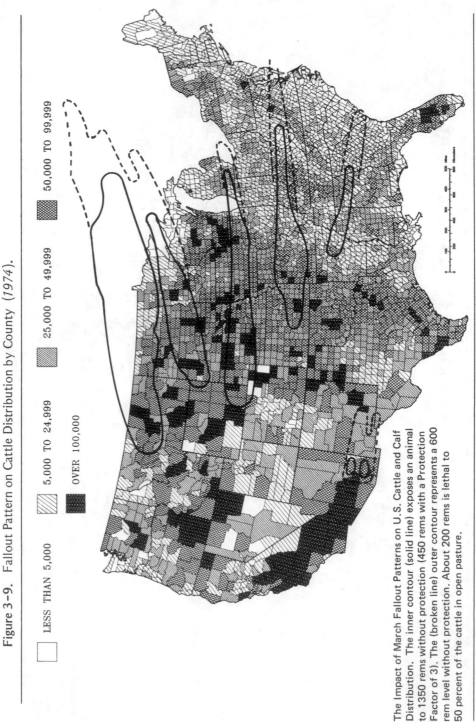

LESS THAN 5,000

5,000 TO 24,999

25,000 TO 49,999

50,000 TO 99,999

OVER 100,000

The Impact of March Fallout Patterns on U.S. Cattle and Calf
Distribution. The inner contour (solid line) exposes an animal
to 1350 rems without protection (450 rems with a Protection
Factor of 3). The (broken line) outer contour represents a 600
rem level without protection. About 200 rems is lethal to
50 percent of the cattle in open pasture.

Source: Analyses of Effects of Limited Nuclear War, Committee on Foreign Relations, U.S. Senate, 1975.

Figure 3-10 illustrates the seriousness of the problem. It shows the fallout pattern attributed to the ICBM bases attacked in an Oak Ridge National Laboratory (ORNL) study.[19] The total megatons used for the ORNL attack is slightly higher, 2,500 megatons, than the approximately 2,000 megatons ground burst against military targets in the OTA attack used in this discussion. The map shows the pattern of radiation exposure after one year without any removal or decontamination. At this juncture radioactive decay will occur at a slow rate, leaving exposure levels steady for long periods. The 0.01 Roentgen/hour contour represents a potential accumulated dose of 0.4 Roentgen/week, a dose that would in three months exceed present occupational standards for radiation workers. This would be a minimum exposure since living in the area would result in continuous exposure—perhaps at a lower level because of decontamination. However, this dose will have to be added to much higher doses accumulated over the first year. "Hot spots," high intensity radiation areas, will make this problem worse. Although few clinical symptoms might be observed initially, the cancer rate should increase for that population over time. In wartime the change would not be perceived as significant, but in peacetime (or limited damage attacks) the exposed population might not view it with indifference.

Losses of sheep, cattle, and pigs, both in barns or in the pasture also would be high. These animals are only slightly more resistant to radiation than humans, and in highly contaminated areas they are unlikely to be in shelters that afford any significant protection against radiation. Figure 3-9 shows the significant portion of livestock, in this case cattle, exposed to high levels of radiation. For a winter fallout pattern (Table 3-3), more than 40 percent of the cattle and 60 percent of the hogs are produced in the most seriously affected states. Cattle production is somewhat complicated since in the United States's system calves are produced on ranches, shipped to pastureland to grow, and then sent to feedlots to be fattened. Many definitions of cattle production or distribution can be used. By any measure—where born, total stock on the farm, or presence in feed lots—more than 40 percent of the cattle are within the most seriously affected states.

Radiation exposure in combination with the diversion of feed (e.g., corn) for direct human consumption should significantly reduce meat availability.[20] The potential for severe meat and dairy price increases, if nothing else, should be evident.

Figure 3–10.   Fallout Patterns Attributed to ICBM Bases, Dose–Rates at One Year.

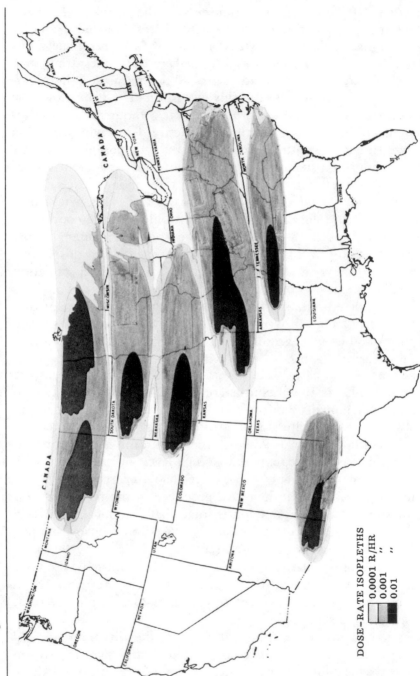

DOSE–RATE ISOPLETHS

0.0001 R/HR
0.001 "
0.01   "

Source: C.M. Hoaland, C.V. Chester, and E.P. Wigner, *Survival of the Relocated Population of the U.S. after a Nuclear Attack* Oak Ridge National Laboratory, ORNL–5401 (June 1976), p. 53.

Grain is a basic food staple both for livestock and humans. North Americans consume about 2,000 pounds per capita, which is about five times the average in less developed countries. Regions VI and IV, the most severely affected areas, contain from 40 to more than 80 percent of the most important grains and animal feed: wheat, corn (grain), rye, sorghum, oats, barley, soybeans, and silage corn (see Table 3-3). The most seriously affected states for a winter attack (those having portions of the state within the 200 rem contour) produce 45 to 80 percent of the grains and feed cited above. Region VI alone contains 50 percent of the wheat and 40 percent of the corn crops.

For the fallout patterns discussed above the critical period will be the spring, when radiation will interfere with the harvesting of some crops, such as winter wheat, as well as the planting of the land for the next fall. These losses will have repercussions within the next six months. By the summer, grain stocks will be significantly depleted, especially if foreign exports continue to maintain needed levels of foreign exchange. (The combination of economic disruption cited above and foreign concerns may make these food sales a critical need.) With the loss of a substantial part of the winter crop and that of the coming fall, it will be extremely difficult to insure adequate supply over the next year. This could be true even if only part of the crop is lost, because unlike past decades, the U.S. stored grain reserves have been quite variable—becoming critically low at times (such as in 1974).

Complicating the prediction of production and supply further is that physical survival, per se, does not insure adequate supply. The trauma to the organizational structure in these regions—a combination of deaths and injuries, evacuation (discussed in Chapter 9), and fear of radiation and new attacks—may leave the production and distribution systems in serious disarray. For areas such as the Northeast (Regions I and II) where food has to travel a thousand miles or more, the combination of reduced production, and the effects of evacuation and social disorganization throughout the food distribution system caused by radioactive contamination may create very serious food supply problems. These problems may be especially severe if a full ICBM/SAC-directed attack takes place. Under these circumstances, relatively undamaged (by radiation) food production capacity and especially distribution centers in the South and Southwest would be affected and disrupted by nuclear attacks on local SAC bases, further degrading the overall system.

Another important result of all these losses is the changing price of food. As noted for livestock (cattle, sheep, and pigs), if a significant reduction in food supply exists even temporarily (for a year or less), the price of food is likely to jump drastically without government controls. The federal government would then be forced to intervene either through instituting fixed prices and allocation policies, or at the least, by forbidding exports to ensure domestic supplies at equitable prices. The economic impact on individual farmers and the agricultural sector could be extraordinary, changing the nature of economic relationships at least temporarily between the farmer and the federal government, and between the U.S. government and foreign buyers.

Moreover, despite higher prices, the immediate and future crop losses sustained by many farmers could force economically marginal and even healthy farms into dire financial conditions, perhaps bankruptcy. Although limited financial disasters in farming are not unusual, the scale of the problem would dwarf previous demands on the federal government.

The importance of these disruptions and dislocations of food supply and distribution can be seen in the Japanese experience in World War II:

> As the war continued, the supplies of fish and rice fell seriously and almost uncontrolled inflation permitted inequities to develop in the distribution of the limited amounts that were available.
>
> *The net result of this situation, the mass of evidence shows, was widespread undernourishment, nutritional disease, social conflict, and depression of the will to resist.* (Emphasis added.)[21]

Seen in the context of a protracted controlled nuclear war requiring massive urban evacuation and causing social and economic disorganization, the problems identified become more real and compelling. Moreover, the social conflict and its political consequences will be highly disruptive (as discussed in the next section). In fact the U.S. Strategic Bombing Survey noted that "consumer deprivations, such as food shortages, were also more important" than the atomic bomb in "inducing certainty of defeat."[22]

The domestic economic impact of food exports deserves further discussion. The United States may find itself in a serious bind. If it sells abroad it can have tremendous effects on prices at home. If the United States does not, then, as noted above, the loss of export income resulting from both restricted food trade and industrial disruption (discussed below) may severely affect its balance of payments. This in turn would dangerously weaken the dollar. Its general effects on the U.S. economy, particularly on the spiraling prices of imports, could be profoundly disruptive. The secondary effect of a weakened dollar on the stability of world oil prices and the prices of other commodities could also be very serious. There is another relevant question—whether the initial crops are even salable because of contamination fears.

Finally, the United States.'s food exports problem could have grave human as well as serious financial repercussions on the rest of the world. North America, especially the United States, has become the breadbasket of the world; grains such as wheat and sorghum, soybeans, and feedstocks are exported in massive amounts. No other area has the capability to provide substantial basic food exports to the rest of the world—especially disaster aid to third world countries threatened by drought (Sahel, Africa) increasing population (Indian subcontinent) and manmade disasters (Cambodia). The implications of a drastic reduction in production are clear. We have only to look at the tenuous nature of the world food reserves and remember the desperation and near worldwide famine of the 1973–1974 period to draw the obvious conclusions. Even if the United States itself can somehow absorb this traumatic blow, how will the rest of the world? The United States has exported 70 percent of its wheat, 20 percent of its corn, 20 percent of its oats, 15 percent of its barley, 25 percent of its sorghum, and 40 percent of its soybean production.[23] In terms of world trade U.S. exports average nearly 50 percent of the wheat[24] (for grain), 70 percent of the corn (for grain), 80 percent of the soybean, and 20 percent of the rice (rough) traded.[25] Thus, even if limited to a few years, a dramatic disruption in U.S. food production capacity leading to significant restriction on the ability or desire to export could have serious and perhaps long-term worldwide repercussions on the international financial structure (stability of the dollar), world food supplies and prices, and even the distribution of world or regional power.

This analysis, therefore, reveals that a significant number of countries should not view themselves as deeply concerned but disinterested spectators to the strategy of limited nuclear war. They should perceive limited nuclear war as a direct threat to their own economic and political stability. The interest of some countries (Japan, India) or areas (Europe, Asia, Africa) in having any controlled nuclear war concept rejected by the Soviet Union and the United States may be very high. The implications of this problem for worldwide politics are very significant, needing serious attention.

In summary, the food production system of the United States will potentially be deeply damaged and normal ways of doing business disrupted by a limited nuclear attack. Ironically, the limited nature of the counterforce attack insures a high level of survival of the U.S. population, which increases the disruptive effects of a counterforce attack by putting an even greater stress on the food production system.

The combination of domestic human and economic disruption as well as worldwide ramifications would be severe. All of these changes must be set against the criterion of a "benign," "controllable" limited nuclear war.

MEDICAL IMPLICATIONS

The estimate of 10 to 20 million casualties during a limited nuclear attack creates a particularly severe impact in the medical care sector. Looking at the available medical care, about 200,000[26] physicians and 450,000 nurses are in the regions most affected—this corresponds to a patient–doctor ratio of between 50 and 100 to 1, and a doctor plus nurse to patient ratio of 15 to 30 to 1. If we assume that only 50 percent of these patients actually require hospitalization and special care this would result in 5 to 10 million patients. These regions have about 600,000 short-term hospital beds available for acute care. Since the proposed attack is assumed not to be seriously disruptive of the society, a minimum of 50 percent of these beds will be occupied, by other patients. Hence, about 300,000 beds will be available to the injured. The ratio is 15 to 30 patients per bed.

These ratios may seriously underestimate the problems because we have not accounted for the casualties among doctors and other medical personnel, the temporary loss of hospital facilities due to fallout, and the social disorganization due to both evacuation and mandatory restriction of medical personnel to shelters (up to two weeks). Even if the whole United States could be used efficiently (which is unrealistic), the patient–doctor ratio would be still on the order of between 25 and 50 patients to 1 doctor, and the short-term hospital beds to patient ratio would be between 10 and 20 to 1. There are approximately 500,000 long-term beds, mostly psychiatric, to deal with rehabilitative needs. Thus, extended medical care requirements will fall most heavily on acute care hospitals.

However, as serious as the gross demands on medical service are, the specific medical and organizational requirements are more overwhelming. As previously stated, to effectively treat radiation problems would require antibiotics, and in many cases blood transfusions and bone marrow transplants. The latter technique would place extensive demands on hospital services for long periods of time (months at a minimum). Moreover, it would be very difficult to distinguish initially which radiation cases were hopeless—thus much medical effort would be devoted to useless work. This would be particularly true in a limited attack such as this one, where the lack of urban destruction would create an image of greater medical capability than actually would exist. Thus, a sense of guilt in not treating individuals under these circumstances might overcome good medical judgment. The combination of the inadequacy of facilities and personnel, and the complex requirements (especially those of long duration) of effective treatment for radiation would impose both short- and long-term burdens on the medical system with which it will not be prepared to cope. Therefore, fallout victims and even patients suffering from normal illnesses are likely to receive significantly degraded care.

There is another aspect that also must be recognized. It is almost certain that a significant portion of patients with fallout injuries and even normal illnesses will have to be evacuated and redistributed throughout the country. At least some contaminated areas will have to be totally evacuated, forcing all patients to leave including those in nursing homes and in psychiatric facilities. The societal impact of transporting and distributing millions of the sick within and outside the affected regions will be enormous. The Three Mile Island discussion in Appendix A illustrates the difficult choices that will have to be made.

Finally, there is one further complicating medical factor. If the postattack period is an unstable and threatening military stalemate, which it is quite likely to be, the full utilization of the medical facilities and personnel of prime urban targets (large cities) will be diminished if not totally eliminated because of unplanned or planned evacuation. This situation could further degrade effective medical care for weeks or months.

Of equal concern will be the complex demands on social services needed to support these movements: distribution of medical records and resolution of any medical payment problems (Blue Cross/Blue Shield, union medical payments, etc.); welfare for patients and their families; relocation and social services for the families of patients requiring long-term care (especially children without healthy parents); and issues like the appropriateness of using workman's compensation and other types of disability (nonwelfare) payments for the evacuated ill.

Taken as a whole, the postattack medical situation will be very serious, and the social impacts stemming from it may present even more demanding problems for the society than the direct requirements of medical care. Moreover, the combination of inadequate food (discussed in the previous section) and medical care should produce destructive results similar to those described below:

> The general health of the Japanese people is deteriorating. There is malnutrition plus lack of medical personnel and facilities for taking care of the sick and the bombing victims. The government admitted during the Diet interpellations in February, 1945, that the physical condition of Japanese youths had declined.
>
> The health situation gives suggestive evidence of the extent and degree of the detrimental living conditions.[27]

Energy

Limited nuclear war will not seriously damage energy facilities or resources such as oil wells, mines, refineries, or power plants. However, due to the United States's heavy use of imported petroleum (20 percent of total energy), substantial problems can arise if, as it is likely, petroleum from foreign sources is cut off. This will be a particular problem since high industrial and population survival implies high demand. The resumption of sales would depend on the favorable termination of the nuclear conflict for the United States (at least back to the pre-attack status quo), confidence in U.S. economic stability, and a high degree of political stability in the oil-producing nations and their regional area. The Persian Gulf, with its proximity to the Soviet Union and its own inherent instabilities, would be a likely candidate for upheaval and extended interruption.

This would affect not only the United States but, more severely, Japan and Western Europe.

Even modest damage to oil refineries may turn out to be deceptive. This damage, coupled with the shut down of Midwest refineries due to heavy evacuation and disorganization from fallout and attacks on nearby SAC bases, could produce a temporary but highly disruptive situation. The extent of this disruption could be measured by the effect even a marginal reduction in oil imports produced in 1979.

The other nationwide issue that may emerge from the introduction of Electromagnetic Pulse (EMP), (Chapter 2, p. 24). This pulse of energy can cause malfunctions of control computers dispatching electricity throughout the system, thus damaging relays and monitor/control circuits which could literally shutdown the national electrical grid system. Even a short period of electrical supply interruption could create the kind of chaos seen in New York City in 1977, a situation that lasted only two days.

POLITICAL AND SOCIAL IMPLICATIONS

Having set the stage through the discussion of a variety of economic and other more quantifiable effects, this section will examine broader social and political issues.

Leadership under Stress

Sociological, psychological, and organizational factors are likely to determine and constrain, directly or indirectly, the type of response permitted a nation's leadership in the event of limited nuclear war, particularly one that is prolonged. (A prolonged stalemate is likely to permit stronger political pressure to be applied to national leadership, while a short-term crisis may insulate leaders more from immediate pressure.) This is especially true since a loss of faith in political institutions and leadership is a likely initial national response to a nuclear attack.[28] A contemporary example, but on a substantially less severe scale, is the enormous distrust of public officials created by the accident at Three Mile Island.

Whether early public reaction would bring an irrational demand for military action, a stunned acquiescence to the initiative of the present national leadership, or a strong move to reject and replace that leadership, is not clear.

A great deal of what would happen depends on the context of the nuclear exchange. Did aggressive acts or provocation occur? What precipitated the exchange? How deeply was the country divided before the exchange—politically, racially, ethnically? In essence, had the government, through a combination of its own policies and because of pervasive division within the country, lose its credibility? Or was the attack perceived as an aggressive and unprovoked attack by a discrete enemy?

If the response is demand for military action or rejection of leadership, it may be totally impossible to terminate the conflict with any reasonable degree of certainty. Even acquiescence does not guarantee swift termination because of the difficulties of completing the actual negotiations.

During World War II Japan was faced with a similar problem. Its leadership was under stress, heavy losses were apparent and defeat possible. The destructive tensions among government officials and the public hostility generated by the growing losses became significant. (They are discussed more extensively on pages 227–229 in Chapter 7.)

Whether the struggle after a counterforce attack will be so divisive that internal stalemate or chaos may result cannot be projected definitively. However, it is of great interest that even when defeat was clearly accepted in Japan, it took months to end the war with a negotiated peace; the U.S. Strategic Bombing Survey reported the decision to surrender was made in May 1945, three months before Hiroshima and Nagasaki.[29]

This raises again one of the most serious problems with the whole limited war concept—that is, how does termination of the crisis come? Does it come through negotiations, inaction, or new nuclear exchange?

Of particular concern in this regard is that in the counterforce scenario no one is defeated in a conventional military or political sense. Thus, the ability of the U.S. or Soviet political leaders to find a formula that implies an acceptable stalemate may require protracted internal as well as external negotiations. This protracted period of indecision leads to the disturbing possibility of what Fred Iklé described in the late 1950s as the "broken back" or unterminated war.[30] His scenario was a nuclear exchange inflicting great damage but with sufficient surviving infrastructure so that a military stalemate with continued fighting resulted.

Limited war strategy ensures a variation of this stalemated situation because a portion of the ICBM–SAC structure remains intact under the terms of the DOD scenarios along with a substantial undamaged Submarine Launched Ballistic Missile (SLBM) force. Under these circumstances, what would be the impact of this type of unterminated war dragging on for weeks and months? And what are the implications for resolving this counterforce conflict?

A pertinent example is the eventual Japanese public reaction against their war leadership during World War II. The public rejected the leadership's claims of omnipotence, power, and courage when damage to the society became evident:

> . . . Toward their other leaders from the prime minister down, the attitude of the people changed greatly. At first the people were proud of and greatly trusted their leaders, but as news of the war reverses began to leak through, and as cabinet changes took place, the confidence of the people in their leadership was rudely shaken and finally utterly shattered . . . the people themselves were not fully united in the latter part of the war.[31]

Resentment toward national leadership, especially in bombed areas, was true of other damaged nations such as Germany, and even Britain. The important point to be made is that while the traumatic effects of a counterforce by itself would be severe, the prolonged terror of an unresolved nuclear conflict would have a corrosive impact on the credibility of national leadership.

Psychological Effects

From a psychological point of view, the imagery of nuclear war, the pervasiveness of casualties, the possibility of massive media (such as TV and radio) exposure, and the intense fear of radioactivity that has been manifested in the United States, should make the nuclear war survivor syndrome (the powerful sense of personal vulnerability described in detail in Chapter 7), to varying degrees, quite widespread. This would be true even without a geographically dispersed SAC-base attack, since fallout would create the imagery of nuclear threat and vulnerability throughout the nation.

There are other psychological facets of this problem—irrational impulses would be at work because of the experience of Hiroshima and the increased awareness of the possibility of fallout and radiation injury. Deep suspicion that the immediate survivors are contaminated with radiation could pervade the unexposed population, even when contamination is not realistic. The symbolic effect of being exposed ("tainted") could lead to the creation of what in Japan became "bomb lepers"—people who survived Hiroshima or Nagasaki, but who then were rejected or shunned by society.[32]

The survivors (*hibakusha*, as the Japanese call them) in these circumstances would become the living symbols of the society's vulnerability and impotence. Thus, like the traditional scapegoat, the exposed could be rejected by the unexposed.[33] Moreover, the feelings of those outside contaminated areas may be translated into antagonism and anger. Just as the English bitterly withdrew their aid to the Irish in the 1840s as the potato crops continued to fail, the populations of undamaged regions, in some instances, will perceive the survivors as an overwhelming burden—a responsibility with which they are unable to cope. Therefore, they might want to reject and escape from them:

> Little sympathy was felt for Ireland; her misfortunes were too frequent, too hopeless, too impossible to remedy. . . .
>
> Even the total failure of the potato in 1848 had not been much noticed, though the failure of 1846 had been universally reported as a horrifying and shattering catastrophe. In the winter of 1848–49 no subscriptions were raised, no philanthropic persons knitted or sewed for the Irish destitute. Compassion for Ireland was dead.[34]

Significantly, the fears of contamination and rumors about contagion persisted for several months after the attack on Hiroshima.[35] This problem was also seen in the continuing distrust and fear of radioactive emissions reported months after the accident in the population neighboring the Three Mile Island plant.[36] Limited nuclear war could aggravate and prolong the period of conflict, especially with the presence of large-scale fallout. Consequently, given the power of the nuclear imagery, the survivors, just as those from Hiroshima, might find themselves isolated, rejected, and denied adequate assistance—a basis for further conflict.

The potential combination of all or even some of the physical and social turmoil discussed in this and other sections of the book, might force the national leadership to an attempt to resolve an essentially untenable situation by military action or negotiations as quickly as possible.

Evacuation

There is another likely result if the nuclear exchange were not terminated immediately—after seeing the impact of the limited counterforce attack, a substantial proportion of the population in major urban areas would demand removal from these areas. (For family members and personnel not performing essential tasks evacuation is certainly likely.) It is also likely that a substantial number of individuals and families would simply leave at their own discretion,[37] as many did during the accident at Three Mile Island, resulting in considerable economic (high absenteeism) and social chaos. Even with planned evacuation, many will flee on their own, reacting to their fear of an ill-conceived evacuation plan. All would see themselves as survivors and potential victims even if they are in undamaged areas; and as survivors or victims, they would be strongly driven by fear and guilt to decrease their own vulnerability.[38] This demand would be very powerful if ICBM radiation impacts were coupled with an attack on highly dispersed (and more visible) SAC bases. All regions of the United States would experience the feeling of increased vulnerability and fear, particularly if censorship does not prevent radio and television coverage of the damage and casualties without evacuation.

Iklé describes the likely response to this experience and the limits of government control. While the description is based on a more urban-oriented attack, the combination of 10 to 20 million injuries, destruction in or near major urban areas, and the continuing threat of radiation from fallout make a comparison realistic and credible:

> More important than the government's views about returning civilians to the cities after attack are the individual decisions of the workers themselves, since the enforcement of an official policy without the co-operation of broad population groups will be very difficult in time of nuclear war. Each individual's decision, as we have seen, will be shaped primarily by the way in which his past experiences are projected into the future. After the first nuclear attacks, the thinking and planning of the survivors will be shaped by the sudden terror of the explosion, by the attendant holocaust of fires, by the widespread, utter devastation, and—above all—*by the shocking number of casualties.* Hence, if further attacks appear likely, the impulse to avoid a repeated experience will be overwhelming. Instead of the expected march back to the cities, there may rather be a further exodus of those survivors who failed to evacuate the first time. (Emphasis added.)[39]

These conclusions are supported by evidence such as " . . . after the big raids (from March on) the . . . majority of workers in (the bombed) areas disengaged themselves from production and became very interested in their own self-preservation. This behavior . . . is gradually deepening the tendency toward defeatism [in Japan]. . . ."[40]

Relating to the hypothetical counterforce attack, evacuation fully or partially of the thirteen most contaminated states for a winter attack (levels of 200 rems or more) could mean moving a substantial portion of the approximately 30 to 40 million most affected people. However, the pressure for evacuation might be even more extensive. There are approximately 140 million people in the 243 standard metropolitan statistical areas (SMSAs).[41] Of the 140 million, about 120 million are in urbanized areas (65 million in the central cities and 55 million in the urban fringe of these central cities). Thus, more than 50 percent of the U.S. population is in compact urban areas constituting less than 1 percent of the total land mass.

More realistically, let us take the largest 157 SMSAs with populations of more than 200,000 people. The total population is 127 million (census statistics for 1970) of which 57 million are in the central city, about 50 million are in the urban fringe, and about 20 million are classified as rural. If just half the population were to be evacuated from the central cities, leaving essential workers, about 28.5 million people would have to be cared for. With 50 percent evacuation of the cities and urbanized areas, implying concern about those potentially within the 1 psi contour, more than 50 million people would be evacuated. Alternately, a complete evacuation of the central city would move over 50 million people. Logistically alone, the government would have to deal with perhaps 30 to 50 million evacuees, in addition to a portion of the 10 to 20 million or more injured and other threatened inhabitants of the highly contaminated regions not accounted for in these SMSA–based estimates. A specific example in Figure 3–11 shows the full evacuation of major metropolitan areas postulated by ORNL.[42] Despite the evacuation, the map shows most of the population in the general vicinity of the major metropolitan areas. The rural areas east of the Mississippi and the West Coast, where the populations are relocated, are overwhelmed as the population per dwelling (Table 3–4) soars over the normal three persons per unit, approaching 15 persons per unit and higher. Complicating the housing density and food distribution problems already

Figure 3-11. Evacuation of Major Metropolitan Areas.

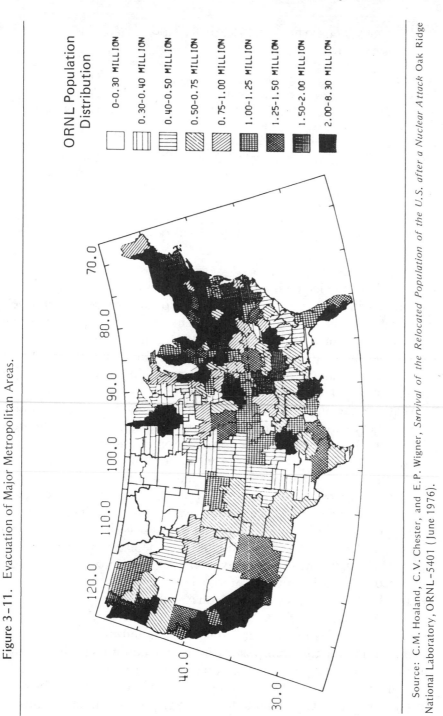

ORNL Population
Distribution

☐	0-0.30 MILLION
▥	0.30-0.40 MILLION
▤	0.40-0.50 MILLION
▨	0.50-0.75 MILLION
▨	0.75-1.00 MILLION
▦	1.00-1.25 MILLION
▦	1.25-1.50 MILLION
▥	1.50-2.00 MILLION
■	2.00-8.30 MILLION

Source: C.M. Hoaland, C.V. Chester, and E.P. Wigner, *Survival of the Relocated Population of the U.S. after a Nuclear Attack* Oak Ridge National Laboratory, ORNL-5401 (June 1976).

Table 3-4. States with Relocation Hosting Factors Greater than Three.

Arizona	5	Maine	6	Ohio	4
California	9	Maryland	4	Pennsylvania	6
Colorado	3.5	Massachusetts	6	Rhode Island	6
Connecticut	6	Michigan	4	Vermont	6
Delaware	4	New Hampshire	6	Virginia	4
Florida	5	New Jersey	6	Washington	4
Illinois	4	New York	6	West Virginia	4
Indiana	4				

Source: C.M. Hoaland, C.V. Chester, and E.P. Wigner, *Survival of the Relocated Population of the U.S. after a Nuclear Attack*, Oak Ridge National Laboratory, ORNL-5401 (June 1976), p. 28.

identified are the large population movements originating in the midwest that will be forced further east and south because of high levels of radiation. The population movement from these areas may be more extreme than postulated by ORNL, increasing already high eastern densities but probably affecting the South most. Evacuation and relocation under these circumstances would be highly disruptive for all concerned.

What are the implications of this massive movement of people? The effects of the economic attack scenarios (discussed in Chapters 5, 6, and 7) provided a realistic indication of the problem. Clearly the most obvious impact is a severe if not total disruption of the whole urban, social, and economic system, on a national scale.

Evacuation from urban areas or whole regions will disperse population and surviving manpower. Food, water, fuel, housing, and medical supplies will be adequate in some areas (at least during an initial period), and only partially adequate or inadequate in others. A significant maldistribution could exist between regional units. Important recovery work required of the cities would also be disrupted because human resources might be unavailable.

Workers could be forced temporarily to live in the cities away from their families or evacuate to rural areas and thus put additional severe strains on the transport system and family stability. Consequently, it will take a major national organizational effort to maintain and integrate resources, equipment, and manpower effectively during a period of unterminated conflict or postattack uncertainty.

During a limited war, effective organization should inevitably include the need for very different (i.e., extensive) short- to midterm governmental powers certainly in terms of 20th century American experience.

These powers would be needed to stabilize a deeply disturbed and fearful population—a population that could undercut the negotiating stance of the federal government by either rejecting its leadership or visibly destroying the outward show of strength (through a disintegrated social and economic climate) needed to negotiate favorably with an adversary.

The limited nuclear war scenario, even more than the smallest economic-oriented attack discussed in Chapter 5 represents a situation similar to the British experience in World War II, in which limited evacuation eventually created class conflict and social disorganization. There the initial period of altruism after the influx of evacuees into the receiving areas disintegrated under prolonged stress, uncertainty, and inadequate social resources (see Chapter 7).

This same situation is possible in a limited nuclear war scenario, particularly if the attack is restricted to ICBMs. Although there is both damage and threat, massive numbers of uninjured individuals could be leaving undamaged urban areas, and the recipients of this "invasion" of evacuees may be less sympathetic if food, housing, and medical supplies become seriously stressed. Under these circumstances, the existence of a normal altruistic period occurring during and after a crisis (hurricane, flood) might be subverted by the large numbers of casualties and evacuees forced to migrate into the rural areas.

Iklé recognized the potential for conflict between rural and suburban populations and urban evacuees. He believed that despite rural resistance, the overwhelming numbers of evacuees would force a grudging sharing of goods. However, this may not be the case. Limited nuclear war is strongly biased by its very nature to create the potential for these conflicts. Moreover, the problem is likely to be exaggerated in the United States. If the central city population is evacuated to the suburban and rural areas, the racial composition of the population will change. Almost 25 percent of the population in the central cities of the 157 SMSAs discussed above is nonwhite, while only 6 percent of the suburban and rural population is nonwhite. Moreover, the income distribution is very different, with the inner cities generally being poorer. Thus a combination of class and racial conflict may exacerbate the social tensions that existed in a situation similar to England in World War II. This will be particularly true if the war remains unterminated for any substantial period of time. This type of emerging racial conflict arose in Japan at the end of World War II: "The Koreans, who have been imported for labor, are feared and suspected of plotting against the Japanese. . . . Rumors and recrimination regarding a scapegoat minority such as the Koreans rose especially sharply."[43]

Given the changing but still unstable state of relations between white and nonwhite, and rich and poor groups in the United States, a dangerous conflict-laden situation might emerge under the conditions of terror and stress. Add to this the normal urban–suburban–rural lifestyle dichotomies, and there is the potential of extreme disruption, perhaps even more long-lasting and threatening to societal stability than the physical damage.

Equally as serious in an unterminated war situation would be the symbolism of a decision not to evacuate. It could be interpreted by minority groups and the poor in the central cities to mean that they were expendable—a situation that would hardly be acceptable. While these scenarios are hypothetical, the basis for these conflicts are firmly embedded in the present social context of the United States, which includes, in the view of some groups and individuals, the continuing lack of credibility of basic social and political institutions, and more quiescent but still unresolved ethnic and ideological conflicts.

A lingering distrust in the effectiveness of the federal government might develop even if the situation did not erupt into additional nuclear exchanges. The sense of continuing anxiety experienced by children subjected to a comparatively mild earthquake in Los Angeles.[44] (in a sense, a loss of trust in the stability of the ground beneath their feet), and the mistrust and fear found after Three Mile Island may have a parallel in attitudes in a limited nuclear war scenario. The experience of evacuation and its anxiety-producing sense of vulnerability may traumatize the evacuees into losing faith in the government in power. Implicitly, this may be translated into a sense that stability and continuity has been lost; that the government has failed in its most basic function, which is to act as a protector, a surrogate parent, in providing security. A loss of this implicit trust cannot help but injure the government's prestige, and thus, its ability to lead.

The imagery of massive casualties experienced directly or indirectly through the media, the confusion and stress of evacuation, the anxiety of not being evacuated, and the fact that the U.S. population has not had direct experience with war and war damage in this century, is a strong argument for this loss of faith. Moreover, inaction or the appearance of a lack of a response to the limited attack may further dissipate the government's credibility. Thus, there will be a strong impetus for the government to provide tangible evidence that it has effectively maintained the preattack status quo.

Organizational problems merge and are reinforced by the credibility and evacuation issues. The U.S. government has had no real experience with extensive natural disasters or domestically fought wars to prepare it for disasters on the scale of a limited nuclear war. Thus, serious errors of judgment in delivering services, planning and executing evacuations, and maintaining an ongoing urban economic life should be expected. This assumption about organizational inadequacies is not made to denigrate the capabilities of the U.S. government to plan effectively for civil defense, but is based on the realistic assumption that because no prior experience exists with regard to nuclear wars of this scale, no amount of planning can anticipate all the subtle but significant problems that could arise. (More extensive discussions occur in Chapters 7 and 9.)

PERSPECTIVE

What would life be like after a counterforce attack? It would be anything but the "limited," "benign" national experience that is required to make this strategy credible.

In contrast to the proposed characteristic of limited destructiveness, the counterforce or limited nuclear war proposals examined lead to these findings:

- The casualties produced—7 to 15 million deaths and 10 to 20 million injuries—will be overwhelming, reinforcing the imagery of extreme threat and vulnerability posed by nuclear war and radioactive contamination.

- The fallout from an attack on ICBM bases will produce significant injury and dislocation of the U.S. food-producing system. Substantial numbers of skilled farmers will be killed, injured, or permanently disabled. Crops will be lost and farms unusable for months or even years (in the case of radioactive hot spots). The distribution system will not work effectively because of social disorganization, evacuation, and hoarding, causing imbalances of food supply among geographical regions. Prices will dramatically rise and major government intervention and controls will be needed.

- Casualties, evacuation, land denial, or restricted access to contaminated areas, will create serious national as well as severe local economic dislocations. The possibility of bottle-necking the economy for many industrial sectors through the disruption of production in key industries also appears very likely. The result would be unprecedented governmental intervention to save industries from bankruptcies, control prices, allocate goods, and determine industrial priorities. The implementation of these policies will be politically explosive.

- The injured and evacuated population would create enormous social service (medical care, welfare, housing, etc.) demands and financial disruptions (deferred mortgages, rents, and time payments; massive savings withdrawals) in a period when the serious economic problems already identified are being most severely felt.

- The medical care system will be initially overwhelmed by the 10 to 20 million injured; both the radiation victims and those ill with conventional problems will receive degraded medical services. Degraded treatment should continue for an extended period because of the extreme and continuing demands of those injured by fallout, the loss of some physicians and hospitals (through contamination) in specific regions and the potential disruption of the manufacture and distribution of medical supplies. The support systems for medical care, medical insurance, and records will be in a chaotic state, particularly because of evacuation.

- Evacuation, particularly in combination with a prolonged war, will generate divisive social conflicts within the population as well as economic and social dislocation. Individual psychological effects of helplessness, fear, and anger will be widespread. They could be easily translated into a loss of trust and support for national leadership. The effect of all these problems is that the organizational needs to bring stability to the society will be overwhelming, and thus governmental intervention will substantially exceed peacetime and recent wartime activities. Conflicts between national effectiveness and individual liberties, particularly property rights, should become serious.

- Internationally, the United States may encounter severe balance of payment difficulties. These difficulties would be attributed to reductions in industrial and food production that would trigger a severely imbalanced import/export trade. This would undercut the dollar's stability and the international monetary system.

Nor are the consequences limited to domestic or international effects on the United States and Soviet Union alone. A perfect example is the United States's key role as a world food producer, an exporter of food to many nations, such as Japan. With a deeply injured food production system, exports should be severely limited, if they are permitted at all. Thus, a significant number of nations may find themselves victims of this attack, with their own stability threatened, although not directly physically damaged. The acceptance by the United States (or the Soviet Union) of the effect of a counterforce assault without an attempt at retaliation of some sort, would almost certainly trigger deterimental international realignments, specifically the dramatic weakening or severing of close ties with the United States (or Soviet Union) of long-time allies, particularly in Europe. As an additional consequence, regional power struggles, reflecting increased international instability, should also occur. Moreover, the oil-producing nations may perceive the massive investments of petrodollars in Europe and the United States as no longer viable, and attempt to reduce their dependency — with further critical financial consequences. In fact these nations may be unwilling to supply any of the combatants, namely Europe, Japan, as well as the United States, until the outcome is clear. The overall international situation would be highly unstable.

What would life be like after a limited attack? Would it be acceptable? Would it be controllable? After examining the effects, and more importantly, the unpredictable and uncontrollable domestic and international forces that will be unleashed, it is difficult to see how a serious national leader could feel comfortable with the risks and uncertainties involved in adopting such a fragile and dangerous strategy.

Still, a lingering question may remain: Could the outcome be different if different assumptions were made? Of course some quantitative changes in targeting could be made, different physical factors (such as wind patterns) could be chosen to modify fallout patterns, but the qualitative effects, especially those related to social disorganization and conflict, psychological fear and distrust, evacuation and economic priorities, and political effectiveness and credibility, would remain. The burden of proof for political acceptability falls on the shoulders of those who propose limited nuclear war, or other forms as yet unspecififed, of "controlled" nuclear conflict. They must convincingly prove that domestic and international effects meet the political acceptability criteria, and then make a credible case for how one simply turns off the conflict at the proper moment. They must be able to tell us: What would life be like after limited nuclear war?

NOTES TO CHAPTER 3

1. *Analyses of Effects of Limited Nuclear Warfare*, Subcommittee on Arms Control, International Organizations and Security Agreements, Committee on Foreign Relations United States Senate, (Washington, D.C.: Government Printing Office, September 1975): Appendix A, p. 101.

2. Ibid., p. 26–27.

3. Limited nuclear war was part of a broader "damage limiting" strategy. This strategy was designed to limit damage to the population and industrial capacity if deterrence failed by reducing the effectiveness of the enemy's attack. Another aspect of the damage limiting strategy was a defensive capability such as the antiballistic missile (ABM) system. Widespread use of this technology was limited in the first Strategic Arms Limitation Treaty (SALT I) in 1972.

4. It should be assumed that "soft" military targets, such as airfields and weapons factories, have always been part of the targeting strategy.

5. *Analyses of Effects of Limited Nuclear Warfare*, p. 20.

6. Silos are blast-resistant enclosures where ICBMs are stored.

7. *Analyses of Effects of Limited Nuclear Warfare*, p. 47.

8. The Secretary of Defense assumed 65 percent of the population with a protection factor (PF) of three to fifteen, while 35 percent are in shelter with a factor of 15 to 100. As a point of reference the first floor of 2-story framed houses are expected to have PF of 3 while basements of an average home 10. Abbreviation SecDef is used in figure 3–5.

9.   Case I contains two 550 Kt weapons, one air burst and one ground burst on each silo. Cases II and III result in higher fatality estimates than Case I (3.2 million), apparently due to lower levels of fallout protection assumed. The base case (II) contains two 550 Kt weapons air burst on each silo, and single air bursts on SAC and SSBN bases leading to an estimate of 6.7 million fatalities.

10. Office of Technology Assessment (OTA), *The Effects of Nuclear War*, Congress of the United States (Washington, D.C.: Government Printing Office, May 1979), p. 84.

11. Roger Sullivan, et al., *Civil Defense Needs of High Risk Areas of the United States* (Arlington, Va.: System Planning Corporation, 1979), p. 22.

12. Office of Technology Assessment, p. 86.

13. Manufacturing value added (MVA) is the dollar difference between the value of a raw material or semifinished product and the final manufactured product.

14. *Census of Manufacturers, 1977*, states: Illinois, Indiana, Kansas, Kentucky, Minnesota, Missouri, Montana, Nebraska, North Dakota, Ohio, South Dakota, and Tennessee for a winter attack. Georgia and Michigan were added, while Ohio and Tennessee were deleted for the March fallout pattern analyses.

15. Alexander Leighton, *Human Relations in a Changing World* (New York: E.P. Dutton & Co., 1949), pp. 70–71.

16. This would be consistent with findings that pre-attack evacuation creates substantial economic disorganization and dislocation leading to serious economic losses. See Richard K. Laurino, Frank Trinkl, Carl F. Miller and Robert A. Harker, *Economic and Industrial Aspects of Crisis Relocation: An Overview.* DCPA 01–75–c–0279 (Palo Alto: Center for Planning and Research, May 1977); and Richard Laurino, Frank Trinkel, Robert Berry, Ruth Schnider, William MacDougall, *Impacts of Crisis Relocation on U.S. Economic and Industrial Activity.* DCPA 01–76–c–0331 (Palo Alto: Center for Planning and Research, Inc., October 1978).

17. Stephen L. Brown and Ulrich F. Pilz, *U.S. Agriculture: Potential Vulnerabilities* (Menlo Park, California: Stanford Research Institute, January 1969).

18. Office of Technology Assessment, p. 89.

19. C.M. Hoaland, C.V. Chester and E.P. Wigner, *Survival of the Relocated Population of the U.S. After a Nuclear Attack*, (Oak Ridge National Laboratory, ORNL–5401, June 1976), p. 53.

20. Office of Technology Assessment, pp. 88–89.

21. Leighton, p. 61.

22. Ibid., pp. 73–74.

23. U.S. Department of Agriculture, *Agricultural Statistics, 1974*, United States, (Washington, D.C.: Government Printing Office).

24. Report of the Secretary General, *General and Complete Disarmament. Comprehensive Study on Nuclear Weapons*, (United Nations General Assembly, A/35/392 English Annex, 12 September 1980, New York), p. 85.

25. Department of Commerce, *Statistical Abstracts, 1978*, (Washington, D.C.: Government Printing Office, 1978), p. 709. For year 1976.

26. We have excluded the Pacific, New England, and Middle Atlantic census divisions. Calculation based on physicians, nurses, and hospital beds for years 1976, 1972, and 1976 respectively. U.S. Department of Commerce, *Statistical Abstracts, 1978*, (Washington, D.C.: Government Printing Office, 1978), pp. 105, 111.

27. Leighton, p. 234.

28. Bruce C. Alnutt, *A Study of Consensus on Social and Psychological Factors Related to Recovery from Nuclear Attack*, prepared for the Office of Civil Defense, Department of the Army, (McLean, Virginia: Human Sciences Research, Inc., May 1971), p. S–3.

29. Leighton, p. 74.

30. Fred C. Iklé, *The Social Impact of Bomb Destruction* (Norman, Oklahoma: University of Oklahoma Press, 1958), p. 190.

31. Leighton, p. 66.

32. Robert Lifton, *Death in Life* (New York: Vantage Books, 1969), p. 106.

33. This is not an atypical reaction to massive disaster. Tuchman reports a similar reaction in the fourteenth century. For example, "the mortality was so great among the people of Normandy that those of Picardy mocked them." Barbara Tuckman, *A Distant Mirror* (New York: Alfred A. Knopf, 1978), p. 97.

34. C. Woodham–Smith, *The Great Hunger* (New York: Harper & Row, 1962), pp. 381–82.

35. Lifton, p. 516.

36. Cynthia B. Flynn, *Three Mile Island Telephone Survey, Preliminary Report on Procedure and Findings* (Mountain West Research, Inc. with Social Impact Research, Inc., NUREG/CR–1093, September 24, 1979), p. 35; and Cynthia B. Flynn and J.A. Chalmers, *The Social and Economic Effects of the Accident at Three Mile Island: Findings to Date* (NUREG/CR–1215, January 1980), pp. 65–67.

37. Roger J. Sullivan, Winder M. Heller, and E.C. Aldridge, Jr., *Candidate U.S. Civil Defense Programs* (Arlington, Virginia: System Planning Corporation, March 1978), p. E–18. A study panel predicted 10 to 30 percent of the population would spontaneously evacuate from risk areas during a crisis period *prior* to any attack.

38. See Irving Janis' and Robert Lifton's discussions of these problems reviewed in Chapter 7.

39. Iklé, p. 108.

40. Leighton, pp. 71–72.

41. *1970 Census of Population*, Department of Commerce.
42. Hoaland, Chester, and Wigner, p. 148.
43. Leighton, p. 246.
44. S. J. Howard, "Treatment of Children's Reactions to the 1971 Earthquake" (American Association of Psychiatric Services for Children, 1971 Convention, Beverly Hills, California, November 20).

4 MASSACHUSETTS
A Case Study

The preceding chapter presented the impact of limited nuclear attack from the national perspective. To complete the picture, this chapter takes a closer look by examining the effects on a specific local site. The regional area examined is in Massachusetts—specifically, the Springfield–Holyoke–Chicopee standard metropolitan statistical area (SMSA). This area contains Westover Air Force Base, a Strategic Air Command (SAC) base, and therefore a counterforce target of interest in Massachusetts. The area would not be significantly contaminated with radiation.

A variety of attacks from one 50 kiloton weapon to the proposed pattern attack[1] by Garwin et al.[2] of three 1 megaton weapons will be postulated. The one 50 Kt is not realistic because the minimum attack used by the Department of Defense (DOD) was a 200 Kt cruise missile, but it does provide a baseline. The more realistic attacks would utilize more than one 200 Kt warhead since the estimated destruction by DOD is only 40 percent of the base with a single weapon of that size.

CASUALTIES

Table 4–1 shows the casualties as killed, injured, and population affected.[3] We have examined a variety of limited war or counterforce

Table 4-1.   Casualties[a]—SMSA (*numbers in thousands*).[b]

Target–Attack	Killed	Injured	Within 1 psi
Springfield			
S-51	10 (2%)[c]	30 (5%)	100 (20%)
S-53	25 (5%)	50 (10%)	205 (40%)
S-201	25 (5%)	70 (15%)	300 (55%)
S-203	70 (15%)	120 (25%)	485 (90%)
S-1A	65 (10%)	130 (25%)	525 (95%)
S-3A	195 (35%)	155 (30%)	530 (100%)
S-3B	290 (55%)	135 (25%)	530 (100%)

Key:

S-51 = 50 Kt, 1 weapon
S-53 = 50 Kt, 3 weapons
S-201 = 200 Kt, 1 weapon
S-203 = 200 Kt, 3 weapons
S-1A = 1 Mt, 1 weapon
S-3A = 1 Mt, 3 weapons
S-3B = Assumptions: 75 percent killed and 25 percent injured within 5 psi

   a. Based on population distribution derived from 1970 Population Census.
   b. Rounded to nearest 5,000.
   c. Not rounded to nearest 5 percent.

scenarios. In order to explore fully the possibilities in the SAC–oriented attack, a range from one 50 Kt (S-51)[4] to three 1 Mt weapons was analyzed. As pointed out, 50 Kt weapons would not be used to ensure destruction of a large SAC base. Nevertheless, the 11,000 killed, 30,000 injured, and 100,000 people within the 1 pound per square inch (psi) contour represent a very high level of damage. It is equivalent to the total number of peacetime deaths for the states of Maine or Rhode Island for the entire year of 1976.

Our minimum attack should be in the three 200 Kt (S-203) range. Here the number of deaths rise to about 70,000, with 120,000 injured and a half million within the 1 psi contour. These mortality totals exceed the annual peacetime death rate for Massachusetts as a whole and equal the total for the entire Vietnam War. Moreover, virtually all the SMSA population is affected. If the attack reaches the level projected in the Congressional analysis,[5] (i.e., three 1 Mt weapons—attacks designated S-3A or S-3B[6]) then, depending on

Table 4-2. Economic Impacts[a]—Springfield-Holyoke-Chicopee SMSA (*MVA*).[b]

Attack Area	Total MVA	Within 5 psi	(%)[c]	Within 1 psi	(%)[c]
Springfield	948				
S-1A (1 1-Mt)		250	(25)	900	(95)
S-2A (2 1-Mt)		600	(65)	948	(100)
S-3A (3 1-Mt)		685	(70)	948	(100)
S-51		25	(2)[d]	200	(20)
S-53		60	(5)	365	(40)
S-201		50	(5)	500	(55)
S-203		165	(15)	660	(70)
State	8,715				

a. Based on MVA derived from 1967 Census of Manufacturers.

b. Rounded to nearest 5,000.

c. Rounded to nearest 5 percent.

d. Not rounded to nearest 5 percent.

assumptions, the number of deaths would be between 200,000 to 300,000 and the 1 psi contour would extend beyond the SMSA boundaries. The impact of this attack at any credible level will generate death and casualties within minutes that are incomprehensible by U.S. domestic peacetime and wartime standards.

ECONOMIC IMPACTS

The economic consequences of a SAC attack on Springfield are shown in Table 4-2. The smaller attacks (one 50 Kt [S-51], three 50 Kt [S-53], and one 200 Kt [S-201]) weapons exhibit serious but not overwhelming potentials for damage. This is in part because the airfield is sited at a corner of the urbanized area. However, three 200 Kt (S-203) and one 1 megaton (S-1A)—more realistic attacks—begin to encompass all the manufacturing value added (MVA) in the SMSA area. However, the economic damage for the state is small. Even the larger attacks, S-2A and S-3A, represent only overwhelming local damage, but do not directly destroy the state's economy in any meaningful sense. Only when coupled to an attack on, Boston or one similar to the part of the economic/urban attack on Massachusetts (see Chapter 8) does the damage become significant statewide. However, this conclusion should be received with caution. Since fallout disrupts the major industrial areas of the Midwest, the functional capabilities of the state's economy may be significantly smaller than the surviving physical capacity would indicate because of evacuation, land denial, or casualties. The SAC attacks would also cause disorganization throughout the rest of the country.

FOOD SUPPLY AND DISTRIBUTION

Food represents a genuine concern. With the possibility of heavy production losses nationally over an extended period of time, the general vulnerability of the Northeast due to limited production capabilities is significant. The largest impacts will be in the meat, flour, cereal, sugar, and sweets categories, which make up almost 60 percent of the protein and about 55 percent of the food energy in an average U.S. diet. The nearest producers of these foodstuffs are outside the Northeast area (see Chapter 8, p. 000 for further discussion). Although it appears unrealistic to assume total losses in any of these categories, the survival of almost the entire U.S. population—the worst estimate is 20 million fatalities, 10 percent of the U.S. population—should, as noted, stretch the capabilities of the U.S. production and distribution systems to their limits and beyond. This would almost certainly mean shortages and regional maldistribution. Thus, demands by the producing regions for first priority on foodstuffs and the distributional problem exaggerated by a possible large-scale evacuation could reduce Northeast food supplies to a depleted, although not necessarily exhausted, state.

The impact would be seen over an extended period as a decrease in the general quality and reliability of the food supply, leading to some increases in ill health and loss of general vigor. Of more significance would be the stress and conflict that could arise over the availability and equity of allocation of limited food supplies. This could create tensions among and within groups. Of particular note is the hostility between regions that could occur. These rifts could degrade general morale, and especially, trust in the impartiality of the national government.

The alternative to modifying these potential tensions is introducing a comprehensive allocation system similar to World War II's rationing systems. The danger is that, along with reactions such as hoarding or black-marketing, the siege mentality that the allocation system should enhance, will increase the sense of threat and vulnerability individuals would experience. It is important to reiterate the fact that these problems have to be measured against our criterion of limited and essentially benign effects (Chapter 1, p. 8). The absence of starvation, therefore, is not a sufficient condition for acceptability under these circumstances.

In summary, while the severity of food problems can vary extensively, the postattack situation will not merely represent an inconvenient but marginal aberration of the normal fluctuations of food supplies. A degree of hardship (i.e., significant shortages) would be introduced by the national and local attack that represents a substantial change in the normal pattern of Massachusetts life. Massachusetts will be part of a nation that has just experienced the explosion of nuclear weapons in every sector of the country—with massive ICBM-oriented fallout producing attacks in some of the United States's major food-producing areas. The general agricultural supply effects would be felt within weeks and would be of indeterminate duration, but the regional political conflict over distribution of food could more seriously affect areas such as the Northeast than the rest of the country.

ELECTRICITY AND FUEL OIL

The direct impact of the Springfield attack on electricity capacity and fuel oil should be limited. The state certainly should not have any short-term difficulties. Fuel storage capacity, electrical generating capacity, distribution facilities, and skilled manpower should be intact. Only the possibility of evacuations or serious interruptions of fuel shipments could change this picture over time. However, the possibility of limited petroleum imports due to fear of radiation and continued war is quite real, especially for the resource-poor Northeast. A prolonged period of limited external supply and internal disruption appear to be the only possible way serious problems would arise in this area.

MEDICAL CARE

Examining attack S-201 (one 200 Kt), we find the 70,000 to 80,000 casualties (dying and injured) have significantly affected the area's medical services. The casualty-to-doctor ratio is about 7 or 8 to 1, or 2 or 3 to 1 if nurses are included. The hospital bed ratio is about 2 or 3 patients for each bed. However, the demand for specialized facilities and personnel involved in effectively caring for children and burn patients makes these figures appear deceptively untroubling. These figures rest on an assumption that about 25,000 beds could accommodate 35,000 to 40,000 patients.

An additional major problem is that a very large proportion of the doctors and a significant portion of the hospital beds are in eastern Massachusetts regions—hours away from the primary damage area. The logistical difficulties here will be enormous and thus the impact on the state and northeast regions, especially in a psychological sense, could be very significant. Psychological effects in this case would not only be the sense of loss, guilt, and impotence of local survivors, but the impact of spreading casualties from Springfield and the other SAC bases of the Northeast through the New England–New York–New Jersey region. The stream of 10,000, 20,000, 30,000, 40,000 or more casualties moving out, just from Springfield, cannot help but have a major social impact. This process should create a sense of vulnerability and threat for the regional population far beyond the areas of severe damage. These emotions will exert a major influence on the strength of the impetus for urban evacuation and subsequently on the nature of the possible political response to national policies.

SOCIAL IMPACTS

Morale could be significantly changed by the type of media coverage of the aftermath of the attack. Censorship, which is not unusual in wartime, could reduce the immediacy of these impacts, but would implicitly acknowledge the gravity of the postattack situation. It would also impose a major wartime control in a situation that has been characterized as resulting only in limited civilian consequences.

We have already dealt with a broad range of general psychological and sociological issues in the previous chapter; they are also discussed in detail in Chapter 7. They have varying degrees of applicability in the context of attacks on Springfield, as part of the larger limited national attack. The most important issues, probably, are evacuation, long-term organizational difficulties, and related psychological effects. We will discuss briefly only the evacuation issue.

Evacuation issues should not be qualitatively different from those already discussed. Though casualties are smaller and restricted to one region, the possibility of forced evacuation of 1 to 2 million people from Massachusetts' cities—either en masse from the central cores or by selective removal of nonessential personnel—is likely, given their obvious vulnerability. The sense of vulnerability represented by the drive toward evacuation could be enhanced, as was pointed out, by the required redistribution of casualties throughout the region, the anxiety produced by an uncertain war/nonwar situation, and the general fear of radiation. Aside from the massive social service requirements (i.e., health care, food distribution, and shelter) and the disruption of basic community and family structure by forced separations in the evacuation of nonessential personnel, the impact of evacuation could cause a sense of unease or insecurity in the population. This again could create powerful forces to terminate or diminish the ambiguity of the postattack period by forceful government actions.

PERSPECTIVE

In general, the effects of limited nuclear war on Massachusetts mirror the damage created in the United States as a whole. However, Massachusetts illustrates the particular vulnerabilities of a resource—poor area: while only modestly damaged, it may be deeply injured by the secondary effects of a limited nuclear attack. The case of Massachusetts also raises questions about the economic stability of a moderately damaged region when it is part of a highly interdependent economy that has been substantially disrupted. Massachusetts' post-attack situation makes clear that even for relatively limited direct damage, factors such as the anticipated threats from fallout, the emotional response to large numbers of injured leaving the damaged area, and the impetus to evacuate vulnerable cities, would combine to produce serious disruptive organizational effects.

A final but predictably disruptive element would be the effect of fallout, no matter how limited. The powerful fears about radioactive contamination prevalent in the United States are likely to drive individuals out of even relatively safe, low-risk areas of Massachusetts. The disorganizing consequences of personal fears and spontaneous population movements could significantly diminish the level of effective control over an already tenuous situation.

NOTES TO CHAPTER 4

1. A specific area, an air force base, is attacked with several weapons to ensure a high probability of complete destruction.
2. Subcommittee on Arms Control, International Organizations and Security Agreements, Committee on Foreign Relations United States Senate, *Analyses of Effects of Limited Nuclear War*, September 1975, (Washington, D.C.: Government Printing Office), p. 47.
3. The casualty estimates were based on data from Hiroshima and Nagasaki.
4. S–51: S = Springfield; 5 = 50 Kt; 1 = the number of weapons.
5. *Analyses of Effects of Limited Nuclear War*, p. 47.
6. S–3B assumes because of the multiple nature of the attack, casualties are 75 percent killed and 25 percent injured within the 5 psi contour.

███ FULL-SCALE
NUCLEAR WAR
Civilian Targets

The previous chapters focused on the impact of a military-oriented, essentially nonurban attack. It was designed to be limited, and acceptable, in its societal effects, thus restraining escalation. In contrast, in subsequent chapters urban attacks specifically designed to produce unacceptable damage will be discussed. The approach will be similar to the discussion of limited nuclear war, developing a scenario — in this case a range of four possible levels of attack — to determine the effects on both a national and regional (Massachusetts) level. Again, a basic objective is to expose the complexity and interactive nature of the problems created by these attacks. In essence, the following chapters will try to expose what life would be like after this type of nuclear war. A second objective is to provide a measure of the actual weapons requirements for a highly destructive, unacceptable attack, and thus address the question, "How much is enough?"

5 NATIONAL ECONOMIC AND POPULATION DAMAGE

In this chapter a series of hypothetical nationwide nuclear attacks directed against the U.S. economy are discussed. They are designed to produce unacceptable damage by inflicting massive immediate economic damage which will prevent an effective and timely national recovery. A key ingredient of this strategy is the destruction of essential industrial sectors, for example, petroleum refining. A strategy of selected destruction was developed to enhance the direct effects by eliminating pivotal industries upon which a variety of other industries depend. Thus, the effects will be felt throughout any undamaged part of the economy. This refined strategy has become possible because the accuracy and numbers of nuclear warheads have increased dramatically in the last decade.

This chapter is designed to introduce the four attacks and present the basic industrial damage and population effects (casualties). The discussion will describe the attack strategy and discuss the industrial and population effects of the attacks on a national level.

METHODOLOGY

The largest, or principal "reference," attack is based on data from *Potential Vulnerabilities Affecting National Survival* (PVANS), a study prepared in 1970 for the Office of Civil Defense by the Stanford Research Institute (SRI) to evaluate the implications of a substantial attack on the American economy.[1] The purpose of the PVANS study was to determine the optimum attack plan for preventing U.S. economic recovery with the smallest number of nuclear weapons. The authors of PVANS proposed to accomplish this objective by inflicting heavy damage on the productive capacity of thirty-four basic, capital goods industries (Table 5–1). The attack design found to be most effective for this purpose included (1) comprehensively attacking, with high-yield (1 megaton) weapons, the industrial capacity in the seventy-one largest U.S. metropolitan areas. (Table 5–2 and Figure 5–1), which contain major concentrations of the thirty-four basic industries as well as other industries; (2) specific targeting of eight of the thirty-four critical industrial sectors with lower yield (100 kiloton) weapons (see Table 5–6).

The 1 megaton (Mt) weapons would destroy 80 percent of all manufacturing capacity in each of the seventy-one urban-industrial areas.[2] Such wholesale destruction of the industrial base would effectively mean, according to PVANS, neutralizing the entire economic capacity located in these areas, including the thirty-four vital industries. The elimination of the entire area as a functioning industrial unit would be the result of damage to the remaining 20 percent of manufacturing capacity and, most importantly, the destruction or elimination of the necessary supporting structure for economic activity (such as utilities—water, gas, electricity; transportation; social services; and labor) in these areas.

The 100 kiloton (Kt) weapons reduce surviving capacity in each of the eight industries to 3 percent or less of the preattack levels.[3] These industries are: (1) petroleum refining; (2) iron and steel works; (3) primary smelting and refining of zinc, copper, lead, and aluminum (nonferrous metals); (4) engines and turbines; (5) electrical distribution products; (6) drugs; (7) office machines; and (8) mechanical measuring devices. The result of this type of attack would be further significant disruption of the national economy. The disruption would be the result of the introduction of severe bottle-necks in industrial production by eliminating the availability of key elements (e.g., iron and steel) upon which numerous other industries (e.g., automobiles and boilers) depend. In addition, the targets for this portion of the attack include some fifty more urban areas (SMSAs) as well as smaller cities—insuring further urban impacts.[4]

Table 5-1. Thirty-four Targeted Manufacturing Sectors.

SIC[a] Code	Manufacturing Sector	SIC[a] Code	Manufacturing Sector
204	Grain mills	334	Secondary smelting and refining of nonferrous metals
262	Papermill products		
265	Paperboard containers and boxes	335	Rolling, drawing, and extruding of nonferrous metals
281	Industrial inorganic and organic chemicals	336	Nonferrous foundries
282	Plastics	339	Miscellaneous primary metal products
283	Drugs[b]		
287	Agricultural chemicals	344	Fabricated structural metal products
291	Petroleum refining[b]		
301	Tires and innertubes	345	Screw machine products and bolts, nuts, and so forth
321	Flat glass		
324	Cement, hydraulic	351	Engines and turbines[b]
327	Concrete, gypsum, and plaster products	353	Construction and like equipment
		354	Metalworking machines
331	Blast furnaces, steelworks, and rolling and finishing mills	356	General industrial machinery
		357	Office machines[b]
332	Iron and steel foundaries	361	Electric distribution products[b]
333	Primary smelting and refining of nonferrous metals[b]	362	Electrical industrial apparatus
		366	Communication equipment
	Zinc	367	Electronic components
	Copper	372	Aircraft and parts
	Lead	373	Ships and boats
	Aluminum	381	Railroad equipment
		382	Mechanical measuring devices[b]

a. Standard industrial classification.

b. Industries reduced to 2 to 3 percent of prenuclear attack capacity in supplemental (100Kt) attack.

Source: Richard Goen, R. Bothun, and F. Walker, *Potential Vulnerability Affecting National Survival* (Menlo Park, California: Stanford Research Institute, September 1970), p. 12.

Table 5-2. Seventy-one Largest U.S. SMSA's Identified by SRI.

1 New York, N.Y. (SCA)	39 Dayton, Ohio
2 Los Angeles, Calif.	40 Bridgeport, Stamford, Norwalk,
3 Chicago, Ill. (SCA)	Conn. (SEA)
4 Philadelphia, Pa.	41 Louisville, Ky.; Indiana
5 Detroit, Mich.	42 New Haven, Waterbury, Meriden,
6 San Francisco-Oakland, Calif.	Conn. (SEA)
7 Washington, D.C., Maryland,	43 Fort Lauderdale-Hollywood, Fla.
Virginia	44 Norfolk-Portsmouth, Va.
8 Boston, Lawrence, Haverhill,	45 Syracuse, N.Y.
Lowell, Mass. (SEA)	46 Fort Worth, Tex.
9 St. Louis, Mo.; Illinois	47 Albany, Schenectady, Troy, N.Y.
10 Houston, Tex.	48 Greensboro, Winston-Salem,
11 Baltimore, Md.	High Point, N.C.
12 Cleveland, Ohio	49 Providence, Pawtucket,
13 Pittsburgh, Pa.	Warwick, R.I.
14 Dallas, Tex.	50 Salt Lake City, Utah
15 Minneapolis-St. Paul, Minn.	51 Akron, Ohio
16 Atlanta, Ga.	52 Oklahoma City, Okla.
17 San Bernardino, Riverside,	53 Toledo, Ohio; Michigan
Ontario, Calif.	54 Wilmington, Del.; New Jersey;
18 Buffalo, N.Y.	Maryland
19 San Diego, Calif.	55 Jacksonville, Fla.
20 Milwaukee, Wis.	56 Worcester, Fitchburgh,
21 Seattle-Everett, Wash.	Leominster, Mass. (SEA)
22 Kansas City, Mo.-Kan.	57 Orlando, Fla.
23 San Jose, Calif.	58 Omaha, Nebr.; Iowa
24 Cincinnati, Ohio; Kentucky;	59 Nashville, Tenn.
Indiana	60 Richmond, Va.
25 Miami, Fla.	61 Oxnard-Ventura, Calif.
26 Indianapolis, Ind.	62 Springfield, Chicopèe, Holyoke,
27 Phoenix, Ariz.	Mass. (SEA)
28 Denver, Colo.	63 Youngstown, Warren, Ohio
29 New Orleans, La.	64 Flint, Mich.
30 Tampa-St. Petersburg, Fla.	65 Mobile, Ala.
31 Portland, Oreg.; Washington	66 Grand Rapids, Mich.
32 Columbus, Ohio	67 Allentown, Bethlehem, Easton,
33 Sacramento, Calif.	Pa.; New Jersey
34 Memphis, Tenn.; Arkansas	68 Charlotte, N.C.
35 Birmingham, Ala.	69 West Palm Beach, Fla.
36 Rochester, N.Y.	70 Albuquerque, N. Mex.
37 San Antonio, Tex.	71 Fresno, Calif.
38 Hartford, New Britain, Conn. (SEA)	

Notes to Table 5-2

SCA–Standard Consolidated Area, incorporation of SMSA's in large metropolitan area.
SEA–Standard Economic Area used in New England to include entire county (ies) within which SMSA is contained.

Source: Richard Goen, R. Bothun, and F. Walker, *Potential Vulnerability Affecting National Survival* (Menlo Park, California: Stanford Research Institute, September 1970), p. 31.

With regard to the urban impacts associated with the 100 Kt weapons one point should be clarified. The primary purpose of this portion of the attack is to destroy the eight industries, not to create general industrial damage or casualties. The physical location of the plant(s) may or may not be in close proximity to the highest industrial and population concentrations in these additional urban areas. Moreover, while a 100 Kt weapon is more than five times larger than those used on Hiroshima and Nagasaki, it is modest by modern standards. While major damage and casualties may be produced on many, perhaps a substantial majority of the targeted cities and urban areas, some areas will receive only modest or peripheral effects. Nevertheless, the detonation of a nuclear weapon in or near these cities will produce major social and organizational disruption, such as panic evacuation, even if no extensive physical destruction occurs. Therefore, when the words *affected* or *impacted* are used to describe the 100 Kt portion of the attack they signify real and highly disruptive changes, but not necessarily, for all areas, the high level of general industrial physical destruction assumed in the 1 Mt weapon attack.

Based on this approach, the authors of PVANS concluded that approximately 500 1-megaton nuclear weapons would accomplish the objective of neutralizing the productive capacity of the seventy-one U.S. standard metropolitan statistical areas (SMSAs) chosen by SRI. In addition, the study calculated that 200 to 300 more 100 kiloton weapons would reduce the eight selected manufacturing sectors to 2 to 3 percent of their total former (preattack) capacity, a level inadequate to sustain economic recovery.

Methodology Expansion

Taking these data as the base, one can examine the influence of a reduction in the number of warheads on the effectiveness of a hypo-

Figure 5-1.   The Basic 71 SMSAs Used as Prime Targets.

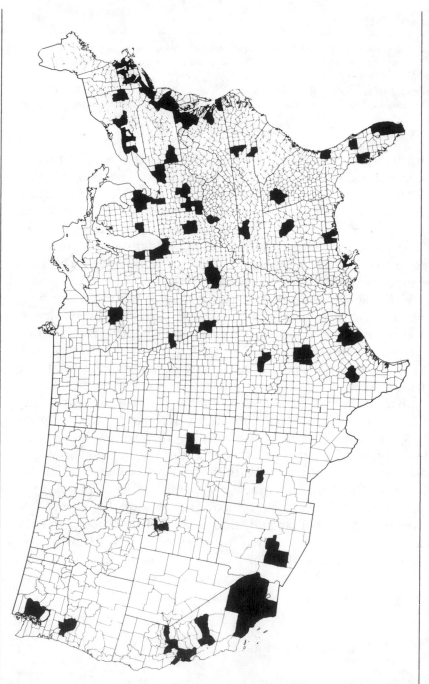

Source: Arthur Katz, *Economic and Social Consequences of Nuclear Attacks on the United States*, Committee on Banking, Housing, and Urban Affairs, U.S. Senate (Washington, D.C.: U.S. Government Printing Office, 1979). p. 6.

thetical attack. The purpose in analyzing the effects of these reduced attacks was to determine whether damage, even at lower levels, could be considered unacceptable, although the attack's ability to prevent economic recovery would be somewhat diminished. This was achieved by postulating a series of attacks (designated A-2, A-3, and A-4) using a reduced number of the 1 Mt warheads, specifically 300, 200, and 100 1 megaton weapons, respectively. The attack using 500 1 megaton weapons (designated A-1) was also included. A representative group of twelve of the seventy-one SMSAs, which differ in such factors as population size and density, were reexamined for all four attacks and used as the basis for projecting the range of overall damage (shown in Table 5-3).

In performing this expanded study, changes were made in the procedure used to make the damage estimates. In particular, the physical damage criteria used here differ from those used by the PVANS analysis. The 5 pounds per square inch (psi) (instead of 9 psi) blast effects contour is the criterion for severe damage to industrial capacity. The radius of destruction is over 4 miles (5 psi) versus about 3 (9 psi). Additionally, casualties were assumed to be 50 percent dead and 30 percent injured within the 5 psi contour; 10 percent dead and 40 percent injured between the 3 and 5 psi contours; and 2 percent dead and 30 percent injured between the 1 and 3 psi contours (Figure 5-2).[5]

These new criteria were considered more realistic than the PVANS criteria for two reasons: (1) the PVANS criteria did not account for destruction and disruptive effects beyond the 9 psi blast effects contour; and (2) they underestimated the effects that the collateral impacts (e.g., transportation losses, disruption of basic services such as electricity, fallout, and so forth), as well as direct damage, would have on the effective utilization of a manufacturing facility. Although even the criteria used in this book may be too conservative, since they do not account fully for the effects of multiple weapon attacks,[6] they are consistent with population impact criteria used by the Defense Civil Preparedness Agency[7] and the Office of Technology Assessment.[8]

To facilitate the discussion, the national consequences of the largest nuclear attack, A-1 (500 1 megaton warheads plus 200 to 300 100-kiloton warheads), are described in terms of physical damage to industrial capacity and casualties. Next, Attack A-1 is compared with the smaller attacks (A-2, A-3, and A-4) to ascertain whether

Table 5-3. U.S. Vulnerability to Nuclear Attack.

Attacks	Percentage of Total U.S. Casualties[a] (a)	Percentage of Urban Casualties[a] (b)	Percentage of Total U.S. Industry Destroyed[b] (c)	Percentage of SMSA Industries Destroyed[b] (d)	Total Megaton Equivalents[c] (e)	Total Weapons Required[c] (f)
A-1	35-45	50-65	60-65	80+	544-566	700-800
A-2	30-40	45-60	45-60	75-80+	344-366	500-600
A-3	25-35	40-50	35-45	55-70	244-266	400-500
A-4	20-30	30-45	25-35	45-55	144-166	300-400

a. Based only on seventy-one SMSAs attacked by 1 Mt weapons. Since the specific targets for the 100 Kt weapons in the fifty additional SMSAs could not be identified, only the damage estimates for the 1 Mt weapons are shown, in order to be conservative. The urban percentage is based on total urban population of 139 million in 1970.

b. Based on manufacturing value added.

c. A 1 Mt attack plus a 100 Kt attack (200 to 300 warheads). A 100 kiloton weapon represents one-tenth the TNT potential of a 1 megaton weapon. A "megaton equivalent" is the weapon yield in megatons raised to the two-thirds power and is a standard measure.

Note: Total U.S. population, 203 million; total population urban, 139 million; total population of seventy-one SMSAs, 110 million. Population based on 1970 Bureau of Census data.

Source: Arthur Katz, Economic and Social Consequences of Nuclear Attacks on the United States, Committee on Banking, Housing, and Urban Affairs, U.S. Senate (Washington, D.C.: U.S. Government Printing Office, 1979), p. 9.

Figure 5-2. Casualties (Death and Injuries) versus Distance (Contours) from Blast Site.

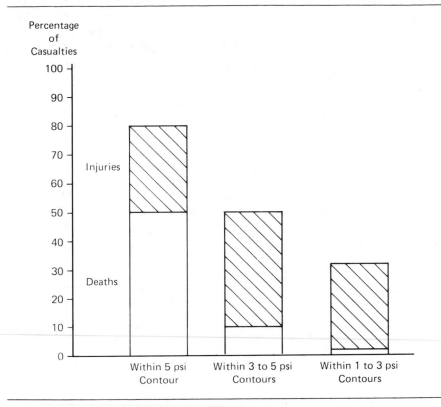

similar damage can be produced from a smaller attack. Finally, in subsequent chapters, the implications of these nationwide or economic attacks and the local (Massachusetts) attacks are discussed in terms of quantitative problems (such as food resources, shelter, fuel and power, and medical care) and the social dimensions of nuclear war.

It should be emphasized that in each of the four hypothetical attacks, it is assumed that weapons of two different yields are employed—1 megaton weapons for general destruction of vital industries and 100 kiloton weapons for the specific destruction of certain categories of vital industry. For any of the four overall attacks, the

Table 5–4. Descriptions of Nuclear Attacks.[a]

A–1 (reference attack)	Basic	500 1–Mt weapons plus
	Adjunct	200–300 100–Kt weapons
A–2	Basic	300 1–Mt weapons plus
	Adjunct	200–300 100–Kt weapons
A–3	Basic	200 1–Mt weapons plus
	Adjunct	200–300 100–Kt weapons
A–4	Basic	100 1–Mt weapons plus
	Adjunct	200–300 100–Kt weapons

a. No effort was made in either the PVANS or this book to develop scenarios that maximize damage to industrial recovery capacity while minimizing civilian casualties, although the possibility of developing target plans to achieve this goal is currently the subject of discussion by American strategists.

damage attributable to the 1 megaton weapons is often discussed separately from the additional damage created by the 100 kiloton weapons. Therefore, references in the text to the basic attack or the 1 megaton attack signify the larger yield weapons portion of the particular attack under discussion. Likewise, references to the supplemental attack, the adjunct attack, or the 100 kiloton attack treat the lower yield weapons portion of the overall attack (see Table 5–4).

INDUSTRIAL DESTRUCTION AND CASUALTIES

The Largest Attack: A Point of Reference

The most dramatic impact of Attack A–1, our reference case, is the virtual elimination of the seventy-one largest SMSAs as productive economic units. These areas contain approximately 110 million people, or 55 percent of the nation's population, and about 60 percent of the nation's manufacturing capacity[9] (measured by MVA). The extent of national industrial destruction is indicated in Table 5–3 and Figure 5–3. As shown in Figure 5–3, the industrial destruction meets or exceeds the range postulated by Secretary of Defense McNamara[10] in the 1960s as representing unacceptable damage. The range should understate the damage, since the urban areas attacked by 100 Kt weapons are not included.

Although the 100 Kt attack's primary importance is bottlenecking the economy, as an adjunct to the major attack, it also has the po-

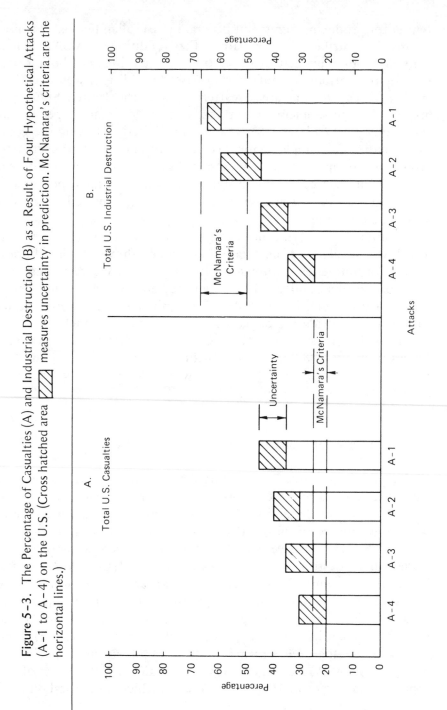

Figure 5-3. The Percentage of Casualties (A) and Industrial Destruction (B) as a Result of Four Hypothetical Attacks (A-1 to A-4) on the U.S. (Cross hatched area ▨ measures uncertainty in prediction. McNamara's criteria are the horizontal lines.)

tential for producing significant general industrial and casualty consequences. It strikes approximately fifty additional SMSAs, which
contain about 7 percent of the national population and about 7 percent of the national manufacturing base. In addition, well over 100
smaller cities or rural areas scattered about the United States are
affected by the supplemental attack. In fact, less than 10 percent of
the country's 120 largest SMSAs are unaffected following the combined basic and supplemental attacks. Six states are projected to
absorb ten or more 100 Kt weapons. Even aiming a few additional
weapons on a state, in some instances, appears to expose potentially
undamaged areas to some level of destruction, thus reducing their
aid-giving potential.

An impression of the destructive potential of the supplemental
attack can be gained from Figure 5-4, which shows the distribution
of U.S. oil refineries. Although many of them are clustered near major urban centers and would be damaged in the 1 megaton attacks
on the seventy-one largest SMSAs, a significant portion of refining
capacity lies outside the damage radius of the basic attacks. Refineries in smaller cities such as Texas City and Port Arthur in Texas and
Lake Charles in Louisiana are untouched by 1 megaton weapons, but
these cities absorb several 100 Kt weapons in the supplemental
attack.

Industrial Damage Assessment

Under attack A-1, for both components of the attack, a combined
total of about 70 percent of total manufacturing capacity is exposed
to destruction or disruption.[11] An examination of Figures 5-5 and
5-6 shows the extent of the attack on a national scale. Twenty-three
states in Figure 5-5 have half their MVA destroyed, while five more
states suffer destruction of over 40 percent of their MVA in the
basic attack against the seventy-one urban areas. The twenty-three
states represent more than 75 percent of the nation's industrial
capacity. Nine states (Arizona, California, Florida, Maryland, Massachusetts, Missouri, New Jersey, New York, and Rhode Island) stand
to lose more than 75 percent of their manufacturing capacity (as
measured by MVA) from the 1 Mt weapons alone. If the effect of the
supplemental attack of 100 Kt weapons is included, the total number

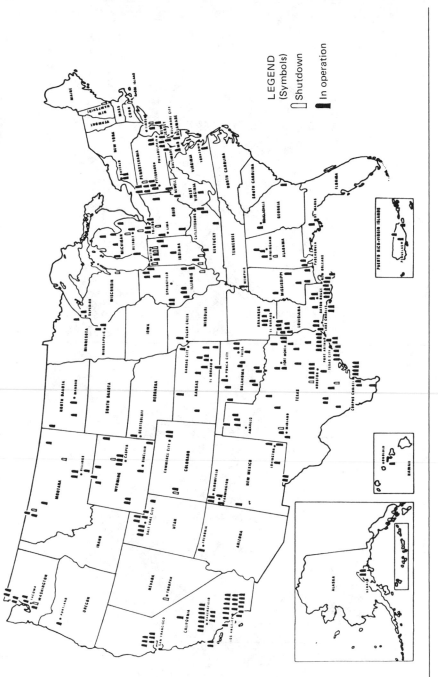

Figure 5-4. Petroleum Refineries in the United States and Puerto Rico.

Source: Department of Interior, Bureau of Mines, Division of Petroleum and Natural Gas.

Figure 5-5. Percentage, by State, of Manufacturing Value Added Effectively Destroyed by 1-Megaton Weapons in Attack A-1.

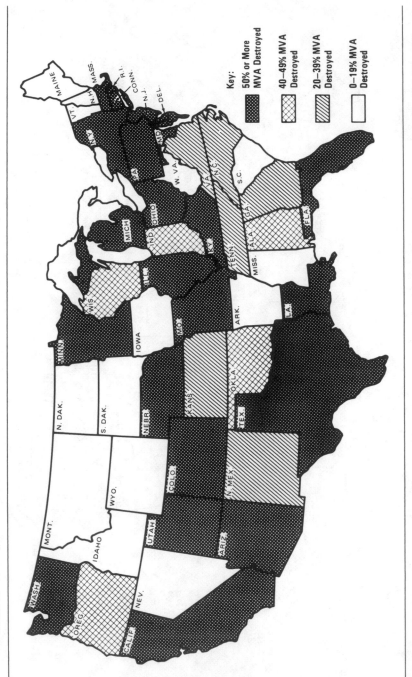

Key:

50% or More MVA Destroyed

40–49% MVA Destroyed

20–39% MVA Destroyed

0–19% MVA Destroyed

Source: Arthur Katz, *Economic and Social Consequences of Nuclear Attacks on the United States*, Committee on Banking, Housing, and Urban Affairs, U.S. Senate (Washington, D.C.: U.S. Government Printing Office, 1979). p. 13.

Figure 5-6. Percentage, by State, of Manufacturing Value Added Exposed to Basic (1 Mt) Attack and Supplemental (100 Kt) Attack.

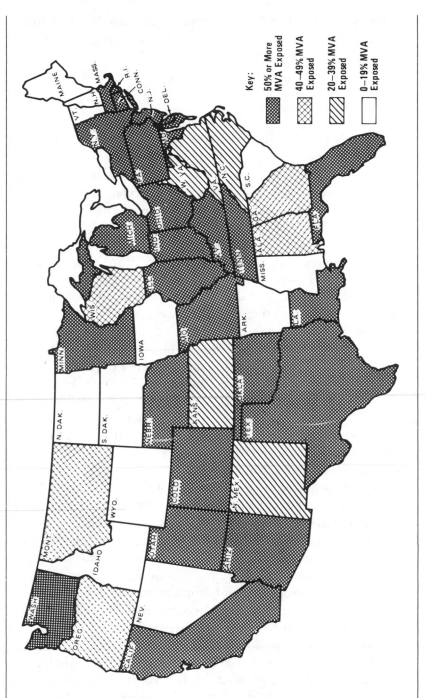

Key:

▨	50% or More MVA Exposed
▨	40–49% MVA Exposed
▧	20–39% MVA Exposed
☐	0–19% MVA Exposed

Source: Arthur Katz, *Economic and Social Consequences of Nuclear Attacks on the United States*, Committee on Banking, Housing, and Urban Affairs, U.S. Senate (Washington, D.C.: U.S. Government Printing Office, 1979). p. 14.

of states having more than 75 percent of their MVA exposed to destruction or disruption rises to fourteen, including Illinois, Louisiana, Ohio, Oklahoma, and Texas.

Regional Effects

As a result of the postulated attacks, several sections of the United States could be seriously injured as economic entities. The extent of this injury is important since the United States has a highly integrated economy. Wholesale losses of regional economic blocks will undercut the national economy and subsequently lead to a precipitous loss of domestic and international power.

The area of primary destruction is the tier of states in the northeast and east-central part of the country from Minnesota to Massachusetts. Every state in this area, with the exception of Wisconsin and Indiana, experiences destruction of more than 50 percent of its industrial capacity in the reference attack, as shown in Figure 5–5.

Because of the particular patterns of industrial concentration, the supplemental attack will not only place in jeopardy areas not exposed to the basic attack but will also increase the damage in certain states already hard hit by the 1 megaton weapons. Texas, New York, Ohio, Oklahoma, Pennsylvania, and Washington will receive ten to twenty-five 100 Kt weapons in the supplemental attack. Massachusetts absorbs two more. However, the two 100 Kt weapons will strike the only major industrial areas in Massachusetts not destroyed in the basic attack of 1 megaton weapons.

With the addition of the supplemental attack of 100 Kt weapons, 60 to 90 percent of the industrial capacity in each state in the northeast and east-central regions (except Wisconsin and Indiana) lies within the areas exposed to attack. As seen in Table 5–5 (last column) and Figure 5–6 even Indiana and Wisconsin have approximately 50 percent of their manufacturing capacity exposed or at risk in the combined basic and supplemental attacks.

If the assumption that an 80 percent level of industrial destruction will incapacitate an SMSA is extended to cover a region as a whole, then the northeast, middle Atlantic, and east-central sections of the country—the largest block of industrial states in the nation, accounting for over 50 percent of its industrial production—is unlikely to continue to function as the country's economic heartland.

Several other industrial regions or states would appear to suffer similar destruction and disruption, making their contribution to the survival or recovery of the surrounding territory very uncertain. Sections of Texas, Louisiana, Oklahoma, and Missouri would be severely damaged, as would Florida and the area covered by California, Arizona, Utah, and Colorado. While twenty-three states experience the loss of 50 or more percent of their industrial capacity, only fourteen states have less than 20 percent of their manufacturing capacity destroyed, as measured by MVA.

With the added weapons in the 100 Kt portion of Attack A–1, substantial damage occurs in all sections of the United States (as shown in Figure 5–6), including the Northwest and the South, which were less damaged by the 1 megaton basic attack. While the actual destruction and casualties may be less severe for the 100 Kt portion of the attack because of weapon size, and the targeting of specific plants rather than general industrial capacity, they are potentially significant enough to imply substantial economic disruption and social disorganization in the postattack period.[12]

These regional patterns of destruction suggest that the assumption that large undamaged areas would exist that could provide either adequate refuge and support for the surviving urban population or the capability to foster a rapid economic recovery is unfounded. Though the concentration of destruction in high density industrial and population areas will leave extensive territory undamaged, this territory will mainly be rural or semirural and largely devoid of the industrial capacity required to ignite and sustain economic recovery on the scale needed to approach current levels of development. Therefore, the magnitude and extent of the destruction of the well-meshed U.S. economy would overwhelm the possible strategies to maintain effective national economic power.

Selected Industries: Critical Lynchpins

The nuclear strategy is even more effective than the gross damage discussed above would make it appear. With the introduction of large numbers of accurate warheads (multiple independent re-entry vehicles, or MIRVs), the gross economic damage strategy can be effectively supplemented and even supplanted to some degree by a major expansion of attacks designed to eliminate pivotal industries. A well-

Table 5-5. Population and Manufacturing Capacity at Risk by State.

| | Preattack Status | | Percentage of Population and Industry Exposed to Urban Attacks[a] | | | |
| | | | 1 Mt Weapons Only | | 1 Mt and 100 Kt Weapons | |
State[b]	Population (thousands)	MVA (millions)	Percent Population	Percent MVA	Percent Population	Percent MVA
Alabama	3,444	$ 3,526	30	40	35	45[c]
Arizona	1,771	995	55	80	55	80[c]
Arkansas	1,923	1,558	0	0	0	0
California	19,953	23,394	80	90	80[c]	90[c]
Colorado	2,207	1,509	55	75	55[c]	75[c]
Connecticut	3,032	6,390	75	65	80[c]	75[c]
Delaware	548	958	85	65	90[c]	65[c]
Florida	6,789	3,683	65	80	65[c]	80[c]
Georgia	4,590	4,684	30	35	35[c]	40[c]
Idaho	713	503	0	0	0	0
Illinois	11,114	20,016	70	75	80[c]	85[c]
Indiana	5,194	10,308	35	40	50[c]	50[c]
Iowa	2,824	3,250	0	0	0[c]	0
Kansas	2,247	2,112	20	30	25[c]	35[c]
Kentucky	3,219	3,636	30	50	35	60[c]
Louisiana	3,641	2,790	40	55	60[c]	85[c]
Maine	992	1,070	0	0	0	0

Maryland	3,992	3,781	85	85	85^c	85^c
Massachusetts	5,689	8,731	80	85	90	95
Michigan	8,875	17,242	60	60	60^c	65
Minnesota	3,805	4,080	50	70	50^c	70^c
Mississippi	2,217	1,635	0	0	0	0
Missouri	4,677	5,395	60	80	60^c	80^c
Montana	694	311	0	0	25^c	40^c
Nebraska	1,483	1,150	30	50	30^c	50^c
Nevada	489	134	0	0	0	0
New Hampshire	738	943	0	0	30^c	18^c
New Jersey	7,168	12,738	80	75	85	80^c
New Mexico	1,016	204	30	30	30^c	30^c
New York	18,237	25,247	85	85	90^c	90^c
North Carolina	5,082	6,607	20	30	25^c	35^c
North Dakota	618	113	0	0	0	0
Ohio	10,652	20,435	65	70	80^c	85^c
Oklahoma	2,559	1,346	25	45	45^c	85^c
Oregon	1,092	2,061	40	45	40	45
Pennsylvania	11,794	19,277	55	60	65^c	70^c
Rhode Island	947	1,351	56	95	55	95
South Carolina	2,591	3,030	0	0	0	0
South Dakota	666	171	0	0	0	0
Tennessee	3,924	4,921	25	30	50^c	50^c
Texas	11,197	10,922	45	55	60^c	80^c
Utah	1,059	777	55	65	55^c	65^c

(Table 5–5. continued overleaf)

Table 5-5. continued

State[b]	Preattack Status		Percentage of Population and Industry Exposed to Urban Attacks[a]			
			1 Mt Weapons Only		1 Mt and 100 Kt Weapons	
	Population (thousands)	MVA (millions)	Percent Population	Percent MVA	Percent Population	Percent MVA
Vermont	444	515	0	0	0	0
Virginia	4,648	4,067	45	30	45	30
Washington	3,409	3,764	45	60	65[c]	70[c]
West Virginia	1,744	2,170	0	0	25[c]	30[c]
Wisconsin	4,418	7,014	30	40	35[c]	45[c]
Wyoming	332	86	0	0	0	0
Total	201,500	261,000	55	61	61.5	68[c]

a. Rounded to the nearest 5 percent.

b. Alaska and Hawaii are excluded, as they were by SRI. Parts of the District of Columbia SMSA have been distributed to the appropriate states, with the MVA of $332 million and population of 750,000 itself unlisted.

c. Indicates that some targets in the 100 Kt portion of the attack were unknown or outside of SMSAs; therefore full percentages could not be given.

Note: Some states reflect no damage because they do not contain any of the seventy-one largest SMSAs or a significant concentration of the eight selected industries specially targeted.

Source: Arthur Katz, *Economic and Social Consequences of Nuclear Attacks on the United States*, p. 8.

designed attack would assure critical basic products or resources were destroyed as well as their logical substitutes. Although the American economic genius has always been innovation and flexibility, the object of this attack strategy is to insure that the requirements for innovation and substitution are so extreme that they will be impossible to achieve, or in achieving them for a small segment of the economy the rest of the surviving economic structure will be distorted. Thus, no balanced economy will be possible and whatever functioning economic power remains will be severely restricted and highly vulnerable. The discussion below illustrates the effectiveness of this specific attack but also identifies more information that supports its general applicability and effectiveness.

The percentages of manufacturing capacity surviving outside the seventy-one largest urban-economic areas (SMSAs) for eight specific industrial categories are shown in Table 5-6, together with the number of weapons required against targets outside the seventy-one urban areas to reduce total capacity in these industries to either 10 percent or less than 3 percent of preattack levels. A combined weighted average of 30 percent of the capacity in these eight selected industries is found outside the seventy-one metropolitan areas. For individual industries, the range of capacity lying outside (beyond the seventy-one metropolitan areas) is 20 to 90 percent. The PVANS study assumed that all the capacity of these eight specific industries inside the seventy-one major urban areas is destroyed by the 1 megaton weapons in Attack A-1. Thus, 300 additional 100 Kt weapons in the adjunct attack will reduce the total surviving capacity in these selected industries to under 3 percent. If just 200 additional 100 Kt weapons are used, total surviving capacity will rise to only 7 percent, as shown in Table 5-7. This indicates that even with a reduction in the size of the adjunct attack, it will nevertheless create high levels of damage in these selected critical manufacturing sectors. Therefore, until the adjunct attack decreases to about one hundred weapons, only a very small percentage of the productive capacity of these sectors lying outside the seventy-one leading urban areas will survive.

Although not among the eight industries specifically targeted for reduction to 2 to 3 percent of former capacity, several other critical industries nevertheless experience a dramatic reduction in capacity as a result of the heavy damage from the attack against the seventy-one SMSAs. Among these are electric components, metal-working machinery, communication equipment, screw machine products, tires

Table 5-6. Weapons Requirements for Damage to Eight Selected
Major Industrial Sectors.

SIC[a] Code	Manufacturing Sector	Percent[b] Surviving Outside 71 SMSAs	Weapons Needed to Reduce MVA to	
			10 Percent	2-3 Percent
Eight Critical Industries				
283	Drugs	20	7	22
291	Petroleum refining	50	40	75
331	Blast furnaces, steelworks, and rolling and finishing mills	25	15	60
333	Primary smelting and refining of nonferrous metals			
	Zinc	80	7	11
	Copper	55	7	15
	Lead	55	2	4
	Aluminum	90	16	24
351	Engines and turbines	30	7	15
357	Office machines	30	7	20
361	Electric distribution products	55	26	60
382	Mechanical measuring devices	25	11	30

a. Standard industrial classification.

b. Rounded to nearest 5 percent.

Source: Arthur Katz, *Economic and Social Consequences of Nuclear Attacks on the United States*, p. 45.

and inner tubes, and electrical industrial apparatus. Therefore, the basic urban attack contains considerable potential for disruption of important segments of the industrial system not specifically included in the 100 Kt attack. Very few additional weapons would be required to reduce the national capacity in these industries by more than 90 percent of preattack values. In view of the thousands of warheads available to the United States and the Soviet Union as a result of the deployment of MIRVs, allocating additional weapons for this purpose would not be difficult.

Table 5-7. Effectiveness of Supplemental (100 Kt Weapon) Attacks on Critical Industries (*based on PVANS estimates; percent of total surviving capacity*).[a]

	Numbers of 100 Kt Weapons Used				
	0	50	100	200	300
Eight industries (petroleum refining, iron and steel works, nonferrous metals smelting and refining, engines and turbines, electrical distribution products, drugs, office machines, and mechanical measuring devices)	30	23	15	7	2-3
Three industries (petroleum refining, iron and steel works, nonferrous metals smelting and refining)	35	15	8	2	< 2

a. Assumes that part of each selected industry lying within the seventy-one primary SMSAs has been eliminated by the basic (1 Mt weapon) attack. For the eight critical industries the proportion within the primary target areas is approximately 70 percent; for the three critical industries, the proportion lying within the seventy-one primary target areas is approximately 65 percent.

Source: Arthur Katz, *Economic and Social Consequences of Nuclear Attacks on the United States*, p. 14.

Additional support for the effectiveness of this bottlenecking strategy is found in a study prepared in 1974 for the U.S. Arms Control and Disarmament Agency by the Metis Corporation.[13] It provides a clearer indication of the type of major interactive effects — namely, the effects throughout the economy from destruction in specific industrial sectors that will be of significant concern. In the Metis study, an economic assessment utilizing the methodology of input–output analysis[14] was used to evaluate the effect of relatively small nuclear attacks (100 to 300 1-megaton weapons) on basic industries vital to defense production in the United States and also a general 10 percent reduction of each input–output sector for the Soviet Union. Although not designed to create the largest amount of general economic damage and disruption, the attacks in the Metis study were nevertheless directed toward the urban–industrial areas containing most of the capacity of these critical basic industries, such as iron and steel production. The attacks of 100 and 300 1-megaton weapons postulated in the Metis study resulted in the destruction of 30 and 53 percent, respectively, of total manufacturing value added. These estimates fall almost exactly in the middle of the ranges of MVA destruction estimated in this book for the smallest attack, A–4 (100 1-megaton weapons destroying 25 to 35 percent of MVA), and the next to largest attack, A–2 (300 1-megaton weapons destroying 45 to 60 percent of MVA), on the seventy-one largest SMSAs.

Besides supporting the general level of economic destruction projected in this book, the Metis input–output analysis indicates that using destruction of MVA as the measure of damage to the economic base may seriously underestimate the actual impact of even small attacks of 100 to 200 1-megaton weapons:

> If nuclear war scenarios are analyzed which result in relatively low levels of attack [1–200 weapons] on [urban industrial] targets, then the use of MVA as a damage criterion can be quite misleading as an indicator of the ability of the surviving economy to sustain a large-scale warmaking effort. Since the economic and institutional activities necessary to sustain a war-making capability are highly interactive, relatively low levels of MVA destruction can lead to significant reductions in the ability to support a war effort.[15]

The use of input–output analysis in the Metis study illustrates the truly interactive nature of a modern industrial economy. For example, changes in the productive capacity of just a few basic industries, such as iron and steel or petroleum products, can influence over 100 other sectors of industry, as shown in Table 5–8. In the cases examined in the Metis study, a 10 percent reduction in the capacity of basic sectors has broad multiplicative effects, reducing output in other defense-related sectors by as much as 30 to 40 percent. Since a portion of the sectors labeled defense related, are critical for the economy as a whole (e.g., trucks, airplanes, and machine tool production), the analysis has broader applicability than it might appear at first. Moreover, the supplemental attack in this book reduces the surviving capacity in various industries to only 2 to 3 percent of preattack levels, instead of leaving 90 percent of preattack capacity surviving as postulated in the Metis study. Such enormous comparative and absolute reductions in the productive capacity of these basic industries will naturally have more widespread and serious ramifications throughout the rest of the economy. In fact the Metis study suggests that the criterion of requiring the destruction of 97 to 98 percent of capacity in critical industries may be overly restrictive,

Table 5-8. Effectiveness of Low-level Attacks to Bottleneck U.S. Warmaking Production.

SIC	Bottleneck Sector[a]	Number of Sectors Satisfied	Final Demand Shortfall (percent)
50	Iron-steel foundries, forging, and miscellaneous products	101	41.2
49	Blast furnaces and basic steel products	107	36.9
42	Petroleum products	107	36.7
81	Electronic components	112	32.3
35	Chemical products	112	30.8

a. With 10 percent destruction of output capacity.

Source: Jack Sassen and Kenneth Willis, "Data Base and Damage Criteria for Measurement of Arms Limitation Effects on War Supporting Industry" ACDA/WEC-242 (Alexandria, Virginia: Metis Corporation, June 1974), p. 45.

and that unacceptable economic disruption will be achieved with less destruction (higher levels of surviving capacity) of basic industries. In any case, the input–output analysis employed in the Metis study shows that attacks of 100 to 300 1-megaton weapons can achieve grave bottlenecks in defense production, and supports this contention for the general economy of the United States. It indicates that damage, as measured by gross losses of MVA, seriously understates the true scope and magnitude of all the economic effects that result from widespread and, for some industries, high levels of destruction. Apparently, similar weapons requirements will achieve comparable results in the Soviet Union (described in Chapter 10).

Although the economic destruction and disruption described above would be impressive in and of itself, there is a supporting, marketing, financial, and monetary structure that will crumble as well. Thus, using this description of damage as the indicator of health of the economy can potentially lead to a serious understatement of economic conditions.

The normal distribution and marketing system will be substantially injured, if not destroyed, though the physical components of the system (trucks, trains) may survive. A massive inventory of surviving supplies and industrial assets, and industrial and commercial consumer needs will have to be reconstructed even to begin to project the proper distribution of materials and goods throughout the United States. The automated and personal (human) parts of the marketing system that assured products were distributed properly and markets were identified is unlikely to exist in any meaningful way because of physical and personnel losses. In addition, fuel—petroleum needed for actual transportation of goods—will have virtually disappeared and is likely to remain restricted for years.

More critically, the present value of money will be destroyed. As noted, "without a monetary system which represents a reliable store of value, complex economic activity could virtually cease."[16] The banking system will be in chaos with no means for borrowers to pay debts, and with records either destroyed or inaccessible to a dispersed population. The insurance system will not function; stock certificates, and records of ownership of property and other goods will be destroyed. What was conceived as serious injury to the financial system as a whole in the counterforce discussion in Part II will become essential destruction after an urban attack. Further, many of the key personnel who could rebuild the system would be casualties or lost for long periods in the postattack confusion. The idea of an effective functional national economy under these conditions appears remote.

The international economic situation is likely to be equally grim. A collapse of the dollar and the present monetary structure is inevitable. U.S. international trade, especially for resources such as petroleum imports, could become virtually impossible in the short run. A prolonged conflict could only further exacerbate the damage to the United States and the international economy. Whatever improvisational strategies might be attempted to regenerate the U.S. economy, the situation could not be anything but desperate.

POPULATION LOSSES

To complement the discussion of the effects on the economy a look at the human dimension of this attack is presented in this section. (Appendix B contains a detailed look at casualties for U.S. cities with a population over 25,000 after the use of different sized nuclear weapons.) To place the implications of the attack strategy in overall perspective the population distribution for the United States (1970 Census) in Figure 5-7 can be compared to the seventy-one urban

Figure 5-7. Population Distribution (1970 Census).

LESS THAN 25,000

25,000 TO 49,999

50,000 TO 199,999

OVER 200,000

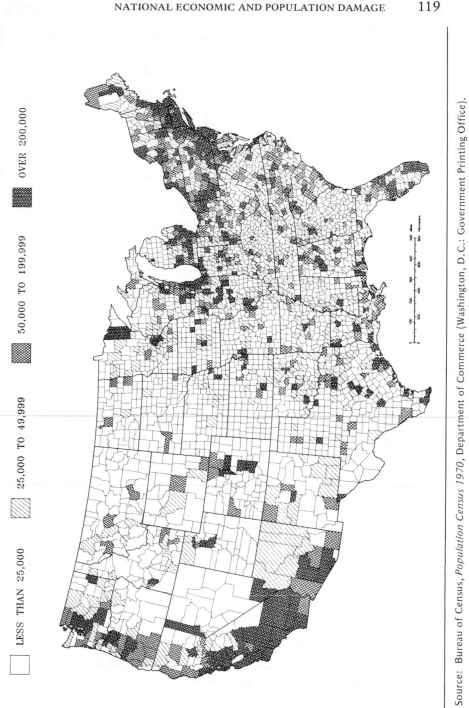

Source: Bureau of Census, *Population Census 1970*, Department of Commerce (Washington, D.C.: Government Printing Office).

areas attacked in Figure 5–1. The overlap is considerable, and the 100 Kt attack is excluded.

Analysis of Attack A–1 indicates that for portions of the urban areas within the 5 psi blast effects contour and absorbing a multiple weapon attack, mortality may range from 50 to 80 percent of the population, with 20 to 30 percent of the population in these areas sustaining injuries. Hiroshima casualty statistics (deaths and surviving injured) show 50 percent of the population killed and 30 percent injured within the 5 psi blast effects contour; as noted, these criteria are used in this book. Casualty estimates based on the analysis of individual cities are shown in Table 5–3, which indicates that mortality and injuries on a nationwide basis for Attack A–1 is in the range of 70 to 90 million people or about 35 to 45 percent of the U.S. population.[17] From 20 to 30 million of these would be injuries, many of a severe to moderate character. For Attack A–1 the casualties would approach 80 percent for most of the seventy-one SMSAs; a conservative range of 65 to 80 percent total casualties for the seventy-one SMSAs has been used.

While the number of deaths is overwhelming, equally as significant is the huge number of injured. They will place a massive burden on the country's surviving human and industrial resources, diverting a substantial portion from recovery and in some cases even from survival requirements to the care of the injured. As indicated in the counterforce discussion in Part II, the long-term social burden of the injured and other dependent persons (such as orphans and the elderly) would become enormous, especially in view of the complexity of the enlarged medical, welfare, and social services needed to care for the victims. Even if imposed upon a stable and essentially undamaged society, the burden would be severe, if not impossible, to cope with effectively. Under these circumstances it is likely to be devastating; moreover, the burden will not be limited to physical demands, the extraordinary level of human damage should cause deep sociological and psychological changes (discussed in Chapter 7).

The worldwide long-term health effects of air burst were computed by the Office of Technology Assessment[18] for a 1 Mt weapon over one and then seventy-eight cities such as Detroit (Table 5–9). As can be seen, without the extensive fallout produced by ground bursts the consequences are relatively negligible.

Table 5-9. The Long-Term Health Effects from Air Bursts.

Estimated worldwide effects from 1 Mt air burst over a city (OTA Case 1):

Somatic effects

Cancer deaths	200-2,000
Thyroid cancers	about 700
Thyroid nodules	about 1,000

Genetic effects

Abortions due to chromosomal damage	100-1,000
Other genetic effects	350-3,500

Estimated worldwide effects from an attack using 78 air bursts of 1 Mt each (OTA Case 2 attack on the United States) are 78 times as great, that is:

Somatic effects

Cancer deaths	16,000-160,000
Thyroid cancers	about 55,000
Thyroid nodules	about 78,000

Genetic effects

Abortions due to chromosomal damage	8,000- 80,000
Other genetic effects	27,000-270,000

Source: Office of Technology Assessment, *The Effects of Nuclear War*, Congress of the United States (Washington, D.C.: Government Printing Office, May 1979), p. 113.

Comparing Effectiveness: How Much is Enough?

Although the focus of the discussion of urban damage to this point has been the largest proposed nuclear attack (A-1), given the level of damage already described, the obvious question is whether unacceptable damage could be achieved by even smaller attacks. Even the largest hypothetical attack represents weapons requirements that are a small fraction, less than 20 percent of the Soviet Union's present nuclear capabilities (as will be seen later the same is true for the United States). Thus, effective smaller attacks have important implications for the meaning of the term "vulnerability" of strategic nuclear forces, and consequently the redundancies (minimum numbers of weapons) needed to achieve a secure deterrent force. Moreover, as the redundant deterrence force becomes a smaller proportion of a strategic force, the increase in targeting flexibility raises important strategic and political policy issues.

When the largest attack (A–1) is compared to other smaller hypothetical attacks, the critical conclusion emerges. Although the postulated Attack A–1 would be devastating, a considerable reduction in the numbers of weapons used would achieve comparable results. This can be seen in Table 5–3, which shows aggregate damage to population and manufacturing capacity, as well as the weapon and megatonnage requirements, for each of the four assumed attacks. The urban damage and disruption from the 1 Mt attack is obvious even at these "low" levels of national attack. However, it is essential not to lose sight of the fact that a well-designed critical industry attack will accompany these attacks, enlarging the dimensions of the economic and social impacts to assure a truly national level of unacceptable damage. Therefore, these attacks will still represent the major economic destruction, devastating industrial bottlenecking, and nationwide organizational and social disruption identified for the largest attack. Subsequent discussion will make the last effect clearer.

To provide some insight into the effects of the smaller attacks, a cross section of twelve SMSAs, representing various parts of the country with different population densities, absolute sizes, and industrial concentrations, was examined, as shown in Table 5–10.[19] Figure 5–8 compares the percentage of manufacturing capacity (MVA) destroyed and casualties for Attacks A–1 to A–4 for the ten of the twelve metropolitan areas allocated more than one weapon. Figure 5–9 shows the comparison for individual SMSAs—New York, Akron, Los Angeles, and Dallas. Attack A–2, employing 300 1-megaton weapons would, for cities hit by more than a single 1-megaton weapon, destroy from 65 to 90 percent of their industrial capacity, cause deaths among the population ranging from 25 to 50 percent, and produce injuries ranging from 20 to 30 percent—or total casualties (dead and injured) ranging from 50 to 80 percent. In the large cities, such as Chicago, New York, Los Angeles, and Milwaukee, the criterion of 80 percent destruction of industrial capacity (MVA) is exceeded, while destruction in most other areas is only slightly below 80 percent. In terms of the criterion of 80 percent damage equaling economic incapacitation, the impact of Attack A–2 is thus only marginally different from that of Attack A–1.

Of greater significance is the destructive power of even a basic attack of 100 1-megaton weapons, as in Attack A–4. A–4 will produce 20 to 65 percent destruction of MVA in the urban areas (SMSAs) hit by more than one weapon, with total casualties ranging

Table 5-10. Effects of Attacks A-1 through A-4 on Twelve Representative Metropolitan Areas.[a]

SMSA	Preattack Population (thousands)	(a) Percent MVA Destroyed				(b) Percent Casualties				(c) Percent Deaths				(d) Percent Injured			
		A-1	A-2	A-3	A-4	A-1	A-2	A-3	A-4	A-1	A-2	A-3	A-4	A-1	A-2	A-3	A-4
More Than One Weapon:																	
New York	16,207	80+	80+	80+	65	80	80	70	60	50	50	40	35	30	30	30	25
Los Angeles	8,452	80+	80+	65	45	80	80	60	40	50	50	30	20	30	30	30	20
Chicago	7,423	80+	80+	80+	60	80	75	70	55	50	45	40	30	30	30	30	25
Boston[d]	3,239	80+	80	70	45	75	70	60	45	45	40	30	25	30	30	30	20
St. Louis	2,363	80+	75	65	50	80	60	55	45	50	35	30	20	30	25	25	25
Milwaukee	1,400	80+	80+	80+	45	75	75	65	55	45	45	35	30	30	30	30	25
Dallas	1,459	80+	65	45	20	65	60	45	40	35	30	20	15	30	30	25	25
Akron	679	80+	80+	80	60	70	65	60	45	40	35	30	20	30	30	30	25
Springfield[d]	583	80	65	50	50	70	55	45	45	40	30	20	20	35	25	25	25
Worcester[d]	612	80	60	55	35	55	50	45	30	30	25	25	15	25	25	20	15
One Weapon:																	
Fort Lauderdale[c]	613	80	50	50	50	60	50	50	50	30	30	30	30	30	20	20	20
Albuquerque	316	80	55	55	55	70	50	50	50	40	30	30	30	30	20	20	20

Table 5-10. continued

SMSA	Preattack Population (thousands)	(e) Percent Population Within 1 psi Contour				(f) Percent MVA Within 1 psi Contour				(g) Numbers of Weapons			
		A-1	A-2	A-3	A-4	A-1	A-2	A-3	A-4	A-1	A-2	A-3	A-4
More Than One Weapon:													
New York	16,207	100	100	90	80	100	100	95	85	60	36	24	12
Los Angeles	8,452	100	100	95	55	100	100	95	60	40	24	16	8
Chicago	7,423	100	100	100	80	100	100	100	80	40	24	16	8
Boston[d]	3,239	100	100	95	80	100	100	100	75	17	10	7	3
St. Louis	2,363	100	100	100	90	100	100	100	90	16	10	6	3
Milwaukee	1,400	100	100	100	90	100	100	100	90	10	6	4	2
Dallas	1,459	100	95	80	70	100	95	90	85	6	4	2	1
Akron	679	100	100	100	75	100	100	100	80	5	3	2	1
Springfield[d]	583	95	85	75	75	100	95	75	75	3	2	1	1
Worcester[d]	612	90	85	75	55	95	80	70	50	7	4	3	1
One Weapon:													
Fort Lauderdale[c]	613	100	90	90	90	100	90	90	90	2[b]	1	1	1
Albuquerque	316	100	100	100	100	100	100	100	100	2[b]	1	1	1

a. Percentages rounded to nearest 5 percent.

b. Only 1 weapon was allocated to these cities under the formula to distribute weapons, a second weapon is added to meet the 80 percent destruction of MVA cited by PVANS. If all 1 weapon SMSA needed an additional weapon it would add an insignificant 10 weapons or 2 percent change to the weapon total.

c. Population in 1970 census.

d. Boston, Worcester, and Springfield are Standard Economic Areas (SEA). Only for Worcester does the SEA contain significantly more population and MVA than the SMSAs within it. Worcester's SEA needs four more weapons than the Worcester and Fitchberg-Leominster SMSAs require for 80% destruction.

Source: Arthur Katz, *Economic and Social Consequences of Nuclear Attacks on the United States*, p. 47.

Figure 5-8. The Range of Industrial Destruction and Casualties for Ten Metropolitan Areas Subject to Attacks A-1 to A-4 (The bars (⊢---⊣) show the range of destruction and casualties for different metropolitan areas).

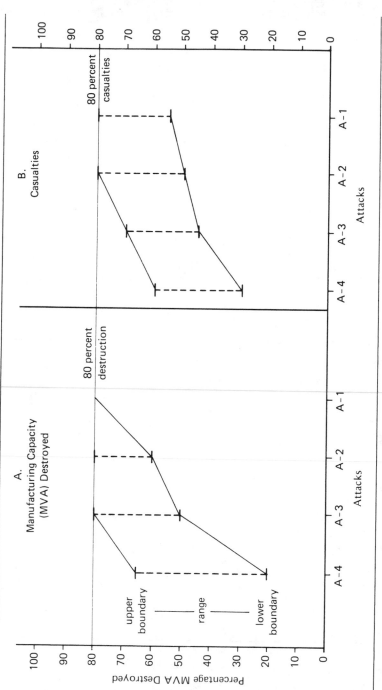

Source: Arthur Katz, *Economic and Social Consequences of Nuclear Attacks on the United States*, Committee on Banking, Housing, and Urban Affairs, U.S. Senate (Washington, D.C.: U.S. Government Printing Office, 1979). p. 47.

Figure 5-9. Manufacturing Destruction and Casualties for Four Metropolitan Areas as a Result of Hypothetical Attacks A-1 to A-4.

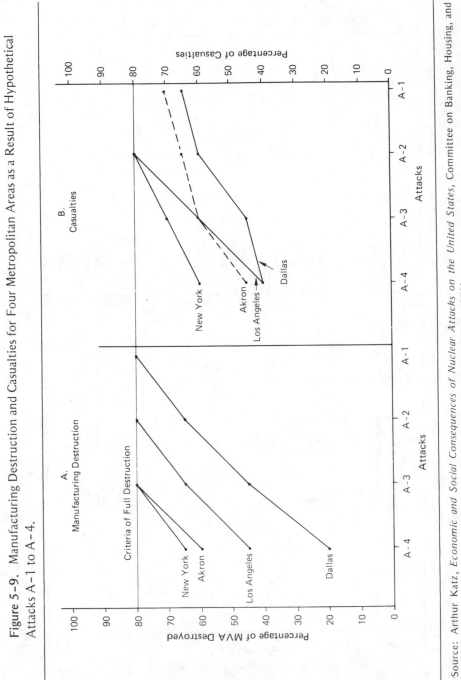

Source: Arthur Katz, *Economic and Social Consequences of Nuclear Attacks on the United States*, Committee on Banking, Housing, and Urban Affairs, U.S. Senate (Washington, D.C.: U.S. Government Printing Office, 1979).

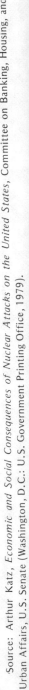

from 40 to 60 percent of the population within these SMSAs. Thus, as shown in Table 5–3, the smallest attack, A–4, would cause about 20 to 30 percent casualties among the U.S. population (Column a), and would destroy 25 to 35 percent of total manufacturing capacity (Column c) and 45 to 55 percent of the manufacturing capacity in the seventy-one largest metropolitan areas (Column d).

These data point to the fact that significant economic disruption and social disorganization could be achieved even with the smaller Attacks A–3 and A–4, since they also produce substantial loss of life and property and significant secondary effects. Presumably, smaller attacks would be designed to strike the highest priority targets. These remain massive levels of destruction. Comparison of economic effects for Attack A–4 is shown for the cities of New York, Akron, Los Angeles, and Dallas in Figure 5–9 and actual damage areas shown in Figures 5–10 thru 5–14, also includes St. Louis.

Urban Concentrations

One of the reasons for this persistent high level of destruction and casualties (in Table 5–3 and 5–8) is that the radius of destruction of nuclear weapons is compatible and comparable to the physical dimensions produced by urban concentration. Nearly 60 percent of the U.S. population lives on only 1 percent of the total land area of the United States. This is a result of the fact that approximately 85 percent of the population included in all SMSAs live on only 10 percent of the SMSAs' total land area. The result is that the population, even within these metropolitan regions, is concentrated in very high density areas.

This is illustrated by the fact that when the number of 1-megaton weapons in the attack is increased fivefold (500 percent), as in Attack A–1, casualties and industrial damage only increase by approximately twofold.

Despite the effects of urban sprawl and industrial migration, industry and population remain concentrated in a relatively modest number of urban areas that present particularly vulnerable targets to nuclear weapons. In other words, population and industry are not really dispersed in terms of the destructive effects of nuclear weapons. This is more true of the Soviet Union, where industry and population are even more densely concentrated than in the United States.

Figure 5-10.   Attack A-4 on New York.

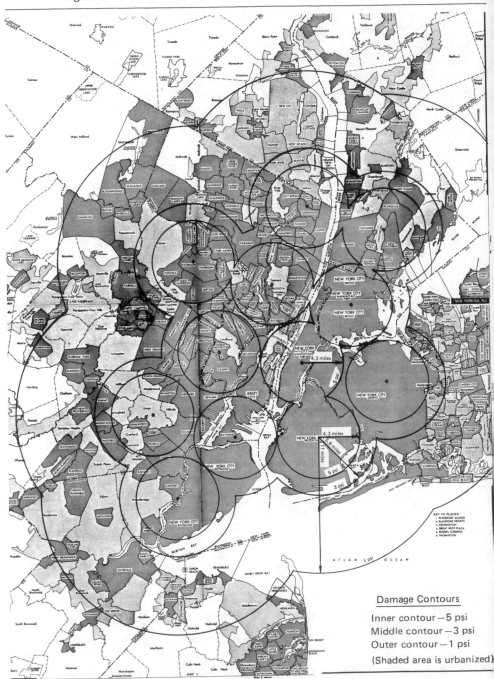

Damage Contours

Inner contour—5 psi
Middle contour—3 psi
Outer contour—1 psi
(Shaded area is urbanized)

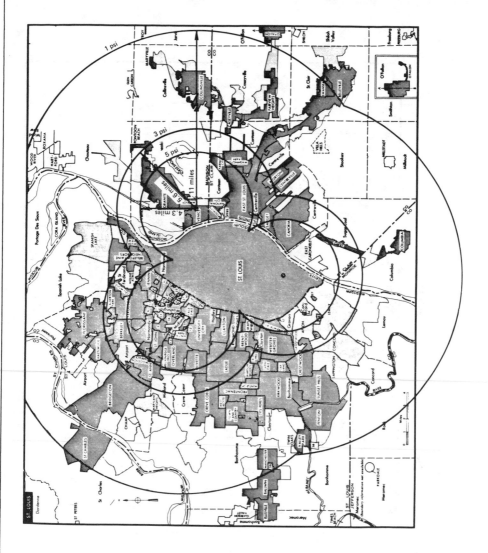

Figure 5–11. Attack A–4 on St. Louis.

Damage Contours

Inner contour —5 psi
Middle contour —3 psi
Outer contour —1 psi
(Shaded area is urbanized)

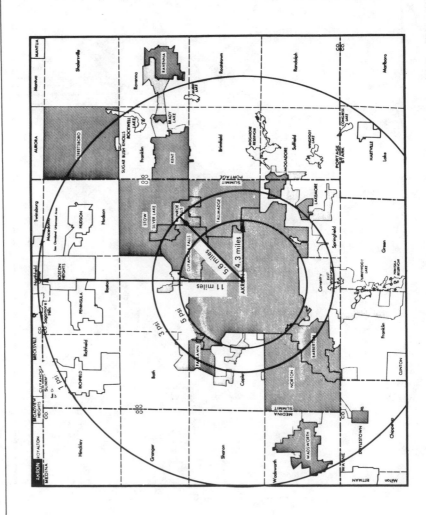

Figure 5-12.   Attack A-4 on Akron.

Damage Contours
Inner contour — 5 psi
Middle contour — 3 psi
Outer contour — 1 psi
(Shaded area is urbanized)

Figure 5-13. Attack A-4 on Los Angeles.

Damage Contours

Inner contour — 5 psi
Middle contour — 3 psi
Outer contour — 1 psi
(Shaded area is urbanized)

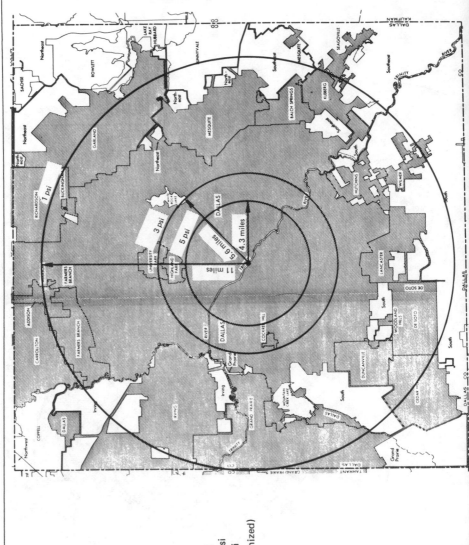

Figure 5-14.   Attack A-4 on Dallas.

Damage Contours
Inner contour—5 psi
Middle contour—3 psi
Outer contour—1 psi
(Shaded area is urbanized)

The consequences of this urban concentration on ten metropolitan areas can also be seen in Table 5-8. It reveals (Columns e and f) that even for the smallest attack, A-4, all but three SMSAs (Dallas, Worcester, and Los Angeles) have 75 or more percent of their manufacturing capacity and population within the 1 psi blast effects contour established as the boundary for minimum damage.[20] By Attack A-3, most have 90 to 100 percent of capacity and population within the 1 psi blast effects contour.

POST-ATTACK ECONOMIC RECOVERY

Is the economic situation as grim as it appears? Can we recover? In the previous sections, we identified the extent of economic destruction and the complex demands even a small urban nuclear attack places on the U.S. society. In this section, an attempt to model the actual path of economic recovery is examined. The Stanford Research Institute's preliminary study of U.S. and U.S.S.R. economic recovery from a nuclear attack basically supports the difficulty of economic recovery and the effectiveness of bottlenecking as a realistic nuclear strategy.[21] The recovery of U.S. Gross National Product (GNP)[22] using a simple input-output model was analyzed. The U.S. economy was divided into 15 large and very general (aggregated) categories such as food and clothing, chemicals, primary metals, automobiles, and so forth. A calculation of recovery after different attack levels using 1-megaton weapons (250, 500, 750, 1000, 1250) was developed. The results for a nine year period are shown in Table 5-11 and Figure 5-15.

It is evident from comparing surviving (Gross National Product) GNP (Table 5-11, Column 1) with the GNP projected for post-attack years that a substantial part of the GNP is unused during the early years after recovery, indicating severe imbalances within the economy. It takes at least 5 years to just equal the projected post-attack surviving GNP levels in all cases, much less reach pre-attack economic levels. The year of full utilization of surviving GNP is described (underlined) in Table 5-11. Except for the smallest attack (250 weapons), the GNP falls substantially below the pre-attack GNP levels even after 9 years. Thus the models, if correct, show a sustained period of severe economic difficulties with investment heavily devoted to rebuilding basic aspects of the economy at the expense of consumer goods and services (quality of life).

Table 5–11. Illustrative Results: Analysis of the Relationship of Surviving Capacity versus Recovery Rate.

(As a Percentage of Preattack GNP)

Type of Attack	Attack Level (No. of Weapons)	Surviving Capacity GNP (1)	Initial Noninvestment Demand (2)	Postattack GNP for Year								
				One (3)	Two (4)	Three (5)	Four (6)	Five (7)	Six (8)	Seven (9)	Eight (10)	Nine (11)
General[a]	250	80.4%	54%	63.1%	60.8%	75.1%	74.4%	79.4%	82.7%	87.0%	91.0%	96.7%
"	500	72.1	47	53.1	51.3	65.0	64.8	69.0	71.9	75.6	79.8	84.0
"	750	67.0	43	47.8	46.1	58.2	58.3	62.6	64.7	67.9	71.0	74.6
"	1,000	63.8	40	44.3	42.8	54.6	55.1	59.6	61.9	65.5	69.1	73.4
"	1,250	61.6	39	42.8	41.3	52.2	52.0	56.7	58.2	61.2	63.8	66.8
Energy[b]	250	85.0	20	23.7	21.6	61.4	70.6	93.7				

a. U.S. Runs with a 15 Sector Model.
Investment cost per dollar of incremental GNP was 2.0 for all runs except energy. 1.5 was used in this case.
The objective function used for optimization was the present value of the future stream of GNP.
The Stipulated lower level for noninvestment was increased at the rate of four percent per year from year two to year nine.
The uniform growth rate from the ninth year on was set at four percent.
The depreciation rate was set at six percent.

b. U.S. Runs with 7 Sector Model.

Source: F.W. Dresch, and S. Baum, Analysis of the U.S. and USSR Potential for Economic Recovery Following A Nuclear Attack (Menlo Park, California: Stanford Research Institute, Strategic Studies Center, January 1973), p. II-7.

The authors also examined a limited number of bottlenecking situations. The results for the energy sector, namely petroleum refining (Table 5-11, row 6), produced even more dramatic impacts in the early post-attack period than those of a generalized attack.[23] The predicted surviving GNP was 85 percent of the pre-attack total, while the functioning GNP was dramatically less, only about 20 percent in the first two years. Moreover, the authors assume the ability to direct a substantial proportion of functioning, surviving industrial production and investment toward assuring the accelerated recovery of the refining sector after two years—a plausible but potentially optimistic assumption.

Although the study shows an extended and difficult recovery period, even these projections are optimistic. The authors themselves concede the models they use provide "upper limits on potential recovery. Projected recovery rates should prove over optimistic when compared with rates actually realized in a real case."[24] If this is the case, then recovery will be a difficult process. The reason for this is that "the recovery models ignore many institutional factors that could make it impossible to achieve the recovery rates projected."[25] Among the shortcomings are the neglect of geographical problems such as "transportation bottlenecks, isolation of particular regions or mismatches in the distribution of surviving populations and plant capacity."[26] Because very large catch-all categories for the economy are used, the problem of being unable to substitute for specific products may be submerged. In this case the combined (aggregate) total of surviving capacity for one of the 15 sectors of the economy may hide the fact that the specific industrial subcategories needed to make the economy function may be badly damaged.[27] Critically, no disruptive effects from organizational or social demands (such as care of injured) are factored into the model. The assumption is that an efficient, planned (central) economy[28] will be immediately in place in the post-attack period, and any curtailment of personal consumption, military activity, and other essential services would be accepted and acceptable.[29] These assumptions taken together as the authors indicated are indeed very optimistic.

While a direct comparison between these attacks and those used in this study are difficult, some gross relationship is possible to devise. The key element is the use of a highly selective bottlenecking component in attacks A-1 to A-4. This component should significantly increase the total effect on the economy even of the smaller attacks

Figure 5–15.   Postattack Recovery Measured by GNP—U.S.[a]

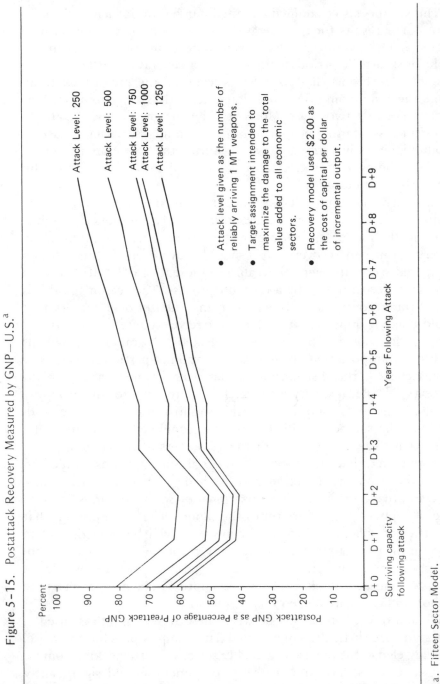

- Attack level given as the number of reliably arriving 1 MT weapons.
- Target assignment intended to maximize the damage to the total value added to all economic sectors.
- Recovery model used $2.00 as the cost of capital per dollar of incremental output.

a. Fifteen Sector Model.

Source: F.W. Dresch, and S. Baum, *Analysis of the U.S. and USSR Potential for Economic Recovery Following a Nuclear Attack*, Stanford Research Institute, Strategic Studies Center, (Menlo Park, California, January 1973). p. II–8.

A-3 and A-4. Therefore, recovery from the effects of 100 1-mega-
ton and 200-300 one hundred Kt weapons in attack A-4 is likely
to be similar to a combination of the 250 and 500 general weapon
attacks shown in the Table 5-11. The larger attacks A-3 to A-1
should be considered as efficient as the 750 to 1250 weapon attacks.
The recovery difficulties for the United States based on these comparisons would indeed be severe even under optimistic assumptions.
In the long term, when more realistic assumptions are factored in,
the situation becomes grim.

PERSPECTIVE

While this chapter is designed to set the stage for the discussion of
the broader social consequences of these urban attacks in following
chapters, it also reveals how deeply damaged U.S. society would
be. The destruction of regional building blocks of the national economy and the lack of an undamaged major regional economic base is
critical. The result is that the U.S. economic system will be parti-
tioned and fragmented, its integration as an effective system seriously in question. Moreover, economic attacks not only damage the
industrial base (factories, etc.), they thin the ranks of the technical
and managerial personnel required to operate a complex industrial
economy. They also destroy and disrupt the supporting financial
structures. The value and utility of money will be thrown into question, as will the value and ownership of goods and property; records
of financial transactions will be destroyed; and the lending and borrowing system (banks and the Federal Reserve) will collapse.

Also associated with extensive industrial damage is injury to the
basic physical support systems. In particular, the urban infrastructure
in the attacked areas—transportation, utilities, housing, fuel and
food distribution systems, sanitation systems, and medical care services—will be badly damaged or of very limited use. Rebuilding these
systems or duplicating them elsewhere will be a lengthy process and
will also divert resources from the economic expansion necessary to
achieve full recovery rapidly.

Further, the casualties (dead and injured) resulting from this type
of attack will be incomprehensible, even if some reduction due to
strategies of civil defense (evacuation) were available. The monumental loss of skilled workers, managers and economic leadership have

already been noted. Key to the reality of the postnuclear attack period will be the staggering social burden of 20 to 30 million injured, many of whom will never again be fully productive contributors to society. Who will care for them? Who will provide the support? What will be the cost to society in delayed recovery and social stability? These are almost unanswerable questions. Thus, it should be clear even at this stage of our inquiry that the complex interdependent relationships that characterize modern industrial societies make them especially vulnerable to nuclear attacks aimed at urban and industrial concentrations. If properly designed, even comparatively small attacks (400 to 500 weapons) against economic targets, particularly basic industries, could result in long-term economic damage and disruption that would be unacceptable to national leaders as well as the general public. The selective attacks against key industrial targets are especially potent since they can bottleneck the economy, exposing the dependencies of many parts of the economic system on pivotal industrial sectors such as steel and aluminum production, oil refining, and turbine and engine manufacture. This type of strategy has become available in the last decade as a result of a combination of increased missile accuracy and growing numbers of warheads (MIRVs), and is not amenable to obvious civil defense countermeasures.

Even with economic change this last point will remain true at least through the end of the century. The numbers of weapons within the existing and projected United States and Soviet arsenals are so large that the additional weapons needed to compensate for industrial growth, some geographical dispersal, and shifts of industry between regions will represent minor overall increases.

Serious additional international conflicts will be triggered by a substantial nuclear exchange between the United States and Soviet Union — causing substantial chaos in the world. Further, the two weakened superpowers would be very vulnerable to economic or military pressures from other nations. Key commodities, such as the massive supplies of U.S. foodstuffs will be lost to world markets for extended periods.

Finally, the basic international monetary arrangements and economic system will have to be restructured. The dollar and most European currencies will be of questionable value after an attack, damaging all nations, particularly those such as oil rich nations, who hold massive sums of petrodollars. In this atmosphere critical goods and resources (such as petroleum) may be withheld because of the lack of a credible basis of economic exchange, and the fear of retaliation for trading with an adversary. This problem will be particularly acute in a prolonged stalemated war crisis.

The discussion in the chapters to follow should be set against this initial description of damaged and disoriented economic, physical, and human systems. While the description already provided may appear a compelling case for declaring that this level of urban attack creates unacceptable damage, it reveals only the first layer of national vulnerability. The following chapters are essential to portray the true extent of damage and its full policy implications.

NOTES TO CHAPTER 5

1. R. L. Goen, R. B. Bothun, and F. E. Walker, *Potential Vulnerability Affecting National Survival* (Menlo Park, California: Stanford Research Institute, September 1970).

2. The study established the geographical distribution, capacity, and location, by plant, of these major industries. The seventy-one largest Standard Metropolitan Statistical Areas (SMSAs) as identified by SRI for 1980 were assumed to be the major initial targets, since they contain the largest concentration of the thirty-four critical industries. For the analysis PVANS examined the geographical distribution of these industries and identified the capacity and location of industrial plants. However, for the detailed siting of targets in the thirty-four standard industrial categories (SIC), the data used by SRI were normalized to the year 1967 using such sources as the Census of Manufacturers. To obtain estimates of weapons requirements, the PVANS study assumed that total destruction of economic capacity would occur wherever the blast effect from a nuclear weapon, as measured by blast overpressure, was 9 pounds per square inch (psi) or greater. For a 1 megaton nuclear weapon, the circle enclosed by the 9 psi blast contour has a radius of 5 kilometers (3.1 miles) and would cover an area of roughly 30 square miles. The number of 1 megaton nuclear weapons needed to reduce each of the seventy-one SMSAs to 20 percent of its preattack manufacturing capacity (the criterion used by SRI) was then calculated.

    To perform the actual calculation, the study divided each of the seventy-one largest SMSAs into 5 kilometer squares, and determined the manufacturing capacity, in terms of manufacturing value added (MVA), in each square. Manufacturing value added is the dollar difference between the value of a raw material or semifinished product and the final manufactured product. Each 1 megaton weapon enclosed all or part of several 5 kilometer squares. The MVA in these squares was added up, giving the total destruction attributed to that weapon. The total number of weapons was determined when 80 percent of the MVA of the particular SMSA was enclosed within the 9 psi contours of the 1 megaton weapons.

Finally, the reader should be aware that the economic calculation in this study presents analyses based on the 1967 Census of Manufacturers. This was done to be consistent with PVANS published in 1970. Nevertheless, checking the detailed analyses against the latest available data at the time of this study, the 1972 Census of Manufacturers, showed relatively small changes. Specific comparisons are discussed in the text or footnotes where appropriate.

3.   Each plant or cluster of plants in one of the eight industries that could be attacked by a 100 Kt weapon were ranked on the basis of the percentage of national manufacturing capacity for the industry contained in the plant(s). The number of weapons needed to destroy 97 to 98 percent of the industry's capacity could then be calculated.

4.   Attacking these fifty SMSAs with nuclear weapons does not necessarily lead to high levels of general industrial destruction for individual SMSAs. The level of MVA loss will be determined by the actual physical location of the target site.

5.   A.W. Oughterson, and S. Warren, *Medical Effects of the Atomic Bomb in Japan* (New York: McGraw–Hill, 1956).

6.   As noted in Figure 2–3, a multiple weapon attack can substantially increase the damage at a single place above what would be expected if only a single weapon was used, because of the overlap of blast waves and thermal radiation.

7.   Defense Civil Preparedness Agency, *Attack Environment Manual* (CPG 2–1A2) (June 1973), ch. 2, panel 3. Now part of the Federal Emergency Management Agency (FEMA).

8.   Office of Technology Assessment, *The Effects of Nuclear Weapons* Congress of the United States (Washington, D.C.: Government Printing Office, May 1979), p. 19.

9.   Based on 1967 *Census of Manufacturers* and 1970 *Bureau of Census: Population Data.* An analysis of the data from the 1972 *Census of Manufacturers* for the seventy-one SMSAs showed 60 percent of the national MVA within these areas; thus they remain as significant as in 1967. In fact, by projecting to 1980, SRI assured that fast growing areas of the nation would be part of this group of seventy-one.

10.   Geoffrey Kemp, "Nuclear Forces for Medium Powers, Part I, Targets and Weapons," Adelphi Papers No. 106 (London: International Institute for Strategic Studies, 1974), p. 25.

11.   Disruption is used to signify the uncertainty introduced by incorporating the 100 Kt estimates.

12. Many U.S. military facilities, such as strategic air command (SAC) bases, submarine bases, and Minuteman (intercontinental ballistic missile (ICBM) sites are located in these less industrialized and less populous regions. Wyoming, Montana, Idaho, North Dakota, and South Dakota, for example, have ICBM sites. If an adversary allocated additional nuclear warheads to some of these strategic military bases in a counterforce supplement to the basic urban attack, the damage to these regions would be greater.

13. Jack Sassen and Kenneth Willis, *Data Base and Damage Criteria for Measurement of Arms Limitation Effects on War Supporting Industry* ACDA/WEC-242 (Alexandria, Virginia: Metis Corporation, June 1974).

14. Input-output tables provide a way of seeing how one industry contributes to the production in other industries and, conversely, how all other industries contribute to production in a single industry. Using a table (matrix) of this type, a picture of the interaction of industries and, more importantly, the identification of which industries play key roles in production by others, can be developed.

15. Sassen, p. 44.

16. J.C. Greene, R.W. Stokley, and J.K. Christian, *Recovery from Nuclear Attack*, DCPA01-78-C-0270 (Washington, D.C.: International Center for Emergency Preparedness, December 1979), p. 13.

17. These estimates may be on the low side, since the impact of multiple weapons has not been taken into account in extrapolating from the Hiroshima casualty data. Also not included are casualties occurring outside the seventy-one largest American urban-economic areas.

18. Office of Technology Assessment, p. 113.

19. To simulate these smaller attacks, the number of weapons used against the specific SMSAs in the main attack, A-1, was reduced proportionally. Hence, Attack A-4 represents 20 percent of Attack A-1 in terms of 1 megaton weapons or 100 1-megaton weapons versus 500 1-megaton weapons. For SMSAs receiving only one weapon in Attack A-1, it was assumed that no reduction took place. While this method is not the most precise, it provides a reasonable, but conservative, basis for comparison. It is certainly not the optimum strategy to achieve the highest level of total national economic destruction.

20. The radius of the blast effects (measured in pounds per square inch of overpressure) varies with the height of the weapon burst. In this book, weapons effects data are based on the assumption that the weapons will be detonated at a height that optimizes blast effects. The approximate radii and square mileage for various blast overpressure contours are as follows:

Contour	Radius of Damage (miles)	Square Miles Affected
1 psi	11.0	380
3 psi	5.6	99
5 psi	4.3	58

21.   F.W. Dresch, and S. Baum, *Analysis of the U.S. and USSR Potential for Economic Recovery Following A Nuclear Attack*, Strategic Studies Center, (Menlo Park, California: Stanford Research Institute, January 1973).

22.   Gross National Product is the total of personal consumption expenditures (what individuals spend for goods and services), gross private domestic investment, government purchases of goods and services, and net exports of goods and services. The national MVA in contrast represents only the manufacturing contributions to the value of the U.S. economy and thus is smaller, about 30 percent of the size of the GNP.

23.   This study used a 7 sector input—output model projected for five years.

24.   Dresch, p. I—16.

25.   Ibid., p. I—16.

26.   Ibid., p. I—11.

27.   Ibid., II—13.

28.   Ibid., II—12.

29.   Ibid., II—3.

6

A WIDENING GYRE
Food, Energy, Medical Care, and Higher Education

The previous chapter described a world in which the United States's economic and human resources were deeply damaged, and a national economic system fragmented and shattered. In this chapter a second level of analysis attempts to portray some of the effects on key elements of society—food supply, medical care, energy supply, and higher education. The delivery of food, medical care, and energy are basic necessities for the functioning of society; higher education is necessary for longer range stability and growth of domestic and international economic, military, and technological power.

From the following discussion a picture should begin to emerge, revealing the depth of the damage to society and the complexity of interaction among different elements of a functioning society. It describes the requirements of coping with a loss of physical resources, and sketches the type of human organizational and management tasks that will be examined in Chapter 7. It also provides another meaningful set of concrete examples of why the official weapons requirements for unacceptable damage are set so artificially high.

FOOD PRODUCTION

Food is one of the basic necessities for survival. Its availability involves several factors: production, distribution, and, to a lesser de-

Figure 6-1. Energy Supply for the U.S. Diet.

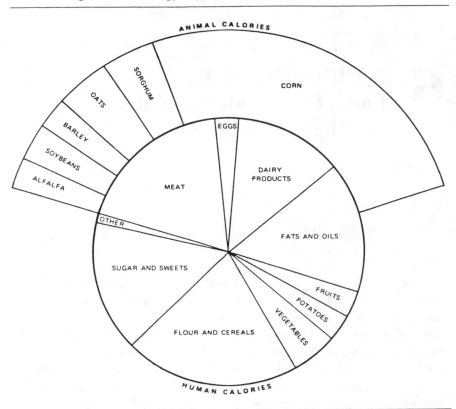

Source: Stephen L. Brown and Pamela G. Kruziz, *Agricultural Vulnerability in the National Entity Survival Context*, Final Report, (Menlo Park, California: Stanford Research Institute, July 1970). p. 64.

gree, processing. All these elements will be weakened in the post-attack period, but the effectiveness of the food distribution system appears to be the major problem. For perspective, the sources of U.S. human and animal food energy needs are shown in Figure 6-1.

Production Requirements

Production of crops and livestock depends on fertilizer, pesticides, irrigation, fuel, farm machinery, and electric power. Surviving hu-

Figure 6-2. Aggregate Crop Yield Response to Fertilizer for Corn.

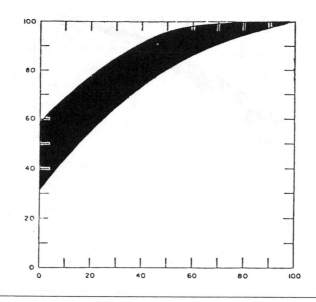

Source: Stephen L. Brown and Ulrich F. Pilz, "U.S. Agriculture: Potential Vulnerabilities" (Stanford Research Institute, January 1969). p. 36.

man resources should be sufficient following attacks A-1 (largest) to A-4 (smallest). However, a massive evacuation and resulting social disorganization could invalidate this prediction because of the urban orientation of these attacks.[1]

Fertilizer. Fertilizer loss will have a substantial impact on crop production. A study by the Stanford Research Institute (SRI) indicates that without fertilizer, a reduction of 50 percent of the yield of major crops is likely, while a 20 percent production loss is possible following a 50 percent cut in fertilizer. Production of corn and wheat, which draw heavily on soil nutrients, would decline by half without fertilizer, as shown in Figures 6-2 and 6-3. Continued planting of these crops with inadequate application of fertilizer could deplete the soil within a few years.[2] Only about one-third of the nitrogen fertilizer applied is available in the soil for the following year's crop.[3] The other principal nutrients, potassium and phosphorus, accumulate in the soil and thus would not be as serious a concern

Figure 6-3. Aggregate Crop Yield Response to Fertilizer for Wheat.

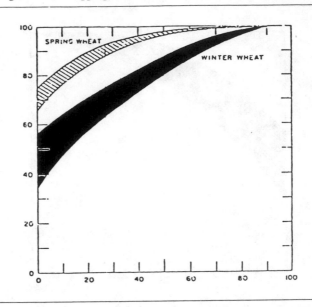

Source: Stephen L. Brown and Ulrich F. Pilz, "U.S. Agriculture: Potential Vulnerabilities" (Stanford Research Institute, January 1969). p. 37.

as nitrogen fertilizer for two to three years. A means of compensating for corn losses would be to divert the feedstocks available for animal production to direct human consumption. This would naturally reduce meat production. Other crops such as potatoes, fruits, and vegetables might experience even more serious losses in productivity as a result of reductions in fertilizer.

The effectiveness of the fertilizer distribution system is an additional limiting factor. In Figure 6-4, consumption and production patterns are shown for primary nutrient fertilizers. The southern and south central states (Regions II and V) are the major production areas, while the Great Lakes and Plains states (Regions VI and IV) are major users. The South contains a major potassium production area; Florida mines almost 75 percent of the nation's phosphate supplies. The south central area (Region V) contains very extensive nitrogen fertilizer production because the hydrogen requirement for ammonia (the major nitrogen fertilizer) comes from natural gas.

The raw material support system is likely to collapse as the result of extensive attacks on refinery capacity in Texas, Louisiana, and

Figure 6-4.   Production Consumption of Primary Nutrients, 1968.

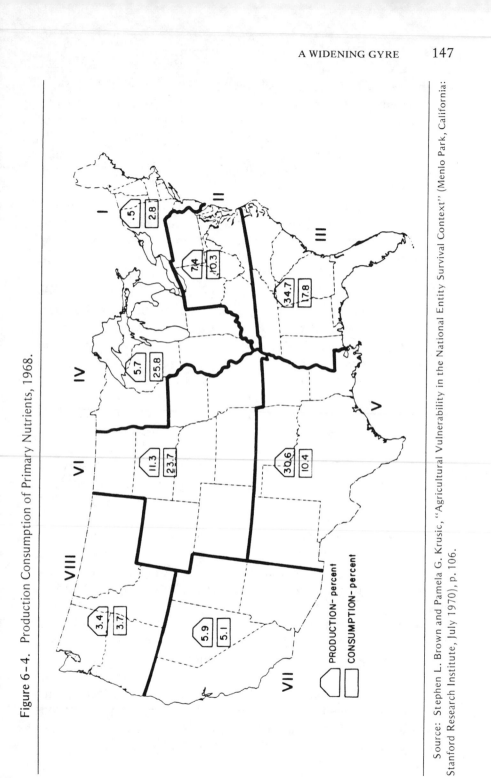

Source: Stephen L. Brown and Pamela G. Krusic, "Agricultural Vulnerability in the National Entity Survival Context" (Menlo Park, California: Stanford Research Institute, July 1970), p. 106.

Oklahoma, destroying petrochemical feedstocks and damaging gas and petroleum product pipelines. The general pattern of destruction in Florida would also have a very substantial influence on fertilizer production. All this would occur even though the fertilizer plants themselves may actually survive because they are located outside the targeted urban-industrial concentrations.

Pesticides.   The most serious effect of a lack of pesticides would be upon potatoes, vegetables, and fruits, though inadequate supplies would also cause reduction in production of major grain crops.[4] Vital fertilizers and pesticides are in many cases petroleum-based or are derived from chemical products, many of which are in turn derived from petroleum. Since the petroleum refining and chemical industries are specifically targeted for virtually complete destruction, heavy losses would be expected in supplies and availability of these products after attacks A-1 through A-4. The adverse consequences of these losses may increase with time. The incidence of pest infestation and soil depletion would increase rapidly unless there was a major modification (e.g., composting, organic farming, and biological controls) of farming strategies. The effective implementation of these new approaches would require several years.

Irrigation.   Irrigation would also suffer from petroleum losses as well as losses of other fossil fuel and electricity, because of the dependence of pumps and related equipment on these energy sources. The loss of irrigation facilities and capacity would have a serious effect on crops such as rice, sugar, beets, potatoes, alfalfa, vegetables, and fruits, but not on major food energy (grain) crops. However, a prolonged disruption of irrigation systems, including the effective use of large-scale water systems, could cause lands to revert to dust bowl conditions.[5]

   Taken together, the serious reductions in all three of these agricultural elements (fertilizer, pesticides, and irrigation) would injure, but probably not destroy, major food production capabilities.

Agricultural Fuel and Power Requirements.   The modern farm depends heavily on electricity and petroleum, which power tractors, harvesting equipment, pumps, trucks, and various types of specialized equipment. Figure 6-5 indicates the dependence of farm pro-

Figure 6-5. Assumed Dependence of Farm Output on Petroleum.

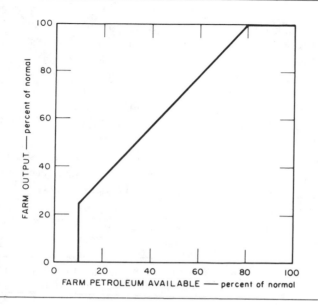

Source: Stephen L. Brown and Ulrich F. Pilz, "U.S. Agriculture: Potential Vulnerabilities" (Stanford Research Institute, January 1969), p. 46.

duction on petroleum availability. Table 6-1 shows some typical farm functions requiring electricity.

Poultry and dairy farms are particularly vulnerable, since both depend upon a high degree of mechanization. This limits their flexibility. A productive milk cow yields thirty to seventy pounds of milk per day. If the farm is large, if electricity is available only sporadically, and if petroleum supplies (for electrical generators) are limited, in a matter of weeks many of these animals would be unable to produce milk or would have a reduced capacity as a result of being unmilked or partially milked for a period of less than one week. If unmilked for only two days, a cow's lactation (milk production) is reduced by about 25 percent.[6] If the period without milking is from four to five days, a cow will dry up and cannot produce milk again until it has calved nine months later. If a cow is only partially milked daily for a period of a week or two, milk production will also be reduced. Without electricity, dairy workers could resort to hand milk-

Table 6-1. Electrical Equipment for Farm Use.

Equipment	
Dairy and livestock	General farm
Milking machine	Grain elevator
Milk cooler	Roughage elevator
Cream separator	Hay drier
Ventilator fan	Grain drier
Milkhouse heater	Feed grinder
Silage unloader	Corn sheller
Pig brooder	Water supply
Fence controller	Pressure system (shallow well)
Poultry	Pressure system (deep well)
Chick brooder	Pump jack
Incubator	
Mechanical feeder	
Egg cooler	

Source: Stephen L. Brown and Olrich F. Pilz, "U.S. Agriculture: Potential Vulnerabilities" (Menlo Park, California: Stanford Research Institute, January 1969), p. 48.

ing. This, it has been estimated, would require three times the present farm manpower at a minimum. However, since efficient milking requires experience, the likelihood is that more than three times the present number of dairy workers would be needed to offset a loss of electricity. While electric power demands may prove less difficult to satisfy, depending on surviving capacity and surviving fuel, power plant reliability problems could also cause significant disruption. Specifically Brown et al[7] expressed concerns about the vulnerability of the electric power system to Electromagnetic Pulse (EMP) produced by a nuclear blast. An SRI report estimated that "at least a 75 percent drop in production could be expected if electricity were cut off more than a few days."[8]

Livestock farming would also experience complex problems. Currently beef cattle are moved from place of birth to pastures for growth, then to feedlots where they are fattened, and finally they are shipped for processing and consumption (see Figures 6-6 and 6-7). Figure 6-6 indicates the extent of concentration of feedlots away from the large population of the East. The cattle may travel 1,000 miles from birth to consumption. This represents a substantial requirement for transportation, energy, and organizational resources.

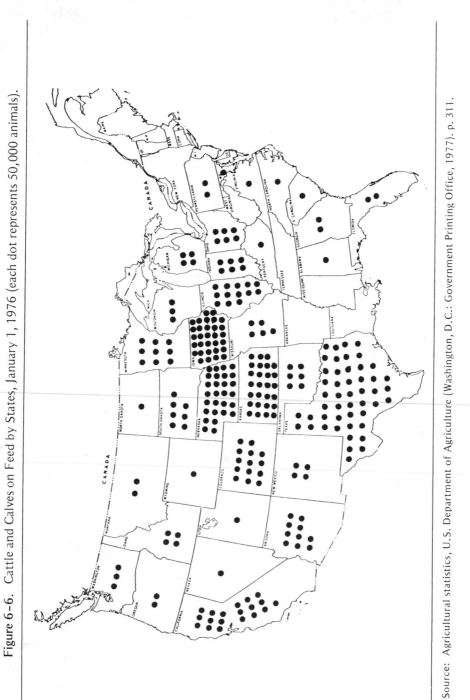

Figure 6-6. Cattle and Calves on Feed by States, January 1, 1976 (each dot represents 50,000 animals).

Source: Agricultural statistics, U.S. Department of Agriculture (Washington, D.C.: Government Printing Office, 1977). p. 311.

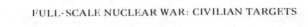

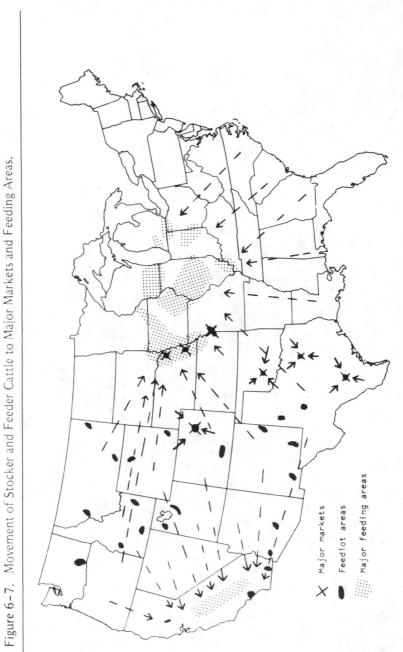

Figure 6–7. Movement of Stocker and Feeder Cattle to Major Markets and Feeding Areas.

✕ Major markets

⬮ Feedlot areas

⠿ Major feeding areas

Source: Stephen L. Brown and Ulrich F. Pilz, "U.S. Agriculture: Potential Vulnerabilities" (Stanford Research Institute, January 1969), p. 52.

With the loss of refinery capacity and potentially major social dis-organization, the prospects of this system working efficiently are not encouraging. These concerns are supported by a Stanford Research Institute report: "Transportation and distribution of livestock and livestock products at all stages of production thus appear to be the most critical considerations in the vulnerability of the livestock prod-uct system."[9]

In the hypothetical attacks oil refinery capacity drops below the production level needed for supplying farm equipment. Farms re-quire about 4 or 5 percent of all oil refinery production, but total U.S. postattack production will be 2 to 3 percent of normal. There-fore, even a reduction in farm requirements by 50 percent would imply a dangerously limited supply. Moreover, the food production system does not end at the farm gate. Transportation and major food-processing requirements will make heavy demands on fuel sup-plies. It appears that four times more energy is required to produce, process, distribute, and store foodstuffs than is directly required to produce food (see Table 6-2). These overall demands, though re-duced because of destruction and casualties caused by the attacks, would prove difficult to satisfy.

Distribution and Processing Requirements

The passage of raw and processed food between various sections of the country and the regional distribution of food production, pro-cessing, and consumption is depicted in Figures 6-8 and 3-6. Table 6-3 provides quantitative details for the distribution of various spe-cific food items.

It should be apparent from these illustrations that the northeast and mid-Atlantic states (Regions I and II) depend heavily on food produced west of the Mississippi (Region VI) and in the Southwest (Region V). California, its adjacent area, and the South also show moderate dependence, although less severe than the Northeast. Em-phasizing the problem of regional resource distribution, Figure 6-9 shows U.S. grain production, and Figure 6-10 an evacuation and redistribution of population proposed by an Oak Ridge National Laboratory (ORNL) study.[10] Even with a major evacuation,[11] the maldistribution is apparent, with major supplies in the Great Plains far from population centers. The ORNL study found that 60 million

Table 6-2. Energy Usage in the American Food System (*all values are multiplied by 10^{11} kcal*).

	1970
Component	
Fuel	282.0
Electricity	68.8
Fertilizer	94.0
Agricultural steel	2.0
Farm machinery	80.0
Tractors	19.8
Irrigation	85.0
Subtotal	526.1
Food processing industry	308.0
Food processing machinery	6.0
Paper packaging	88.0
Glass containers	47.0
Steel cans and aluminum	122.0
Transport (fuel)	246.9
Trucks and trailers (manufacture)	74.0
Subtotal	841.9
Commercial refrigeration and cooking	263.0
Refrigeration machinery (home and commercial)	61.0
Home refrigeration and cooking	480.0
Subtotal	804.0
Grand total	2,172.0

Source: J.S. Steinhardt and C.E. Steinhardt, "Energy Use in the U.S. Food System." *Science* 184 (April 1975), p. 307.

(approximately one-third) of the U.S. population were still located in areas with a grain supply, measured by local production, estimated at two weeks or less, and thirty million others (a combined total of almost half the U.S. population) were in counties with less than two months supply. Since the supply was measured by production rather than stored grains, it may be optimistic. An additional organizational problem is that the South (Region III) and Southwest (Region V) depend heavily on the Midwest for processed food. Based on the information presented here, there is little doubt that all of the

Figure 6-8. Simplified Food Transportation Flow.

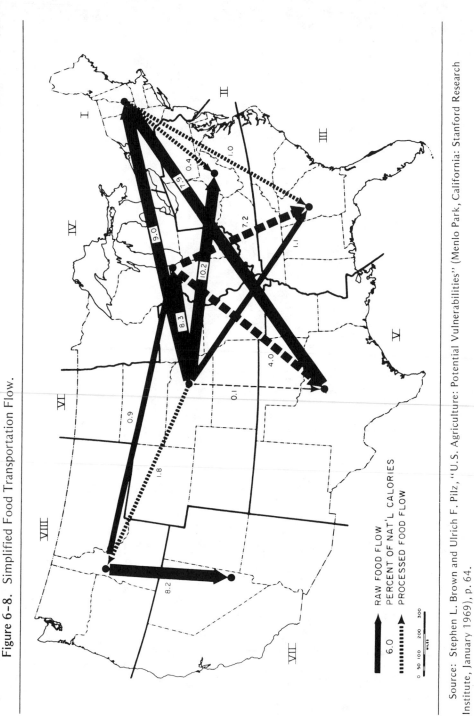

RAW FOOD FLOW

PERCENT OF NAT'L CALORIES

6.0   PROCESSED FOOD FLOW

0 50 100 200 300
MILES

Source: Stephen L. Brown and Ulrich F. Pilz, "U.S. Agriculture: Potential Vulnerabilities" (Menlo Park, California: Stanford Research Institute, January 1969), p. 64.

Table 6-3. Distribution of Food Production and Processing by Region   (percent of U.S. total).

Item	I North-east	II Mid-Atlantic	III South	IV Great Lakes	V South Central	VI Great Plains	VII South-west	VIII North-west
Population	18.2	17.8	14.6	15.7	10.3	7.1	13.1	3.2
Food processing	19.6	17.4	6.4	26.9	6.1	9.0	13.1	1.4
Food value	2.8	7.2	5.3	17.7	14.0	37.6	4.9	10.5
Livestock requirements	3.1	10.1	9.8	22.8	10.2	34.2	5.3	4.6
Feed crops	1.3	8.5	9.6	30.7	7.5	38.6	1.5	2.3
Food grains	0.2	4.0	2.0	9.0	20.0	47.0	3.0	14.0
Sugar	0	2.0	0	17.0	0	32.0	26.0	23.0
Potatoes	22.0	8.0	5.0	16.0	1.0	14.0	9.0	24.0
Meat and eggs	3.0	10.0	11.0	21.0	10.0	34.0	5.0	4.0
Oils	0	9.0	11.0	43.0	11.0	25.0	0	0

Source: Adapted from Stanford Research Institute projections to 1975, Stephen L. Brown and Ulrich F. Pilz, "U.S. Agriculture: Potential Vulnerabilities" (Menlo Park, California: Stanford Research Institute, January 1969), pp. 66–69.

assumed attacks (A–1 to A–4) will seriously disrupt the distribution and processing networks among regions.

Examining the physical survival of the food-processing industry, nearly 77 percent of the nation's capacity is located in the northeast, mid–Atlantic, Great Lakes, and southwestern areas, the regions most severely attacked. This processing capacity constitutes about a 12 percent surplus over the requirements of the population in these regions. Yet the severity of the attacks on these areas will reduce this capacity below levels needed to meet demand within the regions. The loss of an additional 10 percent (for a total of nearly 90 percent) of the nation's food-processing capacity is not inconceivable. Such losses would be very injurious but not necessarily fatal to the nation in the short run. In the midterm, however, the ability to process and store food will be critical to sustained economic and social recovery. It is interesting to note that packaging and containers require almost 10 percent of the energy needs for the entire food system and 40 percent of the energy needs for direct food production. Since containers are important and in some cases essential (e.g., canning) for food preservation, loss of packaging facilities through plant destruction or indirectly through lack of energy and materials, would have severe consequences for the availability of food in distant areas and over time.

Damage to the food distribution system may have the most severe impact on the nation's ability to feed its surviving population in the postattack period. Moreover, intraregional distribution networks could be severely tested. The intra- as well as interregional distribution systems depend on two basic elements—physical resources (railroads, boats, trucks, roads, and fuel) and organizational resources (people, and regional and national allocation systems). The loss of petroleum appears to be the dominant limitation for the former. The adequacy of surviving railroad facilities, highways and port facilities would also be important. Organizational problems could be as severe as fuel issues, if, as expected, there is a significant loss of technical and managerial personnel. Complicating calculations is the possibility of hoarding in food-producing regions.

Destruction within Regions I, II, IV, and VII, coupled with substantial, if not severe, damage in Regions V and VI, will leave the national food distribution system in total disarray. Physical destruction, loss of workers, spontaneous or planned population evacuation (stretching supply lines), fear of radiation, and destruction of

Figure 6-9. 1974 Grain Production.

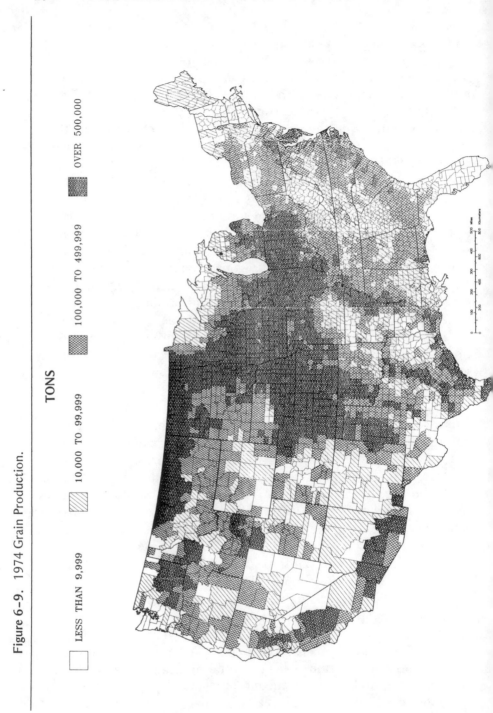

Figure 6-10.   The Redistribution of Population from High Risk Areas (compare changes to Figure 5-7).

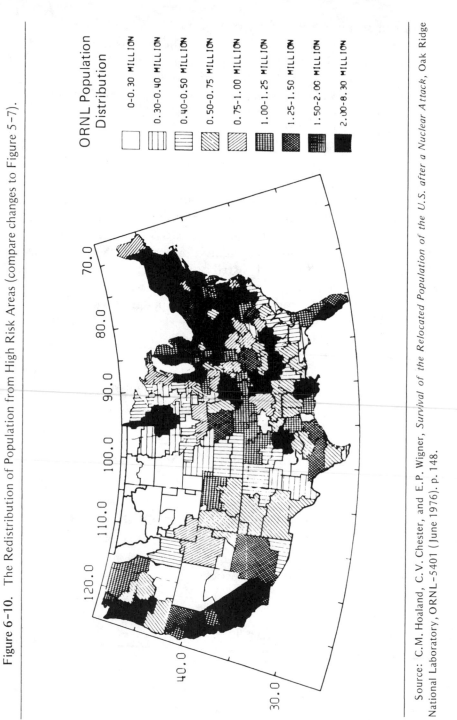

ORNL Population
Distribution

0-0.30 MILLION

0.30-0.40 MILLION

0.40-0.50 MILLION

0.50-0.75 MILLION

0.75-1.00 MILLION

1.00-1.25 MILLION

1.25-1.50 MILLION

1.50-2.00 MILLION

2.00-8.30 MILLION

Source: C.M. Hoaland, C.V. Chester, and E.P. Wigner, *Survival of the Relocated Population of the U.S. after a Nuclear Attack*, Oak Ridge
National Laboratory, ORNL-5401 (June 1976). p. 148.

important facilities (feed lots, storage facilities) will contribute to a significant weakening of the nation's ability to allocate food resources. The surviving organizational resources available to cope with these problems may prove inadequate to the task of improvising a system to replace the existing complex food distribution scheme in the United States.

The experiences of World War II provide additional insights. In general, government control of the food supplies through mass rationing was instituted in Japan, Germany, and Britain in World War II. Beyond the sheer impact of food issues on nutrition, and thus health and vitality, food had an important behavioral and psychological effect in relation to effective economic recovery. It was found that authorities had difficulty keeping workers in bombed cities if the food supply was not sufficient.[12] Moreover, the breakdown in the organization of the food distribution system and the inadequacy of supplies caused evacuation beyond that which actual physical damage would have required. Put simply, people migrated in search of food, further disrupting the economy. (For more detailed discussion of the significance of food supplies in the postattack period, see Chapter 7).

The difficulties and problems caused by the disruption of national food production and distribution systems in World War II would be magnified significantly in an economically oriented attack on an industrialized society today, owing to:

1. The far greater destructive power of thermonuclear weapons;

2. The possibility of achieving nearly simultaneous destruction of large numbers of key target areas, thus limiting the availability of relief from unaffected areas and the opportunity to improvise solutions between attacks;

3. The far more vulnerable, complex, energy-dependent and transportation-dependent food-processing and distributing systems that have evolved since World War II; and

4. A food retailing system in the United States that keeps market and warehouse inventories low—two to three weeks of supply at the maximum.[13]

ENERGY

As few need to be told, the availability of energy is a critical element in national survival and economic power. Since these resources are derived from foreign as well as domestic sources, an added uncertainty—specifically the loss of complete control of petroleum resource allocations—is introduced in a nuclear war. This added uncertainty means the effectiveness of any organizational efforts for stabilization and recovery that rely, as they must, on energy resources are potentially subject to greater failure. In addition to the ambiguities introduced by foreign supplies, the energy system has a number of sequential steps for resource utilization—from mining, to refining and conversion, to distribution—each with their own vulnerabilities. An effective bottlenecking of any critical step in this process would undercut the usefulness of the whole system. The discussion below touches on all of these elements.

The United States depends on fossil fuels (petroleum, gas, and oil) for about 93 percent of its energy needs. Petroleum represents the largest component, providing 49 percent of requirements, while gas and coal provide 26 and 18 percent, respectively.[14]

Petroleum

Attacks A-1 and A-2 would destroy 98 percent of the petroleum-refining capacity of the United States. For A-1 and A-2 the surviving capacity alone could not, as noted, even meet farm fuel demands. Attacks A-3 and A-4 would also disrupt virtually all U.S. refinery capacity, although a smaller amount of refinery capacity will actually be destroyed. The vulnerability of refinery capacity is emphasized by the fact that a recent study found that two-thirds of U.S. capacity could be destroyed by eighty weapons.[15]

The loss of petroleum-refining capacity will have severe consequences in terms of national survival and recovery. These losses would drastically reduce the availability of petroleum for home heating oil, farming, industrial production, transportation, petrochemical products, and power plants. Furthermore, most plants producing complex petrochemicals are located near refineries and are thus

Table 6-4. United States and New England Petroleum Consumption by Source.

	United States	New England
Total consumption, 1976 (million barrels)	6,367	409
Products refined from domestic crude (percent)	59	21
Products refined from foreign crude (percent)	30	56
Direct imports of refined products (foreign crude refined overseas; percent)	11	23

Source: Adapted from Barbara Boynton, "New England Petroleum Product Imports—1976" (Boston, Mass.: Federal Energy Administration, July 1977), p. 12.

themselves physically vulnerable. For example, 60 percent of U.S. petrochemicals are made in Texas Gulf Coast plants.[16]

Foreign petroleum supplies, which now represent over 40 percent of total U.S. consumption, might be available for recovery (see Table 6-4). Yet such supplies are unpredictable even in peacetime, and perhaps inadequate for long-term recovery. In the aftermath of a nuclear war the reliability of these sources could be uncertain for months, particularly if the United States lacked money (or barter) or if exporters were guided by other national political priorities, including fear of retaliation by an adversary.

Another disturbing factor is that approximately 75 percent of the foreign petroleum comes to the United States as crude petroleum and thus requires American refining capacity; only about 10 percent of normal petroleum needs are satisfied from foreign refineries.[17] Thus, if U.S. refinery capacity were destroyed, using the import levels without qualification gives a deceptively optimistic picture of the amount of usable petroleum products actually available for the U.S. economy. Even if the foreign contribution of petroleum products could represent substantially more than 10 percent of U.S. post-attack needs (because initially energy demand is significantly reduced), the uncertainty of foreign supplies, and especially the political implication of extraordinary dependency on foreign sources, raise very serious questions about both the United States's postattack economic recovery and its international political status.

Direct attacks on petroleum product and crude petroleum pipelines, which carry about one-third and three-quarters, respectively, of total U.S. volume in these categories, would reinforce the disruptive effects of refinery destruction.[18] The importance of an effective crude and refined petroleum distribution system is shown by the different geographic distributions for petroleum production (Figure 6–11) and population (demand) centers (see Figure 5–7). The transportation issue is a good example of how many facets a nuclear war problem may have.

One of the key crude oil pipeline problems is the Trans–Alaska Pipeline System (TAPS). Approximately 7.5 percent of the total crude petroleum to all U.S. refineries in 1977 passed through this pipeline.[19] In a recent report, the General Accounting Office (GAO) concluded: "There is no alternative transportation system for moving Alaskan crude should TAPS become inoperative."[20] Thus, an attack on this pipeline would result in losses of an important domestic resource.

This GAO study also reported that the Capline system, which supplies 25 percent of the crude oil needs (7.5 percent of total crude in the United States) of Midwest refineries, and the Colonial pipeline, which handles 9 percent of total refined petroleum products domestic demand, but an average of 40 percent to thirteen Eastern states, were also both vulnerable to sabotage (and thus to nuclear attack). The destruction of pumping stations and centralized computers that remotely operate key pipeline facilities (in the case of Colonial pipeline located in the target city of Atlanta, Georgia) could cause losses of these key installations for six months—reducing or eliminating pumping capacity. Supporting these concerns is the fact that automation has reduced the number of skilled personnel manually able to operate the pipelines if computer controls were destroyed. Moreover, improvements in pipeline technology have reduced the numbers of maintenance personnel. In the event of a nuclear exchange, even the limited number of skilled personnel may be lost through death, injury, or evacuation. Thus, serious shortages would result.

The GAO also pointed out "that pump stations or other key facilities would almost certainly require a special order for replacement . . . a manufacturer may require from six to twelve months to fill an order for a specific replacement pump."[21] Despite the high priority these needs may receive in the aftermath of a nuclear war, the extensive destruction of the nation's industrial base should impose significant delays (perhaps years) for replacement of these key items.

Figure 6-11. Percentage Distribution of U.S. Petroleum Refinery Capacity by State.

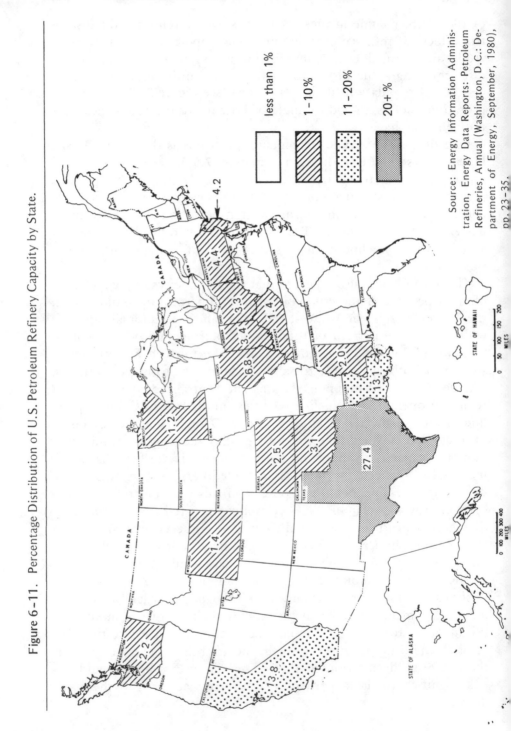

less than 1%

1–10%

11–20%

20+ %

Source: Energy Information Administration, Energy Data Reports: Petroleum Refineries, Annual (Washington, D.C.: Department of Energy, September, 1980), pp. 23–35.

The GAO study concluded: "Damage to key facilities on just a few pipeline systems could greatly reduce domestic shipments, causing an energy shortage exceeding that of the 1973 Arab oil embargo."[22] This conclusion was of course based on a fully intact nation.

The PVANS study also examined the pipeline issue and supported the significance of the impact. It estimated that ten additional weapons hitting three of the major petroleum product pipelines would severely disrupt 63 percent of the pipeline capacity for the delivery of refined petroleum (based on barrel miles).[23]

Waterborne traffic also carries substantial amounts of crude and refined petroleum (13 percent to the Atlantic coast and 25 percent to the Midwest), so that some substitution of transport capabilities might be possible if port facilities survive. In fact, it is quite probable that many ports with major oil-handling facilities will be destroyed or badly damaged.[24] However, even if this substitution were possible, it would result in further demands on motor carrier systems for extended trips in order to distribute petroleum products from these ports. This, in turn, would result in increased fuel use and would depend upon a high degree of organization:

> To place this transportation problem in perspective, two pipelines, the Plantation and the Colonial . . . [are] supplying about two-thirds of the oil for the New York–New Jersey area. If these two lines were severed by a nuclear strike, it would require from 200 to 250 T-2 tanker equivalents to move this liquid from Galveston, Texas, to New York. . . . This operation would use all of the U.S. tankers, and the ports at each end, if they were not destroyed by the attack, would be so crowded that a complete traffic jam would result.[25]

While petroleum demand from the New York–New Jersey area would obviously be drastically reduced after Attacks A–1 to A–4, nevertheless, it should be clear that even supplying a decreased level of U.S. demand would be quite difficult.

Crude Petroleum Production. Further complicating the petroleum availability problem is the vulnerability of crude oil production shown in Figure 6–12. The refineries and petroleum port facilities destroyed in the Southwest are adjacent to major production areas. Although many wells themselves may not be destroyed, the substantial destruction of nearby urban areas may cause widespread casualties among experienced oil personnel, as well as very substantial

Figure 6-12.   Oil Production by County.

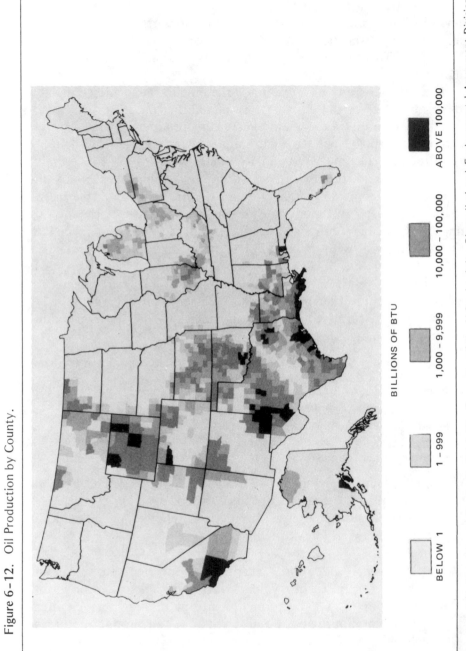

BILLIONS OF BTU

BELOW 1   1 – 999   1,000 – 9,999   10,000 – 100,000   ABOVE 100,000

Source: Frank R. Drysdale and Charles E. Calef. *The Energetics of the U.S.: An Atlas*, Biomedical and Environmental Assessment Division, National Center for Analysis of Energy Systems (Upton, New York: Brookhaven National Laboratory, October 1977).

social disorganization. (This disruption should also be true of California, another oil-producing area.) These problems coupled with possible losses, in the general attacks, of manufacturing capacity for petroleum exploration and operation equipment, should mean short- to midterm reductions of domestic crude oil supply.

To summarize, the direct damage to refinery capacity poses the most serious, perhaps insurmountable, postattack problem for short-term stability and certainly a critical one for long-term recovery. Additional disruptions of petroleum transportation and production capacity would add other significant elements of uncertainty with regard to petroleum supplies.

Coal

Coal is the most abundant fossil fuel resource in the United States. It is used predominantly for electricity production, producing 45 percent of the electricity generated in the United States, and for industrial purposes such as process steam. The substitution of coal for oil would be difficult in the short term. Limitations on the interchangeability of fuels in many industries and in residential heating would complicate survival and recovery.

The coal supply itself would also be uncertain because of losses of vital infrastructure in the coal-producing areas of the East (shown in Figure 6-13), especially in Pennsylvania and West Virginia. Strip mining of coal for power plant fuel and other uses would require equipment, such as drag lines, which also utilize substantial quantities of petroleum fuels and electricity. Deep mining also relies on electricity. However, in both cases, this electricity comes from the normal grid and is not generated on site. Thus, all the uncertainties and vulnerabilities of the postattack electrical supply system (discussed below) must be factored into estimates of coal production.

Coal is transported by railroad, barge, and, increasingly, trucks for short hauls. Railroads are diesel-powered and trucks also use diesel fuel or, in some cases, gasoline. Thus, besides damage experienced by railroads or highways, both modes of transportation may be seriously curtailed because of petroleum product shortages due to refinery losses. Even coal-burning power plants that provide electricity for mining could be affected, if rail and truck transportation systems

Figure 6-13. Coal Production by County.

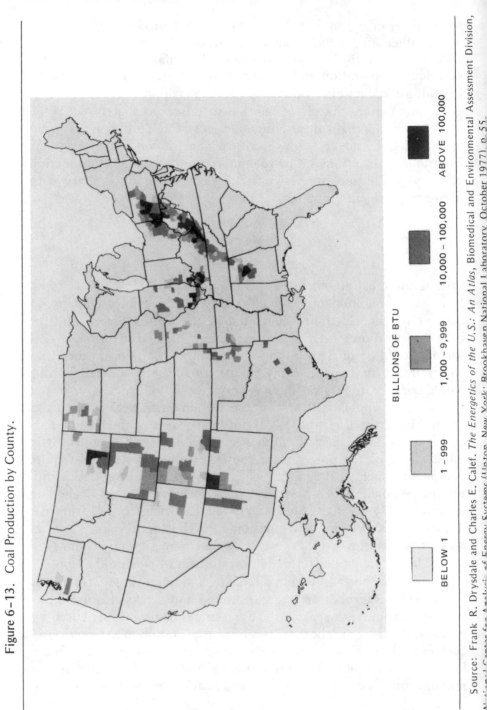

BILLIONS OF BTU

BELOW 1   1 – 999   1,000 – 9,999   10,000 – 100,000   ABOVE 100,000

Source: Frank R. Drysdale and Charles E. Calef. *The Energetics of the U.S.: An Atlas*, Biomedical and Environmental Assessment Division, National Center for Analysis of Energy Systems (Upton, New York: Brookhaven National Laboratory October 1977) p. 55.

cannot supply the fuel for power plant operation. The obvious conclusion is that anticipated damage to several vital and related factors
of production makes it doubtful that coal can be substituted for significant amounts of petroleum for a year or more after an attack.

Natural Gas

Texas and Louisiana produce 74 percent of American natural gas,
while Oklahoma, Kansas, and New Mexico account for much of the
remainder (Figure 6–14). These five states consume about one-third
of all natural gas themselves. The midwest, north central, and middle
Atlantic states and California are other major consuming areas. Virtually all gas moves by pipeline; pathways are shown in Figure 6–15.
Pipelines have compressors to maintain gas flow at 40 to 200 mile
intervals. Selected destruction of compressor stations and related
pipelines would prove very disruptive to industrial and residential
users.[26] As previously noted, the economic disruption and deprivation caused by comparatively mild natural gas shortages in the winter
of 1976–1977 and by the coal shortage in the winter of 1977–1978
provide indicators of how dependent the American economy is on
these fuels and how vulnerable they are to curtailment at the source.

Electric Power

The physical damage to electric power-generating capacity and
power-transmitting capability is substantial, but should not be overwhelming, under the postulated attacks. Stored fuel at the generating
plant should be adequate for three to six months of operation, if
power consumption is drastically reduced.

On the basis of fuel supply and plant capacity available, it appears
that a limited but sufficient supply of electric power will be available
for essential needs in most areas. However, availability of skilled
workers and maintenance capabilities complicate the picture. Personnel to operate and service generating and transmission facilities effectively may not exist in the required numbers.

Further problems could result from the disruption and destruction
of the electrical system, especially computers that are essential for
distributing electricity throughout the nation's grid system.[27] The

Figure 6–14. Natural Gas Production by County.

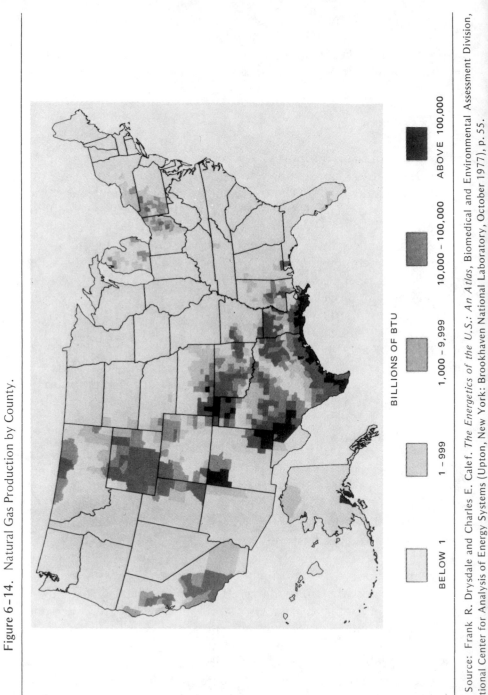

BILLIONS OF BTU

BELOW 1   1 – 999   1,000 – 9,999   10,000 – 100,000   ABOVE 100,000

Source: Frank R. Drysdale and Charles E. Calef. *The Energetics of the U.S.: An Atlas*, Biomedical and Environmental Assessment Division, National Center for Analysis of Energy Systems (Upton, New York: Brookhaven National Laboratory, October 1977), p. 55.

Figure 6-15. 1970 Intrastate Natural Gas Movement.

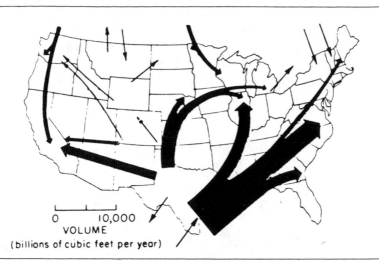

0   10,000
VOLUME
(billions of cubic feet per year)

Source: From *Gasfacts*, American Gas Association, 1973.

consequences of failure of this system was amply indicated in the blackout of the northeast United States in 1965. As noted, this problem could be produced by Electromagnetic Pulse (EMP). It can be caused by the detonation of a few nuclear weapons at high altitude (12.5 to 25 miles above the surface of the earth) or many air or ground burst around the nation. The Defense Civil Preparedness Agency concluded that because of EMP "no reliance should be placed on the presumed availability of electric power during and immediately following a nuclear attack."[28] While countermeasures against EMP effects are possible, at present the civilian electrical power system is not extensively protected.

Power plants generally require one month of maintenance per year, during which operations are halted; continuous attention is needed for the rest of the operating time. Since large numbers of skilled workers would be killed or seriously injured in urban areas, the ability to maintain operating efficiency could be sharply reduced or capacity eliminated altogether in the critical early months of the postattack period.

Complicating these difficulties will be the lack of spare parts and replacements for inoperable equipment. The turbine and electric motor industry would be destroyed in the postulated attacks, along with iron and steel works. In view of the individual design of each power plant, cannibalization of parts from other power plants may be of limited usefulness. Therefore, while power-generating capacity appears adequate in the postattack period on first examination, many unquantifiable problems remain that may substantially reduce electric capacity and power transmission.

MEDICAL CARE

Of all the problems that most deeply touch the individual, the family, and the society, the delivery of effective medical care and the personal burden of illness and death are among the most potent. It is a scene from the movie "Gone with the Wind," a panoramic view of endless rows of wounded southern soldiers as Atlanta falls, which begins to convey an accurate emotional sense of the immediate impact of the enormous numbers of casualties produced almost instantaneously in these attacks. It is the sense of helplessness and the inadequacy of limited medical and human resources when confronted with the massive accumulation of human suffering, that is both touching and demoralizing. This powerful emotional response is lacking in any attempt to quantify and dispassionately discuss the effects of nuclear war. Our discussion of effects does not portray the sense of continuing powerlessness, anger, and self-pity that injured individuals and those around them, including medical personnel, must face in a world deprived of the elements—abundant food, medical equipment—that would most effectively support their recovery. Thus, discussing interactive medical effects does not properly frame the personal emotions and their disorienting effects on society. Perhaps only a novelist can complete this picture and do justice to this dimension of life after nuclear war. Given these limitations, the following discussion will focus on creating an accurate picture of the implications of our hypothetical attacks on the medical system.

In the initial postattack period, severe medical care problems will occur on a nationwide scale because of the masssive increase in the number of people who will require medical care for burns, radiation sickness, blast effects, shock, and other injuries; and the absence of necessary medical services and supplies due to the wholesale destruction of hospital facilities, widespread deaths and injuries among medical personnel, and the almost total destruction of the drug industry.

Other serious health problems are likely to appear later. For example, while epidemics are unlikely to occur during the early postattack period because the large reservoirs of disease carriers will be absent, nevertheless, prolonged contact in crowded conditions necessitated by extended shelter life or fuel and housing conservation measures would increase the long-term probability of epidemics.[29] In addition, the appearance of diseases not normally seen in the United States, such as plague, typhus, cholera, and so forth, may generate fear (magnified by the postattack atmosphere) that will cause spontaneous or planned isolation of specific areas, and diminish the effectiveness of postattack recovery programs.

The most serious immediate postattack medical problem will be treatment for burns, blast injuries, and radiation exposure. This will be complicated by the likelihood of multiple injuries—that is, combinations of burn, blast, and radiation injuries. Analysis of data from the atomic bombings of Hiroshima reveals that some 40 percent of the survivors sustained multiple injuries.[30] Radiation exposure complicates the treatment of other injuries. Tests of animals with both burn and radiation injuries showed a significant increase in mortality over death caused from burn injuries alone because of increased vulnerability to infection.

Yet, there are only twelve burn care centers in the United States, and of the nation's 6000 general hospitals, fewer than 100 provide specialized burn care. Two hundred severe burn cases would saturate all existing facilities.[31] Though burn center care is important to survival rates for serious burn victims of all ages, flame injuries affect children more severely than adults. For eight year olds burned over 60 percent of their bodies, the survival rate in hospitals is only 20 percent, but it increases to 50 percent for those treated in burn care centers.[32] Few if any of these facilities will survive nuclear attacks on metropolitan areas.

The prognosis for seriously exposed radiation cases or multiple injury patients will depend on nutrition, rest, and medical care. In radiation cases, the hematological system is seriously disturbed, including blood cell production by the bone marrow and storage by the spleen. Resistance to infection is severely limited. For patients with substantial radiation exposure, antibiotics, transfusions, and in cases of exposure to over 300 R, the depression of the white blood count (leukopenia) can be successfully treated with sophisticated medical treatment, including bone marrow transplants. But the likelihood of the availability of this treatment on a large scale is inconceivable in a postattack environment.

Under the attacks envisioned in this book, medical care for the injured will be further complicated by the virtual elimination of the pharmaceutical industry, one of the eight critical industries targeted for maximum destruction. Even simple protection against infection will be difficult, because infection control requires antibiotics and other prophylactics. Urban stocks of these medicines will be in large measure destroyed, and new supplies will be unavailable as a result of the destruction of the pharmaceutical industry and limitation of foreign trade. These losses will also be critical for chronically ill individuals (heart disease, diabetes, and so forth) who depend on drugs for their capacity to sustain physical activity or life itself.

In summary, under postattack conditions for any of the attacks, A–1 to A–4, even basic care could be limited or completely unavailable in the urban-industrial areas. Given the magnitude of the casualties nationwide (twenty to thirty million) and the loss of specialized medical facilities and personnel, even simple protection against infection will be difficult. Infection control would require antibiotics and other prophylactics, stocks of which would be exhausted immediately, with little possibility of rapid supply due to the destruction of the drug industry. The Dean of the Harvard School of Public Health, Dr. Howard Hiatt, summed up the reality of the post-nuclear attack world by stating that "Treatment would be virtually useless and the costs would be staggering."[33]

Physicians and Hospitals

The potential losses in medical resources are shown in Table 6–5. It demonstrates the degree of urban concentration of medical resources in the United States: 68 percent of the physicians and 64 percent of the dentists are found in the seventy-one largest urban areas, while these urban areas contain only 55 percent of the total populace. Likewise, 71 percent of U.S. physicians and 68 percent of its dentists reside in the areas exposed to both the 1 megaton weapon basic attack and the 100 kiloton adjunct attack, though these areas contain only 61 percent of the total U.S. population. Thus, physicians and dentists are comparatively more vulnerable than the general populace to the effects of nuclear weapons.

Table 6-5. Impact of Attack A-1 on Physicians, Hospital Beds, and Dentists.

	Physicians			Hospital Beds			Dentists		
	Preattack Total	71 Largest SMSAs (percent)	All Exposed SMSAs (percent)	Preattack Total	71 Largest SMSAs (percent)	All Exposed SMSAs (percent)	Preattack Total	71 Largest SMSAs (percent)	All Exposed SMSAs (percent)
United States	301,323	68	71	842,986	54	57	111,043	64	68
Urban United States (all SMSAs over 200,000)	231,613	89	92	528,258	85	92	81,322	88	92

Source: Arthur Katz, *Economic and Social Consequences of Nuclear Attacks on the United States*, p. 92.

Other medical resources are also concentrated and therefore vulnerable, as shown in Table 6–6, which compares the proportion of the American populace living in the seventy-four largest urban areas (standard metropolitan statistical areas, or SMSAs, with over 500,000 population) and in the 218 medium to large urban areas (SMSAs with over 50,000 population) with the percentage of medical specialists and hospital beds found in these same urban centers.

Although not identical to study categories shown in Table 6–6 they are similar, particularly the seventy-four SMSA category, and thus furnish corroborating evidence. The 50,000 and 500,000 categories do confirm that physicians of all types, especially hospital-based physicians, surgeons, and medical specialists, are proportionally more numerous in the cities than would be expected on the basis of the general distribution of population. Many of these specialists will be among the types of medical personnel most needed for adequate care of postattack survivors. A prominent example would be burn care experts.

As a consequence of these urban concentrations, the expected loss of medical personnel and the large number of casualties will dramatically change the patient-to-doctor ratio, with both short- and long-term implications for the quality of health care. If three-quarters of the physicians in the seventy-one major metropolitan areas are killed or incapacitated during Attack A–1, the ratio of injured (from the attack alone) to functioning doctors may rise to 200 to 1 or even 600 to 1, depending on the extent to which physicians can be imported to the targeted metropolitan areas—or, conversely, patients transported from damaged to undamaged areas. Initially the patient load would be even higher, perhaps on the order of 1000 casualties per doctor, because many of the dying injured would still be alive. This should be compared to an average of 90 to 110 office visits per week, with only 20 percent judged medically serious or very serious.[34] A slightly higher estimate of 130 patients per week is given by the American Medical Association.[35] One might estimate 25 patients per day as the upper part of the average range.

Under Attacks A–3 and A–4, the casualty load would be less severe, perhaps 100 to 300 casualties per doctor, but still an impossible ratio in terms of providing adequate medical care. Although surviving paramedical personnel will be able to assist, their numbers will also be reduced proportionally, and their training for attending to the seriously and multiply injured is limited.

Table 6-6. Percentage of Medical Resources in U.S. Cities by Type as Compared to Percentage of Population.

City Size	U.S. Population (percent)	Hospital Beds	Physicians	Medical Specialists	Surgeons	Other	General Practice	Hospital-Based Physicians
Over 50,000	73	74	84	88	84	88	67	93
Over 500,000	54	54	67	70	63	69	50	79

Source: Center for Health Services Research and Development, American Medical Association, "Physician Distribution and Medical Licensure in the U.S., 1974" (Chicago, 1975), p. 16.
Arthur Katz, *Economic and Social Consequences of Nuclear Attacks on the United States*, p. 20.

Similar conditions would pertain for available hospital beds and special care facilities. A combination of casualties ranging from 20 to 30 million and pervasive destruction of hospital beds would create ratios of thirty to forty patients per available bed, compared to normal hospital occupancy rates of 75 percent, or three patients for every four beds. Even though hospitals are prepared to expand capacity under emergency planning, coping effectively with this magnitude of patient influx seems highly unlikely. Moreover, any surviving burn care units, which are usually found only in major hospitals and number ten beds on the average, will be faced with the prospect of treating hundreds of thousands of burn victims. Although the Military Surgical Hospital concept, which processes high volumes of injured in wartime, could be applied to these circumstances, it ultimately depends on transfer to well-equipped medical facilities for success. Unfortunately this second element of this system will not exist. These circumstances would force physicians to be extremely selective concerning the patients they will treat during the initial postattack period. Doctors and other medical personnel are likely to practice triage, that is, denying care to those who are likely to survive without it and to those who are unlikely to survive with it—while concentrating on those for whom medical care will make the greatest difference. Even then medical care will be superficial and primitive. In addition, many survivors with existing medical problems, especially those requiring drugs (e.g., insulin) or other special treatment (e.g., kidney dialysis machines), will be particularly vulnerable and may die or become seriously incapacitated within the first few weeks or months after an attack.

The national prognosis for the quality of early medical care is therefore very poor. Inadequate numbers of medical personnel and supplies, overwhelming numbers of casualties, and destruction of many large hospital facilities, combined with massive physical and social disruption, provide little basis for anything but crude medical care. These deficiencies will have a serious influence on the functioning of the society as a whole. According to Iklé's study:

> With the undestroyed hospital filled to capacity, relatives or hosts will undertake to nurse people through radiation sickness in homes or temporary billets. Many patients may require care for months. This burden of disease may constitute an excessive drain on the nation's manpower. The slow recoveries or disappointing deteriorations of the sick people who are scattered among families will tax large population groups more severely than the material

devastation and initial fatalities, thus diverting much time and energy from rehabilitation or from the war itself.[36]

The decline in medical care would not just be a drain of physical resources but it will create severe psychological trauma for patients, relatives, and doctors as well. As noted in the introduction to this section these groups would have to confront their inability to obtain and provide adequate medical services. The result, particularly for medical personnel, could be anger and disillusionment about their impotence—their inability to cure what was previously curable or at least treatable. The impact on morale could be devastating.

A further complication identified in the previous discussion of limited nuclear war is the extreme disruption of the medical support system (such as records and insurance payments) and the demands on the social service system (survival support). They were evaluated in terms of a disrupted society. Under the circumstances of our hypothetical attacks those demands for support will increase, but the ability of the system to make any reasonable adjustments to provide this support will be shattered. Where records were inaccessible but for the most part ultimately available under the limited war case, they will be in large measure destroyed under these scenarios. Thus an entire support system will have to be reconstructed. The survivors and ultimately the nation's recovery strategy will be burdened by the enormity of this task.

Finally, probable food shortages, difficulties imposed by substandard facilities, and possible casualty evacuation would further tax the injured, denying them the nutrition and rest that is so vital to full and speedy recovery. Overall the medical prognosis for the injured and in fact for the entire population is gloomy.

HIGHER EDUCATION

American economic and military power derives in large measure from its ability to maintain its technological leadership. Higher education plays a central role in maintaining this lead. The universities and colleges do not simply provide the trained personnel to assist in scientific and technological development but are themselves an essential component of the technological infrastructure. They provide the institutional framework for basic research that becomes the basis of scientific discovery and technological innovation. The existence of a viable system for higher education is an essential component of national military and industrial strength; it could likewise make a crucial long-term contribution to the strength and speed of post-attack economic recovery.

Yet measures to cope with the requirements of immediate relief and survival conflict in many respects with measures to ensure effective and sustained recovery over the long term. This is true for education. The demand for industrial and agricultural labor, resulting from losses in equipment, fuel, and labor force, will necessitate the diversion of students and teachers, or would-be students and teachers, from academic pursuits. At the same time, satisfying the material requirements of the educational system (classrooms, libraries, laboratories, teaching aids, etc.) will face competition from more urgent needs. Postattack human and dollar investments in education are likely to be quite low for several years. If hostilities are sustained or terminate in an ambiguous truce, military manpower needs may also reduce the emphasis on all but the most basic aspects of education.

The Japanese experience in World War II provides an indication of the extent and character of these demands:

> The whole education system is disrupted. After a period in which there was drastic curtailment of colleges, middle schools, and even some technical schools, and after children were evacuated and then permitted to move back again, finally all schools in March 1945 were made secondary to the mobilization of students for production needs.[37]

A failure to recognize this relationship can be self-defeating.

An indication of the extent of the vulnerability of the higher education system is given in Table 6-7. The numbers and percentages of institutions of professional and higher education and their professional, graduate, and undergraduate populations found in the seventy-one primary urban targets are shown. The proportions of graduate and undergraduate students falling within the seventy-one largest SMSAs (56 and 54 percent, respectively) reflect the distribution of the general population in these SMSAs (55 percent). More than half of the higher education system would be either destroyed or severely disrupted in the postulated attacks. Significantly, professional schools (e.g., medical and social work schools), show a much higher concentration (72 percent in these seventy-one urban areas), indicating a substantial vulnerability.

Table 6-7. Urban Concentration of Higher Education Centers
and Advanced Students–1976.

	Institutions of Higher Learning	Under-graduate Students	Graduate Students	Professional Students
U.S. total	3,055	8,247,408	1,267,548	243,958
Within seventy-one largest SMSAs	1,362	4,452,651	707,923	174,885
Percent (rounded to nearest 5 percent)	45	55	55	70

Source: Arthur Katz, *Economic and Social Consequences of Nuclear Attacks on the United States*, p. 100.

Another significant issue is educational quality. In a study of the vulnerability of higher education to nuclear war, King and Kleiner found that larger universities and multiuniversity centers in the United States are heavily concentrated in cities or metropolitan areas.[38] More than 85 percent of the largest schools (20,000 or more students) are located in cities with populations of 100,000, and 38 percent of these institutions are in cities of more than one million. As the authors noted, these larger universities and the next rank of colleges with more than 5,000 students provide the basic research and professional training infrastructure. Their size and the economies of scale allow them to produce a disproportionate share of the nation's professional (e.g., medicine, law) and graduate-trained (e.g., engineering, social scientists) personnel. The physical plants and the faculties of trained professors and researchers are the foundation for successful research efforts. In addition, the university centers attract large numbers of highly trained professional researchers in neighboring industries, consulting and professional firms, and private research institutions. The vulnerability of these resources to nuclear attack is very great.

Of the large colleges and universities (more than 5,000 students) in this study, 53 percent are in the seventy-one targeted SMSAs. Of colleges and universities with more than 20,000 students, 65 percent are found within the seventy-one largest SMSAs.[39] It should be noted that for all the categories discussed above, the seventy-one SMSA base represents the minimum damage to national higher edu-

Table 6-8. Concentration of Top-Ranked Professional Graduate Schools in Seventy-one Targeted SMSAs.

	Percent in Top Ten [a]	Percent in Top Fifteen or More [b]
Biological sciences		
Biochemistry	80	70 (32)
Botany	30	50 (22)
Developmental biology	90	65 (29)
Entomology	50	40 (16)
Microbiology	70	65 (29)
Molecular biology	90	65 (32)
Pharmacology	70	75 (21)
Physiology	90	75 (29)
Population biology	50	45 (20)
Zoology	60	80 (22)
Chemistry	80	60 (38)
Physics	70	70 (30)
Engineering		
Chemical	50	60 (17)
Civil	50	65 (18)
Electrical	70	70 (28)
Mechanical	70	65 (20)

a. Rounded to nearest 5 percent.

b. Numbers in parentheses are actual number of schools in top fifteen or more.

Source: Arthur Katz, *Economic and Social Consequences of Nuclear Attacks on the United States*, p. 101.

cation resources since the urban areas targeted by 100 kiloton weapons are not included.

To determine whether there exists any measurable qualitative differences between the universities within and beyond the seventy-one major target areas, the ratings of graduate and professional schools were compared. Table 6-8 shows the distribution of top-ranked biology, chemistry, physics, and engineering schools.[40] Excluding engineering schools, Table 6-8 indicates that based on the numbers ranked within the top ten schools and the top fifteen or more schools, the number of quality institutions within the seventy-one SMSAs exceeds the proportion expected simply on the basis of distribution of graduate students (55 percent). Specifically, for nine out of twelve of the graduate science specialties ranked on both indexes,

Table 6-9. Concentration of Top-Ranked Professional Schools
in 71 Targeted SMSAs.

	Percent in Top Ranking [a] (rounded to nearest 5 percent)
Architecture	65
Business	85
Dentistry	45
Education	60
Engineering	55
Law	90
Medicine	90
Nursing	90
Pharmacy	50
Public health	70
Social work	80

a. Authors did not use the same number of institutions in each of the categories above; instead, a category included nine, ten, or eleven schools in the top ranking group.

Source: Arthur Katz, *Economic and Social Consequences of Nuclear Attacks on the United States*, p. 101.

over 60 percent of the highest ranking institutions are found within the seventy-one SMSAs. Only in three instances does any percentage fall below 50 percent. Graduate science programs were chosen because of their relation to technological strength.

The distributions for professional schools are shown in Table 6-9.[41] In this case, the distribution of high-quality professional institutions has the expected average, 70 percent, as the median. This is not terribly surprising since these schools are already disproportionately concentrated in the seventy-one SMSAs.

The data indicate that serious qualitative as well as quantitative losses would occur nationally within the higher education system under the basic nuclear attack scenarios postulated. The qualitative data should be interpreted carefully since they by necessity contain a substantial element of subjectivity.

PERSPECTIVE

The severe limitation of energy supplies, particularly the loss of petroleum refining capacity; the loss of key chemicals (such as pesticides and fertilizers); and the regional and national economic and social disorganization resulting from any of the attacks postulated (A-1 to A-4) will deeply affect the nation's food. The results of Attacks A-1 through A-4 on the nation's food distribution, processing, and production system will be first, survival of sufficient basic production capacity in most food categories in the midrange but real limitations on the use of this capacity due to possible combinations of inadequate fuel and electricity, shortages of fertilizer and pesticides, uncontrolled population migration and social disorganization, and, possibly, radioactive fallout; second, a severely disrupted transport system, raising the possibility of a sufficient total food supply with great maldistribution; and, third, insufficient food-processing capacity, even if supplies of raw foodstuffs are adequate, causing spoilage and shortages.

Further, while mechanization, automation, and widespread use of chemical fertilizers and pesticides have made American food production comparatively very efficient, they have also created a situation in which large urban populations are totally dependent for food supplies on a system that is highly vulnerable to nuclear attack.

A final critical point as we noted in the discussion of limited nuclear war, is that it is not just the U.S. urban population that will be affected but a substantial number of other nations that depend on U.S. food production. A disruption or partial destruction of U.S. agriculture will have widespread ramifications throughout the world food market, dramatically cutting supplies and increasing prices. For surviving supplier nations food could quickly become a major political weapon; for consumers it could become a focal point of desperate conflict in international affairs. From a humanitarian and political perspective this vulnerability is a serious concern.

The overall postattack energy picture includes the following features:

1. Petroleum availability will be severely curtailed, with serious implications for economic recovery efforts. The uncertainty of foreign sources of petroleum, especially refined petroleum products, and the cost of foreign petroleum cloud the picture even further.

2. Coal supply will not be as severely constrained but complex production, transportation, and substitution problems are likely to restrict the use of this resource for some time into the future.

Figure 6-16. 1974 Electric Generation Fuel Sources in the United States.

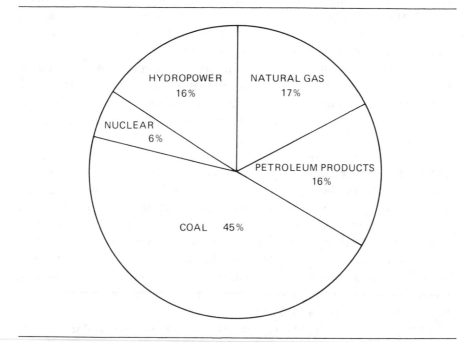

Source: "New England Hydroelectric Development Potential," Hydroelectric Facilities Workgroup, Energy Resource Development Task Force, New England Federal Regional Council, June 1976.

3. Supplies of natural gas should be able to return to preattack levels with comparative ease, assuming any damage to pipelines can be readily repaired.

4. Electric power plant capacity should be adequate for essential postattack needs, if power plants are not specially targeted[42] and if fuel problems can be solved (see Figure 6-16). However, some difficulties may be expected in the area of plant maintenance and the survival of critical computer and electrical equipment needed for the system to function efficiently.

Inasmuch as postattack economic recovery will be critically dependent on the availability of energy—and thus on the availability of fuel, refinery capacity, transportation, and generating and transmission capacity—the most significant effects of damage to these components of the national energy system is likely to be felt in the middle to long term after the attack. As several authorities have noted, the rebuilding of a viable economy (to say nothing of an expanding economy) is a race between the recovery of industrial output and the depletion of surviving resources.[43]

The initial damage from the postulated attacks would reduce energy dramatically, but the system may be able to meet the minimum essential requirements in some areas. However, as full economic recovery is pursued, enormous demands will be made on the damaged energy system, even if stringent limits are placed on individual consumption by rationing the use of fuels and electricity. Whether the badly damaged economy with its output greatly curtailed will be able to generate the enormous sums of capital and other resources required to refurbish the national energy system and to purchase foreign petroleum (assuming it is available) remains doubtful. It is not a far-fetched prospect that the victim of an urban-oriented thermonuclear attack will find itself in the position of many of today's least developed countries—in a vicious circle where current, essential consumption prevents accumulation of the surplus resources required to expand productivity and output.

Emerging from the discussion of medical effects are some very obvious mid- and long-term problems beyond the overwhelming short term medical demands:

1. There will be a heavy burden of long-term, chronically, or permanently injured survivors that will continuously stress the reduced medical capabilities and disoriented social service support system.

2. There will be a general deterioration of health care for everyone including the loss of major medical research facilities throughout the United States; and the medical eduational system will be badly damaged and its objectives greatly changed.

3. Nutritional problems will exacerbate medical problems if the food supply system proves ineffective.

4. There will be serious mental health problems stemming directly from the impact of the attack or from the stress of coping in the postattack recovery period.

Epidemics are unlikely, at least in the early period, but may appear quickly if immunization programs break down and the other measures used to insulate the United States from reservoirs of hazardous disease fail.

The implications of the combined effects of all these problems is a society burdened and preoccupied with human suffering, unable to successfully cope with its demands. The credibility of the remaining leadership, and its ability to focus resources for recovery may very well hinge on how it copes with the medical effects of nuclear war. Finally, given the massive scale of population losses and casualties after nuclear attacks, it is likely that the concept of the function of the university would also change. Its role would be a more narrowly vocational and professional training ground. Moreover, the training may be at a very basic level. The result would be that many important intellectual pursuits and professions could decline. Most seriously injured may be the basic scientific and technological infrastructure. The justification for basic research during the postattack recovery period would be questioned, and any diversion of energies in this direction is likely to be challenged. In this regard, many complex scientific experiments that required extraordinary collaboration among scientific groups and extremely expensive and sophisticated equipment would be eliminated or delayed for very long periods. The quality of research and the vital contribution to technology by the university will diminish drastically in almost any foreseeable nuclear attack on the U.S. economy.

Higher education depends on three elements: human resources — a reservoir of students and well-trained and experienced faculty and researchers (including technicians); physical facilities reflecting the interest and economic capabilities of society; and finally, most critically, the attitude of the society toward learning. In the aftermath of nuclear war attitudes toward education and its uses and purposes could radically change. Certainly the institutions themselves would be decimated and their economic and social base severely undercut.

For the nation, the heavy losses absorbed by institutions of higher education will mean severe long- as well as short-term recovery problems with potentially significant implications for the economic, political, and military roles of the United States in the global arena.

NOTES TO CHAPTER 6

1. Major problems would occur if radioactive fallout is introduced in agricultural areas. The most probable way this could occur is an attack on U.S. intercontinental ballistic missiles (ICBMs). Thus, a military attack would be combined with the postulated industrial attacks. In such an event, a combination of manpower losses (through illness or death) and land denial (potential crop contamination and fear of exposure to fallout) would result in severe production problems. The agricultural problems from fallout have been discussed in Chapter 3.

2. Stephen L. Brown, and Ulrich F. Pilz, "U.S. Agriculture: Potential Vulnerabilities," Contract no. DAHC–20–67–C–0116, OCD Work Unit 3535A (Menlo Park, California: Stanford Research Institute, January 1969), pp. 23–28.

3. Stephen L. Brown, and Pamela G. Krusic, "Agricultural Vulnerability in the National Entity Survival Context," Contract no. DAHC–20–69–0–0186 (Menlo Park, California: Stanford Research Institute, July 1970), p. 114.

4. Brown and Pilz, p. 81.

5. Stephen L. Brown, H. Lee, J.L. Mackin, and K.D. Moll, "Agricultural Vulnerability to Nuclear War," Contract no. DAHC–20–70–C–0395 (Menlo Park, California: Stanford Research Institute, February 1973), p. 30.

6. Ibid., p. 89.

7. Ibid., p. 78.

8. Ibid., p. 90.

9. Ibid., p. 48.

10. C. Haaland, C. Chester, and E. Wigner, *Survival of the Relocated Population of the U.S. After a Nuclear Attack*, (Oak Ridge, Tenn.: Oak Ridge National Laboratory, June 1976).

11. Distance traveled was limited to 200 miles except for California and New England.

12. Fred G. Iklé, *The Social Impact of Bomb Destruction* (Norman, Oklahoma: University of Oklahoma Press, 1958) p. 151.

13. J.W. Billheimer, F.J. Jones, and M. Myers, *Food System Support of the Relocation Strategy*, vols. I and II (Systan, Inc., September 1975), p. 106

14. Energy Information Administration, Department of Energy, *Annual Report to Congress 1978*, vol. 2 (Washington, D.C.: Government Printing Office, 1978) p. 7.

15. Office of Technology Assessment, *The Effects of Nuclear War*, Congress of the United States (May 1979), p. 65.

16. Ibid., p. 69.

17. Barbara Boynton, "New England Petroleum Product Imports—1976" (Boston: Federal Energy Administration, July 1977), p. 12.

18. U.S. Senate, "National Energy Transportation," Committee on Energy and National Resources and Committee on Commerce, Science, and Transportation, 95th Cong., 1st sess., (Washington, D.C.: Government Printing Office, May 1977), pp. 183–84.

19. General Accounting Office, "Key Crude Oil and Products Pipelines are Vulnerable to Disruptions," EMP–79–63 (Washington, D.C.: Government Printing Office, August 27, 1979).

20. Ibid., p. ii.

21. Ibid., p. 24.

22. Ibid., cover page.

23. R. L. Goen, R. B. Bothun, and F. E. Walker, *Potential Vulnerability Affecting National Survival* (Menlo Park, California: Stanford Research Institute, September 1970), p. 59.

24. Office of Technology Assessment, p. 69.

25. Haaland, Chester, and Wigner, p. 137.

26. M. M. Stephens, "Vulnerability of Total Petroleum Systems, Office of Oil and Gas," Department of Interior (Washington, D.C.: Government Printing Office, May 1973), p. iv.

27. The Energy and Defense Project, *Dispersed, Decentralized and Renewable Energy Sources: Alternatives to National Vulnerability and War*, Final Report, for Federal Emergency Management Agency (DCPA 01–79–C–0320), (Washington, D.C.: Government Printing Office, December 1980), pp. 301–306.

28. Defense Civil Preparedness Agency, *DCPA Attack Environment Manual*, Chapter 4, CPG 2–1A4, Department of Defense (Washington, D.C., June 1973), Panel III.

29. Private communication, Craig Llewellyn, head of epidemiology, U.S. Army Consultation Service, 1970.

30. A. W. Oughterson and S. Warren, *Medical Effects of the Atomic Bomb in Japan* (New York: McGraw-Hill, 1956), p. 89.

31. Howard H. Haitt, *Journal of the American Medical Association*, vol. 244, no. 20, November 21, 1980, p. 2314. Hiatt was quoted as describing the demands of a single burn patient on a well equipped hospital.

A 20-year-old man was recently hospitalized in the burn unit of one of Boston's teaching hospitals after an automobile accident in which the gasoline tank exploded, resulting in extensive third-degree burns. During his hospitalization, he received 281 units of fresh-frozen plasma, 147 units of fresh-frozen RBCs, 37 units of platelets, and 36 units of albumin. He underwent six operative procedures, during which wounds involving 85 percent of his body surface were closed with homograft, cadaver allograft, and artificial skin. Throughout his hospitalization, he required mechanical ventilation and monitoring with central venous lines, arterial lines, and an intermittent pulmonary artery line. Despite these heroic measures, which stretched the resources of one of the country's most comprehensive medical institutions, he died on his 33rd hospital day. His injuries were likened by the person who supervised his care to those described for many of the victims of the atomic bomb that exploded over Hiroshima.

32.   "America Burning," Report of the National Commission on Fire Prevention and Control, cited in Colman McCarthy, "Caring for Burned Children," *Washington Post*, April 22, 1978.

33.   Howard H. Hiatt, p. 2315.

34.   National Center for Health Statistics, *National Ambulatory Medical Care Survey*, Series 13, no. 33 (PHS, HEW, 1975).

35.   American Medical Association, *Profile of Medical Practice*, (1978).

36.   Iklé, p. 26. Although Iklé focused in his discussion on radiation sickness, burn and other types of injuries create similar demands.

37.   Alexander H. Leighton, *Human Relations in a Changing World* (New York: E.P. Dutton & Co., 1949), p. 234.

38.   R.B. King, Jr., and A.M. Kleiner, *Social Institutions and Thermonuclear War—A Case Study of Higher Education* (HRB–Singer, Inc., January 1967).

39.   Data provided by the Congressional Research Service, from Opening Fall enrollment 1975–1976, NCES.

40.   These rankings are based on the quality of faculty; K.B. Reese and C.J. Anderson "A Rating of Graduate Programs" (American Council on Education, 1970).

41.   These rankings are based on graduate school dean ratings; see P.M. Blau and R.Z. Margulies, "The Reputation of American Professional Schools," *Change* (Winter 1974–75): 42. Engineering as a profession was used as a general category; no attempt was made to differentiate graduate and undergraduate quality as in Table 6–8.

42.   In recent years there has been a trend toward large generating plants of 600 to 1,000 megawatts capacity, with two or four plants clustered at one site. While remote siting improves the probability of survival from urban nuclear attack, the advent of MIRV warheads makes additional specific attacks on those remote locations quite feasible and effective in terms of the economical allocation of destructive power to high priority targets.

43.   See Sidney G. Winter, Jr., "Economic Viability after Thermonuclear War: The Limits of Feasible Production," RAND Memorandum, RM–3436–PR (Santa Monica, Calif.: The RAND Corporation, September 1963), p. vi; and Fred C. Iklé, pp. 181 and 190–202.

7 SLOUCHING TOWARD BETHLEHEM
Psychological, Social, Political, and Institutional Effects

In the two previous chapters the consequences of the economically oriented nuclear attacks have unfolded. It was observed that a well-designed nuclear attack could deliver a crippling economic blow to the United States, destroying productive industrial capacity, under-cutting the utilization of even surviving physical plants, and severely damaging the domestic and international monetary and financial systems that support the U.S. economy. The physical destruction of the value of money, and in turn, the value of assets such as property and insurance, as well as unemployment, and the absence of basic necessities are the translation of these losses to an individual level. The human loss in terms of skills and emotional trauma is incalculable. The burden of massive numbers of injured, many of whom could no longer be productive, would remain a continuing drain and diversion of goods and, most importantly, human resources and emotional energy. However, even the diversion of these energies only promises social service and medical systems that are shadows of their former selves. The reconstruction of the medical system will be a particularly slow, frustrating, and demoralizing process. To see death, when formerly there had been life, cannot be anything but personally debilitating, and a direct challenge to the survival of leadership. But, as we have seen, life after nuclear war will be even more disorienting. While surviving physical resources for food production such as land and farm machinery will be initially

191

adequate, other critical elements such as energy will not be available. Also in question will be the organization of remaining food production capabilities and remaining supplies to support survival and recovery, both in the short and long run. The lack of supply and the maldistribution of existing food reserves will have widespread effects on national unity and political credibility as well as personal survival. As just noted, energy supply will play a pivotal role in assuring the availability of basic necessities from the standpoint of distribution of goods and production. Critically, the international economic system, including the trading of petroleum, will be thrown into chaos by the collapse of key currencies, particularly the U.S. dollar. Finally, the loss of a major part of the higher educational system and associated technological research capability will have direct effects on military and economic strength. Of equal significance are the large-scale organizational demands that will occur in many sectors to draw together resources and develop priorities that incorporate short-term survival requirements and longer term national recovery strategies. The latter will be needed to maintain the United States's international standing.

Placed in this context of disruption and destruction, human suffering, and disorientation, is the final component of our inquiry into life after nuclear war—the social, psychological, political, and institutional demands society will experience.

In the final analysis, the question of how, when, or whether a nation will effectively recover from a nuclear attack will depend in large measure on the damage to complex social relationships. Without the political and social consensus that binds disparate groups into a nation, the organization necessary to guide and focus recovery effort, and the individual's ability to confront and overcome disruptive personal emotional demands, all the surviving economic and military capability will be of little use.

This chapter will analyze psychological, social, and political effects likely to result from a nuclear attack. Although modern man has never experienced the simultaneous widespread devastation that would accompany the nuclear attacks postulated in this book, it is possible, based on experience with strategic bombing in World War II and on human behavior in both large-scale and local disasters, to identify some of the most likely major problems. Of particular interest are problems—often not examined in studies of nuclear attack effects—that have the potential to produce lasting changes in social organization and political behavior and therefore have an important bearing on the question of the acceptability of nuclear war. Thus, this chapter will focus on the response of social institutions to large-scale destruction.

DIFFERING EFFECTS OF LARGE- AND SMALL-SCALE DISASTERS

The magnitude of a disaster has an important influence on its effects. This becomes clearer when the attributes of large-scale catastrophes are contrasted with the patterns of activity typically found following or during small-scale disasters. Unless this distinction is made, the attributes that make small-scale disasters frightening but tractable could be assumed to exist in large-scale catastrophes. This would lead to a substantial overestimate of our ability to cope competently with the problems raised by nuclear war. Thus, a meaningful appreciation of the implications of this distinction needs to be developed before the subsequent discussion of social, psychological, political, and institutional effects. The model used here for small-scale disasters is based on one developed by Allen Barton in his study, *Communities in Disaster*.[1]

In a small-scale disaster, there is a reasonably well-defined process that occurs between the event and the return to normal life. These stages are defined by Barton as predisaster to postdisaster phases. Normally, a period of unorganized response appears after the initial stress of a small-scale disaster. This unorganized response may include individuals and groups helping neighbors and nearby survivors who are injured or trapped, as well as nonadaptive behavior such as withdrawal or ritualistic activity (for example, sifting through wreckage aimlessly). During this period, leadership may emerge both for specific local situations and for broader disaster problems. This leadership may come from normal authority figures such as mayors, organizational heads, and civic leaders. In many cases local figures with skills that are adaptable to disaster situations (such as mechanics and army veterans) can also emerge in the role of leaders. They become role models for the people around them and provide a framework for others to evolve adaptive behavior.

Serious problems can develop in adaptive behavior if the "natural" leadership does not respond adequately. One of the most significant difficulties under these circumstances is role conflict. Conflict develops between protecting one's family and performing one's organizational or civic functions, between personal emotions (family loss) and community roles. This phenomenon can significantly reduce the adequacy of the early disaster response.

Most early responses are centered around small-scale rescue operations and a general reorientation to the disaster situation. The next stage is entered when a more organized response occurs. This response may take several forms simultaneously. Disaster organizations within the community may mobilize and begin to perform their functions. In addition, other functionally relevant agencies and institutions may be mobilized to help. Further, help from a larger community may begin to appear—police and medical aid, as well as army and national guard, if necessary. The most significant phenomenon that occurs as part of the response of the larger community is "mass convergence," a movement of individuals into the disaster area. The consequences of this movement are ambiguous. Properly directed, these individuals constitute a pool of human resources to aid in the disaster relief operations. However, by their numbers and ambiguous motivation (some are simply voyeurs), they can overload disrupted transportation facilities and carry out only aimless and unproductive work.

At this stage in the postdisaster period a number of significant functional roles must be fulfilled, such as organizing relief efforts and providing communications. Organization is the most crucial of these tasks, since there is a need to direct and focus work in productive channels. This requires an understanding of techniques for coping with specific problems, such as casualties and fire. Also required is a set of goals that will help to stabilize the disaster situation. The leadership must have the ability to adapt its organizations or authority to the effective utilization of resources and volunteers. Part of this adaptive process is successful two-way communication—to inform and direct the population within and outside of the disaster area, and to obtain crucial information such as the type, location, and numbers of casualties from the community.

If these functions—organization and communication—can be performed well, the supply of food, clothing, shelter, and medical assistance can be effectively distributed. This application of resources forms the bridge between the termination of the immediate, critical postdisaster period and the rebuilding of the community.

Ideally, the third phase is a period of relative harmony and cooperation within the community itself. This is the period of the "altruistic" society, when energies focus on rebuilding and reconstituting normal life. Finally, there is an attenuation of the altruistic society, and a return to normal relationships occurs. This completes the disaster life cycle. While the logistical problems are often formidable and confusion may reign in the early postdisaster period, the situation is usually well controlled in a short period.

In nuclear war, the situation will be quite different. The impulse is to flee, not to enter, the area, because of the terrible destruction and the fear of contamination by radioactivity. The mass convergence of external resources would be far less likely to occur in this type of disaster. It is questionable, given the scope of nuclear war, whether significant outside resources would be available under any circumstances. In addition, destruction could also overwhelm the indigenous resources and leadership that survive, as in Hiroshima. This loss would severely limit any ability to reconstruct leadership and organizational roles. As a German Jesuit witness to the Hiroshima disaster, Father Siemes, reported: "Among the passersby, there are many who are uninjured. In a purposeless, insensate manner, distraught by the magnitude of the disaster, most of them rush by and none conceives the thought of organizing help on his own initiative. They are concerned only with the welfare of their own families."[2] Other personal accounts of Hiroshima and Nagasaki suggest that the main pattern of behavior was to help family members and sometimes neighbors and then to escape from the city of ruins and fires into the countryside, ignoring the plight of strangers.

Everywhere the victims needing help outnumbered the potential helpers and rescuers. Moreover, the physical condition of great numbers of victims was too serious for nonprofessionals—or even professionals lacking equipment and supplies—to cope with successfully. The emotionally overwhelming nature of this experience appears to have prevented spontaneous organization of rescue and relief groups. Further exacerbating these problems was the fear of renewed bombing.

Given these extremely negative circumstances, the distribution and movement of leadership and technical experts, equipment, and essential supplies into damaged areas will pose difficult logistical and motivational problems even if the conflict terminates immediately. However, should nuclear or conventional warfare continue, these remaining resources will be claimed in large measure for the prose-cution of the war effort (e.g., for sustaining and fueling essential defense industrial production; providing replacement troops and offi-cers; caring for combat casualties; maintaining active forces; and transporting military goods and units) and will be available for civil-ian relief only in limited and probably inadequate quantities.

To overcome shortfalls in vital relief commodities, it may become necessary for the government, if it is still functioning on a central or regional basis, to commandeer or requisition private stocks held in undamaged or less damaged areas and to conscript human resources for civilian relief efforts. Whether the population in the undamaged areas will readily acquiesce in such measures remains to be seen. The experience of other countries in analogous circumstances, treated in subsequent sections, indicates that this will pose a significant prob-lem for the authorities.

In the absence of adequate supplies to meet minimum relief requirements, logic suggests that there is little possibility for the growth of the spirit of community cooperation and selflessness—the "altruistic community"—that is essential for effective postattack reconstruction and recovery efforts.

Furthermore, the loss of human resources will add to the diffi-culty of completing tasks that in peacetime are taken for granted. For instance, in an attack concentrated on highly productive urban areas, the loss of technical, managerial, and leadership personnel will be especially high. The loss of their natural replacements—whether from death, injury, or evacuation—will also be large because of their location in similar areas. These human resources are especially criti-cal in a highly complex, industrialized society where both technical skills and leadership experience are accumulated only over time. This includes losing not only personnel involved in economic production and service fields, but also individuals who perform other necessary social roles, such as clergymen, civic leaders and volunteers, teachers, psychologists and psychiatrists, professional counselors, and a variety of other professionals or paraprofessionals to whom citizens look for role models and assistance, especially in times of stress. These human resources also staff society's institutions and organizations. In these roles they transmit society's values and norms and maintain the social relationships upon which any functioning society depends.

With this combination of human and material losses, new or latent social divisions among groups may arise and be aggravated by the individual struggles to survive. The maldistribution of resources among groups and within and especially between regions has the seeds of significant social conflict. Social conflict may be especially acute between the population of areas where survival resources may be adequate or marginal and incoming evacuees who may strain or are perceived to strain the region's resources. Intergroup problems could have severe and debilitating political and social implications if scapegoating replaced national unity during the critical initial stages of postattack recovery. The ability to fend off a continuing external threat could be substantially diminished.

All the elements that make a small disaster tractable—limited damage; modest casualties; surviving leadership; a diminishing incidence of role conflict; and large reservoirs of external, easily mobilized skilled workers, material resources, and organizational skills—will be lacking, especially if hostilities continue or their resumption is threatened. Therefore, nuclear war should be viewed as having a qualitatively different character than small-scale familiar disasters and even catastrophic incidents in wars such as the fire bombing of Hamburg.

NUCLEAR AND CONVENTIONAL BOMBING: CONTRASTS AND SIMILARITIES

The experience of World War II provides an important historical record for evaluating war-related social effects, since it involved the heaviest and most widespread damage to civilian populations and institutions hitherto known to man. It must be remembered, however, that for the most part, bomb damage in World War II accumulated over an extended period of time; it was not confined to a few hours or weeks. The fire bombing of Coventry, Dresden, Hamburg, and Tokyo and the atomic bombing of Hiroshima and Nagasaki were somewhat exceptional, but even in these cases not all substantial portions of the major urban areas of a country were struck at once, as they would be in a major nuclear attack.

Attacks of the kind envisioned under most nuclear war scenarios differ from strategic bombing during World War II in two important respects—scope and timing. The difference in scope means that the attacked areas will not be able to count on an influx of resources from undamaged areas to aid in recovery. In the case of Hiroshima, for example, electricity was restored in less damaged areas on the day following the attack, train service to the city was resumed on the next day, certain streetcar lines were operating on the third day, and telephone communications were restored in some sections within ten days. This relatively rapid recovery of some basic services was made possible by the very small size of the attack bomb used (as compared to nuclear and thermonuclear weapons currently available), by the fact that only one weapon was used, and by the availability of human and material resources from the many other functioning areas.

In addition, while the semblance of normal life became possible in heavily damaged cities during World War II within months of strategic bombing raids, the productive capacity of these important economic areas was greatly reduced and did not reach prewar levels until after there had been large infusions of American capital and other assistance. It is difficult to see how and where similar external resources could be obtained following extensive damage from a nuclear war involving the United States and the Soviet Union and perhaps other leading industrial economies. Even if a country can in time make good the losses in capital goods, manpower, and technical competence resulting from widespread nuclear attacks, its role in world politics and economics is likely to be considerably diminished during the lengthy rebuilding period.

Less easy to assess in this context are the effects of differences in scale between continental industrial powers such as the United States and the Soviet Union and the countries most heavily damaged by World War II bombing, chiefly Germany, Japan, and Britain. All three of the latter are compact economic entities, a fact which makes them in several respects more vulnerable to the consequences of strategic bombing. Yet heavy and widespread damage to larger political and economic units will severely strain the ability of central control mechanisms—the federal government and other institutions—to make and execute nationwide plans and policies. The damage to communications and transportation systems will be especially important in this respect. The desire or necessity for regional autonomy and other centrifugal tendencies will add to the burden on national authorities and perhaps permanently weaken their control. The erosion of central control will have significant consequences for postattack recovery, for the nation's postattack role in the world, and for the longevity of the central government.

While the long duration of World War II doubtless aggravated many social and economic effects, the time span also provided an opportunity for conscious or unconscious adjustment to conditions that deteriorated relatively slowly as compared to the sudden cataclysm of widespread nuclear attacks. The time between bombing attacks and other setbacks permitted more gradual improvisation and experimentation with expedients. A semblance of normal life could often be achieved between the repeated shocks, which made it more possible to cope with each successive blow. Even with considerably more time for adaptation, the social, political, and economic effects of strategic bombing in World War II were severe for victor and vanquished alike.

In a nuclear exchange, by contrast, survivors and surviving institutions will have no time for gradual adaptation to a more drastically altered environment. The change from a normal world to a devastated world will be far more abrupt, occurring virtually overnight. In the absence of an adaptive period, the strains imposed on political, social, and economic institutions and mechanisms are likely to be even harsher than those confronted incrementally in World War II. The possible consequences of these enormous stresses would be to retard seriously an adequate national response to postattack conditions for periods of up to several years, while individuals and society readjust to dramatically changed circumstances. The sudden shock of widespread nuclear destruction may permanently alter fundamental social, political, and economic values and institutions. Thus, the shift from a viable, intact nation to one that is deeply injured due to nuclear war is likely to be far more disruptive than that produced by conventional strategic bombing in World War II.

The availability of resource assistance and time for an adaptive process is particularly important because, as studies of wartime Britain show, preattack emergency planning will not necessarily be relevant to disaster conditions and may fail to meet actual requirements. This appears to be especially true of social policy, where government plans fail to account for significant social variables that arise in crisis situations.

Hence, while it is possible that some of the problems described in the following sections will be mitigated by national and local preparedness and civil defense measures, previous experience with large-scale prewar social planning for emergency conditions does not permit a high degree of confidence in the success of such efforts. This is especially true where such planning is directed toward events that have no true precedents, as would be the case for simultaneous nuclear attacks against major urban and industrial areas.

With this in mind, the following sections attempt to describe in greater detail some of the major noneconomic problems that will be faced following a nuclear attack. Though for the sake of convenience the discussion is divided into psychological, social, and political problems, these are often related, and the division is at times arbitrary.

PSYCHOLOGICAL EFFECTS OF NUCLEAR WAR

Robert Lifton's evaluation of the psychological effects of the atomic bombing of Japan, *Death in Life*, concludes that the reality of such an event overpowers the normal human capacity to absorb and integrate an experience in a useful way. The imagery of a totally shattered human environment created by such catastrophe further magnifies the emotional impact. Lifton found that the experience stripped away normal psychological protection. Even protective mechanisms such as psychic numbing and denial (refusal to accept the existence of a threatening and frightening occurrence) were so distorted that this experience eventually became the basis for pathological behavior. Effects of this kind are potentially the foundation for apathy, antisocial behavior, and psychological disorganization seen in other postdisaster situations.

Judging from the studies of the Hiroshima and Nagasaki survivors, the image produced by a nuclear attack in the mind of a survivor is one of annihilation, loss of continuity, and a total break with previous reality. The extent and scale of the destruction creates an atmosphere of overpowering involvement: "A sudden and absolute shift from normal existence to an overwhelming encounter with death."[3] All the normal connections with everyday experience and human continuity are broken: reality is radically transformed into a terrifying and all encompassing image of the death of human life and even of nature. There is "the replacement of the natural order of living and dying with an unnatural order of death-dominated life."[4]

For the Hiroshima survivors, nuclear attack, in Lifton's terms, amounted to a "death immersion" followed by an escape from death's grasp. Escape for some represented personal failure or impotence and resulted in what was termed subsequently "death guilt." According to Lifton, this guilt was derived from a combination of factors, all related to the magnitude and overwhelming terror of the atomic tragedy. Thus, while the instinct for survival will remain the primary human response to a nuclear attack, survival may be purchased at an emotional price. For some, this price could be very high, the result of abnormal or aberrant personal behavior patterns during the initial confrontation with the catastrophe. At Hiroshima, personally unacceptable behavior took the form of running away. Later, the survivors had to confront this behavior; shame and guilt were often the legacy of this confrontation.

The sense of failure arose from the inability and, at times, the unwillingness of many survivors to extend adequate assistance to family, friends, or strangers in need during the initial terrifying minutes and hours after the explosion.[5] This gave rise to "survivor's guilt," a common reaction stemming from the survivor's inability to fulfill basic human responsibilities and, to some extent, from the conflict of feeling joy in surviving when they believed they should have died. Those who died, some survivors believed, had made it possible for the survivors to live.

Even those who tried to remain and help were unable to cope, physically and psychologically, with the magnitude of the destruction and the number of casualties. They, too, experienced guilt related to feelings of helplessness, impotence and shame.

All survivors eventually had to attempt to confront and integrate into their lives this fear and guilt. Unfortunately, these emotions were tied to an annihilating experience that was so psychologically overwhelming that it left many of them fixated on this small portion of their lives.[6] For some, a substantial portion of their productive energy was thereafter devoted to coming to terms with their terrifying experience. While these reactions are likely to occur to some degree in other types of disaster, the confrontation with death would have a well-defined terminal point in most cases, and the survivors would be freer to renew their lives. The process of living and experiencing, then, helps to mitigate the power of these tragic events and to permit survivors to find some way of coming to terms on a personal level with their experiences.

In the atomic attacks on Japan, a unique and significant element came into play, insuring greater long-term difficulties in adjustment. This element was the slowly evolving recognition of the effects of radiation: delayed death from initial radiation effects; increased incidents of leukemia, cancer, and genetic disease; and a vague but continuing feeling of ill-health and lack of vigor called "A-Bomb Disease." The survivors and the event were thus linked by a connection through the survivor's body that could never be discarded. All survivors' paths to reestablish their connection with their former lives were in a sense barred. Moreover, their children could carry this hazard through their genetic material.

Adding to the complexity of the situation is the fact that the effects of radiation are unpredictable for a single individual. Thus, a clear-cut verdict on the personal fate of individual survivors was, and is, impossible. Because of this continuing uncertainty, fear at either a conscious or unconscious level and the memories of Hiroshima may remain mixed together, reinforcing each other and strengthening the continuing emotional effects. While highly personal, the powerful long-term emotional responses described by Lifton could play a deeply disruptive role. This disruption would be achieved by diverting energies needed by the society to cope with survival and recovery to debilitating self-destructive or inappropriate behavior—a psychological reaction likely to influence individual productivity and, therefore, economic recovery efforts.

Besides guilt, helplessness, aimlessness, and aberrant behavior, Irving Janis found in studying Hiroshima records that "one of the most frequent types of sustained emotional disturbance appears to have been a phobic-like fear of exposure to another traumatic disaster. This reaction consisted in strong feelings of apprehensiveness accompanied by exaggerated efforts to ward off new threats."[7]

This understandable response has been widely noted in recent studies of disaster or crisis victims, such as the survivors of the 1972 earth dam failure at Buffalo Creek, West Virginia,[8] the hostages taken in various terrorist raids or aircraft hijackings, and the residents near the nuclear accident at Three Mile Island (discussed more extensively in Appendix A).

While the emotional impact on the survivors themselves will be the strongest, this phobic reaction may exist even among populations not directly affected by nuclear blasts. The fear of radiation, combined with exposure to large numbers of the dying or surviving injured, could make most of the population perceive themselves as survivors of the nuclear detonations, as indeed, in a sense, they will be. After multiple nuclear detonations, the kinds of reactions seen at

Hiroshima and Nagasaki may not be limited only to those in the vicinity of the blast area but will spread to the larger population as it becomes aware of the magnitude of destruction. An illustration that this is likely to be true is the extensiveness of the physical area where emotional reactions created by the accident at Three Mile Island were found.

Janis also points out that the severity of the emotional and phobic reactions is proportional to the severity of specific injuries and the manner of dying:

> Apparently it was not simply the large number of casualties but also the specific character of the injuries, particularly the grossly altered physical appearance of persons who suffered severe burns, that had a powerful effect upon those who witnessed them. Hence, it appears to be highly probable that, as a correlate of the exceptional casualty-inflicting properties of the atomic weapon, there was an unusually intense emotional impact among the uninjured evoked by the perception of those who were casualties.[9]

Iklé described another potent effect, the "Perception of Danger Principle," evoked by the sight of casualties:

> Nothing can make people more fully aware of the risk of death and injury from bombing than seeing air-raid casualties around them. Therefore, if there is a threat of further attacks, city dwellers are impelled to action to avoid the risk of death or injury. In the event of very large disasters, such as nuclear explosions, where shelters and ordinary precautions may not offer sufficient protection, many urbanites will leave the city. *This exodus [is] probably one of the most important morale effects from nuclear bombing....* (Emphasis added.)[10]

Thus, the impulse to escape will be very strong, even outside the directly and severely affected areas. This will make unplanned evacuation a high probability and lead to uncontrolled migration of both the healthy and the injured from attacked regions. If this occurred on a large scale, it would compromise and complicate some of the relief and recovery efforts, which to be effective will require orderly movement and distribution of refugees.

Of equal concern is the ultimate impact of this experience on economic recovery. The likely reality is that unlike the experience after conventional bombing in World War II, where "essential personnel usually favored a return to the cities, so that they could quickly resume work in industries only partially damaged,"[11] there will be

little motivation for—or more accurately, a deep aversion to—returning to the cities to rebuild the economy. "And thus a very different situation will exist from that envisaged in most civil defense
plans."[12] If the threat of further bombings or even the irrational fear
of war remains, this impulse to avoid danger would be strong. Under
these circumstances it is unlikely that "all able-bodied men will
march back into the devastated cities to rebuild, repair, and resume
industrial production as soon as possible and that the government
will not permit a prolonged evacuation of the workers."[13] Rather
more likely, in Iklé's view, is that "not only nonessential persons but
most of the workers will remain evacuated as long after the first
nuclear attack as further attacks appear likely."[14]

Although Iklé uses tactical nuclear war[15] as an example, the same
principle is applicable to any situation in which follow-up attacks are
possible. This would include limited, selective strategic war, unlim-
ited strategic nuclear warfare at any level of attack, or even a civil
defense evacuation in anticipation of a nuclear attack. In the last
eventuality, the inability to predict in advance when the attack will
occur and whether the targets will be military or urban-economic
areas will pose special problems, since evacuees will be reluctant to
return to the cities even if the first attacks center on military forces.

Phobic reactions to actual or anticipated nuclear attacks, causing
planned or uncontrolled population migration, can have significant
negative consequences not only for the postattack recovery process
but also for the operation of the economy during a crisis leading
up to an attack. This will be especially true if essential personnel
spontaneously leave their jobs in large numbers. Genuine danger
could arise if, during a tense preattack period, there was a significant uncontrolled migration, leading an adversary to believe that a
planned evacuation was taking place prior to launching a first strike.
In an unstable and ambiguous situation like this, the adversary's
response might be to launch its own nuclear attack preemptively.

Supporting the likelihood of a strong negative reaction is the fact
that unlike the long period of acclimation for the general population[16] that accompanied the Blitz, any of the nuclear attacks assumed
by this book will constitute one discrete event for which there would
be no comparable prior experience. This has particular significance
for the United States, which has not endured the devastation of war
on its territory for more than 110 years and which has never experienced the effects of strategic bombing or other aspects of modern,

high technology warfare. The U.S. populace is therefore unlikely to be psychologically prepared for the destruction possible from nuclear attacks. Finally, contributing to the intensity of the reaction is the highly threatening perception of radiation. Even assuming a general understanding of the effects of radiation on the part of the public, the fear of its effects is not necessarily diminished and may even be enhanced. The highly emotional controversy over civilian nuclear power that began in earnest in the 1970s is evidence for the accuracy of the last observation.

Therefore, so far as there are relevant empirical data, it is apparent that nuclear attacks exposing large populations to the actual or perceived threat of devastation will have a significant disruptive psychological impact on the survivors. The range of emotional responses discussed will greatly complicate the mobilization of human resources for continuing a war effort or for reconstituting the society and restoring the economy.

In a review of the overall social consequences, Bruce C. Allnutt noted:

> Among the most significant results [of the panel's review] are quantitative estimates of the impact of such social and psychological factors on the availability and efficiency of the surviving labor force . . . the results indicate, for example, that, *one month after the attack, less than half of the potential labor force could be expected to work without immediately beneficial compensation, and that, of these, one in five would be able to function only at a level greatly degraded from his normal abilities.* (Emphasis added.)[17]

A Sense of Isolation

An important social factor that influences the course of events in any postdisaster period is the growth or disappearance of a sense of isolation for individuals, communities, classes, regions, and, judging from the history of World War II, even for whole nations. In this regard, assistance from outside the stricken area is important not only for its material benefits, but also for the psychological benefit of creating a bond with the larger world that it comes to symbolize. This connection with a more normal society helps to provide the impetus for rebuilding the damaged society, creating a sense of vitality and competence to dispel the continuing perception of isolation. These psychological benefits are important because symbols—in this case linkages to a familiar outside world—have important functions in binding societies together. They restate a common thread of hope and shared aspirations.

The material and other links that Britain maintained with the United States and the Commonwealth throughout the war made its situation different from the experience of Japan and Germany toward the end of the war. There, an increasing sense of isolation added to the demoralizing effect of war losses.

While feelings of isolation operate differently and produce effects of varying seriousness depending upon the circumstances, in combination with other effects of a catastrophe their impact could be significant. For example, as noted above, an acute form of defensive apathy known as "psychic numbing"—a type of psychological protection against the overwhelming consequences of the disaster—is frequently seen following serious catastrophes such as earthquakes and floods. This apathetic attitude may deepen if the stress that engenders it is not removed. An isolated and disrupted postattack community or society may be able to provide little relief; instead, the type of destructive behavior found in Japan near the end of World War II could increase:

> A drift toward accomplishing personal and private aims rather than those which are national . . . farmers who are slacking off in their efforts . . . growing little more than is required for their own subsistence needs . . . considerable hoarding in both town and country and extensive black market activity. Suspicion and uncertainty are weakening the will to follow the Government leads and even leading to oblique and passive forms of resistance.[18]

In the two cities struck by atomic bombs, these types of reactions and behavior were intensified. Persons entering Hiroshima and Nagasaki immediately after the attack found an apathetic and disorganized population. For months after the bombing, the Hiroshima survivors did not function effectively.[19] It was the intervention of outsiders with resources and leadership that revitalized Hiroshima and played the dominant role in its later boom town recovery.

The effect of this type of demoralization has been seen before, in other shattering tragedies:

> In the countryside peasants dropped dead [from the Black Death] on the roads, in the fields, in their houses. Survivors in growing helplessness fell into apathy, leaving ripe wheat uncut and livestock untended. Oxen and asses, sheep and goats, pigs and chickens ran wild and they too, according to local

reports, succumbed to the pest. . . . The sense of a vanishing future created a kind of dementia of despair. A Bavarian chronicler of Neuberg on the Danube recorded that "Men and women . . . wandered around as if mad" and let their cattle stray "because no one had any inclination to concern themselves about the future." Fields went uncultivated, spring seed unsown. Second growth with nature's awful energy crept back over cleared land, dikes crumbled, salt water reinvaded and soured the lowlands. With so few hands remaining to restore the work of centuries, people felt, in Walsingham's words, that "the world could never again regain its former prosperity."[20]

The world did survive, but reconstruction of society was long and painful despite the survival of the basic physical resources. The availability of intact resources is in contrast to the widespread destruction of a post–nuclear war period.

Drawing the threads of this discussion together, the picture of the psychological effects that emerges from our scenarios and from any other using nuclear weapons distributed throughout the nation, is the creation of a sense of impotence from acute, then lingering, nagging fear, self-pity and self-doubt, shame and guilt, isolation, panic, aversion, and for some, withdrawal and death. For all, it would be a shattering personal experience. The results of this emotional response will confound organizational efforts for recovery in some cases, and create, in others, a sense of betrayal and loathing for surviving leadership. If it is difficult to imagine these circumstances, think of the collapse of Cambodia in the late 1970s. This is the psychological stuff out of which a viable independent national power must be constructed.

SOCIAL DISORGANIZATION AND STRATEGIC WARFARE

Some of the other issues likely to confront a society under the stress of a large-scale nuclear attack against the civilian population are illustrated in the experience of the United Kingdom and other nations during World War II. While the correspondence between the response of the British and others to the strategic air war and postnuclear attack problems is not perfect in any sense, the former does highlight the complexities of the social situation during and after a major catastrophe involving evacuation (planned or unplanned), heavy loss of life, and extensive damage to economic and social infrastructure.

The British case is particularly relevant for the United States, because of the general cultural and political similarity of the two societies.

The principal differences are that the British faced a significantly lower level of physical destruction and had more time to adapt to circumstances, since the bombing of major cities did not occur all at once. While the British experience with strategic bombing and strategic (preattack) evacuation is examined as a predictor of problems that will arise in the United States following a strategic nuclear attack, the wartime history of Japan and Germany are also relevant. The importance of the German and Japanese data is that they illustrate that the British experience is not unique either culturally or in terms of the level of physical damage.

Under Air Attack

Even before bombing attacks began in earnest, the British were faced with the need to evacuate certain residents from their cities and to adapt basic social services, such as health care, welfare, and education, to conditions of stress and uncertainty. Soon the problems of coping with bomb destruction and caring for the homeless were added to this burden. These conditions and the institutional response to them were analyzed in R.M. Titmuss's official study, *Problems of Social Policy*, published in 1950. After looking at life under threat of bombing, the lessons learned are drawn in the sections below.

Impact on Society. The Titmuss study provides an instructive overview of the actual demands that are made on a society battered by air attacks. He points out that the original concerns over the level of casualties were overstated and misplaced and that the problem that emerged was:

> *The amount of social disturbance, and particularly the number of homeless people, were found to have been greatly underestimated before September 1940.*
>
> *The central problems of this period [air war] were not, as things turned out, in the field of casualty work; of treating the injured and burying the dead. They were largely concerned with reducing social distress and finding remedies for the general disorder of life under air bombardment.* The effects of dropping explosive and incendiary bombs on the highly organized business of a great city, where the orderly functioning of one tiny part of the whole

organism depended upon automatic union at just the right point in time with many other interdependent parts, disturbed the lives of individual citizens in countless ways, and created for the Government a host of urgent social problems. (Emphasis added.)[21]

One of the first and most urgent problems was simply to establish an organization and a reliable physical communication system that worked effectively enough so that government could function in its other tasks. However, demands were more widespread and basic:

The provision of clear water for drinking, of dirty water for fighting enemy-action fires, of power to run transport and industry, of heating to cook meals and warm houses, of unbroken pipes to carry away sewage and avoid the risks of disease; all these were among the tasks which could not wait upon leisurely processes.[22]

In this regard, the British were not unique. The Japanese suffered much the same disruption. Reviewing the situation in 1945, the Foreign Morale Analysis Division found:

definite trends toward organization breakdown, confusion, decreasing effort, and resistance to the adjustments and compensations imposed by the needs of the war situation. There is a drift toward the accomplishment of immediate private and personal aims rather than national objectives. *In part, this confusion and disorganization stems from major changes brought by the war, such as the breaking up of families, the closing of schools, evacuations due to bombings, migrations of industrial workers, the absorption of a large part of the male population into the armed forces, the entrance of women into new occupations and the severe deterioration of the transportation and communication facilities.* (Emphasis added.)[23]

Government Response. The British response to the stress described is significant and revealing. A major finding that emerges from Titmuss's study is that despite a serious attempt to anticipate the impact of air war on civilian populations, the British government failed to perceive adequately the complex social issues that would arise. For example, the evacuation of large populations demanded an ability to anticipate requirements for social services and then to effectively redistribute them geographically. This effort was impeded by the lack of governmental institutions flexible enough to make these transitions easily, and foresighted enough to anticipate the social conflicts likely to arise between populations with different life-styles and values.

In addition, the effectiveness of social service planning was further reduced by faulty assumptions. For example, medical services were initially structured so heavily toward air war victims that the sick became victims of their own government's planning, especially during the initial phase of the war:

> Patients in an early operable stage of cancer were sent home untreated; expectant mothers were refused admission for what were likely to be difficult and dangerous confinements; children in plaster of paris were deprived of the care they needed; bedridden patients—the arthritic, the diabetic and heart cases—were discharged to the care of relations heedless of the fact that these relations might now have evacuated, leaving the house empty; highly contagious tubercular patients were sent to crowded homes with young children, perhaps to die, perhaps to infect their families. "Surely never before," she [a volunteer] wrote, "has a nation inflicted such untold suffering on itself as a precaution against potential suffering. . . . Why should it have been considered less disastrous for anyone to die untreated of cancer, appendicitis or pneumonia than as the result of a bomb?"[24]

In addition to the underestimation of social impacts, the problem of uncertainty (in this case, about when, how, and what type of air war and about the use of gas, secret weapons, and threat of invasion) created significant distortions in the ability to plan and act. This meant the diversion and immobilization of human resources and equipment that could have been utilized in other ways. Coping with the unknown and the need to provide for these contingencies became the "dominating strategical necessities of the home front."[25]

Complicating this problem further is the likelihood that a period of uncertainty will follow a nuclear attack, especially for the less destructive attacks discussed in this book.[26] Despite the assumption of a single quick nuclear exchange, it cannot safely be assumed that the postattack period will be free of ambiguity about follow-up attacks; continued combat with conventional or tactical nuclear weapons; or protracted stalemate, with a return to open warfare possible at any time. Therefore, the organizational preoccupation and misallocation associated with an extended period of anticipated warfare is likely to be a serious impediment to postattack civilian recovery efforts.

The Family Unit. While there have been many changes in social organization during the past several decades (such as a mobile and suburbanized population, dispersion of the extended family and sub-

sequent decline in its function as a viable social unit, expanding numbers of women of childbearing age in the work force, more single
parent families, increased responsibility on the educational and social
service system for the socialization and care of children, and an
increase of the elderly population), the nuclear family is nonetheless
the basic social unit in the United States. The family and the social
institutions that support it (schools, churches, day care centers) typically experience severe stress in times of war; an even greater toll
may be expected following a nuclear exchange.

In many cases, families will be broken up by death, by injury or
disease, by evacuation, or by military or labor force conscription.
Where the family remains intact, the ordeal of the attack, injuries,
sustaining life in deprived circumstances, awaiting resolution of the
military situation, altered expectations, and losing or being evacuated from neighbors, relatives, and supporting institutions (such as
church, school, day care centers, job, and civic and social organizations) will place severe stress on adults and children alike. While the
emotional needs of children can be expected to increase and require
more immediate attention, the ability of surviving parents to supply
these needs without adequate external assistance and while facing
their own traumas may become seriously diminished. The ability of
national or local authorities and private organizations to provide
more than basic assistance with food, shelter, and medical care is
likely to be small for a considerable period after an attack, leaving
few resources for social problems described above.

The stress on the family unit will change, both in degree and character, when families are evacuated, in either the preattack or the
postattack period. Evacuation, however, will not eliminate these
problems, especially if it is prolonged as a result of an unresolved military situation or the requirements of rebuilding urban areas. Stresses
will remain because the willingness and the ability of host areas to
absorb large numbers of evacuees and the capability of the evacuees
to adapt to their new setting are likely to be quite limited. (This
collision of host and evacuee values or expectations created profound problems, which will be discussed in more detail later in this
chapter.)

The British experience is again illustrative, not only of the types of
problems that will be encountered, but also of how these problems
necessarily alter the character of programs originally established only
to save lives. Titmuss identified a number of problems "of home and

school life—mothers in factories, fathers in uniform, interrupted education, crowded homes, lack of children's shoes and so on."[27] He found that because of the stress of the war, "some mothers and fathers were less able or less willing to make the home a place of warm activity. . . . Simultaneously, the performance of many schools in their roles of educational and civilising agencies deteriorated."[28]

Because of these problems the character of the evacuation program changed. Increasingly, from 1941 onward, the children who came under the government's evacuation scheme reflected the deprivations and inconsistencies of the times:

> It became, not so much a scheme for preserving the lives of children in areas relatively safe from air attack, but a scheme whose primary task was to find temporary homes for children whose mothers were out working in factories, were ill or were expecting a baby, for children out of parental control because of the absence of fathers, for children who needed on educational grounds to be linked up with a particular evacuated school, and for an assortment of other reasons. In short, it acted as a safety-valve for social distress in the cities and it gave to some children some of the elements of care which the family, when not separated by war, strained by bodily and economic ills or broken by dissension, was best fitted to provide.[29]

In brief, the very measures designed to cope with the effects of strategic war, such as evacuation, will themselves create significant negative and unanticipated side effects for this basic social unit. Similar measures (evacuation, mobilization of the civilian work force, closing of the schools) had similar consequences for families in Japan, as one observer noted, the social dislocation was "detrimental to Japanese family structure and the feelings and values that go with it."[30]

While the long-term significance of these side effects cannot be ignored in assessing the acceptability of nuclear war, of more immediate importance is their impact on the process of social and economic recovery. The availability and motivation of leaders, technicians, workers, and all classes of personnel required in the recovery effort will be affected by family considerations, especially for families with children. Concern for the well-being and safety of relations will often be in conflict with the needs of the larger society, causing some to drop out of the work force entirely or, at a minimum, producing high absentee rates and lower productivity. For some adults, the loss or injury of spouses and children will rob them of any incentive to care for themselves, much less contribute to the general rebuilding of the nation. They will thus impose additional burdens on the recovery effort rather than shoulder them. Children without parents will also require special care because of their profound social traumas. However, such care may be limited, since attempts to remedy this situation by providing special care can divert substantial quantities of productive energy from recovery needs. Ironically, the consequence of such limited care may be children lacking the normal motivation and self-esteem needed to become productive citizens.

Stress on the family unit will not be limited to those families in the attacked areas. Families in the host areas receiving evacuees will also be affected by conflicts arising from differences between the hosts and the evacuees and between the more fortunate and less fortunate evacuees, particularly as a consequence of the spreading social trauma of the nuclear attacks themselves.

Quite apart from individual psychological reactions related to nuclear war, therefore, damage to basic and supporting social institutions such as the family can have serious implications for postattack recovery. The effects will emerge not only as increased abnormal behavior and antisocial attitudes, which impose additional burdens on substitute social structures, but also as of weakened individual motivation and support needed for the effort to rapidly rebuild the economy and the society.

Housing as a Social Problem. One of the most formidable tasks facing authorities after strategic air attacks, whether nuclear or conventional, is the provision of basic housing for evacuees and those whose homes have been destroyed or otherwise made unfit to live in. In World War II, strategic bombing produced long-term housing shortages in Europe. Worse shortages may follow nuclear attacks.

The British experience is again illustrative of the magnitude of the task, of the inability of authorities to foresee its nature clearly, and of the unintended consequences of efforts to cope with the problem. The task was complicated by the fact that "the authorities knew little about the homeless who in turn knew less about the authorities."[31] Adding to the misconceptions and miscalculations were totally unexpected problems that nevertheless had to be addressed. For example, unexploded bombs made many homeless although their homes were not destroyed. An analogous effect in a nuclear war would be the necessity to abandon undamaged homes because of high levels of radiation, the suspicion of lingering radiation, or the lack of supporting services (electrical power, potable water, sanitary facilities, police and fire protection). Furthermore, in nuclear attacks of the type hypothesized in this book, a much greater proportion of the housing stock will be destroyed than was the case in wartime Britain.

In the British case, casualties were overestimated, while the numbers of homeless were underestimated. The consequence was the overcrowding of already inadequate, temporary "rest centers," which were initially lacking in such basic amenities as toilets and blankets. No provision was made for loans or other means of replacing lost or damaged furnishings or for making repairs for damaged dwellings. Also unanticipated was the social class resistance to relocation in new neighborhoods or areas, which were perceived as foreign and threatening, despite the lack of proper shelter in their original neighborhoods.

Short- and long-term problems were also raised by the need to cope with the reconstruction of the physical housing stock itself. In Britain, nearly a quarter of a million homes were destroyed or damaged beyond repair, while 3.5 million homes suffered repairable damage. Because of the diversion of resources to other pressing needs, these losses could not be replaced during the war.[32]

In addition to the lack of dwellings, there was a shortage of household equipment and furnishings, either for new construction or to replace worn out or damaged items. Titmuss summarized the housing situation: "The physical shell [of the home] was not so good; there was less room because there were fewer houses and—since so much was destroyed and so little made—furniture and equipment steadily deteriorated."[33]

In cases where there are high levels of housing destruction combined with high population survival rates, as occurs with preattack evacuation, the population density per dwelling unit does not increase in direct proportion to housing losses—that is, the surviving population does not simply double up. In both Japan and Germany, Iklé found that the destruction of the housing stock did not result in corresponding increases in housing density:

> Only a certain percentage of the homeless survivors find accommodations within the city, and *this percentage declines gradually as the number of homeless survivors becomes larger in relation to the undestroyed housing resources.* Although housing density apparently increases as the number

of homeless persons becomes larger, it does so at a slower rate. (Emphasis added.)[34]

Part of this phenomenon may be attributed to the loss of important utility services (water, electricity, sewage), the ability of some survivors to find accommodations distant from the stricken areas, the avoidance of crowded living conditions, and physical damage that makes surviving dwellings unattractive for habitation, if not unfit. Whatever the causes, it is clear there are serious limitations on the utilization of surviving housing stock to accommodate fully the survivors of the areas. This is important because, under these conditions, additional population migrations away from even the undamaged areas of the attacked cities may take place. This could spread the problem of caring for the survivors over a broader area where resources cannot be concentrated so readily and therefore used efficiently. It could also promote conflict among survivors for favorable living situations if evacuation is severely limited.

The specific experience in Hamburg during World War II summarized in Figures 7–1 and 7–2 shows the difficulties in the cycle of evacuation and housing utilization cited above. Figure 7–1 displays the population in Hamburg (dark line) from preattack to the postwar period. Figure 7–2 shows the variations in population per housing unit for the same period. The population density per dwelling unit did indeed increase, from below three to about four persons per unit, indicating that a portion of the homeless were reaccommodated in the surviving dwellings in Hamburg. The population of Hamburg was about 1.1 million after reaccommodation, while the surviving dwelling units remained at about 280,000, down from at the beginning of the war. However, a very significant portion of the population, about one-third, did not return during the war.[35] Had they returned, the density would have risen to approximately six per unit (1.6 million people in 280,000 dwelling units). Even after the war, housing density remained below five persons per unit.

Hamburg, thus, supports the observation that a variety of social factors and the destruction or disruption of supporting urban services and infrastructure can combine to prevent the maximum theoretical utilization of the surviving housing stock as a consequence. The demand for alternative shelters outside the damaged cities would increase, causing population migrations that will further tax the housing capacity and other resources in the areas near these cities.

Figure 7-1. Evacuation and Return Compared with Housing Destruction in Hamburg during World War II.

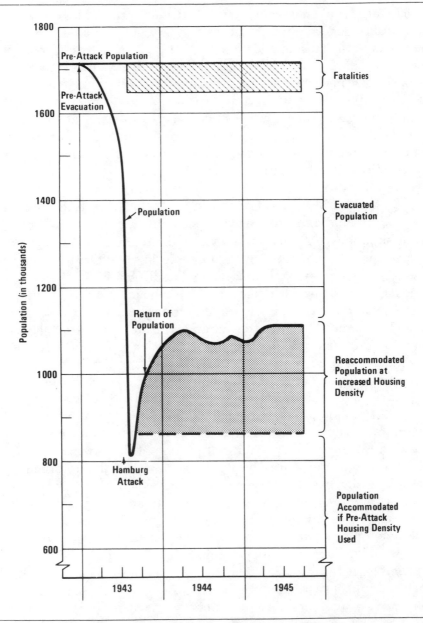

Source: Modified from Fred C. Iklé, *Social Impact of Bomb Destruction*, p. 104.

Figure 7-2. Housing Density (persons per dwelling unit) Before and After the Hamburg Fire Raids.

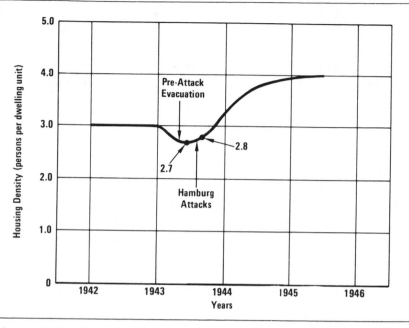

Source: Arthur Katz, *Economic and Social Consequences of Nuclear Attacks on the United States*, Committee on Banking, Housing, and Urban Affairs, U.S. Senate (Washington, D.C.: U.S. Government Printing Office, 1979), p. 125.

World War II experience shows that rebuilding of the housing stock is not rapid. Because of the long-lived or chronic nature of the housing problem population migrations also become long term— even, in some measure, permanent. This would be true in both the damaged and the undamaged areas. The latter may experience housing shortages from efforts to accommodate long-term or permanent refugees from the cities.

A specific illustration is again Hamburg, which—while losing 50 percent of its housing in major air raids—rebuilt only a very small percentage by the war's end. This is quite consistent with the British experience described previously. Following a nuclear attack, with far greater potential for destruction and with the added problem of radioactive fallout, similar conditions of widespread substandard housing could be expected to persist for at least a decade or more.

Poor housing may result in health problems. Even domestic stress is likely to be exacerbated by overcrowding. These problems could in turn result in further social instability, affecting economic recovery.

The British faced a combination of all the problems discussed above. As Titmuss notes, it was only after a considerable passage of time following the onset of air attacks that the British authorities were able to recognize the extent and magnitude of the problem and remedy the deficiencies in their own preattack planning. They at first failed

> to plan intelligently, sympathetically, and in detail to meet the social consequence of air attack.
>
> When the attack came, the rest centre and communal feeding services had to be completely re-organized. Many new services, for needs hitherto unvisualised or only partly glimpsed, had to be hurriedly established; administrative and information centres; mobile feeding canteens and mobile Assistance Board offices; furniture for rehousing, and the salvage, removal and storage of furniture from damaged houses; hostel and billeting schemes; removal grants, and immediate cash compensation for the loss of furniture, clothing and essential tools.
>
> Practically all this had to be done without devising any new executive machinery; in other words, local government as it existed in 1939 had to be used. (Emphasis added.)[36]

Providing shelter for both evacuees and the homeless is thus a task that goes well beyond erecting tents or wooden barracks or assigning additional occupants to surviving dwellings. While national, state, and local authorities will not have to contend with the complexity imposed on the governmental machinery such as Britain's poor (welfare) law, neither will they have quite the same time to adapt and improvise.

Thus, planning for the postattack period will be hampered, as it was in Britain, by the inability to foresee how long the evacuees will have to remain displaced or how long the homeless will remain without housing, as well as by ill-prepared social planning and service agencies (if they survive). Exacerbating these problems will be the antagonisms and resistance discussed earlier that arise in times of general social dislocation. Housing measures that are geared to short-term evacuations (the model for both American and Soviet nuclear war planning) will be inadequate for extended evacuations or for very large numbers of the permanently homeless. Their implementation can waste precious housing resources and time, as occurred in Britain, should longer term programs prove necessary. The ability of authorities to meet basic requirements successfully, such as those for housing, will not only test the resourcefulness of authorities, it will test whatever political credibility authorities may retain following widespread nuclear attacks. Failure to meet this challenge will have significant implications for the political viability of the government in the postattack period.

Impact on Age Groups. Typically, strategic war has a particularly severe effect on the young and the elderly, the age groups requiring the most care in society. According to the official British history, children and old people died literally of neglect. Infant death increased during the early years of adjustment at the beginnings of the war. Fatalities among the young due to road accidents increased because of "less schooling, less supervision. . . ."[37] Increases in child deaths from suffocation in bed and from food were also noted. Both the elderly and the young died of accidental burns at an increased rate. Titmuss recorded the impact on the elderly: "The effect of the war environment on the loneliness and limited capacity of old age to help itself led to an excess mortality during 1939–41 of over 2,300 elderly people from falling downstairs, out of bed, elsewhere in the home, out of doors and in unknown circumstances."[38] The wartime mortality for children under fifteen and adults over sixty-five exceeded the prewar mortality rates for these age groups. These indirect deaths were equal to 10 percent of the more than 60,000 deaths directly attributable to the air war. The increased level of stress and the diversion of energies of survival demands can only exacerbate this problem in the post nuclear war era.

Response to Food Shortages. Major food shortages are certain to occur after a nuclear attack, at least in some areas, and may become prolonged, for reasons analyzed in Chapter 6. Though the causes of similar shortages in World War II were somewhat different, the negative effect of inadequate food supplies on morale, individual behavior and social cohesion, and relief and recovery efforts will probably be at least as severe after a nuclear exchange. Of particular concern is the inability to use food as an effective incentive to keep or attract workers to high risk or damaged cities. The impact of strategic bombing on food distribution is illuminated by the consequences of an attack on Coventry, where food processing was relatively decentralized as compared to the present-day system in the United States.

> The notorious raid . . . on the night of November 14–15, 1940, was the first of a series that, while they never produced a breakdown of food supplies, caused officials to reflect upon the narrow margin of safety they possessed, not indeed in food stocks, but in the help that was available to a community temporarily reeling under a blow. In Coventry, gas, electricity, and water supplies were all interrupted in whole or in part; all bakeries, except one that relied on oil fuel, were therefore out of action, as were milk-pasteurizing and bottling plants. Bread, to the extent of 100,000 loaves in a single day, had to be brought from Birmingham and Stoke-on-Trent; milk from other towns. So many people had lost both ration book and retailer that rationing had to be suspended. (It had to be restored 10 days later because of the influx of visitors.) Many local tradespeople, including the chairman and vice-chairman of the Ministry of Food area provisions and groceries committee, were killed or missing; of those that survived nearly all, reported the Divisional Food Officer, were stunned for a couple of days and dazed for some days afterwards.[39]

Germany and Japan experienced even more severe problems:

> A plentiful food supply, more readily obtainable within the city than outside, is one of the most effective incentives for workers to remain in a partially damaged city. . . . During the later years of World War II, food became so scarce in German cities that workers resorted to week-end trips to the country to round out their food rations through purchases or foraging in farm areas. This caused absenteeism and increased the load on the overtaxed transportation system. The food scarcity in Japanese cities was generally worse than in German cities. It is reported from Kobe that day laborers, badly needed in the war industries, fled to the country after the heavy raids because of food shortages in the city.[40]

The inability of the government to deal with the problem in Kobe:

> forced the immediate evacuation of air-raid victims. Over 12,000 tons of rice—the complete stock of Kobe's emergency supplies—were destroyed in the March and June attacks. After the June attack, food distribution was completely disorganized and never got back to anything approaching normal. As a consequence, black market activities and absenteeism due to the necessity of foraging became extremely serious despite efforts to mitigate the problem at key factories by direct food distribution.[41]

Thus, while in the earlier part of the war when food was still reasonably abundant, release of additional supplies was timed to bolster morale in the aftermath of air raids, such surpluses were eventually exhausted, with significant consequences for morale and for industrial recovery after the attacks.

Leighton's discussion of this issue in relation to Japan during World War II sums up the problem. He identified the results of the inequities that developed in the distribution of a rapidly diminishing food supply, particularly fish and rice.

> The net result of this situation, the mass of evidence shows, was widespread undernourishment, nutritional disease, social conflict and depression of the will to resist. . . .
>
> While the drastic reduction in the food supply helped to undermine confidence in leadership and intensified the cleavage between the "haves" and the "have-nots" among Japanese civilians, the consequent competition for the necessities of life, together with heightened nervous tensions and mounting difficulties brought on by air raids struck at the nerves of individuals. . . . In answer to the question "Did the people's attitudes and conduct toward each other change during the war?" almost half the responses indicated growing tension among the civilians. A middle-class housewife of Ogaki expressed herself this way:
>
> "Yes, definitely—everyone became inconsiderate. Stores didn't extend services; riding trains and streetcars was a mad commotion. I think the people became irritable due to lack of food. They are always hungry and dissatisfied and naturally they try to blame their suffering on someone."[42]

ANTAGONISM AND HOSTILITY

As the earlier discussion of Britain illustrated, wartime measures often foster the emergence among the population of a variety of social conflicts and antagonisms that are latent or muted in peacetime. Deep rifts can appear within a society under the stress of a long period of deprivation and uncertainty.

The Japanese encountered this problem. They experienced a "trend toward social disorganization and hence disorganization of the war effort. . . ." This trend was associated with "hostility between urban and rural people, the city dwellers feeling that the peasants are hoarding and falling down on production, while the farmers feel that those who live in the big towns are the cause of heavy taxes, lack of fertilizer and low prices for country produce. There is also an influx of city people into the country as a result of evacuation, and these are a strain on rural housing and subsistence facilities."[43]

The maldistribution of resources also fosters significant conflict between the residents of areas where survival resources may be adequate or marginal, and numerous injured or healthy incoming evacuees who are perceived to strain the region's resources. This would especially be true of rural areas adjacent to heavily damaged areas. "Because of their poor adjustment to rural life and the strain they constitute on housing and subsistence facilities, the city people are further increasing the hostility of the peasants."[44]

In fact, much of this hostility had a basis in the relationships that existed within the society prior to the deprivation of war. As the report quoted by Leighton notes: "Various economic, political, social and regional conflicts that existed before the war between different kinds of Japanese have become heightened."[45]

In addition to the urban–rural divisions, the report pointed out that:

> To a lesser extent there is mistrust felt by the residents of different cities for each other. Osaka has been singled out especially for adverse comment by people from other areas.
>
> Wider and larger regional differences also play a part. It is well known that the inhabitants of Okinawa have been long regarded as not quite Japanese and hence to some degree inferior. To a lesser extent Hokkaido is considered as a place apart. Regions responsible for the production of commodities that are painfully scarce, such as coal, are probably targets for the resentments of other districts. Traditional clan loyalties and differences of view also play a part in regional cleavages.
>
> The Koreans . . . are an obvious scapegoat of considerable importance. It may be recalled that in the earthquake and consequent fire in Tokyo in 1923 great numbers of Koreans were massacred.[46]

A population divided among itself in this way can readily undermine efforts to coordinate war production or a speedy economic recovery from the effects of war.

The existence of similar conflicts in a postattack U.S. society is supported by a panel of military officers, civil defense planners, and scientists engaged in disaster and postattack research, assembled for a 1971 study for the Army on the effects of a nuclear attack on the United States. They predicted that in the event of nuclear war:

> an increase in conflict between sections of the country, between advocates of varying war policies, and between urban and rural populations . . . such conflict would pose serious problems . . . and many participants in the study pre-

dicted racial or class conflict as well. Such conflict, most panelists noted, as well as that between families and other small groups, would necessitate the imposition of martial law or other authoritarian systems in many localities, and the widespread use of troops to maintain order. . . .[47]

The implications for a society with racial, ethnic, cultural, or economic differences and tensions is clear. With the range of potential conflicts that could emerge in a postattack society, the assumption, based on previous disaster experience, that for at least the initial postattack period conflict would be minimized in an atmosphere of cooperation may be tenable only if the period of stress is quite short. A prolonged period of stress, uncertainty, and inadequate resources coupled with rising numbers of incoming evacuees could significantly erode this mood. The loss of cooperative attitudes may in turn seriously undercut an effective national mobilization of human resources for the recovery effort.

Ironically, the impact of nuclear war may be greater for the social structure if large numbers of casualties and evacuees are forced to migrate into rural areas (as in Attacks A–3 and A–4), instead of dying in the initial attacks. The number of evacuees might reach 50 or 100 million before or immediately following a nuclear attack, when uncertainty about targets, size of initial attack, and the possibility of follow-up attacks would lead to massive spontaneous or planned migrations from potential target areas. Such evacuations are likely to increase group tensions and could severely strain, if not overwhelm, the ability of civil authorities to control the situation. Any prolongation of this condition would accentuate the fear and uncertainty and aggravate the interpersonal and intergroup conflicts. As a consequence, efforts to reestablish civil authority and begin the economic recovery could be inhibited.

DISRUPTION OF POLITICAL AUTHORITY

The complexity and variety of fundamental problems associated with organizational and institutional recovery requirements are indicated in the study by Allnutt. Though the panel questioned in the study produced generally optimistic conclusions about the long-term probability of rebuilding American institutional and material strength, it nevertheless noted many specific and severe problems, similar to those discussed here, that seem to contrast with the panel's general optimism. The report states, for example:

> Major institutions and organizations were seen as fragmenting in most cases and collapsing in others, but the seriousness of this result would be relieved somewhat by the irrelevancy of many of them to the early stages of recovery, and by the ability of social structure to spring back into action where physical conditions permit. The Federal Government would make serious mistakes and suffer a loss of power and prestige, but not a loss of faith so serious as to favor the possibility of revolt. Financial institutions would be modified greatly, and barter would be a widespread reaction to inflation, but money was not seen as going out of style, nor was a barter economy foreseen. Legal, judicial, and enforcement systems would similarly undergo great strains, being overwhelmed entirely in some areas, but again, due process, though delayed, would not be lost in *principle*. Industries and commercial organizations were expected to fragment into autonomous, local entities until communications and transportation systems were repaired, but the goals of such corporations would not be greatly changed. . . .[48]

In contrast to these complex demands in the areas heavily damaged in the hypothetical nuclear attacks, the ability of civil authorities to respond to the emergency will be severely constrained by a drastic reduction in the technicians, professionals, managers, and public leaders, who are heavily concentrated in the urban areas, as noted in the earlier discussion of small scale disasters. The ranks of potential replacement personnel will also be significantly thinned, since the apprentices, management trainees, junior executives, and lower level civil servants are concentrated in these same areas.

These losses will not occur as a result of fatalities alone. Some personnel will be injured, making them unfit for technical, management, or leadership roles. Others will suffer role conflict, perhaps fleeing the stricken areas or at least failing to make themselves available to assist the community. Some may be forcefully evacuated, intentionally or unintentionally.

The loss of these key personnel will reduce the capacity of public and private organizations to function effectively, just when this capacity is most needed. At the same time, certain political forms and conventions (such as electoral procedures and administrative law) will have to be ignored or suspended temporarily, due to the lack of time for their observance or because of the loss of personnel, such as the members of state legislatures or city councils. Where executive authorities (mayors, city managers, governors) do not survive, their duties will fall upon individuals either not competent in terms of ability or not regarded as competent to assume these duties from a legal standpoint. The loss of recognized political leaders and the disruption of political norms could call into question the political legitimacy of those attempting to exercise leadership in the immediate postattack period. This can have several consequences.

First, the state or federal government can impose martial law and appoint a civilian or military officer to govern by decree. If this person's decisions are unpopular, as many doubtless will be, the lack of political legitimacy may, in the eyes of some, be sufficient reason to disobey his or her edicts. This impulse will be particularly strong not only among existing antisocial or criminal elements, but also among normally law-abiding citizens whose desire to escape, survive, or pursue less rational courses (i.e., returning to dangerous areas to search for lost relatives or property) may be in direct conflict with the needs of the community as perceived by the appointed or surviving civil authorities.

An illustration of the effect of social disintegration in Hiroshima after the bombing, is that the city became "infested with burglars," whereas, before the atomic bomb, the government had been able to leave military supplies unattended at airports and in warehouses because theft was an insignificant problem.[49]

The loss of political and civic leaders and the disruption of political institutions can have other negative consequences. At a local level, competition among surviving politicians or public officials over who has the competence to be the true political leader will impede relief efforts and increase fear and uncertainty among the survivors. At the same time, disagreements between local authorities on the one hand and equally hard-pressed state and federal authorities on the other are likely to increase, if only as a result of the different perspectives, resources, and needs of the various levels of government. The national government or the state government could easily be paralyzed by this dissension, leading to major organizational disruption lasting a significant period of time before it could be remedied. The demoralizing and administratively debilitating effect of repeated governmental reorganizations in wartime Japan has already been noted.

No doubt, as often happens under emergency conditions, there will be cases where previously unrecognized leaders will come to the fore. Yet the emergence of new leaders to fill vacancies cannot be guaranteed in every instance. Hence it would be imprudent to count heavily on this phenomenon of new leadership or on the willingness of new leaders who do emerge to forego exploitation of their newly adopted mantles of authority. The literature of social and political disintegration under conditions of extreme stress indicates that many of those who assume leadership roles are gifted opportunists.[50]

An additional concern is the reaction of the American public to the suspension of laws and legal norms and to the imposition of numerous controls needed to deal with the exigencies of the post-attack period. Distribution of property and resources; direction of all facets of the recovery effort; the movement of goods and people; coordination of industrial production, transportation, and communications; organizing the workforce and, in general, the economic, social, and political aspects of life, will be assumed, in all likelihood, by a centralized authority at the national or regional level under special powers granted for this purpose. Indeed, preparedness planning in the United States already includes draft emergency legislation, executive orders, and regulations to achieve this end.

As in World War II in Europe, citizens may be organized in work patterns or brigades; they may be assigned specific jobs, not necessarily their preattack positions. Housing, food supply, and transportation will be allocated or otherwise controlled by the government, as will the movement of citizens beyond their home areas. Private or individual control of resources would not exist in many regions. Precluding private decisionmaking and initiative, except on a restricted scale, would be limited resources, the requirement for national survival and recovery, and the threat of conflict among contending individuals or groups. The imposition of controls will require delegation of authority and a suspension of basic property, legal, and individual rights far more sweeping than America experienced in either the Civil War or World War II, when many personal freedoms were suspended.

Introduction of societal controls will not only make extraordinary demands on institutions at a time of severe loss of organizational and leadership resources; it will also require that individuals in power, the institutions they command, and the actions they take be viewed as legitimate. Yet the legitimacy of the government will be undercut to the extent that its measures alter or conflict with preattack social, political, legal, or economic norms and behavior. It will be undercut by its inability to successfully convince the population that it is meeting essential social needs as well as promoting economic recovery. It will be undermined further by the introduction of new administrative structures such as are contemplated in American civil defense planning. These new or reorganized bureaucracies may be required to deal with emergency circumstances, but they will be unfamiliar and will therefore lack the legitimacy of preattack agencies. Maintaining society will be difficult, but ultimately essential. If the discrepancy between preattack national values and postattack realities becomes too great, the difficulties facing political leaders will be intensified. A significant risk of total loss of political legitimacy may develop, accompanied perhaps by real efforts on the part of survivors to change the leadership or the system forcibly or, at a local level, to take matters into their own hands.

While a sense of national emergency and solidarity may operate to sustain the support of survivors for some time into the postattack period, the failure of government at any level to actually achieve or at least to create the widespread perception of achieving meaningful recovery progress, to explain satisfactorily the causes of the attack, or to demonstrate a genuine concern for social needs and preattack values could lead to widespread disaffection. The result, again, would be serious challenges to the authority of government itself.

Taken as a whole, then, the various issues discussed raise some important questions about the ability of the political leadership in the postattack period to implement any massive organizational efforts. Once again, the experience of World War II appears relevant, even when allowance is made for the difference in timing between a sudden and a protracted cataclysm. The case of Japan is instructive:

> In politics, cleavages between different factions are becoming more evident. These political moves indicate not only scheming and counter-scheming but also dissolution of solidarity, hostility between cliques, lack of clarity as to aims and methods and, above all, a roughened sea of rising public fear, hostility and confusion.[51]

Radical opposition awaited its opportunities:

> There are a small number of radical secret societies operating below the surface who would like to see the Allies win because it would discredit the ruling groups and give themselves a chance to develop political power.[52]

There was also a deepening crisis of confidence:

> The Government and the public generally blame each other for the war situation. The people accuse the Government of bungling, interfering, red tape, lack of trust in the people, concealing information and economic

muddling so that the food situation is desperate and the black markets are uncontrolled.

Recent rumors, scribblings and [other] manifestations are numerically increasing. . . . They say that the Japanese war leaders, or the leading circles, are responsible for the decisive battle against Japan proper, for intensified air raids, shortage of food stuffs, acute inflation, etc. . . . This indignation against the ruling class was shown in criticisms of military strategy and misrepresentation of the attitude of military circles. Others speak ill of government measures and government communiques. They explicitly assume a hostile attitude toward the government circles. Some others dare to speak of class antagonism.[53]

This crisis of confidence was not unique to the Japanese. Janis noted that there were a number of reports of British resentment and hostility against the government stemming from the effects of the air war. Populations experiencing bomb damage naturally gave the most evidence of this hostility. Significantly, the resentment remained after improvements in population protection:

Control observations made at some of the same areas at a later period, when air defenses and rescue organizations were much more effective, showed that, although diminished in quantity, the quality and to a large extent the direction of these social responses remained unchanged. Resentment was again directed primarily at home authorities; but the onus of criticism was not exclusively upon the lack of care, foresight or effective defense; criticism spread to such matters as the political and military conduct of war or alleged incapacities of the Government on the domestic and industrial fronts. Even when, as was often the case, such criticisms were already current, they were strongly reinforced after raids.[54]

Hostility against the political leadership was also observed in Germany:

In Germany, the heavy air attacks to which civilians were subjected had the effect of increasing aggression against home-front authorities, according to the USSBS morale report:

"Bombing did not stiffen morale." The hate and anger it aroused tended to be directed against the Nazi regime which was blamed for beginning air warfare and for being unable to ward off Allied air attacks.

Typical of the evidence cited is the finding that hostile feelings toward national leaders were related to bombing experience. For example, 62 per cent of the people in unbombed towns expressed trust in the leaders, as against 48 per cent in heavily bombed towns.[55]

The strain of large-scale damage and physical deprivation, coupled with the sense of impending military defeat, was also reflected in fissures within the military and between the military and civilian leaders in Japan:

> The Army has been losing prestige in the eyes of the general public as a result of its defeats, and has been reacting to this by trying to strengthen its hand wherever it can on the home front. At the same time, its old enemies, in the business interests, the civil Government and the Navy, are taking a stronger stand against it. Although opinion is not uniform within the Army, a major clique advocates a fight to the end, with the hope and perhaps expectation that they can inflict such losses on the Allies that a compromise peace will be achieved. They are trying, therefore, to extend their control, especially over industry and home defenses.
>
> Business groups, on the other hand, are resisting Government control, and especially Army control, wherever they can. . . .
>
> The Navy is smarting under its loss of prestige, and even more under its loss of ships. Traditional hostility between it and the Army has been increased. It is trying in a rather frantic manner to secure public recognition, even claiming a fictitious victory at Formosa and playing up the fighting of its sailors on land in the Philippines.
>
> The regional administrative councils are in conflict with local Army and Navy commanders.[56]

While nothing can be said in any definitive sense about the post-attack political context, it is evident that a prolonged war situation or even an implicit and stable military stalemate (i.e., a tacit understanding of truce) could leave the political leadership in turmoil and seriously cripple its national reconstruction efforts. Additionally, though it is difficult to predict with certainty the effects of unparalleled damage on political conditions in the United States or, indeed, in any other country, the results observed in historical cases from similar societies provide at least plausible models for developments. Unpredictability itself counsels prudence in planning assumptions. The unique and unprecedented character, suddenness, and destructiveness of nuclear war, therefore, combine with history and prudence to suggest that strategic planning should be based, not on optimistic assumptions about national attitudes and behavior, but on pessimistic yet plausible contingencies.

EVACUATION—LESSONS TO BE LEARNED

The threat of bombing attacks—whether conventional or nuclear—raises the issue of the effectiveness of evacuation strategies. The British and other experiences in World War II are useful points of departure for this discussion, which will be expanded in Chapter 9.

Conventional War

In World War II the British Government decided to protect women and children against the expected air war by evacuations. There were two such evacuations, the first at the outbreak of war in August 1933, during the so-called "phony war" when there was no strategic bombing, and the second, more modest effort after attacks had begun against civilian targets in major cities. The first phase is perhaps the most interesting, since it revealed major problems and also shaped subsequent evacuation policies. The later policies, as noted earlier in this chapter, became extremely constrained and custodial in nature—that is, limited to real cases of social distress rather than general population movements. One of the reasons for this change was that the first evacuation had eventually met with considerable resistance, due to the social disorganization and tension caused by deficient government planning. This experience was not forgotten by British officials. In addition, considerable resistance to evacuation emerged among much of the population arising from a desire to "die among their own."

The initial British evacuation involved one and a half million women and children. The operation of the evacuation turned out to be disastrous itself. Neither the social service needs of these evacuees—schools, medical care, welfare—nor the institutional requirements to implement these services were anticipated.

> To organise quickly and smoothly a group of new social services for evacuees demanded, in the reception districts, a well-regulated system of day-to-day administration and a sufficient number of people equipped with that kind of practical experience which knows how to get things done, in the right order, and within the limits set by central policy. These requirements were not generally available in the reception districts in 1939. And even when substantial

improvements had been made the standard of performance was by no means uniform over the whole country.[57]

The social burden that fell on the individual hosts in evacuation áreas was thus severe and the source of considerable tension. Complicating and expanding this burden was the government's lack of appreciation of the sociological or psychological effects of removing children and women from their social milieu and placing them in poorly structured way stations where familiar social cues and responsibilities were missing. In this atmosphere, relatively simple problems became major issues. Bedwetting, head infestations, and the burden of supplying clothing for poorly clothed evacuees became significant conflict points.

> The complaints that were made about the evacuees took various forms. It was said that the children's clothing was generally inadequate and, very often, in a filthy condition; that many of the mothers and children were dirty, verminous and affected with scabies, impetigo, and other skin troubles; that a large proportion of the children wetted their beds and soiled their clothes, and that many mothers were reckless, irresponsible, ungrateful and deplorably mannered.[58]

Though based to some degree in fact, this perception was aggravated by the social differences between host and evacuee and by the condition of protracted crisis *without actual bombing*.

The protracted and hollow nature of the crisis changed heroic sacrifice into sullen hostility:

> Both sides were, when they met, expecting too much. Disillusionment set in from the first day, and the local and national press were soon fiiled with protests from indignant householders.[59]

These reactions and tensions could easily be repeated in a similar strategic evacuation prior to nuclear attack, perhaps with more severe side effects.

These experiences are not limited to predisaster circumstances. In 1953, large floods in the Netherlands caused similar problems between evacuees and hosts. The key factor identified by Iklé in this case was not the lack of real hardship or heroic sacrifices, as in the first British evacuation, but the long-term nature of the evacuations, that is, a temporary act of good will turning into a prolonged, fundamental change in the host's life pattern.

The same increase in social tension [as in the British experience] is borne out by studies of the Dutch evacuation of 1953. Apparently, people can adjust remarkably well to great hardships if an early end is in sight. Furthermore, the initial adjustment between host and evacuee is aided by an outburst of altruism and sympathy on the part of the hosts and by a prevailing feeling of solidarity in times of national crisis. However, when the prospect of long inconvenience appears and when the original hospitality wears off under the continuous inroads on privacy and the daily occasions for friction, social tensions will gradually increase. The factors which seemed to be particularly related to the incidence of tension between hosts and evacuees in Holland were differences in religious beliefs and income levels. The latter became important only in the long run. Furthermore, evacuated families with children experienced significantly more tensions than those without children, probably because the children placed a great burden on the hosts.[60]

The Japanese experience supports the observation that the dislocating impact of evacuation, particularly conflict between host and evacuee, will occur even under the assumed uniting effect of shared suffering—especially during extended periods of stress.

Evacuees had a most unsettling effect upon the communities in which they sought refuge. They went everywhere, spreading news of disaster and eating into the meager resources of their hosts.

Their leaving [home] resulted in disorganization of family life and the abandonment of passive defense against bombs in the communities from which they came.

In nearly all the communities which received evacuees, the commonest complaint of the people was the increased black-market activities and the consequent rise in the price of commodities. The people blamed the black market upon evacuees who, they charged, being rich, were willing to pay high prices to obtain goods otherwise unavailable.

Even had organizational efficiency remained at a high level, this vast migration would have been a calamity. But the very scope of the evacuation dissolved organization, already under heavy strain from physical results of bombing. The combination was disastrous.[61]

Nuclear Attack Conditions

Current U.S. descriptions of large-scale urban evacuation during nuclear war threats rest on the assumption of "strategic warnings"— that is, a period when a worsening political situation will give notice of impending attack and thereby permit rapid and widespread city evacuation. Quite apart from the uncertainty over predicting the timing and nature of an attack, the rapidity of such an evacuation will considerably aggravate some of the problems encountered in Britain, allowing less time for planning, adaptation, and reestablishment of basic services. Furthermore, whole cities, not just selected categories of the populace, will be evacuated, adding further to the burden on the host areas. If a nuclear attack comes, many of the refugees may become more or less permanent residents—squatters—in the host areas, at least for the extended period during which decontamination and reconstruction of the damaged urban areas takes place. Therefore to a very real degree, if a nuclear war does occur, large-scale evacuation implies significant *permanent* population resettlement—a problem that civil defense planners and national policymakers cannot ignore.

If postattack conditions do continue to be severe, efforts to carry out this resettlement and to replace losses in the housing stock will be seriously constrained. Hamburg, as noted, lost 50 percent of its housing stock in major air raids in 1943 and was able to replace only 2 percent of these losses five months later. If government at the state and local levels is also destroyed in the nuclear attacks, the problems of providing housing for the survivors will become even more difficult to cope with.

To gain an insight into the possible implications of evacuation in the United States, especially for housing needs, the magnitude of postattack migration was examined in relation to the lightest assumed attack (M-4) and the heaviest assumed attack (M-1) on Massachusetts cities. To evacuate all or most of the individuals within the damaged areas (defined by the 1 psi blast contour) would require moving a total of over 2.5 to 3.0 million people. This is approximately double the number of persons evacuated over an extended period throughout Britain at the beginning of World War II. The evacuation would include 900,000 dying and injured following attack M-4 and 1.4 million dying and injured following attack M-1. Additionally, if war continued unterminated after a relatively light initial attack such as M-4, all survivors from the centers of major undamaged urban areas, could be expected to become evacuees. In that case, the number of evacuees would increase by about another 500,000, raising the total to between 3.0 and 3.5 million, many of them injured. This would mean accommodating over half of Massa-chusetts's population in the undamaged suburban–rural portions of the targeted standard metropolitan statistical areas (SMSAs) in the Springfield–Boston region, since transportation to more distant points would be an unlikely option for all but a few survivors.

In the case where suburban or lightly populated areas surrounding the attacked cities and the suburban, but not the central, parts of the unattacked SMSAs are used as reception areas, the density per dwell-ing unit would increase three times above pre-attack levels follow-ing attack M–4 and four times after attack M–1.[62] Nine to twelve persons would occupy dwelling units that before the attack housed three. In an alternate example, if exposure to possible further attacks were to be seen as an acceptable risk, then all housing in the undam-aged SMSAs and outside the 3 psi blast contour in the attacked SMSAs would be available. Under these circumstances density in-creases would be halved to about five to six persons per unit. Popula-tion densities per dwelling unit would grow still higher if a successful preattack evacuation were to be carried out and if fatalities were held to a level of less than 10 percent.

The considerable difficulties that Massachusetts would face in pro-viding shelter at reasonable population densities for survivors and evacuees is supported by the data produced in a ORNL study for an attack larger than A–1, including military as well as urban targets.[63]

The study evacuated 80 percent of the population from urban tar-gets and areas where very high radiation levels would exist (ground bursts were also used). Figure 7–3 shows the 2 psi contours from the attack and Figure 7–4 the evacuation pattern for the Northeast. The study indicated that Massachusetts and all the states surrounding it had housing density increases on the order of six times normal levels (Table 3–4)—that is, going from an approximate level of three peo-ple per dwelling unit to eighteen. Comparing Iklé's finding that even under wartime conditions the numbers of individuals per dwelling unit tend to reach upper limits and the levels of population density per dwelling unit projected by ORNL for the postattack period, it seems to be evident that very substantial problems of overcrowding would exist under the most favorable conditions.

As indicated in the historical data analyzed in the earlier sections on social needs, not only will government at all levels be facing the immediate difficulties of effecting and controlling the mass migration of populations, they will also be facing other complex social and eco-

Figure 7-3.   Two Psi Blast Circles on the Northeastern United States.

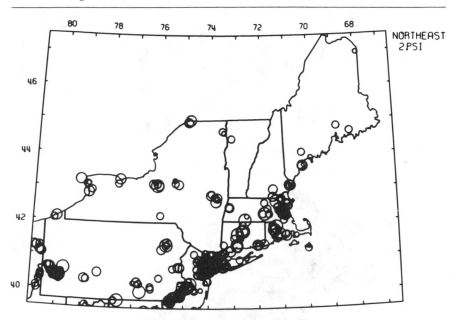

Source: C.M. Hoaland, C.V. Chester, and E.P. Wigner, *Survival of the Relocated Population of the U.S. After a Nuclear Attack*, Oak Ridge National Laboratory, ORNL-5401 (June 1976), p. 25.

nomic problems. Ironically, the more successful the evacuation—that is, the more lives saved, the more demanding will be the postattack task of providing for basic survival (food and shelter) and social service needs.

This is also true for the economy. Urban destruction and permanent resettlement implies dramatic economic dislocation with a huge reservoir of people competing for limited job opportunities. This problem will be profound since, as noted in Chapter 5, the financial system will be disarray, if not destroyed. Key industries with surviving production capacity will be "bottlenecked" because of selective and general destruction. As even the optimistic models of recovery in Chapter 5 indicated, these effects will not be short-lived. Significantly, these problems may be complicated by the fact that evacuees or refugees may not necessarily remain concentrated in the undamaged portions of urban areas or in the designated reception areas nearby, where their needs can be more easily met and where their

Figure 7-4. Relocated Population, Northeast.

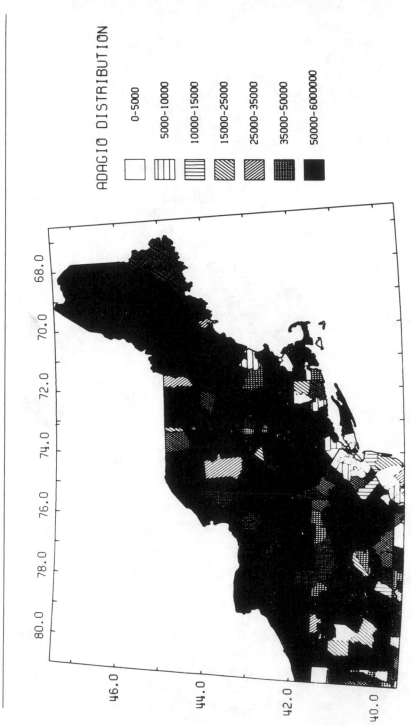

ADAGIO DISTRIBUTION

0-5000

5000-10000

10000-15000

15000-25000

25000-35000

35000-50000

50000-6000000

Source: C.M. Hoaland, C.V. Chester, and E.P. Wigner, *Survival of the Relocated Population of the U.S. After a Nuclear Attack*, Oak Ridge National Laboratory, ORNL–5401 (June 1976), p. 29.

own contribution can be used most effectively. They may flee in an uncontrolled fashion from all damaged urban areas, in response to the desire to (flee) escape confronting extreme destruction (described above by Irving Janis). Less likely, because of the combination of massive destruction, the powerful aversion created by the extraordinary numbers of casualties, and the strong fear of radioactive contamination, is the drive to return to the cities—even those under attack—seen in World War II. As Iklé noted, "The premature return of German evacuees was so prevalent that city authorities tried to take measures to prevent it. . . . This premature return of nonessential evacuees during World War II shows the great strength of the backward pull of the city."[64] Evacuation of whole cities may minimize or eliminate this factor.

While the drive to flee further from the cities or return to them depends on the level of actual damage and, as importantly, on individual perception of danger, nevertheless, for the civil defense planner or policymaker, this additional uncertainty can only make their already formidable task that much more difficult.

Twenty years ago when the Federal Civil Defense Administration had just scrapped its city evacuation plans as a response to the far less numerous and less capable nuclear weapons of that era, Fred C. Iklé described the practical problems of large-scale evacuation. He noted that the major emphasis had been on motivating people to evacuate rather than evaluating the sociological demands of evacuation particularly permanent evacuation. He warned: *"However, the war will not end miraculously after the people have been moved into the nearest fields, and further problems of evacuation will then arise."* (Emphasis added.)[65]

In the near term, when saving lives is the paramount consideration, stress on practical or logistical difficulties seems appropriate. However, over the longer term, as Iklé states, the sociological problems, together with economic and political problems, will assume the dominant role, as the nation seeks to reconstitute its prewar economy and society. The case studies of World War II evacuations illustrate, there are vast difficulties in terms of social organization even when time and resources are relatively abundant and when the survival of most of the government at various levels can be assumed.

The preoccupation with the numbers of dead and the degree of economic damage, while understandable, has diverted attention from examining the problems that the living will face immediately and for many years after a nuclear exchange. As Richard Titmuss wrote of the British experience: "Those visions of panic-stricken crowds and of mutilation and death had obscured the plain and humdrum problems of maintaining as going concerns the institution of the family and the business of living in cities."[66]

Foreseeing these problems and avoiding the shortsightedness that afflicted governments in World War II is a necessary first step in minimizing their impact, if war comes. Similarly, appreciating the complexity and magnitude of these problems is the key element for making comprehensive and realistic judgments about the "acceptability" of nuclear war. What is clear, however, is that evacuation in the context of conventional war has not been a notable panacea.

LONG-TERM SOCIAL COSTS: A CHANGING MIND-SET

One neglected aspect of society's response to nuclear war is the philosophical changes toward life and society. It represents a profound but intangible influence on the course of postattack society. The effects of the Black Death illustrate how these changes could intrude into the philosophical and ideological framework of society. The magnitude of these changes could reshape people's perceptions of their world and, concomitantly, their ideas and actions. An indication of the strength of this influence is the theme of death that permeated medieval perceptions and affected lifestyles and philosophies. "Together the frescoes marked the start of a pervasive presence of Death in art, not yet the cult it was to become by the end of the century, but its beginning."[67]

This is not an experience unique to the middle ages. It was seen also in the Hiroshima survivors' fixation on their experience and in the profound effect of the Depression of the 1930s on society's values. Massive and powerful physical and social events clearly shape the actions and values of generations to come, indelibly distorting or reorienting intellectual as well as physical life. Barbara Tuchman described this process in terms of a contemporary as well as medieval tragedy:

> An event of great agony is bearable only in the belief that it will bring about a better world. When it does not, as in the aftermath of another vast calamity in 1914 and 1918, disillusion is deep and moves on to self-doubt and self-disgust. In creating a climate for pessimism, the Black Death was the equiva-

lent of the First World War, although it took fifty years for the psychological effects to develop.[68]

Nuclear war would no doubt have an equally profound and negative impact. One can only speculate on the "philosophical changes" after a nuclear exchange, but the outcome of even the smallest of the hypothetical attacks discussed bodes ill. The political, military, and economic implications of a loss of hope, a national destruction of the human spirit is summed up in this symbolic footnote in history:

> In Siena, where more than half the inhabitants died of the [Black] plague, work was abandoned on the great cathedral, planned to be the largest in the world, and *never resumed*, owing to loss of workers and master masons and "the melancholy and grief" of the survivors. The cathedral's truncated transept still stands in permanent witness to the sweep of death's scythe. (Emphasis added.)[69]

PERSPECTIVE

In this chapter a deeper and broader understanding of the scope of the effects of nuclear war has been developed. A layer of complexity has been examined that, though necessarily lacking specificity in terms of application to individual nuclear attacks, nevertheless identifies fundamental questions: Can the present political and organizational structure adapt to and fulfill the overwhelming demands of the post-attack period? Even if the nation survives, will it retain its democratic political system? These questions represent the keys to understanding and judging life after nuclear war. They cannot and must not be ignored, but seem to be conveniently misplaced in most public discussions and analyses.

The experience of nuclear war is likely to have devastating psychological effects, especially for Americans, whose homes and institutions have largely escaped the ravages of recent wars. The very short period required to carry out highly destructive nuclear attacks will increase their emotional impact, particularly those reactions associated with denial of the true extent of the damage and those fostering flight from damaged areas and resistance to reentering them.

A high incidence of abnormal behavior, ranging from the nonfunctional to the antisocial, can be anticipated. Specific psychological effects would include disorientation, fear, doubt, apathy, and antipathy toward authorities.

Families will be particularly vulnerable to the effects of widespread nuclear attacks; they will be broken up by death, severe injury, or disease; evacuation; or military and labor conscription. The young, elderly, and handicapped will suffer disproportionately since they are most dependent for support on society's material and institutional resources.

The loss of material and institutional resources in urban-industrial attacks will make survival in the postattack period difficult for individuals and groups alike, compounding the psychological stresses of the attack itself. Satisfying even the simplest requirements of survival—food, shelter, and clothing—will become major tasks.

The loss of human resources will be severe due to their concentration in major urban areas. If the nation's ability to provide adequate leadership and resources from outside the attacked areas is limited, as it is likely to be, the demoralization of the population will be even greater, further retarding effective relief and recovery efforts.

Significant interpersonal, intergroup, and inter-regional conflicts are likely to arise. Ethnic, racial, regional, and economic conflicts present in the preattack society, while minimized in the period immediately after an attack, will be heightened by the extent of the deprivation and the resulting tensions after only a limited time. New antagonisms will develop between hosts and evacuees or refugees over the possession and use of surviving resources.

If hostilities persist or if there is a prolonged threat of renewed war, the changes in the social fabric would be even more profound. Major, possibly permanent, changes in social values and institutions can be expected as society seeks to adjust to a radically altered environment dominated by the question of physical survival, both personal and national.

Economic destruction, loss of political leadership (especially at the local level), and the need to mobilize resources for relief and recovery will present extraordinary demands on weakened political institutions. In the interest of implementing survival programs, legal norms and practices will have to be suspended for prolonged periods in many areas. The character of political institutions and authorities is almost certain to change, especially if hostilities or the threat of hostilities persist. Both old and new political structures are likely to suffer from greatly reduced confidence and credibility. Decentralization of political power and more authoritarian methods of political, social, and economic control are likely responses to postattack conditions. Widespread disaffection may ensue. Consequences of this kind will have an important bearing on the acceptability of nuclear war.

The beginning of this chapter set a scene, a grim description of economic and human damage, and the vulnerability of key structures supporting society's short- and long-run goals. What should have emerged from this chapter is a realization of how inadequately even that picture described life after nuclear war. What it lacks is a sense of the uncertainties and ambiguities associated with effectively using the surviving physical and human resources, reestablishing social bonds, and promoting political trust. While profoundly disturbing in terms of human survival and, particularly, prolonged human suffering, the importance of the pivotal integrating psychological, social, political, and institutional effects of nuclear war, should also be considered within a different framework.

These effects should be evaluated in terms of effective national power. National power is a bellwether of genuine survival, for ultimately it is the indicator of success to military and national leaders. Survival of individuals in political and social terms has little meaning, unless they continue to function as part of a viable national economic power or military force. Therein lies the importance of the levels of destruction and of weapons use necessary to achieve the compromise of this power. This discussion indicates clearly that compromised power is attained in the range of the smallest rather than the largest hypothetical attacks. For the general and the politician, this should speak volumes about the mandatory level of survival of nuclear forces the former must assure, and the fragility of the political power that the latter seeks to retain. In each case, the present debate is misleading—overestimating both weapons requirements and the strength and durability of political structures.

NOTES TO CHAPTER 7

1. Allen H. Barton, *Communities in Disaster: A Sociological Analysis of Collective Stress Situations* (Garden City, N.Y.: Doubleday and Co., Inc., 1969).
2. Father Siemes, "Hiroshima—August 6, 1945," *Bulletin of the Atomic Scientists* 1 (May, 1946): 2–6.
3. Robert Lifton, *Death in Life* (New York: Vantage Books, 1969), p. 31.
4. Ibid., p. 30.

5. This type of response to overwhelming and incomprehensible disaster is timeless. A prime example in another era is the Black Death:

    Angolo di Tura, a chronicler of Siena, recorded the fear of contagion that froze every other instinct. "Father abandoned child, wife husband, one brother another," he wrote, "for this plague seemed to strike through the breath and sight. And so they died. And no one could be found to bury the dead for money or friendship. . . . And I, Angolo di Tura, called the Fat, buried my five children with my own hands, and so did many others likewise."

    There were many to echo his account of inhumanity and few to balance it, for the plague was not the kind of calamity that inspired mutual help. Its loathsomeness and deadliness did not herd people together in mutual distress, but only prompted their desire to escape each other. (Barbara Tuchman, *A Distant Mirror* [New York: Alfred A. Knopf, 1978], p. 96.)

6. Interestingly, an increase in stress-related neurosis anticipated as a result of conventional strategic bombing did not materialize, because the war provided not only dangers but also opportunities to perform useful tasks and to show leadership qualities and compassion. This suggests a possible qualitative difference between the psychological impact of nuclear attacks and conventional bombing. This may be attributable to the grossly different level of destruction and the compressed time scale of a nuclear attack. For the British experience, see R.M. Titmuss, *Problems of Social Policy* (London: His Majesty's Stationery Office and Longmans, Green and Company, 1950).

7. Irving Janis, *Air War and Emotional Stress* (New York: McGraw-Hill, 1951), p. 46.

8. See Gerald M. Stern, *The Buffalo Creek Disaster* (New York: Random House, 1976).

9. Janis, pp. 16–17.

10. Fred C. Iklé, *The Social Impact of Bomb Destruction* (Norman: University of Oklahoma Press, 1958), pp. 28–29.

11. Ibid., p. 107.

12. Ibid., p. 107.

13. Ibid., p. 107.

14. Ibid., p. 108.

15. A ground war, similar to that proposed for Europe, where "small" and short-range nuclear weapons are used.

16. The reaction, as noted above, would be different for those individuals experiencing a particularly gruesome and traumatic incident.

17. Bruce C. Allnutt, "A Study of Consensus on Social and Psychological Factors Related to Recovery from Nuclear Attack," HSR–RR–71/3–D1 prepared for the Office of Civil Defense, Department of the Army, (McLean, Va.: Human Sciences Research, Inc., May 1971), pp. S-4.

18. Alexander H. Leighton, *Human Relations in a Changing World* (New York: E.P. Dutton & Co., 1949), p. 251.

19. However, psychological difficulties were also aggravated by the loss of the city's leadership resulting from the destruction of central Hiroshima.
20. Tuchman, pp. 98–99.
21. Titmuss, pp. 239–240 (footnote 6).
22. Ibid., pp. 239–40.
23. Leighton, p. 234.
24. Titmuss, p. 195.
25. Ibid., p. 241.
26. That war termination is an especially difficult problem is illustrated by the fact, previously noted, that the Japanese leadership decided to surrender as early as March 1945 but was unable or unwilling to put this decision into effect before the atomic bombings in August of that year.
27. Titmuss, p. 423.
28. Ibid., p. 423.
29. Ibid., p. 423.
30. Leighton, p. 234.
31. Titmuss, p. 278.
32. Ibid., p. 96.
33. Ibid., p. 330.
34. Iklé, p. 58.
35. This can be accounted for by several factors, including fatalities, experience during evacuation period, military and industrial manpower requirements, further evacuation to other regions, lack of services, poor quality of surviving dwellings, and reluctance to live in quarters crowded to maximum theoretical occupancy levels.
36. Titmuss, pp. 296–297.
37. Ibid., p. 334.
38. Ibid., p. 334. "Excess" accidental deaths are those above the prewar norms in these age groups.
39. R.J. Hammon, *Food, Vol. I. History of the Second World War*, United Kingdom Civil Series, ed. W.K. Hancock (London: H.M. Stationery Office, 1957), p. 156.
40. Iklé, p. 151.
41. The U.S. Strategic Bombing Survey, Pacific Report No. 58 (Washington, D.C.: Government Printing Office, 1946–1947), p. 166.
42. Leighton, pp. 61, 71.
43. Ibid., p. 66.
44. Ibid., p. 245.
45. Ibid., p. 253.
46. Ibid., pp. 243–246.
47. Allnutt, pp. S–3 and S–4.
48. Allnutt, pp. S–3.

49. Thomas Stonier, *Nuclear Disaster* (Cleveland: World Publishing Co., 1963), p. 91.
50. This is borne out, for example, in studies of German politics and society after World War I, at the end of the Weimar Republic, and again at the close of World War II, as well as in studies of Russia during the period of consolidation of the Bolshevik Revolution between 1917 and 1920.
51. Leighton, pp. 67–68.
52. Ibid., p. 68.
53. Ibid., pp. 68–69.
54. Janis, p. 128.
55. Ibid., p. 129.
56. Leighton, pp. 248–49.
57. Titmuss, p. 150.
58. Ibid., p. 114.
59. Ibid., p. 114.
60. Fred C. Iklé, *The Social Impact of Bomb Destruction* (Norman: University of Oklahoma Press, 1958), p. 119.
61. Leighton, p. 67.
62. These calculations ignore the use of surviving schools and other public buildings to house survivors, which will alleviate housing pressures to some degree; however, many such facilities will be in use as aid stations, makeshift hospitals, relocation sites for private and government offices, and the like, reducing their availability for housing purposes.
63. C.M. Hoaland, C.V. Chester, and E.P. Wigner, *Survival of the Relocated Population of the U.S. After a Nuclear Attack* (Oak Ridge National Laboratory, ORNL–5401, June 1976).
64. Iklé, p. 90.
65. Ibid., p. 84.
66. Titmuss, p. 327.
67. Tuchman, p. 124.
68. Ibid., p. 124.
69. Ibid., p. 96.

8 MASSACHUSETTS
Regional Effects

In order to gain a better appreciation of the impact of economically oriented nuclear attacks, the effects of Attacks M–1, M–2, M–3, and M–4 (defined below) on Massachusetts will be examined in detail in this chapter. The examination is primarily of Massachusetts but also includes New England.

The full-scale attack, M–1, involves the use of seventeen 1 megaton (Mt) weapons on the Boston metropolitan region. This includes not only the Boston standard metropolitan statistical area (SMSA) but also the SMSAs of Lowell, Haverhill, and Lawrence as shown in Figure 8–1. In addition, in this attack, the Worcester and Leominster–Fitchburg SMSAs absorb three weapons, as does the Springfield–Holyoke–Chicopee SMSA. Massachusetts thus receives a total of twenty-three 1 megaton weapons. Attack M–1 uses four fewer weapons than the national attack A–1, which targets twenty-seven 1 megaton weapons on Massachusetts. New Bedford and Pittsfield are subject to attacks by 100 kiloton (Kt) weapons, although their effect will not be extensively analyzed.

The other attacks, M–2, M–3, M–4, contain twelve, seven, and three weapons respectively. They are shown in Figures 8–2, 8–3, and 8–4. In the text, the four attacks are referred to as the twenty-three-weapon, twelve-weapon, seven-weapon, and three-weapon attacks. It should be noted that Attacks M–2 through M–4 contain

Figure 8–1. Impact of Attack M–1 on Massachusetts. (SMSAs Attacked by 1-Megaton Weapons are Shown).

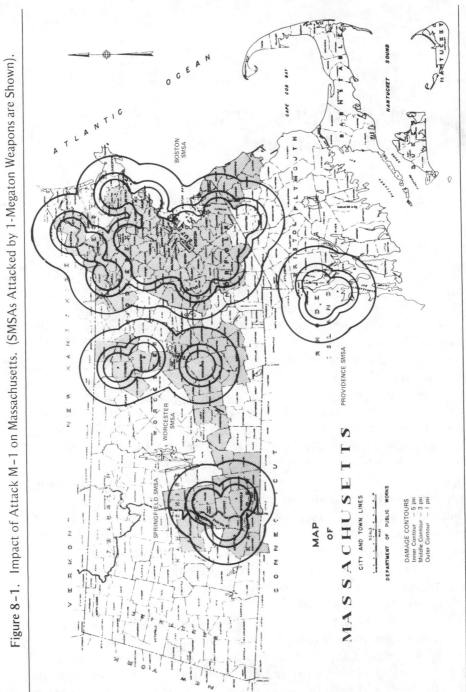

Source: Arthur Katz, *Economic and Social Consequences of Nuclear Attacks on the United States*, Committee on Banking, Housing, and Urban Affairs, U.S. Senate (Washington, D.C.: U.S. Government Printing Office 1979), p. 52.

Figure 8-2. Impact of Attack M-2 on Massachusetts. (SMSAs Attacked by 1-Megaton Weapons are Shown).

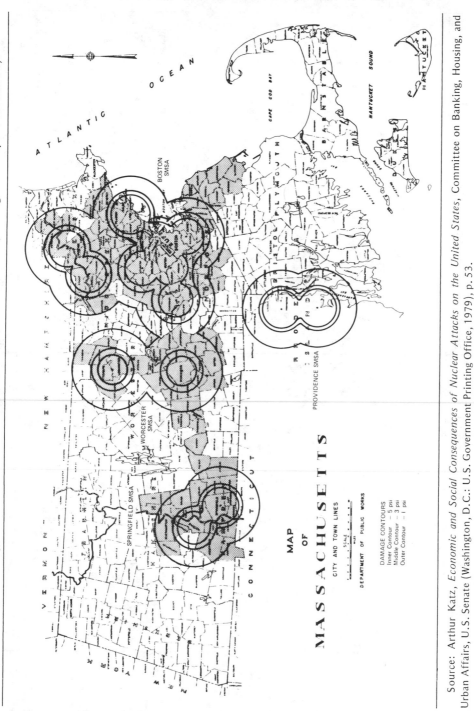

Source: Arthur Katz, *Economic and Social Consequences of Nuclear Attacks on the United States*, Committee on Banking, Housing, and Urban Affairs, U.S. Senate (Washington, D.C.: U.S. Government Printing Office, 1979), p. 53.

Figure 8–3.   Impact of Attack M–3 on Massachusetts.   (SMSAs Attacked by 1-Megaton Weapons are Shown).

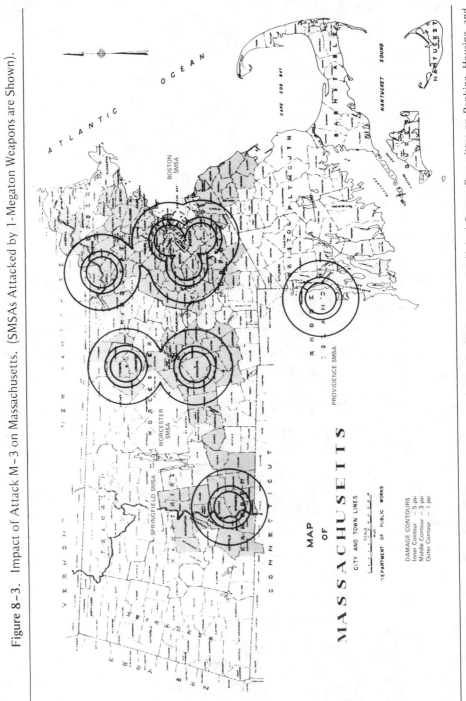

Source: Arthur Katz, *Economic and Social Consequences of Nuclear Attacks on the United States,* Committee on Banking, Housing, and Urban Affairs, U.S. Senate (Washington, D.C.: U.S. Government Printing Office, 1979), p. 54.

Figure 8–4. Impact of Attack M–4 on Massachusetts. (SMSAs Attacked by 1-Megaton Weapons are Shown).

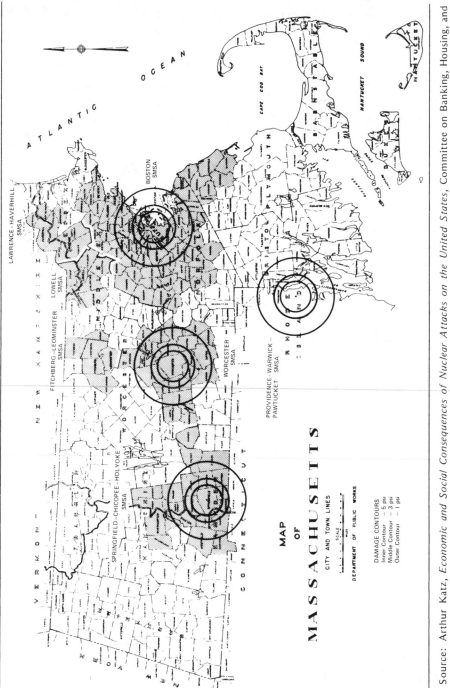

Source: Arthur Katz, *Economic and Social Consequences of Nuclear Attacks on the United States,* Committee on Banking, Housing, and Urban Affairs, U.S. Senate (Washington, D.C.: U.S. Government Printing Office, 1979), p. 55.

fewer weapons than what would be expected from the Massachusetts equivalents of A-2 through A-4—that is, M-4 uses three weapons instead of the five weapons expected from A-4; M-3 uses seven not the eleven in A-3; and M-2 uses twelve instead of the sixteen in A-2. The reason for this reduction was an attempt to look at a broader variation in the numbers of weapons in order to reveal impacts with a few weapons. For comparison, the manufacturing value added (MVA) and casualty impacts on Boston, Springfield, and Worcester standard economic areas (SEAs) are shown in Table 5-10. The discussion of the Massachusetts case, however, does essentially parallel the analysis of nationwide physical, economic, and social effects.

CASUALTIES

Table 8-1 shows the casualties produced by Attacks M-1 to M-4 on a statewide basis and for the cities of Boston and Springfield. The casualty estimates are again based on data from Hiroshima and Nagasaki.[1]

Even the smallest attack encompasses over half the state population within the disrupted areas—that is, the 1 psi contour. Approximately 600,000 people (10 percent of the population) are killed, and 900,000 (15 percent of the population) are injured. More than 50 percent of the population (3 million people) is within the 1 pound per square inch (psi) contour.

When Attack M-3 is considered, casualties are nearly 50 percent statewide and even higher in the two major cities. To provide a measure of the magnitude of the casualties, a single hypothetical 1 megaton weapon on Springfield generates more than twice the total number of U.S. deaths as the Vietnam war; instead of causing these fatalities over many years, they happen virtually instantaneously, the majority occurring within minutes or hours.

This case study raises one additional point about casualty estimates for attacks using several large yield or numerous small nuclear weapons. Besides the vastly increased potential for conflagration, physical damage, and radiation exposure from the overlapping of the blast and thermal impacts of these nuclear weapons, the distance needed to escape the affected areas will increase. Whereas only one or two miles were needed to escape from the damaged area of

Table 8-1. Massachusetts Casualties for Attacks A-1 through A-4 (*in thousands rounded to nearest 10,000*).

Locale and Scope of Attack	Killed	Injured	Percent of Population Within 1 psi Contour[a]
Statewide total			
M-4 (3 Mt)	600	900	55[a]
M-3 (7 Mt)	1,150	1,200	70
M-2 (12 Mt)	1,500	1,300	75
M-1 (23 Mt)	1,800	1,400	80
Boston			
M-4	350	650	75
M-3	900	900	95
M-2	1,200	1,000	100
M-1	1,400	950	100
Springfield			
M-4	130	130	75
M-3	130	130	75
M-2	160	160	85
M-1	200	210	100
M-1a[b]	290	150	100

a. Rounded to nearest 5 percent.

b. Assumes 75 percent killed and 25 percent injured within 5 psi contour because of multiple weapons detonations.

Source: Arthur Katz, *Economic and Social Consequences of Nuclear Attacks on the United States*, p. 57.

Hiroshima or Nagasaki, for the Boston area, in the larger attacks, an individual will be required to travel fifteen to twenty miles to reach lightly damaged areas and forty to fifty miles to reach undamaged areas. Conversely, no quick rescue will be possible because of fallout and radiation fears; thus, removal and treatment of the injured would be dangerously slow.

Fallout: An Added Dimension of Effects

In addition to the discussion of casualties from direct (blast, thermal, and radiation) effects, the consequences of nuclear fallout on casualty estimates have been analyzed and the implications for survival and recovery evaluated. Although the national attack data assumed only air bursts (maximizing destruction), it is not unreasonable to assume for argument's sake that a portion of the large quantity of weapons (many of which seem redundant) will be ground burst. The reduction in blast and thermal effects is compensated for by the disruptive and destructive results of fallout. These include increased casualties inside and outside the area of direct impact; denial of rescue service, survivor care (distribution of food and medical aid), and fire control in large portions of the region for a short period of time; and psychological impacts, such as fear produced by concern and confusion over the inability to predict consequences when the extent of individual exposure is either unclear or not, at least immediately, fatal. The importance of this psychological problem is discussed in Chapter 7.

Winter (Figure 8-5) and Summer (Figure 8-6) attacks for different Massachusetts cities were postulated to assess effects of different wind patterns. However, these estimates are based on idealized wind patterns; while they are indicative of possible problems, they do not represent definitive predictions. Table 8-2 gives the number of individuals within the 100 to 500 R (Roentgen), the 500 R or more, and 2,000 R or more contours for specific cities. The impact of individual 1 Mt ground bursts were examined for Boston, Worcester, Lawrence, Lowell, Springfield, and Fitchburg. Boston, Worster, and Springfield were examined for the summer.

From Table 8-2, it should be clear that for a single ground burst, hundreds of thousands, and in some cases up to 1 million, individuals fall within these contours. Moreover, the 500 R contour represents the lowest exposure at the outer edge of the area; the actual radiation exposure inside will reach several thousands of Roentgens (400 to 500 R, which is approximately equivalent to X- or gamma ray radiation doeses of 400 to 500 rems, is considered lethal to 50 percent of those exposed) and will enclose hundreds of thousands of people, as shown for the 2,000 R contour in Figure 8-7. Mitigating this factor is the shelter available, which will provide some type of radiation protection and reduce exposure.

We have assumed that the radiation exposure received is only 10 percent of the actual exposure in the area, so that 1,000 R general exposure would result in an actual exposure for individuals of 100 R. The protection factor (PF) of ten is standard for a basement

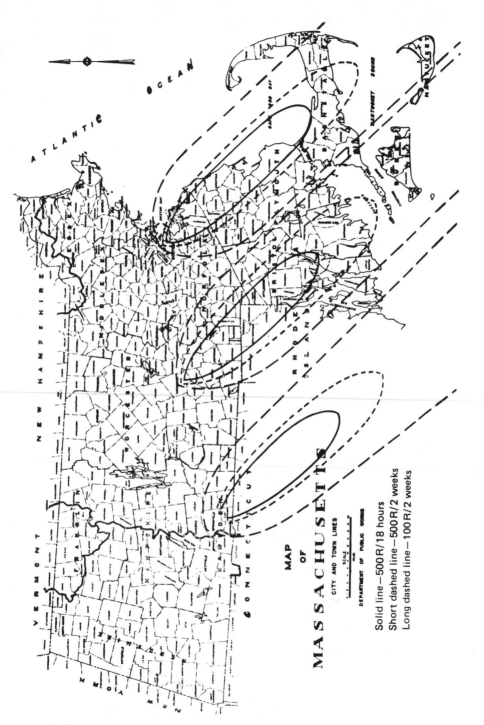

Figure 3. Fallout Patterns for a Winter Attack on Three Cities—Boston, Worcester, and Springfield.

MAP
OF
MASSACHUSETTS

CITY AND TOWN LINES

SCALE

DEPARTMENT OF PUBLIC WORKS

Solid line—500 R/18 hours
Short dashed line—500 R/2 weeks
Long dashed line—100 R/2 weeks

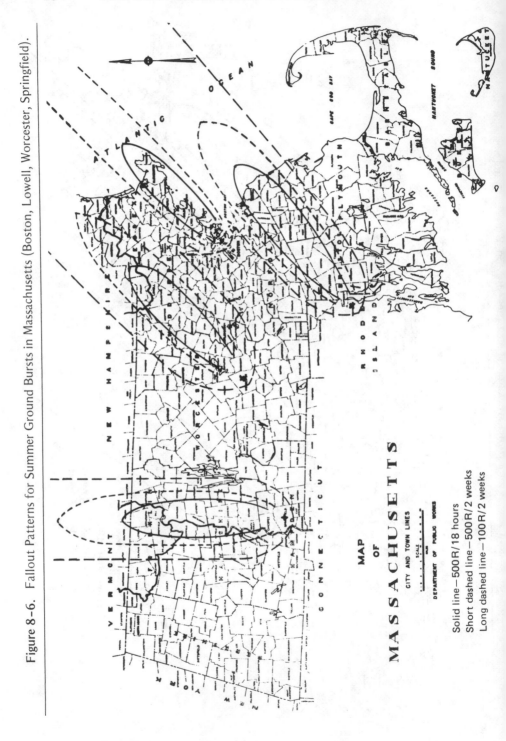

Figure 8-6. Fallout Patterns for Summer Ground Bursts in Massachusetts (Boston, Lowell, Worcester, Springfield).

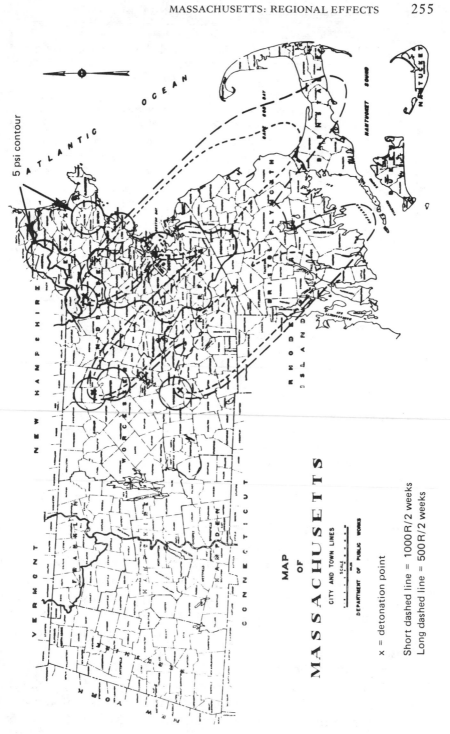

Figure 8-7. Fallout Patterns for Weapons Detonated on Four Cities—Boston, Lowell, Fitchberg, and Worcester.

Table 8-2. Exposed Population from Fallout in Massachusetts.[a]

	Winter Attack		
	Ground Burst Between 500–100 R Contours	Ground Burst 500 R Contour	Ground Burst 2,000 R Contour
Boston	150,000	700,000	400,000
Worcester[b]	150,000	475,000	225,000
Springfield[b]	150,000	50,000	
Fitchberg	625,000	700,000	400,000
Lawrence	425,000	425,000	
Lowell	1,400,000	1,050,000	900,000

	Summer Attack	
	Ground Burst Between 500–100 R Contours	Ground Burst 500 R Contour
Boston	400,000	550,000
Worcester[b]	400,000	600,000
Springfield[b]	225,000	250,000

a. Rounded to nearest 25,000

b. Only Massachusetts population.

Source: Based on Census Bureau, 1970 Census of Population, Department of Commerce (Washington, D.C.: Government Printing Office).

of a one or two family house. This seemed reasonable and, in fact, in some areas perhaps optimistic.[2]

To provide a measure of the real effects, two cases will be considered. The first is a set of scenarios where only one 1 Mt ground burst is used to attack Boston during a typical summer or winter day (Table 8-3). The calculated deaths and injuries combine blast and fallout effects. Because of the Boston wind patterns, the more densely populated western part of the metropolitan area is not affected and thus the total affected population (defined as those persons within the 100 R plus 1 psi contour) is somewhat smaller than that affected by the 1 Mt air burst. However, the killed and injured are similar to the air burst situation, and the affected land areas are

Table 8-3. Casualties for a 1 Megaton Attack on Boston (*with and without fallout*).

	Killed	Percent	Injured	Percent	1 psi + 100 R Contour	Percent
Winter						
1 Mt air burst	35	13	670	24	2,125	77
1 Mt ground burst	38	14	675	25	1,650	50[a]
Summer						
1 Mt ground burst	38	14	635	23	1,525	50[a]

a. Includes 1 Mt and 100 R contours.

much larger. Moreover, no cancer or long-term radiation effects were calculated; thus, additional deaths as well as land denial would be expected over time.

The second case describes a situation where several ground bursts might be used to enhance the Boston-directed attack. Ground bursts in Lowell, Boston, Fitchburg, and Worcester were used as an example. As can be seen in Figure 8-7, almost the whole of eastern Massachusetts is within the 500 R contour for a winter attack; a summer attack is less pervasive and effective. For the winter attack, almost 3 million people are in areas with more than 1,000 R of radiation, and 2 million are in areas of 2,000 R. If all those exposed within the 1000 R contour received the minimum exposure of 100 R (1,000 R divided by the protection factor of ten), the number of cancers produced over the population lifetime is potentially in excess of 50,000 to 150,000[3] —an increase of 10 to 30 percent. In addition, 100 rems (approximately 100 R) fall in the range of the predicted dose needed to double genetic defects. Actually the impact will be much greater, because 100 R is a minimum exposure. Perhaps 25 percent, or 750,000 people, will be exposed to 450 R, which, as noted above, produces a biological dose (rems) from which 50 percent of these individuals will die. Thus, the immediate casualties will include hundreds of thousands of deaths, and the long-term cancers will be in the tens of thousands.

The impact of a combined full-scale nuclear attack plus these ground bursts is shown in Table 8-4. The impacts for the four ground bursts (Lowell, Boston, Fitchburg, and Worcester) discussed above[4] have been examined as part of Attack A-1.

Table 8-4. Casualty and Mortality from Fallout for Casualty
Assumptions (*Massachusetts total population 5,639,000*).[a]

	Total	Immediately Injured	Initially Uninjured
Exposure to 100-200 R	450,000	225,000	225,000
Exposure to 200 R or more	1,525,000	600,000	925,000
	1,975,000	825,000	1,150,000
Total (injured and initially uninsured)			
Additional deaths		350,000	
Additional casualties[b]		1,050,000	
Total casualties (from direct effects and fallout)			
Deaths		2,200,000	
Surviving injured		2,200,000	
Total		4,400,000	

a. Rounded to nearest 25,000.
b. Initially uninjured by direct weapon effects (blast, thermal, radiation).

For a winter attack, the increased deaths would be on the order of
350,000, and the injured would increase by about 1 million. Significantly, more than 1 million of 1.4 million casualties were among
those portions of the population (both within and outside the
impact areas) that were previously predicted to have survived uninjured.

The consequences of a summer attack are somewhat different.
About 500,000 fewer people are affected by fallout. Southeast Massachusetts, as well as the Pittsfield area, will suffer a very high degree
of isolation caused by the vast damage and possible fallout in contig-
uous areas of New York, Rhode Island, and Connecticut.

The combination of direct effects and fallout will leave Massachusetts with approximately 2 million dead and more than 2 million
injured for a winter attack (100,000 less for a summer attack) out
of a population of 5.7 million. Fallout will make the most severely
affected areas uninhabitable for two weeks except by those persons
in fallout shelters, and of limited use for months. Moreover, rescue
and assistance to the injured will be impossible in the early postattack period. Using the nuclear attack pattern for the winter, east-

ern Massachusetts would be isolated by fallout. Accordingly, the sanctuaries for refugees that could have existed in southeastern Massachusetts (near Cape Cod) and mid–Massachusetts if only air bursts were used will be denied to both refugees and inhabitants. For a summer attack, northeastern and north central Massachusetts will be the areas potentially most affected. Other ground bursts in Albany (New York), Springfield, Hartford (Connecticut), and Providence (Rhode Island) could add to the disruption and isolation.

Therefore, it should be clear that a modest portion of a large-scale nuclear attack diverted to the production of fallout can have substantial effects. The fallout victim will require extended care, utilizing resources such as food, medical supplies, and health care personnel. This care will be complicated in the case of survivors suffering other types of injuries besides radiation exposure.

ECONOMIC IMPACTS

The Boston region is a service-oriented area, with federal and state government centers and insurance and consulting firms. Research, electronic, and high technology firms are located along Route 128 (now I–95), which circles the Boston metropolitan region. The majority of the service-related jobs are in the Boston core. Thus, even a 1 megaton attack on Boston is severe in terms of damage to the service and government sectors.

Specifically, in Attack M–4, the core of Boston would be destroyed and with it the governmental–medical–academic complex that is an important ingredient in the economic vitality of the region. Table 8–5 shows the level of destruction of MVA. The percentage of MVA destroyed in Attack M–4 is 30, 50, and 55 percent, respectively, for Boston, Springfield, and Worcester.

Attack M–4 encloses a substantial portion of the manufacturing capacity for these SMSAs within the 1 psi contour, to the level of approximately 65 percent or more. Combining all the destruction for Attack M–4, approximately 25 percent of the MVA of the entire state of Massachusetts is included within the 5 psi contour, and over 60 percent is within the 1 psi contour even for the smallest attack. Massachusetts would clearly be severely damaged.

Comparing Attack M–4 and the individual 1 megaton attacks to larger industrially oriented attacks, the level of assured destruction

Table 8-5. Massachusetts Manufacturing Capacity Subject to
Destruction (*percentages are of statewide or SMSA-wide totals*).

	MVA Within 5 psi (percent)	MVA Within 1 psi (percent)
Statewide destruction		
M-4	25	60
M-3	40	70
M-2	55	75
M-1	75	90
Boston		
M-4	30	65
M-3	50	95
M-2	70	100
M-1	90	100
Springfield		
M-4	50	75
M-3	50	75
M-2	65	95
M-1	80	100

Source: Arthur Katz, *The Economic and Social Impacts of Nuclear Attacks on the United States*, p. 56.

rises with larger attacks, but the total MVA in the affected areas out to the 1 psi contour is not dramatically altered. Attacks M-3, M-2, and M-1 produce major statewide damage, which reaches approximately 80 percent with Attack M-1. Using the PVANS formula (80 percent damage equals complete functional industrial destruction, see p. 94), all of Massachusetts, and not just the three major metropolitan areas, could come to a virtual economic standstill under Attack M-1. This may be an understatement of the problem, since New Bedford and Pittsfield are also expected to receive 100 kiloton blasts.

Attacks M-2 and M-3 also represent the virtual destruction of the Boston, Springfield, and Worcester SMSAs as functioning economic entities. Even at the level of damage of Attack M-4, and certainly in Attack M-3, nearly all the MVA in these urban centers are within the 1 psi contour.

The importance of the physical damage to the region between the 1 and 5 psi contours is that it causes disruption of basic urban functions such as sanitation, fire, and police, and perhaps sewage disposal and water supply. This disruption can create serious difficulties in utilizing both the areas between the 1 and 5 psi contours and inside the 5 psi contour.

A similar problem would arise with respect to fallout. Air detonations, of the type used here, produce minor radioactive fallout and thus less severe medical effects. However, fear generated by confusion in a postattack period may lead to the belief that fallout is not limited. Therefore, given the image of radioactivity, even the possibility of its existence, could strongly inhibit early utilization of economic facilities. This would further complicate recovery.

FOOD PRODUCTION

Under the scenarios examined for this book, Massachusetts would be a badly damaged area highly dependent on other regions for its food. The northeast region, including New England, New York, and New Jersey, produces only 15 percent of its food needs under normal circumstances. Stated differently, about 3 percent of the nation's calories are produced in the Northeast, while its population consumes 18 percent of the nation's calories.[5]

Therefore, the Northeast must receive approximately 85 percent of its foodstuffs from other parts of the country, largely from beyond the Mississippi River. For Massachusetts, grains come from the central states of Kansas and Nebraska, cattle products from the Southwest, and vegetables and small fruit (raisins, plums, etc.) from Florida, California, and Arizona.

The region, according to the Stanford Research Institute (SRI) study cited above (footnote 5), has food-processing capacity in excess of regional needs — 19.6 percent of national capacity versus 18.2 percent of national consumption. Yet only 5 to 10 percent of Massachusetts's food-processing capacity lies outside the 5 psi blast effects contour for the largest attacks. Most of the state's processing capacity would thus be lost in an attack the size of M–1.

The critical consideration for survivors in Massachusetts is therefore a functioning national distribution system. With some contamination and substantial destruction occurring throughout the heart of the production areas in a nuclear attack, a distribution system extending over 1,000 to 1,500 miles to Massachusetts will provide a questionable and uncertain lifeline. Thus, Massachusetts is likely to receive inadequate supplies from outside the region. This could lead to severe food shortages within weeks that would last for an extended period, depending on the effectiveness of reconstruction and decontamination procedures.

The resources available in Massachusetts and neighboring states to cope with this problem are, as noted, sparse. In the immediate postattack period and for several months thereafter, Massachusetts residents will have to rely heavily on stored supplies and local food production. Yet in terms of food storage, Massachusetts will not have substantial supplies. Because of the containerization revolution of the last decade, foodstuffs are no longer stored in large inventories at local warehouses. Most stores (especially supermarkets) have supplies on hand for only one to two days of normal demand. Moreover, approximately a week's supply is kept in Massachusetts warehouses. These warehouses are largely in the major urban areas, which would be heavily attacked. The expanding use of frozen foods may make some of these estimates too optimistic because of the potential loss of electricity. However, even if the warehouses remain undamaged, only about two weeks supply of food would exist for survivors in the state, assuming consumption is drastically reduced.

If warehouse food reserves are as inadequate as present stocks indicate, Massachusetts will be very dependent on its own production and that of other New England states. As Table 8–6 indicates, Massachusetts produces very little of its own requirements in a number of important food categories: meat (25 percent), noncitrus fruit (66 percent), vegetables (10 percent), milk (32 percent), potatoes (12 percent), and eggs (32 percent). Only corn, apples, and cranberries are produced in abundance. Fish is a major food resource available in quantities substantially above Massachusetts's own needs (200 percent). Milk, eggs, and potatoes are available from other New England states (Vermont, New Hampshire, and Maine, respectively). Although dairy and poultry farming are regular sources of food, they depend heavily on electrical equipment. Any disruption in fuel supply or electricity will impair dairy and poultry productivity.

Massachusetts food production will also be reduced by the direct and indirect effects of the assumed attacks. The only staples produced in significant amounts are fish and dairy products, the former an important source of food energy. Fishing centers such as Boston, Gloucester, and New Bedford will sustain direct damage to fishing

Table 8-6. Sources of Food Energy and Protein in Average U.S. Diet and Percentage of Total Massachusetts Consumption Produced in Massachusetts (*percent*).

	Food Energy Supplied[a]	Protein Supplied[b]	Total Massachusetts Consumption Produced in Massachusetts
Meat	19.9	41.2	25
Eggs	2.0	5.3	32
Dairy	11.6	23.1	32
Fats and oils	17.9	0.1	0-10
Citrus fruit	0.9	0.5	0
Other fruit	2.2	0.6	66
Potatoes	2.7	2.3	12
Vegetables	2.8	3.6	10
Beans-nuts	2.9	5.0	0
Flour and cereal	19.3	17.8	0
Sugar and sweet	17.1	0.0	10
Miscellaneous	0.7	0.5	10
Total	100.0	100.0	

a. USDA, 3,290 calories average daily consumption per person.

b. USDA, 100 grams protein average daily consumption per person.

Sources: Agricultural statistics, USDA, p. 560.

Arthur Katz, *Economic and Social Consequences of Nuclear Attacks on the United States*, p. 74.

fleets, equipment, and manpower in the larger attacks. In addition, the lack of electricity, the fear or presence of fallout contamination, the evacuation of survivors to rural areas, and general disorganization may eliminate as producing units many of those farms adjacent to the targeted areas. In Attack M-1 (the largest), over half the poultry and dairy farms in Massachusetts are within the 1 psi contour and thereby are exposed to effects of nearby detonations. Those that continue to operate will experience reductions in production levels from lack of supplies, fuel, and equipment. Any surpluses produced by these farms may be absorbed by hoarding or withheld from use for other reasons, such as the lack or uncertainty of compensation.[6] In Attacks M-3 and M-4 (the smallest), food production losses attributable to the direct effects of nuclear weapons will range from 5 to 20 percent of preattack levels, with additional reductions likely as a result of indirect effects. Even if attack-related deaths and population migration reduce state consumption by a substantial amount in relation to losses in warehouse food stocks, regional food production capacity, and imports from other regions, there still remains a prospect of serious local food shortages in the immediate postattack period. Food scarcity in Massachusetts may be prolonged, depending on how quickly the national processing and distribution system can be reconstructed, how much local farmland is abandoned or not worked, and whether the damage to the Massachusetts fishing industry can be repaired.

Figure 8-8 portrays the food value (energy) and protein available for different estimates of surviving population under three different food production scenarios.[7] The figure shows average calories and proteins available to the surviving Massachusetts population compared to normal requirements for moderate and light activity. Scenarios F-1, F-2, and F-3 represent optimistic, moderate, and pessimistic views of food availability following a nuclear attack.

The criteria for evaluating the adequacy of food supplies are the minimum amount of protein and food energy (calories) needed by an individual to survive and the minimum amount of protein and calories needed to work effectively in a postattack environment. For simple maintenance of life an average adult requires about 2000 calories per day. This is 60 percent of the present consumption for an average male.[8]

However, postattack survival and recovery activity is likely to require at least moderate, if not strenuous, physical work. To sustain moderate activity, the combined average requirement for adult males and females is about 2,700 calories or 80 percent of the present average U.S. energy intake. In terms of protein, 30 to 40 grams per day, or 30 to 40 percent of the current intake, is the estimated requirement.

An important relationship exists between calories and protein. When calorie intake is insufficient, two effects occur: (1) protein is used for energy rather than for its normal functions of growing, repairing tissue, or other biochemical functions; and (2) there may be inadequate energy at a cellular level to utilize the available protein effectively. Thus, protein requirements may be understated, and the

Figure 8–8. Postattack Calories and Protein Available in Massachusetts under Various Estimates of Surviving Population and Food Production.

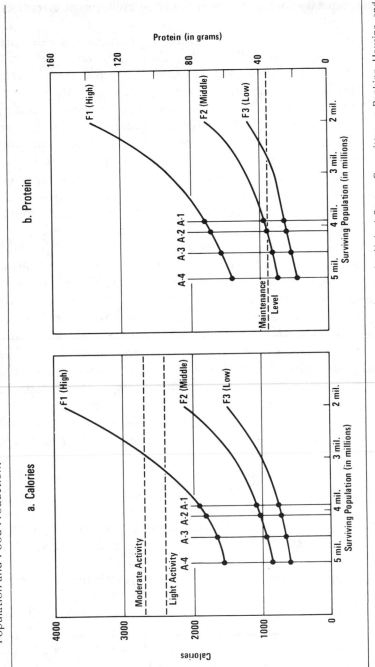

Source: Arthur Katz, *Economic and Social Consequences of Nuclear Attacks on the United States*, Committee on Banking, Housing, and Urban Affairs, U.S. Senate (Washington, D.C.: U.S. Government Printing Office, 1979), p. 75.

human capacity to use this essential food component effectively may be degraded.

Scenario F-1 assumes availability of potatoes and dairy products from other states, as well as high utilization of corn, fish, and other foodstuffs produced in Massachusetts. Scenario F-2 represents a reduction in the availability of fish products due to damage to Boston, New Bedford, and Gloucester and more pessimistic assumptions about the availability of other foods. Scenario F-3 assumes very little food assistance from outside Massachusetts (except for potatoes) and reductions on the order of 50 percent for instate production.

Scenario F-1 does not appear realistic under the attacks assumed in this book, because of the direct destruction of food production capabilities, the loss of petroleum supplies, and an unreliable electrical supply generating capacity, coupled with food distribution difficulties throughout Massachusetts and New England. In addition to the losses of ships and human resources in Boston and possibly in Gloucester and New Bedford, lack of fuel and damage to processing facilities will reduce fish supplies. Finally, if processing capacity (canning, freezing) is lost or reduced by limitations on fuel or electricity availability, fresh fish may have to be consumed quickly before they spoil. The extensive destruction in eastern Massachusetts caused in Attacks M-1 through M-3 would curtail transportation from the coast to refugees, evacuees, and inhabitants in the western part of the state, further reducing the utility of these fish catches.

Assuming that an average of 2,450 calories and 30 to 40 grams of protein per day are needed by adults for survival (light activity) during the early postattack period, then only under the most optimistic food scenario (F-1) and the lowest survival rates (Attacks M-1 and M-2) is there a possibility of a reasonable individual consumption level. For Attack M-4 (5 million surviving), even food scenario F-1 (just above 50 percent of present food resources from sources within and outside Massachusetts) is not likely to provide acceptable consumption levels.

High population survival under heavy attacks similar to M-1 and M-2 would, therefore, exacerbate, rather than reduce, food availability problems. Moreover, large surviving populations would require extensive evacuation, especially from eastern and urban Massachusetts. This spreading population would severely strain the food distribution system. If some ground detonations are used, fallout from a summer attack could further deny the use of Gloucester and probably isolate southeastern Massachusetts. In a winter attack, fallout would seal off the coast of Massachusetts and disrupt southeastern Massachusetts. At a minimum, the fish supply for western Massachusetts may be reduced significantly, while farmland would be lost for spring planting.

In sum, under the least damaging attacks, M–3 and M–4, (comparable though smaller than A–3 and A–4), Massachusetts may face marginal human survival conditions, even if the food distribution system continues to work well. If both local production and outside assistance fail, caloric and protein deficiencies would begin to affect some survivors—especially children and the elderly, injured, or sick—within a month of the attack. For those already seriously injured and weakened by radiation, the substantial decline in the general nutritional level would have very serious consequences for long-term survival. Because of their reliance on external food production and distribution, Connecticut, Rhode Island, New York, Massachusetts, and, to some degree, New Hampshire, Vermont, and Maine may experience serious deficiencies in food supplies within two to three months after a heavy attack, whether it occurs in summer or winter.

Thus viewed from a regional or national level the food production and distribution system will not function effectively for months, perhaps years. Aside from the significance of this damage for society, the most important lesson to be drawn is that food, though not directly attacked under these hypothetical scenarios, is severely affected by the indirect changes created in the rest of the social and economic systems of the nation.

ENERGY SUPPLY

In 1975, New England imported over 98 percent of its major energy resources from other parts of the United States or from abroad. In addition, New England is more dependent on petroleum than the rest of the United States, relying on imported petroleum for 80 percent of its needs, while the rest of the country needs only 40 percent.[9] New England therefore suffers far more than other regions from an interruption of petroleum supplies.

For this book, the surviving reserves of fuel oil in Massachusetts after Attacks M–1 and M–4 were calculated to determine the resources available in relation to fuel needs.[10] Given consumption pat-

Table 8-7.　Massachusetts Fuel Surviving Attacks M-1 and M-4 (*rounded to nearest 5 percent*).

Percent distillate oil surviving	
Attack M-1	10
Attack M-4	40
Percent residual oil surviving	
Attack M-1	45
Attack M-4	70
Percent gasoline surviving	
Attack M-1	10
Attack M-4	30

Source: Arthur Katz, *Economic and Social Consequences of Nuclear Attacks on the United States*, p. 83.

terns and the distribution of storage capacity in Massachusetts, analysis showed that about 60 percent of the distillate fuel lies within the 5 psi blast effects contour in Attack M-4 and is thus assumed destroyed. For Attack M-1, 90 percent of distillate fuel stored in the state is within the 5 psi contour and is destroyed. Table 8-7 shows the proportions of fuel inventories surviving by type of fuel.

Space Heating

An estimate was made of fuel remaining after Attacks M-1 and M-4 using surviving storage and the amount of heating oil available in home storage tanks. Projected total heating fuel on hand in the state is calculated by combining the amount of fuel in surviving storage and home fuel tanks. It is assumed that the latter are filled to two-thirds of an average capacity of 275 gallons—a standard size for home-heating fuel tanks. The estimated fuel required by month under normal consumption for dwelling units surviving Attacks M-1 and M-4 is compared with the fuel available after an attack in December or an attack in February. This comparison is shown in Table 8-8. From the standpoint of heating surviving dwellings, an attack early in the winter would have more adverse consequences than one later on, since the surviving fuel supply may not last through the remaining winter months.

Table 8-8. Massachusetts Heating Fuel Demand and Supply after Attacks M-1 and M-4 (*in millions of gallons; rounded to nearest 5 percent*).[a]

Attack Scenario	Dec.	Jan.	Feb.	Mar.
Attack M-1				
Fuel required	75	80	75	65
Fuel available after December attack	105			
Fuel available after February attack			90	
Attack M-4				
Fuel required	255	280	250	215
Fuel available after December attack	355			
Fuel available after February attack			300	

a. Uses 1977 data from *Weekly Statistical Bulletins*, American Petroleum Institute, for February and December.

Source: Arthur Katz, *Economic and Social Consequences of Nuclear Attacks on the United States*, p. 84.

For both attacks, M-1 and M-4, the fuel available does not vary significantly for the months examined. This implies a rather constant level of stored fuel during the winter months. However, the surviving storage capacity amounts to only a little more than one month's supply assuming normal consumption. If fuel is consumed more slowly, it might last for two months or more, depending on weather conditions. A severe winter could change this prognosis substantially. Certainly for the ill, injured, or elderly, reduced space heating may represent a serious hardship in the postattack period. Wherever possible, increasing the number of occupants in surviving dwelling units will aid in the conservation of limited stocks of heating fuel.

In the case of Attack M-1, such a large proportion of the population will be killed that despite a 90 percent loss of residual storage capacity, adequate supplies should remain available in the near term. Thus, unless an early winter attack is coupled with some unanticipated fuel supply and distribution problems, supplies would be sufficient for the small surviving population, but only for meeting home-heating needs and not for industrial or commercial requirements. If commercial or industrial distillate fuel demands were included, the actual supply picture presented would appear too optimistic.

About 25 percent of the dwelling units in Massachusetts are heated by gas-fired units and electric space heating, with the former predominating. Damage to natural gas production and distribution facilities or diversion of gas supplies at points along the pipeline is conceivable and would have a severe impact in New England, which is located at the end of the gas pipeline system.

An adequate distribution system is even more essential for western Massachusetts than for the eastern counties, since most surviving storage capacity is located in eastern Massachusetts. The western part of the state also consumes fuel at a faster rate than the eastern part, causing a differential in the rate of depletion of reserves. The western part of the state would be isolated in terms of access to fuel because eastern Massachusetts, Rhode Island, and Connecticut will sustain heavy losses of distillate storage capacity in both Attacks M–1 and M–4. The other route for supplying fuel to western Massachusetts is to use water transportation to Albany and tanker trucks into Massachusetts. However, Albany and other major cities (Buffalo, Syracuse, Rochester) will be destroyed in the economic attack, while New York City, and New Jersey with its refinery capacity, will also be heavily attacked. Supply from these areas will be uncertain at best. Vermont and New Hampshire fuel reserves are not sufficient to be helpful.

Eastern Massachusetts, specifically eastern Essex County, could be supplied by truck from Maine. Survivors in Middlesex and Worcester counties, however, are not likely to be helped in Attack M–1, except through evacuation to New Hampshire and Vermont. The counties in southeastern Massachusetts (Plymouth, Bristol, Barnstable, Dukes, and Nantucket) will have meager fuel reserves after Attack M–1, yet they would have at least one port open, either at Fall River or New Bedford. Newport County in Rhode Island might have surviving reserves, but not enough to export. Since almost half of all slightly damaged or undamaged housing units will be in southeastern Massachusetts, and almost half of the surviving fuel reserves will be in this area, distribution problems may be less serious than in western Massachusetts.

New England as a whole will experience long-term fuel shortages, since nearly all U.S. refinery capacity will be destroyed. As noted, the region derives approximately 80 percent of its energy from petroleum products, as opposed to over 40 percent for the nation as a whole (Figure 8–9), and is heavily dependent on imported petro-

Figure 8-9. Comparison of New England and U.S. Energy Resources, 1974.

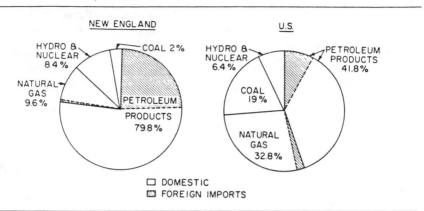

□ DOMESTIC
▨ FOREIGN IMPORTS

Source: Arthur Katz, *Economic and Social Consequences of Nuclear Attacks on the United States,* Committee on Banking, Housing, and Urban Affairs, U.S. Senate (Washington, D.C.: U.S. Government Printing Office, 1979), p. 85.

leum.[11] New England imports its fuel oil mainly from the Caribbean and the Middle East. Nearly 80 percent of the petroleum products used in New England is either refined abroad or produced domestically from foreign crude, as shown in Table 8-9. In a period of post-attack instability or unresolved war, there is a strong possibility that no foreign nation will want to risk shipping to the United States, especially to a highly damaged region, even if the port facilities are available.

Table 8-9 indicates the estimated surviving residual oil and gasoline capacity. The surviving capacity for stored residual, which is used in power plants and some manufacturing processes, might be substantial because of the more remote siting of power plants. The availability of gasoline is more difficult to judge. Initially a limited amount of gasoline should be available from surviving service stations as well as major storage capacity. This may be sufficient for several months, if transportation is government controlled and restricted to essential services, as one would expect. Civil and military authorities will presumably have the power to expropriate and control fuel and other essential commodities as well as prevent the growth of black marketeering.

Table 8-9.   Sources of New England Petroleum Products by Type in 1976.

	All Types	Residual	Distillate	Gasoline	Other Oil
Total consumption (millions of barrels)	409	122	119	129	40
Percent domestic (U.S. crude refined in the United States)	21	7	31	25	23
Percent indirect imports (foreign crude refined in the United States)	56	23	68	73	59
Percent direct imports (foreign crude refined abroad)	23	70	1	2	18

Source: Barbara Boynton, "New England Petroleum Product Imports—1976," (Boston: Federal Energy Administration, July 1977), p. 12.

Electricity

A considerable portion of the electric generating capacity in New England will survive the proposed nuclear attacks, as shown in Table 8-10. In Attacks M-1 and M-2, the operation of the NEPEX (New England Power Exchange) system, which coordinates and directs the operation of all major generating and transmission facilities in New England, may be affected by the destruction of its central control facility in West Springfield. Distribution of electric power in New England can be handled by four NEPEX subcenters, or if these subcenters are disrupted, the individual power plants would be able to coordinate operations through radio communication. Basic generating capacity and the system for coordinating this power grid are likely to be adequate in the postattack period.

Since oil, and especially imported oil, will be in short supply, in the first few months after an attack, the flexibility of the surviving generating capacity and the ability of fuel stocks to meet the demand for electricity is of importance. This is particularly true since most of New England's nonnuclear power plants are oil fired (Figure 8-10).

Table 8-10. Surviving Generating Capacity in Massachusetts and Connecticut.

	Percent Surviving		
	Massachusetts		Connecticut
Type of Plant	M-1	M-4	M-1
Fossil fuel	65	85	55
Nuclear fuel	100	100	100
Total[a]	67	87	67

a. Weighted average based on generating capacity in each category.

Source: Arthur Katz, *Economic and Social Consequences of Nuclear Attacks on the United States*, p. 86.

Figure 8-10. Sources of Fuel for Electric Generation in New England.

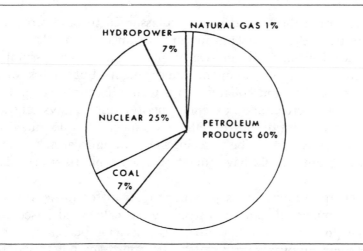

Source: "New England Hydroelectric Development Potential," Hydroelectric Facilities Workgroup, Energy Resource Development Task Force, New England Federal Regional Council, June 1976.

The data for damage caused by Attacks M-1 and M-4 indicate that with resupply of fuel, Massachusetts will have enough surviving electric generating capacity to satisfy surviving demand; without resupply, it will have sufficient fuel for several months, especially if consumption diminishes. Serious problems would result from unexpected breakdowns, excessive numbers of operating personnel killed or injured, and damage to the electrical distribution system.

The effectiveness of surviving electrical capacity after Attack M-1 in both Massachusetts and Connecticut was analyzed. Approximately 20 percent of the combined generating capacity in these two states is in nuclear plants. These plants could operate at full capacity for one year and for another year at diminishing capacity due to gradual fuel exhaustion. These reserves would be significant if fossil fuels are in short supply. Nuclear plants, if not specifically attacked, have a better chance of surviving and operating because of remote siting and their large internal fuel capacity. None of the nuclear plants in Massachusetts and Connecticut would be damaged by the hypothetical attack. New London is a likely target from a military point of view, however, because of its submarine pens and adjacent shipyards. Therefore, the loss of or damage to nuclear plants at nearby Montville and Millstone (1,230 megawatts total generating capacity) is possible in a combined attack on economic assets and strategic military facilities.

Plants within the 5 psi contour are assumed to be destroyed, and those outside the 5 psi contour are assumed to be damaged but repairable. This may be an overly pessimistic set of assumptions, especially for heavy containment nuclear plants, but the loss of transmission capability and collateral injury to adjacent areas may make the plant ineffective for an extended period despite physical survival. Under this assumption nearly half of Connecticut's nonnuclear generating capacity would be lost in the economic attack. Surviving fossil fuel plants would have fuel stocks available for thirty days of operation.

The energy requirements per month for different demands (residential, commercial, and industrial) were calculated based on the surviving portions of each sector. The surviving percentage of commercial demand was considered to be approximately equal to the residential demand. Table 8-11 shows the four consumption scenarios that were examined: (1) full normal energy use by surviving residential, commercial, and industrial facilities; (2) half normal

Table 8-11. Electrical Capacity Available in Massachusetts after Attacks M-1 and M-4 Under Various Demand Conditions.

Demand Scenario	Capacity after Attack M-1	Capacity after Attack M-4
1	12 months	3 months plus (25 percent)[a]
2	12 months	8 months plus (45 percent)
3	12 months	5 months plus (25 percent)
4	12 months	3 months plus (25 percent)

a. Percent of requirements satisfied by nuclear power at 60 percent capacity through twelve months.

Source: Arthur Katz, *Economic and Social Consequences of Nuclear Attacks on the United States*, p. 88.

use; (3) half normal use for residential and commercial facilities only, with full industrial consumption; and (4) half normal use for residential and commercial, but double for industrial consumption for economic recovery purposes. Even under the most demanding assumptions (1 and 4), Massachusetts will have three months of electric power at full capacity after Attack M-4 and a twelve months' supply at full capacity after Attack M-1. For Attack M-4, even after full electrical generating capacity is lost (due to exhaustion of fossil fuels), in Scenarios (1) and (4), 25 percent of the capacity is available through the first year following the attack; this is attributable to nuclear plants. Connecticut, if its extensive nuclear power capability is undamaged, will have approximately a one year's operating capability under all assumptions except in Scenario (4) for Attack M-1.

Combining Massachusetts's and Connecticut's surviving capacity after Attack M-1 provides more than six months of electric power for the two states (Table 8-12). Generating facilities in Vermont, New Hampshire, and Maine are undamaged. These states should be in a favorable position during the first six postattack months, barring major plant breakdowns; more than 40 percent of their combined capacity is nuclear. Rhode Island is in the most vulnerable position, but could draw from nearby undamaged capacity in Massachusetts and Connecticut. Therefore, only an inability to obtain fossil fuel within months of the attack and nuclear fuel in the long term (more than one year) should create serious generating problems for New England. However, this conclusion is predicated on the assumption that the plants operate well during this period—not a trivial matter.

Table 8-12. Electrical Capacity Available in Massachusetts and Connecticut after Attack M-1 Under Various Demand Conditions.

Demand Scenario	Capacity after Attack M-1
1	11 months plus (70 percent)[a]
2	12 months
3	12 months
4	7 months plus (60 percent)

a. Percent of requirements satisfied by nuclear power at 60 percent capacity through twelve months.

Source: Arthur Katz, *Economic and Social Consequences of Nuclear Attacks on the United States*, p. 88.

Even in peacetime, nuclear and fossil fuel power plants experience frequent malfunctions in operation, in addition to normal shutdowns for maintenance. For example, individual nuclear plants vary in operating performance. Experience at the two Massachusetts plants has been that one performs near the 60 percent average capacity for all nuclear plants while the other, larger, one has performed below average. Therefore, the actual generation of electrical supply for Massachusetts will depend on adequate maintenance, skilled workers, and the availability of spare parts. Spare parts may be a particular problem since the turbine and other related supplier industries will be destroyed or badly damaged. Competition among various economic sectors and regions for spare or replacement parts will be great. The Northeast may be viewed as a low priority area because of the extent of damage. Parts not available on site might not be accessible for months or even years.

In Attacks M-1 and M-2, the effectiveness of the electrical distribution system may come into question. This system depends heavily on the survival of transmission lines. Most surviving generating capacity available to Massachusetts will be in the southeastern portion of the state, in southeastern Connecticut, and in southern Vermont, New Hampshire, and Maine. Although some essential transmission lines connecting surviving plants and undamaged areas are well out of the regions of severe destruction, many of the key transmission lines would pass through devastated regions such as Worcester, Springfield, Holyoke, Chicopee, Hartford, Providence, and Bridgeport. This becomes another element of uncertainty.

To summarize, direct damage from Attacks M-1 and M-4 does not appear to be the critical element in determining the availability of electric power unless the plants themselves are specifically targeted. Plant reliability and the supply of skilled personnel and replacement parts appear more crucial for assuring power plant availability, with fuel supply becoming a severe problem six months after the attack.

In particular, the well-designed nuclear attacks described above will create such widespread damage and disruption in Massachusetts and New England that while some of the prerequisites may exist for maintaining the surviving population in the short run, the availability of expanding energy supplies for the midterm recovery period is very uncertain. On a national level New England draws attention to the fact that the severe supply curtailments caused by destruction or disruption of parts of the major energy resources systems, such as petroleum refining and pipeline transportation, are amplified by the complexity of actually running power plants, locally distributing power, or assuring residential heating supplies are available. A well-integrated national energy system requires more than that physical resources be in place, it demands sufficient skilled human resources and a management strategy that integrates human survival and economic recovery needs. For the national attacks discussed here all these elements are unlikely to be available for effective early national recovery.

The discussion of electricity and energy supplies illustrates a further important general observation. It points up the difficulties of making confident predictions about the availability of key economic and industrial resources (e.g., electricity) when they are themselves highly dependent upon the accessibility of other material or human capabilities (e.g., skilled power plant personnel). The complex and subtle interdependencies among different economic and social elements in technologically advanced societies need to be acknowledged even if uncertainties prevent unambiguous conclusions. This becomes a particularly important cautionary note when we attempt to describe the effects of traumatic human events such as nuclear war in terms of narrow physical indicators such as surviving power plant capacity.[12]

MEDICAL CARE

The medical care problems of Massachusetts would mirror those found on the national level following nuclear attacks. Table 8-13 shows the very large medical consequences even for a small attack such as M-4. Out of approximately 11,000 doctors in Massachusetts, more than 40 percent are within the 5 psi contour for Attack M-4, and approximately 70 percent are within the 1 psi contour. Conservatively, about 4,500 (40 percent) of the doctors in Massachusetts are killed, injured, or incapacitated in this smallest attack. When compared to the projection of approximately 900,000 to 1.1 million injured, the ratio of injured to available doctors ranges between 135 and 165 to 1.[13] If all the 10,000 doctors in the neighboring New England states were pressed into service, the ratio would be almost 60 to 1 (see Table 8-14). However, very few of these additional doctors will be available, given the extensive damage in the northeast area.

The larger attacks (M-1 to M-3) increase the number of deaths faster than the number of injured. Despite this, the ratio of doctors to injured increases by a factor of ten (1,000 to 1) because doctors tend to be concentrated more heavily in urban areas and therefore, as a group, will suffer proportionally more casualties. Nurses and paramedical personnel are also clustered in the same urban areas with hospitals and doctors. Thus, of the nearly 30,000 nurses in Massachusetts, the percentage of killed and injured would be similar to that for doctors. About 17,000 nurses should be available, bringing the ratio of medical personnel to injured down to about 40 or 45 to 1 for the smallest attack, M-4. Military and private disaster teams still functioning will also be severely taxed, because of two factors. The strategy of military forward medical units, as previously discussed, is to deal with the traumatic effects quickly and send casualties back to support medical units. No support units will exist in any substantial numbers to deal with the overwhelming numbers of casualties. Also in drastically short supply, as previously noted, will be the specialized personnel and facilities needed to treat the large numbers of burn and radiation exposure victims. As geneticist Dr. James Neel, formerly Director of Field Studies for the Atomic Bomb Casualty Commission, reported to the Senate Foreign Relations Committee: "The major medical center with which I am associated

Table 8-13. Vulnerability of Massachusetts Hospital Beds and Doctors.

Statewide Totals	Hospital Beds (51,000)[a]				Doctors (11,200)[b]			
	Within 5 psi Contour		Within 1 psi Contour		Within 5 psi Contour		Within 1 psi Contour	
	Number	Percent[c]	Number	Percent[c]	Number	Percent[c]	Number	Percent[c]
Massachusetts:								
Attack M-4	15,000	30	23,000	45	4,700	40	7,800	70
Attack M-1	30,000	60	45,000	90	8,900	80	10,100	95
Boston: Attack M-4	10,200	20	17,000	35	4,000	40	6,500	60

a. American Hospital Association Guide to the Health Care Field, 1975 Edition (Chicago, Ill.: American Hospital Association, 1975), pp. 111–117.

b. Tri-state Regional Medical Program "A Report on Physician Manpower in the Tri-state Region," (Boston, Mass.: Medical Care and Education Foundation, Inc., 1970).

c. Rounded to nearest 5 percent.

Sources: Arthur Katz, Economic and Social Consequences of Nuclear Attacks on the United States, p. 94.

Table 8-14. Medical Resources in States Adjoining Massachusetts.

	Physicians[a]	Dentists[a]	Nurses[a]	Hospitals[b]		Hospital Beds[b]	
				Total	Short Term	Total	Short Term
Connecticut	5,853	1,772	15,438	68	40	21,200	10,800
Rhode Island	1,549	418	3,073	22	13	7,900	3,500
New Hampshire	1,060	313	3,521	36	30	6,500	3,300
Vermont	877	181	1,836	21	17	4,200	2,200
Maine	1,304	356	4,051	52	45	8,000	4,400
New York	43,539	12,372	74,280	415	329	175,200	84,800

Sources: a. Arthur Katz, *Economic and Social Consequences of Nuclear Attacks on the United States*, p. 95.

b. U.S. Bureau of the Census, *Statistical Abstract of the United States: 1975*, (Washington, D.C.: U.S. Department of Commerce, 1975), p. 80.

at the University of Michigan has a special burn unit which receives referrals from all over the State; it can handle exactly 10 acute patients at a time."[14]

The hospital beds in Massachusetts totaled about 50,000; of these, about 26,000 are short-term beds. Most of the others are psychiatric beds. Almost 25,000 of the 50,000 beds are within the 1 psi contour even for the lightest attack, M–4, and about 15,000 beds are inside the 5 psi contour, where damage will be very severe. Assuming only these 15,000 beds are eliminated, 35,000 beds remain for 1 million injured people or one hospital bed for about thirty injured. These calculations ignore the fact that many hospital beds will be occupied before an attack.

Even if all the approximately 50,000 beds in the rest of New England were available, the ratio is still one bed for about ten injured. Should half of the injured not require any significant hospital treatment and assuming a low 50 percent preattack occupancy rate, the ratio of ten to one obtains.[15]

Only by spreading the casualties over a very large section of the Northeast could the problem be made tractable.[16] Moving the seriously injured to hospitals in undamaged areas in Vermont, Maine, and New Hampshire would require very rapid mobilization of organizational capabilities, large transportation resources, and paramedical or volunteer personnel. If military units and other resources can be diverted for this purpose, such massive medical evacuation, combined with the use of existing packaged disaster hospitals and military field hospitals (if they are available), may reduce some of the enormous medical care problems. At the same time, available hospital beds are not an absolute limitation on the provision of emergency and long-term medical care. The less seriously injured can, at least for short periods, be retained in the corridors of surviving hospitals or in adjacent structures. School infirmaries, clinics, and similar facilities will also mitigate to some degree the effect of the damage done to primary hospital centers.

Nevertheless, hospitals and other medical facilities are geared to the average demand for medical services, not to catastrophic conditions. Only a limited number of operating theaters and other specialized facilities will be available. For example, only three hospitals in Massachusetts have special burn care units.[17] All three are in Boston, within the most severely damaged area even under Attack M–4, the lightest attack postulated. Similarly, it is the large community of university-associated hospitals that offer the widest range of medical services and have the most specialized personnel. These, too, tend to be in urban centers and are therefore very vulnerable to destruction. Finally, the task of providing emergency and long-term medical care will compete for scarce resources (fuel, emergency generators, food, etc.) with other essential postattack requirements. The very severe decrease in medical facilities following even a light attack will mean agonizing decisions for those allocating surviving resources and a long-term burden on recovery efforts. It will also mean additional fatalities among those who might otherwise have survived their injuries or preexisting maladies if the routinely accessible preattack medical care had not been drastically reduced.

These findings are consistent with the destruction experienced in World War II as recorded by Dr. Iklé:

> Even if there were no cases of radiation sickness, the medical resources remaining after a nuclear attack would not permit adequate treatment of all nonfatal casualties. Medical facilities and personnel, which are largely concentrated in central areas of cities, are themselves subject to attack. In Nagasaki, over 80 percent of the hospital beds were completely destroyed, and the mortality of the patients and medical staff who were in the hospitals at the time of the explosion was about 75 to 80 percent. Hamburg lost 14,000, or 66 percent, of its 21,105 hospital beds during the big raids. In comparison, only 45 percent of Hamburg's dwellings were destroyed in these raids.[18]

Most of the foregoing analysis of the availability of medical care facilities is based on the effects of a light attack, M–4. As postulated attacks grow in destructive force, the already serious difficulties grow worse, as shown in Table 8–13.

Since many of the casualties will suffer from burns, blast injuries, and radiation exposure, they will require the skills of plastic surgeons, dermatologists, orthopedic surgeons, and opthalmologists. A critical need will exist for those in the fields of preventive medicine and public health. Though the numbers of physicians in various specialties would be inadequate even if all survived, it is apparent from Table 8–15 that the potential losses in these categories (and in the whole medical community) are substantial.

At the lowest level attack (M–4), 40 to 60 percent of these specialized physicians are within the 5 psi contour, with about 60 percent or more inside the 1 psi limit. The geographic distribution of these specialists is similar to that of other doctors. With larger attacks, the losses become larger, as shown in Table 8–15. Only

Table 8-15. Impact of Attacks M-1 and M-4 on Massachusetts Medical Specialists.

| | | Percent[a] | | |
| | | Percent[a] Within Metropolitan Areas | Attack M-4 | Attack M-1 |
	Total			
All specialties	8,127	90	40	75
Cardiovascular disease	93	95	50	80
Dermatology	111	95	45	80
Gastroenterology	38	100	65	90
General surgery	801	85	65	75
Internal medicine	1,187	90	45	80
Neurological surgery	65	100	60	90
Neurology	95	100	55	85
Obstetrics-gynecology	446	95	35	75
Ophthalmology	230	95	40	80
Orthopedic surgery	241	95	40	75
Plastic surgery	29	95	50	85
General preventive medicine	25	95	40	90
Public health	25	95	50	70
Radiology	284	95	40	75

a. Rounded to nearest 5 percent.

Sources: Medical Care and Education Foundation, Inc., "A Report on Physicians Manpower in the Tri-state Region" (1970).

Arthur Katz, *Economic and Social Consequences of Nuclear Attacks on the United States*, p. 97.

about twenty dermatologists (20 percent), two hundred surgeons (25 percent), four plastic surgeons (15 percent), sixty orthopedic surgeons (25 percent), fifty opthalmologists (20 percent), three preventive medicine physicians (10 percent), and eight public health physicians (30 percent) would be outside the 5 psi contours for Attack M-1. Of the categories of medical specialists analyzed under Attack M-1, only one category, public health, had more than 25 percent of its personnel outside the 5 psi damage contour.

Beyond forcing physicians to be extremely selective in choosing the patients they will treat, the losses of medical facilities and supplies will make treatment superficial. As noted above, many survivors in or beyond target areas will be people who depend on drugs and special treatment. In Massachusetts, sufferers from chronic diseases such as diabetes (100,000), heart disease (170,000)[19] and high blood pressure (200,000)[20] will suffer from reduced care.

Massachusetts will also face the national problem of limited medical supplies due to the destruction of the drug industry. As in Hiroshima, the medical supplies, facilities, and personnel will initially be inadequate to meet demand. Unlike Hiroshima and Nagasaki, however, no massive and rapid influx of personnel and supplies can be expected from the outside because of the extent and magnitude of the damage experienced in these economic attacks.

Medical Recovery

The long-term adequacy of medical care is closely tied to teaching and research facilities. Boston contains a complex of medical institutions (e.g., Massachusetts General Hospital and Massachusetts Eye and Ear Infirmary) that represents a significant medical resource. Tied to these institutions is a complex of medical schools (Harvard, Tufts, Boston University), as well as the Harvard School of Public Health. The destruction of these valuable teaching and research resources will be a severe long-term loss. To restore these complex and vital resources will be difficult and may prove impossible in the case of larger economic attacks if the demand for basic health and survivor care is as significant and overwhelming as predicted in both the short- and long-term postattack periods. Not only will a substantial portion of the medical personnel be killed or seriously injured, but a significant proportion of the basic institutions required for replacing these losses will be gone. The impact on various types of medical specialization illustrates the problem most dramatically. Many specialists require four years of training beyond medical school. With many teaching facilities, particularly major university or university-affiliated hospitals, destroyed and a large portion of instructors and practicing specialists killed, both an immediate and, possibly more critical, and medium- and long-term shortage of these vital skills will ensue.

HIGHER EDUCATION

Massachusetts reflects similar problems found in educational effects at a national level, but it is an extreme case in many ways, since it has a unique concentration of academic and professional communities. There is a large concentration of students, professors, and professionals in the Boston metropolitan area and also, to a lesser degree, in the Springfield area, at a large number of academic institutions known for their quality. Attracted to these institutions and interacting with them are high technology industries and a large class of professionals employed in consulting firms.

What might be called a medical–academic complex has made the Boston metropolitan area a fertile place for innovation and research. It has also become an important training ground for many professionals in both the medical and the technological communities. Substantial destruction of physical plants and human resources would have wide ramifications for long-term social and economic recovery well beyond the borders of Massachusetts. Moreover, those surviving components of the complex may have their energies focused for very different purposes and thus diminish their contribution in the area of sophisticated research and development.

The vulnerability of the academic complex to nuclear attack is evident from Table 8–16. Approximately 45 percent of the academic institutions (both two- and four-year), 65 percent of the professional and graduate student population, and 50 percent of the undergraduate students are within the 5 psi damage contour for Attack M–4. This increases to 75 percent of the institutions and nearly 90 percent of the graduates for Attack M–1. Even the smallest attack will seriously, perhaps irreparably, degrade the higher education system in Massachusetts.

PERSPECTIVE

Because of the high concentration of urban targets, the destruction after a nuclear attack on Massachusetts (and indeed, on the entire Northeast) will be devastating. Moreover, the Northeast again serves as an illustration of the problems faced by a resource-poor region, a region literally at "the end of the line" for food and energy

Table 8-16. Exposure of Massachusetts Students to Attacks M-1 and M-4.

	Undergraduates (248,986)				Professional–Graduate (59,880)			
	Within 5 psi		Between 5 and 1 psi		Within 5 psi		Between 5 and 1 psi	
	Number[a]	Percent[b]	Number	Percent	Number	Percent	Number	Percent
Attack M–4	119,000	20	47,000	30	39,000	65	10,000	15
Attack M–1	181,000	75	38,000	15	52,000	90	7,000	10

a. Rounded to nearest 1,000.

b. Rounded to nearest 5 percent.

Source: Arthur Katz, *Economic and Social Consequences of Nuclear Attacks on the United States*, p. 102.

resources. The combination of economic destruction, casualties, resource deprivation, and physical and psychological isolation, suggests that an area like the urban Northeast might be "written off"; in short, given up for dead. On the other hand, through evacuation and permanent population migration, the area may write itself off, relegating itself to a low-priority status for recovery assistance. In this scenario, an area known for extraordinary medical, educational, and high technology resources would be transformed into a virtual wasteland, and its future would be bleak in terms of its economic vitality and prospects for receiving postattack support.

NOTES TO CHAPTER 8

1. The estimates are conservative for multiple weapon attacks. Hiroshima and Nagasaki were small individual bombs (12.5 to 22 Kt). The multiple weapon attack presents new problems. Total casualties within the 5 psi contour could easily reach nearly 100 percent, with 75 percent killed.

2. Within 5 psi, many buildings with survivors (most of whom would be injured) will be badly damaged, thus affording less protection than one might expect. Within the 3 to 5 psi contours, varying damage will occur, but since this area is suburban–rural, where one to two family houses should predominate, the assumption appears reasonable. However, outside the 1 psi areas this factor may underestimate protection.

3. Because of age distributions the actual impact may be less.

4. In order to compute casualties and mortality from radiation level, a number of assumptions have been made. First, those exposed to less than 200 R will survive; second, 50 percent of the injured exposed to 200 R or more within 5 psi will die (within 1 to 5 psi contours, 20 percent mortality will occur); and finally, those initially uninjured (those escaping injury from the initial effects of blast, thermal, and radiation effects) will have only 10 percent mortality for exposure over 200 R. Although a dose of 200 R is not considered the Lethal Dose (LD50), at which 50 percent die, over half of those within these contours will experience dose levels at or above 450 R. Moreover, most of the injured will be severely hurt; thus, the impact of exposures to 200 R and above will place them in serious jeopardy from infection and breakdown of the hematological system.

5. Stephen L. Brown and Ulrich F. Pilz, *U.S. Agriculture: Potential Vulnerabilities* Contract No. DAHC–20–67–0116, OCD Work Unit 35335A (Menlo Park, California: Stanford Research Institute, January 1969), p. 60.

6. A recent study for the Defense Civil Preparedness Agency by the Oak Ridge National Laboratory (ORNL) suggests the use of federal promissory notes to pay for foodstuffs, noting that "it is unlikely that sufficient federal law enforcement or military personnel will be available to confiscate food in face of widespread opposition by local authorities. See C. Haaland, C. Chester, and E. Wigner, *Survival of the Relocated Population of the U.S. After a Nuclear Attack* (Oak Ridge, Tennessee: Oak Ridge National Laboratory, March 1976), p. 161.

7. For the average american diet food value is 3,290 calories per day per person, while protein utilization is 100 grams per day per person. U.S. Department of Agriculture, *Agricultural Statistics*, (Washington, D.C.: Government Printing Office, 1974), pp. 559–60.

8. Joint Food and Agricultural Organization/World Health Organization Ad Hoc Expert Committee, *Energy and Protein Requirements (1973) Report*, World Health Organization Technical Report Series, No. 522. (Geneva, World Health Organization, 1973).

9. J.P. Brainard, J.S. Munson, and P.F. Palmedo. *The Energy Situation in New England* (Upton, New York: National Center for Analysis of Energy Systems, BNL 50580, November 1976).

10. The approximate number of housing units using oil, gas, and electricity for heat was established after dividing the state into the western and eastern sections to account for differences in space heating. The eastern part of the state, east of Worcester County, contains about 1.45 million dwelling units, while the western part of the state has some 450,000 units. The number of housing units within the 3 psi blast effects contour—the limit for severe damage to housing—was then calculated, assuming that most residential units within the 3 psi contour would be uninhabitable because of direct damage, fallout, or loss of vital services such as water and gas. These units were excluded from calculation of postattack consumption of energy reserves. (If the 5 psi blast effects contour is used as the limit for damage, instead of the 3 psi contour, the number of housing units severely damaged changes by less than 100,000 units or 10 percent of the total. In addition, vulnerable frame houses are more common in the suburban areas within the 3 psi blast effects contour, so that lower blast pressures would achieve damage equal to that inflicted on the multiunit brick structures found in greater numbers within the 5 psi blast effects contour.)

    Space heating was assumed to require 1.2 times as much fuel in western Massachusetts as in the eastern portion of the state (based on degree day information, *Yankee Oilman*, March 1971, p. 18). In eastern Massachusetts, a dwelling unit is estimated to use an annual average of about 1,100 gallons of fuel. To obtain a truer picture of fuel use, the percentage of total consumption for various months was calculated. The winter months account for a significant percentage of the total amount of fuel consumed each year. Using the average annual consumption per dwelling unit, 1,100 gallons, the number of gallons of fuel oil consumed in the eastern and western sections of the state for the months of December through March was estimated. Fuel use for home heating was then calculated by month for both western and eastern parts of the state.

Next, the storage capacity for various types of fuel for all New England states was examined by percentage per state. Massachusetts has 28 percent of the distillate storage capacity in New England (see J. F. Maglio and S.K. Reskin, *New England Fuel Storage Capacity* [New England Regional Commission, MIT-NEEMIS-76-012TR, November 1976]). Distillate fuel stored in Massachusetts was estimated to be 125 million gallons in February 1977 and 260 million gallons in December 1977 based on the average of four *Weekly Statistical Bulletins* from the American Petroleum Institute for February and December 1977.

11. New England Regional Commission, *New England Energy Management Information System*, September 1976, pp. 6–7.

12. For a lengthier analysis of the relationship of surviving resources to the short-term and long-term survival of the population, see Sidney G. Winter, Jr., *Economic Viability after Thermonuclear War: The Limits of Feasible Production*, RAND Memorandum RM-3436-PR (Santa Monica, Calif.: The RAND Corporation, September 1963).

13. The 11,000 physicians may overstate the actual numbers available since it includes everyone (practicing or not) who holds a medical degree. Estimates based on Medical Care and Education Foundation, Inc., "A Report on Physician Manpower in the Tri-State Region" (Boston, Massachusetts, 1970).

14. Testimony of Dr. James V. Neel, in *Effects of Limited Nuclear Warfare*, Hearings before the Subcommittee on Arms Control, International Organizations and Security Agreements, Committee on Foreign Relations, U.S. Senate, 94th Cong., 1st sess., September 18, 1975 (Washington, D.C.: Government Printing Office, 1976), p. 12.

15. The actual rate of occupancy is 75 percent; moreover, hospital care would be complicated by outpatients who require hospital facilities.

16. American Hospital Association, "Hospital Statistics" (Chicago, Ill., 1976).

17. American Hospital Association, *American Hospital Association Guide to the Health Care Field, 1975 Edition.* (Chicago, Ill.: American Hospital Association, 1975), pp. 111–117.

18. Fred C. Iklé, *The Social Impact of Bomb Destruction* (Norman: University of Oklahoma Press, 1958), p. 25.

19. Based on national average for those on medication given in U.S. Department of Health, Education, and Welfare, Public Health Service, Health Resources Administration, *Prevalence of Chronic Conditions of the Genitourinary, Nervous, Endocrine, Metabolic, and Blood and Blood-Forming*

Systems and of other Selected Chronic Conditions, U.S.-1973, National Health Survey Series 10, No. 109, (Washington, D.C.: Government Printing Office, March 1977), p. 7.

20.   Based on national average for those on medication given in U.S. Department of Health, Education, and Welfare Public Health Service, Health Resources Administration, *Prevalence of Chronic Circulatory Conditions, U.S., 1972*, Health Survey Series 10, No. 94, (Washington, D.C.: Government Printing Office, September 1974), p. 6.

9 EVACUATION
Can the Center Hold?

Over the last decade evacuation has become the centerpiece of U.S. civil defense planning. The shelters of the 1950s have given way to plans for mass movements of people as the focus of governmental energies.[1] Evacuation, or crisis relocation, has been proposed as a strategy to reduce the effects of nuclear war by minimizing casualties and dispersing human resources geographically to help assure recovery.

Interest in this policy also arose from the proposal that civil defense could be used as an offensive strategic weapon. Its offensive rather than defensive character stems from the projected ability of an attacker to remove its vulnerable urban populations while holding its adversary's cities hostage to a full scale attack—thus gaining a strategic advantage. For example, the Soviet Union might pursue this approach as a complement to limited nuclear war, as described in Chapter 3.

Evacuation is basically a simple strategy—get people out of the high-risk (target), urban areas. People, then, become the basic resource for survival. The number of people saved in the initial round of destruction, if it comes, forms the criterion of success. Recovery is implicitly equated with simple human survival.

Although apparently straightforward in conception, there are a number of questions raised by this approach. Among the foremost

291

is whether evacuation will be effective in minimizing the effects of nuclear war. A number of complex problems have been identified in previous chapters that raise serious doubts about whether large scale strategic evacuation can assure a nation's successful nuclear survival. We have already learned (in Chapters 3, 5, 6 and 7) that the nation's economic and social systems are quite vulnerable to damage, which large scale evacuation and population survival may only serve to increase. These problems include political and host–evacuee conflicts; the government's inability to deliver key social services (medical care, education), basic necessities (food and shelter), and its subsequent loss of credibility; and the economic mismatch between the huge reservoirs of survivors and the limited job opportunities stemming from destroyed or bottlenecked industrial capacity. Although evacuation may have some useful influence on the postattack environment by providing a semblance of political and social organization, the historical and analytical evidence is not convincing that, at the levels of destruction and disruption identified for nuclear war, it can have a pivotal effect on overall recovery. At best, evacuation may have only a marginal positive benefit, and even that is not entirely clear.

There are other issues of equal importance about preattack evacuation as a component of strategic policy. Will it offer the political and social flexibility in a prolonged crisis needed to avoid a nuclear exchange? In this regard, the underlying assumption that preattack evacuation, like limited nuclear war, is a benign instrument of strategic policy must be tested. Does preattack evacuation leave society intact and functioning, and the population confident and supportive of its leadership? Will it be perceived by the nation as highly threatening rather than protective of U.S. society? Will it be seen by an adversary as provocative, thus increasing tension under highly volatile circumstances? Will it meet the test of the acceptability criterion used to evaluate limited nuclear war? Will it lead to a situation that will jeopardize the government's ability to control events in a rational manner during a nuclear confrontation? If the answer to this last question is yes, then preattack evacuation would be an extremely brittle, limited, and therefore dangerous instrument of strategic policy.

Finally, might this policy be regretted? Regret in this case would mean undercutting the overall goal of minimizing the extent of physical and social damage, or most critically losing the flexibility to resolve crises before they become war. Indeed, there is a certain irony in accepting this concept, since portraying successful evacuation as an attainable objective enlarges the circumstances under which nuclear war fighting *appears* to be acceptable. This effect could be achieved by asserting that preattack evacuation will successfully protect society and assure its recovery, despite significant physical damage and casualties. Under these circumstances, the public perception of the damage produced by a nuclear attack could be altered. Nuclear war would then appear less frightening and dangerous, creating a gray area of apparent acceptability that would erode the effectiveness of deterrence. Thus this concept must be examined with great care.

The following section will examine some of the effects of preattack evacuation. Since attack scenarios have been discussed previously, the primary focus will be the economic, social, and ethical problems raised by an evacuation when no subsequent attack occurs. The no-war situation is an important indicator of the real flexibility of this strategy, as well as its pitfalls.[2]

ECONOMIC EFFECTS

The economic effects of preattack evacuation on U.S. society are severe and complex. Laurino et al.[3] examined this problem involving 400 urban areas containing 135 million people. They identified a variety of effects on individuals, government and industry which occur prior to actual evacuation and extend well beyond its termination. Table 9-1 summarizes them for different institutions and crisis periods.

In the precrisis period, evacuation of perhaps 10 to 20 percent of the population (13-26 million people) would not be unexpected. This would begin to disrupt the economy because of the absenteeism of key workers, and resulting in inefficient operation or preattack shutdowns, and a 10 percent slowdown in industrial activity that would double the unemployment rate.[4] Salaries and other payments might be disrupted by the loss of personnel responsible for these functions. Heavy demands on personal finances could occur during this period. Businesses would begin to liquidate their inventories in high-risk areas to minimize their losses. Small businesses would be faced with heavy demands for prepayment of goods, which they

Table 9–1. Summary of Effects of Crisis Relocation (CR).

Operational Phase	The Individual	Business
Pre–CR Crisis	Selective unemployment Changed consumption Reduced savings Reduced access to savings and investments	Production shutdowns Inventory liquidation Deferral of payments and expenditures Reduced access to assets Reduced access to credit
CR–Initiation	Stoppage of income Emergency costs Cash shortage Lower acceptability of checks and credit cards	General shutdown Freeze on assets and payments Security problems Distribution stoppage
CR–Maintenance	Loss of employment income CR–Maintenance expense Cash shortage Restricted access to liquid assets Overdue obligations Security of assets	Shutdown of most risk area business Support of essential industry Expansion of host area industry Stoppage of accounts receivable Distribution problems
CR–Reconstitution	Slow re-employment Lower income Reduced liquid assets Overdue obligations Changed consumption patterns Reduced savings	Slow buildup of production Slow buildup of demand Depleted inventories Inadequate working credit Production inefficiencies Loss of asset values Reduced financial stability Reduced access to credit

Table 9-1. continued

Operational Phase	Financial Institutions	Local and State Government
Pre–CR Crisis	Increased withdrawals Reduced savings Reduced receivables Reduced interbank funds Management controls	Reduced tax receipts Increased costs Delayed inter-government payments Increased cash flow
CR–Initiation	Shutdown of risk area bank services High service demands in host areas Security problems Shutdown of exchanges	Curtailed service income Greatly increased emergency costs Restricted access to liquid assets
CR–Maintenance	Control of withdrawal Credit restrictions Increased net borrowed reserves Curtailed interbank borrowing Reduced profits Reduced debt payments	Reduced regular income Increased emergency costs Controlled access to funds Accelerated payment Dependence on inter-government revenue
CR–Reconstitution	Check clearing backlog High level of float Maintenance of bank liquidity Excessive credit demands Records updating Low savings rate Phase out of controls	Reduced revenue Inter-government claims Increased welfare costs Payment of accrued obligations Depleted liquid assets Reduced asset values Reduced tax base

Source: Richard K. Laurino, F. Trinkl, R. Berry, R. Schnider, W. MacDougell, *Impacts of Crisis Relocation on U.S. Economic and Industrial Activity* (Palo Alto, California: Center for Planning and Research, Inc., October 1978), p. 5–8.

might be unable to meet, because of fear of the destruction of these businesses after an attack. Financial institutions, especially banks, would be faced with increased withdrawal of money, particularly large withdrawals by other nations or individual foreigners. This could have a rapid and highly disruptive effect on U.S. banking and U.S. currency in the world market. The price of gold and other commodities might explode. Little lending would also be expected during this period to business and local and state governments. Hoarding and panic buying in both high- or low-risk areas in anticipation of a crisis is likely to occur. State and local governments in low-risk areas would have to prepare for the potential incoming evacuees. The stress on their modest resources would be great.

At the start of the evacuation, unemployment would dramatically increase and essential industries would have to shut down. If the 400 areas mentioned above were completely evacuated, unemployment would skyrocket, reaching approximately two-thirds of all nongovernment workers.[5]

There would be an attempt to keep key workers in or near high-risk areas to maintain critical industries. But the evidence of families separating under stress (role conflict) creates some reason to be seriously concerned about successfully accomplishing this objective. Especially in light of the reaction to nuclear imagery[6] seen with the Three Mile Island experience, this will be a difficult task. Individuals and families would be confronted with the need for using only the cash on hand, which for the urban poor would be extremely limited. Governments at all levels would have to prepared to begin the support of tens of millions of poor and even financially secure individuals. Credit cards, bank accounts and any other normal instruments of financing would be inoperable because of the massive shift of financial workers and operations.

While business would be shutdown, goods in transit would have to be rerouted to be useful during an evacuation period. The logistics of redistributing these goods would be a nightmare, exacerbated by the fact that 90 percent of central management employees and 95 percent of corporate headquarters are in metropolitan areas which will be evacuated.[7] Moreover, many industries in non-risk areas that depend on risk-area suppliers would have to attempt to find alternate supplies or begin to reduce production, or shutdown.

Financial institutions would also have to be shutdown, particularly to protect themselves against chaotic and massive withdrawals of money. Employees and functions would have to be moved. All inter-bank transfer of money for checking and other purposes could not take place. The flow of cash for mortgage and other payments of debts to these risk area banks would cease and not start again until after the crisis ended.

The actual crisis period, which could last two weeks or longer, would require a major organizational effort just to maintain the sem-blance of a functioning economic system. Individuals would have to be fed and housed during this period, requiring either money pay-ments to individuals and families or a highly regulated distribution system for food and necessities involving the entire nation. In essence a massive public support system would be needed to protect the entire population. Even cash would be of questionable value with a nuclear war in prospect. Black or gray markets for bartering com-modities—gold, silver, food—could easily spring up. Credit would be highly restricted, if it existed, and hoarding might be expected. The ability to maintain a functioning support system for individuals and families would depend heavily on host–evacuee cooperation. As we have discussed previously, that assumption is highly uncertain when massive numbers of intruders (evacuees) are forced to remain for extended periods of time—even for a few weeks—in low-risk areas. The friction and competition for goods and services between and even within these groups would be severe.

Industries and business would be shutdown in the risk areas, and many in the non-risk areas. The loss of urban banks where rural accounts are held would also pose problems. Inventories of goods would also be stripped during this period in many industries. The implications for the postattack period will be serious since competi-tion in some industries for meager remaining supplies will be severe. These effects could include industrial or regional dislocations and dramatic rises in price. This problem would grow if remaining inven-tories in risk areas were also heavily used during evacuation.

Essential industries such as food production would have to con-tinue in risk areas. Some substitution and increased production in non-risk areas would be helpful. However, the possibilities of being unable to gather and organize the skilled workers, managers, and public utility (energy, water) support workers to labor in risk areas might pose a grave problem. Role conflict, fear, and disorganization would all contribute to this problem. As the crisis period continued, the organizational stress (depleted inventories, reduced credit, uncertain payments, worker absenteeism and role conflict) would grow and undermine efficient industrial production in all geographical areas.

Financial operations would be seriously handicapped during the evacuation period. The non-risk area banks depend on larger high-risk area banks for many services, including check clearing and record keeping, and thus would be without these services. The transportation system, which moves currency and checks, would be heavily stressed. The mail service, which is used for some of these transfers, is likely not to function at all. The money in risk area banks would not be available, in many cases, making it very difficult for banks in non-risk areas to keep adequate reserves. Banks functioning in either area would have to face the problem of being continually drained of funds during this period. Increasing the confusion would be delays in loan repayments and uncertainty of the value of securities, particularly from risk area businesses or city governments. Most stock exchange and commodity markets would be closed, further freezing assets. For state and local governments in non-risk areas, this would be the period of greatest stress. They would be required to expand their basic services such as water and sanitation and to assume the role of the distributor for financial support.

The end of the crisis, even if no attack were to occur, would not be an end of the disruption of society. In fact, estimates show that it would take at least one to two years[8] to return to a normal economic situation if all went well.

On returning to the cities, individuals and businesses would face accumulated debts coupled with potential delays in industrial start-up and reemployment. Commercial businesses and industry would confront depleted physical resources and a desperate need for money (credit) to operate. However, banks, already suffering from heavy outflows of money and losses from overdue payment, would restrict loans. Without support, many marginal business or industries could easily go bankrupt during this period. Industrial and commercial start-up could also be delayed by a drop in demand as individuals and businesses sort out debts, inventories, and financial viability. Added to this would be the basic problem of just getting organizational and physical systems, such as transportation, functioning efficiently. The combination of these effects would cause reduced industrial production, resulting in an extended period of unemployment or underemployment. The effect on individuals, particularly low income workers, of restricted employment and accumulated unpaid debts, would be severe financial hardship. In turn, businesses in low income areas dependent on low income workers, or those already financially marginal before the evacuation, could collapse as late as a year or two after the evacuation ends under these disrupted circumstances. The collapse of smaller businesses could lead to serious financial problems for large companies because of losses due to the default on outstanding debts and the collapse of demand from these customers.

Financial institutions would have a pivotal role in recovery, yet they too would be in great difficulty. They would be under pressure to expand credit but, as noted, they would suffer from high pre-evacuation withdrawals, delayed or slow debt service repayments, lower savings rates, and the difficulty of interbank loans (to improve reserves). Without government support and control, some banks could collapse, setting off a chain reaction. Of equal concern is that banks are likely to restrict credit and discriminate against even essentially sound customers. The resulting policy of selective financial support would lead to effects both destructive to and biased against certain sectors of the economy. The government, forced to intervene, would then be faced with severe competition among industries and individuals for credit. Under these circumstances it would inevitably confront politically explosive decisions. Politically explosive as well would be the question of whether the economic burden had been equitably distributed between risk area and non-risk area workers during this recovery period. Moreover, until the economy reached equilibrium and the financial community believed the crisis truly over, commitment to reestablishing all preevacuation financial services would likely be resisted. Of particular concern would be a sudden heavy withdrawal of assets, frozen during evacuation, by foreign nations and individuals, and the investment or transfer of money outside the United States by U.S. corporations and citizens to protect its value. In general, world financial markets are also likely to be in chaos during this recovery period, unless the underlying factors producing the military crisis have been definitely eliminated.

Specific dollar estimates of the losses occurring in a two-week evacuation are shown in Table 9–2. Laurino et al. projected an approximate cost of 50 billion dollars during the crisis period and at least another 50 billion during the postevacuation recovery period of one to two years.[9] These losses are based on a number of underlying

Table 9-2. Selected Direct Costs Associated with CR-Maintenance Phase.

Cost Factor	Direct Cost (1975)	
	$ Billion/day	$ Billion in 2 Weeks
Salaries (non-government)	$1.3	$18
Risk area business (MVA)[a]	2.0[b]	28[b]
Risk area business (fixed costs)[c]	0.35	5
Financial sector (added costs)[d]	0.02	0.3
State and local operations added cost[e]	0.3	4
Subsistence of evacuees	0.5	7
Other evacuation costs: commuting	0.03	0.4
relocation and return	N.A.	2
Shelter upgrading and recovery (for evacuees)	N.A.	6-18
Local government revenue loss	0.05	0.7
Total	$2.5	$43-55

a. Less government, financial, and agriculture.

b. Not included in total; salaries and fixed costs are added to the total as separate factors.

c. Not including salaries.

d. Added check clearing costs plus interest loss due to 15% depletion of demand deposits.

e. Own personnel only; 12-hour day plus minimum operating logistics.

Source: Richard K. Laurino, F. Trinkel, R. Berry, R. Schnider, W. MacDougell, *Impacts of Crisis Relocation on U.S. Economic and Industrial Activity* (Palo Alto, California: Center for Planning and Research, Inc., October, 1978), p. 5-9.

assumptions. They are predicated on effective organizational control of key financial and industrial institutions by a central authority. Political stability and restored public confidence, particularly in the value of goods and money, is also assumed. Most importantly, the problem of a renewed evacuation is not addressed, although concerns over an extended evacuation period are identified. A second evacuation period would raise serious questions about the stability of society under this type of stress. Therefore, while the authors attempted to incorporate a substantial level of reality in their estimates, they are still generally optimistic.

Laurino et al. did identify possible strategies to mitigate the economic and industrial problems identified. They indicated that substitutes for cash payments such as invoices and free goods would be used for essential needs for approximately one half of the U.S. population who are evacuees. Limited bank withdrawals would be used for other purposes. This system might be extended into the period after the crisis is terminated. They estimated essential production, such as food processing, in risk areas could be reduced substantially, minimizing the use of risk area industrial capacity and the recruitment of workers. However, to attain risk area production reductions of more than two-thirds becomes increasingly dependent upon reaching levels of near perfection for the distribution of products and services throughout the U.S.[10] In general, the mechanism proposed, while useful, still assumes excellent planning and near perfect execution by responsible government agencies, and the minimum of social and political conflict and psychological distress.

SOCIAL DISRUPTION

Host–evacuee conflicts, as already indicated, can develop after any sustained period of evacuation, especially one associated with deprivation (lack of food and other basic resources and services). Increased, too, is the likelihood of tensions and hostility, and the political impact arising from not evacuating, or selectively evacuating, various groups or urban areas. If the British experience of a long-term, unresolved crisis without an actual attack is repeated, the government will again be faced with the difficult choice of either retaining evacuees in host areas where they are difficult to support and increasingly less welcome, or returning them to the cities that may be subject to attack at any time. As previously indicated, if the evacuees are retained in the host area for any extended period, their massive social service needs will only grow. This will further stress the organizational capabilities of the local and national governments, and by implication, test their credibility through their performance. Judging from the historical evidence, an added complication will be the possibility that many urban residents may return to the evacuated urban areas of their own accord (unless barred by force). The powerful need to remain with community and family was, as noted, the reality that undermined the British evacuation plans. Perry et al.[11] emphasize the need for keeping the family unit together as a prerequisite for effective evacuation.

If a significant number of essential personnel remain in the cities, the forces of cohesion will be particularly strong. However, even if the entire population is removed, social problems not extensively experienced by the British could draw individuals back to the city. With police and military personnel likely to be needed elsewhere, looting will be extremely difficult to prevent in sprawling suburbs and downtown high-rise areas. Evacuees forced to leave behind prized possessions, but knowing that these undamaged items will be prey to theft, could be reluctant to remain in host areas for a lengthy period of displacement. For example, after the accident at Three Mile Island, the fear of looting made some members of the population reluctant to evacuate (see Appendix A).

Taken as a whole, the conflicting desires of the government and the evacuees can create the worst of all possible worlds—disorganization in both host and urban areas. However, even a decision to return evacuees to the cities during uncertain conditions is fraught with dangers. Returning to the cities with the international conflict unresolved is an implicit admission of an error in judgment that can undermine the credibility of any subsequent decision to evacuate. The dangers of a government allowing itself to be caught in this dilemma should be obvious.

Titmuss described evacuation as a traumatic experience in the host areas and in British society in general, even in the absence of war. His depiction of the British experience serves as a graphic illustration of the effects of preattack evacuation:

> To millions of people in Britain the war was already real enough, the shifting of population—the hurried movement from the cities, the migration of industry and commerce, schools and other institutions, and then the filtering back to the towns—directly affected the daily lives of from one-quarter to one-third of the people. The social stresses which accompanied and followed a movement of people and homes on such a scale cannot be measured; for it was not just a matter of separated families and invaded homes. The framework of social service upon which modern communities have come to depend was—in parts in different places—violently wrenched into disorder. The metropolitan area and other large cities were stripped for action; stripped of schools, evening institutes, clubs, nurseries, clinics, maternity homes, hospitals and the essentials of staff, equipment and buildings. Meanwhile, the reception areas were overloaded with population and short of all these things. . . .

The expected war on civilian society had not come. The Government, in preparing to meet an immediate air onslaught, had put into operation its civil defense schemes and had by so doing, upset the working of the peacetime social services.[12]

Thus, even those not directly touched by the formal evacuation plans were not immune to its impacts on society.

The process of instituting civilian defense measures created disorder resistance, antagonism, fear, and anxiety among the populace on behalf of whom the measures were implemented. The social dislocation mirrored all too well war itself. Leighton summarized the impact of evacuation on Japan: "Evacuation, then was bad for the morale of the evacuees, bad for the morale of their hosts, and bad for the morale of those whom they left behind. *It materially disorganized the economy and the social life of the entire country.*" (Emphasis added.)[13]

ETHICAL CHOICES

There is another set of social issues generally not adequately discussed. These are the momentous ethical and social decisions that must be confronted during preattack evacuation, decisions that will affect the lives of a number of vulnerable and dependent groups in society.

Urban areas are the site of major medical complexes, generally the receiving hospitals and clinics for the ill from surrounding rural as well as metropolitan areas. In these hospitals are critically and seriously ill individuals and those awaiting sophisticated diagnosis. Shall these critically ill be moved, and if so, to where? This is a particularly ironic question since it is just these urban areas vulnerable to attack that contain the key elements of our medical support systems. In the Three Mile Island area (Appendix A) plans were made to move hospitalized small children to a major pediatric clinic in Philadelphia, a most unlikely possibility under these circumstances in view of general urban evacuation. Who shall make the decision to risk the death of individuals during evacuation, or later due to inadequate care in host areas, as opposed to allowing them to stay in an evacuated area? Who shall stay to assist these people (workers and relatives?), and will the support systems—utilities such as water supply and garbage collection—be available? Many will survive under any circumstances, but who shall be responsible for those who die, especially if no attack occurs? What would be the price in terms of the credibility of the government?

What shall be done with those in nursing homes or in mental institutions? Who shall care for the elderly or handicapped who, though not in a nursing home or institution, still need a variety of support services unlikely to be fully available in host areas because of limited resources? Where will the prisoners go? Will those less dangerous be released in the interest of reducing the public burden, as planned for those in the area around Three Mile Island? Can the national leadership answer these questions and will that leadership survive those answers and their inevitable mistakes?

EVACUATION AND PREPAREDNESS

The impact on society of a major urban evacuation before a nuclear attack will be comparable in many ways to the economic and social dislocation of war. Large-scale evacuations are logistically formidable under benign conditions and face special difficulties in the stress of a crisis or war, when the attacker controls timing and targets.

On the basis of the data, no one would suggest that accepting the risk of a nuclear attack is preferable to experiencing an evacuation, but previous experience does indicate that evacuations are difficult to implement and have undesirable side effects for which the authorities must be prepared, particularly if the evacuation is in any way premature. First, governments must be able to meet more than simple demands for food and shelter, especially if the evacuation lasts longer than a week. Second, control of the evacuation process and of the evacuees will not be easy; if the process must be carried out rapidly, populations are unlikely to cooperate uniformly with the authorities. Third, even if no undesired reaction from an adversary is provoked, premature evacuation—with its economic and social dislocation and losses—will waste government resources and significantly reduce the effectiveness and strategic value of any subsequent attempt at large-scale evacuation.

Even in wartime the difficulty of pinpointing accurately the time of an adversary's attack and the time for safe return to the cities (either because the crisis has been resolved or because the attack has come and no follow-up attacks can be expected) poses especially troublesome—and perhaps even insurmountable—problems for national leadership and civil defense planners in the nuclear age. If the evacuation is unplanned (people beginning to empty the cities at their own discretion), or if it is uncontrolled (people using routes, transportation, and host areas of their own choosing), then the problems of protecting and supporting the population while prosecuting a war effort will be magnified many times. Part of these difficulties could be attributed to some individuals and groups who will be reluctant to cooperate with the evacuation plans of authorities; many, for example, will be unwilling to abandon their property or familiar surroundings, while others will leave in an uncontrolled fashion, seeking to secure the most favorable circumstances for survival. This further complicates control of the evacuation, especially if the process is to be carried out rapidly and with a minimum of preattack training or notification to prevent panic.

Weather, premature migrations, and particularly the reactions of residents of the host areas can be major sources of additional difficulty. Ironically, even deciding the goals of evacuation will create difficulties. Are we evacuating on the assumption that there will be attack, or are we hoping to avoid an attack? As Laurino et al.[14] have pointed out, the organization and operation of evacuation would not necessarily be compatible, depending on our choice of strategy. For example, if an attack is expected, all workers and as much industrial equipment as possible would be removed. If evacuation is viewed as strategic policy to provide the least economic damage and most political flexibility, then the inclination might be to keep the economy in urban areas functioning, retaining workers and equipment in those high-risk areas. These questions create interesting dilemmas.

Clearly, preattack evacuation is not a neutral instrument of strategic policy. A nuclear attack during the evacuation process is likely to increase casualties. If poorly timed or badly implemented, it runs the risk of undermining governmental legitimacy and credibility when these factors are critically important. A premature or false evacuation will be perceived as an unnecessary exposure to deprivation due to incompetent government planning. This perception may seriously impair the effectiveness of subsequent evacuations or even limit their use. The political implications of these limitations are significant. The country's leadership would be in considerable trouble if it ordered another false evacuation; thus, its ability to use this option in an international crisis would be seriously compromised.

Evacuation can also impose another major constraint on international flexibility, since preattack evacuation, like military mobilization, can be interpreted as a preparation for war and therefore a provocative act, perhaps a signal for the initiation of hostilities.

Because mass evacuations disrupt the national economy, particularly the economic systems that support urban centers, the ability of authorities to house, feed and otherwise support the evacuated populations would be severely strained. If the evacuated population must remain dispersed for a prolonged period of time, either because the abandoned cities are largely destroyed or because the crisis remains unresolved, the problem of satisfying basic survival needs will be substantially magnified.

PERSPECTIVE

Evacuation and preparedness programs in World War II show that preattack planning cannot be limited solely to the short-term problems of immediate physical survival, but must also provide for meeting basic social needs and coping with long-term disruption. Plans for protecting the population and mitigating the effects of strategic bombing involves widespread changes in family, community, and larger social structures. This effort would require a qualitatively different approach to civil defense than even the most ambitious efforts presently discussed. The United States would have to adopt a strategy of nuclear war fighting in its most expansive sense, and the mindset of fear, distrust, and grave foreboding of Soviet intentions and international events would be needed to sustain such a strategy. A vast non-urban social service structure would have to be prepared along with a major strategy of undergrounding and geographical dispersion of key facilities—with economic and energy impacts as well as the requirements of political control of industrial decisions. The effectiveness of even this strategy would be highly questionable because of the proliferation of accurate warheads. A more modest urban evacuation policy without a long-term support system would leave tens of millions of people without the physical or social resources to support themselves after an attack. A nation staggering under that burden might quickly begin to look like Cambodia or Bangladesh instead of a first rate world power.

Thus, civil defense as represented by improved initial survival of an urban population after a nuclear attack is a modestly effective instrument *only* in the event that no prolonged evacuation occurs, no significant urban damage occurs, and the war is terminated within days. Even under these circumstances the social and economic price will be substantial. However, there is little likelihood of achieving all these conditions simultaneously. In terms of military planners, the regret for incorporating evacuation as an effective part of strategic policy would be overwhelming. Effective large scale civil defense might have been a possibility in the 1950s and early 1960s when limited numbers of weapons constrained the flexibility of a nuclear attack, but in the 1980s, its value undercut by increased numbers of warheads and sophisticated targeting, evacuation seems a dangerous misconception.

NOTES TO CHAPTER 9

1. Although improving industrial protection against blast effects has been considered, evacuation remains the focal point of U.S. strategy.
2. Certain distinctions are pertinent. Evacuation can be selective, as it was in World War II Britain. It can occur prior to an attack if there is adequate warning, or it can occur immediately afterwards as a consequence of the unlivability of the damaged cities. Evacuation can be planned or unplanned, controlled or uncontrolled. Whatever the type of the evacuation, such mass migrations will pose serious problems for the surviving authorities, although the extent and severity of these problems are certainly not independent of the type of evacuation used.
3. R.K. Laurino, F. Trinkl, C.F. Miller and R.A. Harker, *Economic and Industrial Aspects of Crisis Relocation: An Overview*, DCPA 01-75-c-0279, (Palo Alto, California: Center for Planning and Research, May 1977); and R.K. Laurino, F. Trinkl, R. Berry, R. Schnider, W. MacDougell, *Impacts of Crisis Relocation on U.S. Economic and Industrial Activity*, DCPA 01-76-c-0331, (Palo Alto, California: Center for Planning and Research, October 1978).
4. Laurino et al. 1977, p. 33.
5. Ibid., p. 33.
6. Ronald Perry, Michael Lindell, and Majorie Greene, *The Implications of Natural Hazard Evacuation Warning Studies for Crisis Relocation Planning*, Final Report (Seattle, Washington: Battelle Human Affairs Research Center, February 1980), p. 24.

7.   Laurino et al., 1977, p. 53.

8.   Laurino et al., 1978, pp. 5-11.

9.   Ibid., pp. 5-10.

10. Ibid., pp. 5-6.

11. Perry, Lindell, and Greene, p. viii.

12. R.M. Titmuss, *Problems of Social Policy* (London: His Majesty's Stationary Office and Longmans, Green, and Company, 1950), pp. 137-38. It is important to recall that the prewar social services mentioned by Titmuss do not represent the far more extensive programs inaugurated by the Labor Party after it came to power in 1946 but are the comparatively basic services of the 1930s. By contrast, the services now provided by local, state, and federal governments in the United States are more extensive.

13. Alexander H. Leighton, *Human Relations in a Changing World* (New York: E.P. Dutton & Co., 1949), p. 67.

14. Laurino et al., 1977, pp. 8-9.

10 VULNERABILITY OF THE SOVIET UNION

While this book focuses on the United States, many of the implications of the hypothetical attacks directed at this country have considerable relevance for the Soviet Union. Perhaps, in some ways, the effects described for the United States understate the seriousness of the possible impacts for the Soviets. The United States, despite its ethnic and racial conflicts, does not suffer from the centrifugal forces created by distinct regional nationalities and formerly independent nation states. Nor do vulnerabilities created by ideological or historical neighboring adversaries exist. Social disorganization, industrial fragmentation, and the loss of the political credibility of existing leadership in this context may not mean just a floundering, second-rate nation state but the disintegration and fragmentation of the Soviet Union itself. Thus, while this chapter addresses only a restricted set of industrial and population vulnerabilities of the Soviet Union, the superposition of the social issues raised in the context of the United States will have profound implications for the meaning of these strategic issues for the Soviet Union.

In trying to compare the Soviet Union and the United States, some key questions have been raised about their relative vulnerabilities. The first is whether their geographical distributions of economic activity and population are different enough to make one nation or the other significantly more vulnerable to nuclear attacks. The second is whether, after heavy damage to U.S. nuclear forces, an effective retaliation can be mounted against the Soviet Union. A related question is whether current civil defense efforts in industrial and population protection by the Soviet Union can assure a dramatic reduction in its economic damage and casualties. If such efforts were effective, it would raise troubling questions about the effectiveness of the concept of mutually assured destruction (MAD).

This chapter will briefly address these questions by reviewing some recent studies evaluating Soviet vulnerabilities. It is not intended as an exhaustive survey, but instead as a basic framework within which the effects and vulnerabilities found in our study of the United States can be evaluated in terms of the Soviet Union and other industrialized nations.

A 1978 report by the Arms Control and Disarmament Agency (ACDA)[1] provides a useful starting point for the question of general vulnerability. Its purpose was to describe the efficacy of Soviet civil defense against nuclear war, by looking first at some crude indicators of vulnerability and then evaluating some specific attacks. Figure 10-1 compares the land area that encloses U.S. and Soviet urban populations.[2] It should be readily evident that the Soviet Union urban population is considerably more compact,[3] since the graph shows that the Soviet Union has 100 percent of its urban population within a land area of 5,000 nautical miles square (NM^2)[4] and the United States reaches that point at almost triple that figure (14,000 NM^2).

For comparison, Soviet urban areas are less than one tenth of one percent of its land area, while the ACDA study's projection is five tenths of one percent for the United States. More surprising is that despite the larger Soviet land mass, the rural population of both nations live within similar areas, 2 to 2.5 million NM^2 (Figure 10-2). Most instructive is Figure 10-3. The number of individual nuclear weapons is described in terms of their areas of destruction, in this case, a circle 1.5 nautical miles in radius is equivalent to a single weapon. The number of weapons (in this case circles) needed to destroy a particular percentage of industrial installations for the United States or the Soviet Union is shown on the horizontal axis. The circles represent the destructive radius of a medium-sized weapon, a 40 kiloton warhead of a MIRVed Polaris missile or perhaps a bomber carrying 200 Kt short-range attack missiles (SRAMS), depending on the assumptions.[5] The graph was produced starting with the circle

Figure 10-1. Distribution of Urban Population According to Land Area.

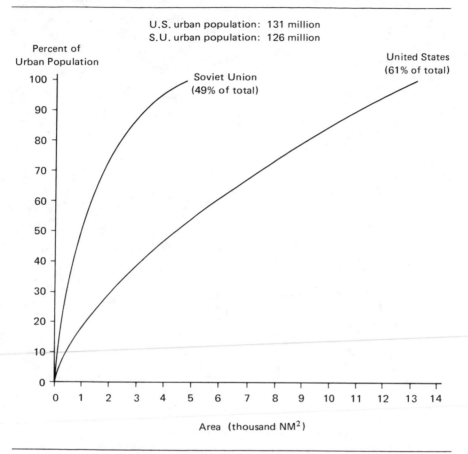

U.S. urban population: 131 million
S.U. urban population: 126 million

Percent of
Urban Population

United States
(61% of total)

Soviet Union
(49% of total)

Area (thousand NM^2)

Source: United States Arms Control and Disarmament Agency, *An Analysis of Civil Defense in Nuclear War* (Washington, D.C.: ACDA, December 1978), p. 3.

containing the largest number of industrial installations, then the circle containing the next largest was added, and so on, until all industry was covered. What should be clear is that the United States and Soviet Union have similar concentrations of industrial capacity, at least for targeting purposes.[6] As a basis of comparison, the ACDA study pointed out that to destroy 70 percent of the industrial installations of either nation (horizontal line), would require approximately 1,300 weapons (circles). This would be a devastating blow, at

Figure 10-2. Distribution of Rural Population According to Land Area.

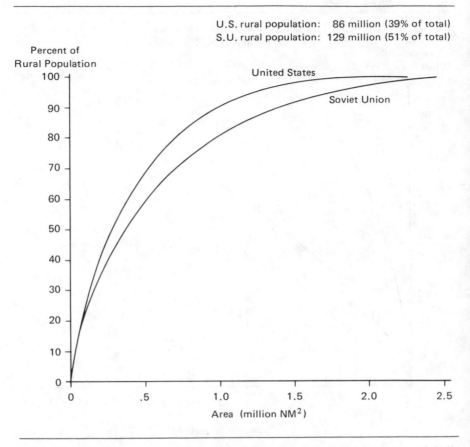

U.S. rural population: 86 million (39% of total)
S.U. rural population: 129 million (51% of total)

Source: United States Arms Control and Disarmament Agency, *An Analysis of Civil Defense in Nuclear War* (Washington, D.C.: ACDA, December 1978), p. 4.

least comparable to the largest attack (A-1) examined for the United States.[7]

Finally, in Table 10-1, the collocation of industry and population is shown. The Soviet Union has a higher percentage (31 percent versus 22 percent in the United States) of its population living in close proximity to industry (less than 1.5 nautical miles). The ACDA study stated:

> In conclusion, the answer to the question, "Does the Soviet Union have an inherent advantage over the U.S. because of population and industrial distribution?" is clearly "no."

Figure 10-3. Comparative Collocation of U.S. and Soviet Industrial Installations.

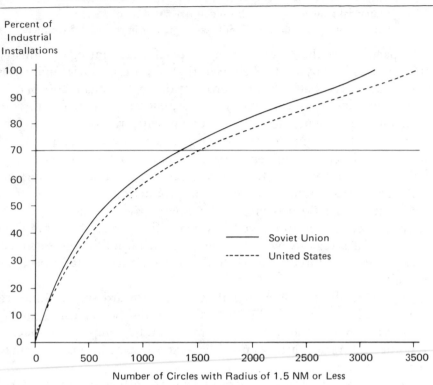

Source: United States Arms Control and Disarmament Agency, *An Analysis of Civil Defense in Nuclear War* (Washington, D.C.: ACDA, December 1978), p. 5.

Table 10-1. Location of Population Nearby Industry (*percent of population*).

Percent of Population Living Within:	U.S.	S.U.
1.0 NM	9	16
1.5 NM	22	31
2.5 NM	45	44
5.0 NM	68	52

Source: U.S. Arms Control and Disarmament Agency, *An Analysis of Civil Defense in Nuclear War* (Washington, D.C.: ACDA, December 1978) p. 6.

— Urban density is greater in the Soviet Union.
— Rural density in both countries is similar.
— Industrial concentration in both countries is similar.
— Population collocation with industry is greater in the Soviet Union.[8]

Expanding on these points, a more specific accounting of industry and key facilities by ACDA[9] showed that important Soviet industries have more than half of their production in less than 200 plants. These facilities produce primary metals, chemicals, petroleum, construction equipment, agricultural equipment, railroad equipment, synthetic rubber, and electric power generations. For example, there are only eight copper refineries, sixteen heavy machine plants, thirty-four sizable petroleum refineries, eighteen integrated iron and steel mills, and fifteen agricultural machine production plants. Nine tractor plants make 80 percent of the Soviet Union's entire output. Chemicals are largely produced in twenty-five cities. The entire Central and Volga regions, with a population of 60 million gets its electricity from three hydroelectric and nuclear plants located near large cities.[10]

The vulnerabilities described above point toward similar and serious difficulties for both the United States and Soviet Union in the event of a nuclear attack. Three more studies employing specific hypothetical nuclear attacks provide greater insight into the accuracy of this observation.

Geoffrey Kemp,[11] in a study evaluating the effectiveness of a small nuclear capability (such as France's), examined in detail the urban industry and population at risk in the Soviet Union. His approach was to analyze a range of attacks to determine what strategic forces were needed to deliver a specific level of damage successfully.

The effects of several levels of nuclear attack, D–1 through D–4, on the Soviet Union are shown in Table 10–2 and Figure 10–4. D–1 is an attack on the 10 largest Soviet cities excluding the Moscow area; D–2 covers the 10 largest cities including the Moscow area; D–3 is on the 50 largest Soviet cities; and D–4 is on the 204 largest Soviet cities.

Table 10–2 first shows population and industrial categories at risk (columns *a* to *c*). Columns *d* to *g* show the number of weapons needed to perform Attacks D–1 to D–4. Note that D–1 is the smallest attack. Two weapon sizes, 50 kiloton (Kt), Columns *e* and *g*, or 1 megaton (Mt), Columns *d* and *f*, are used—they illustrate the weapon requirements with high and low explosive power.

Figure 10-4. Comparison of Population (A) and Industrial Capacity (B) at Risk (within 5 psi destruction contour) for Attacks D–1 to D–4 Against the Soviet Union. McNamara's Criteria for Unacceptable Damage are Shown with Broken Lines.

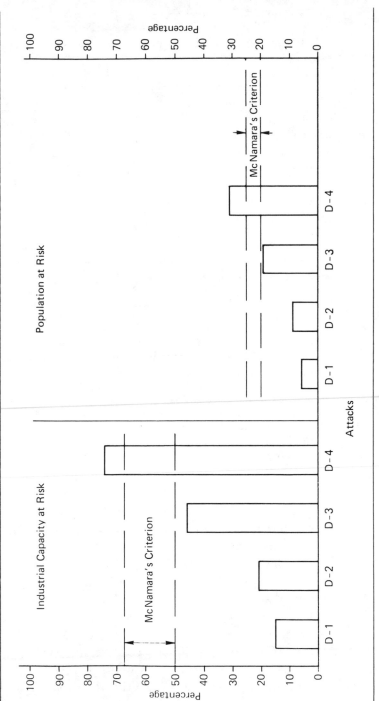

Source: Geoffrey Kemp, *Nuclear Forces of Medium Powers Parts II and III: Strategic Requirements and Options*, Adelphi Papers, No. 107, (London, England: The International Institutes for Strategic Studies, 1974).

Table 10-2. U.S.S.R. Vulnerability to Nuclear Attack.

Attacks	Total Population at Risk (millions) a	Percentage Urban Population at Risk b	Percentage Industrial Capacity at Risk c	Total Megaton[a,b] Equivalents		Total[b] Weapons	
				1 Mt d	50 Kt e	1 Mt f	50 Kt g
D-1	15	11	15	26	25	26	181
D-2	21	16	25	90	40	90	300
D-3	46	34	50	144	86	144	631
D-4	74	55	62	303	138	303	1,014

a. Illustrations Table 10-2 state requirements in terms of numbers of weapons (warheads and bombs) and "megaton equivalents." Equivalent megatons (EMT) are defined as N(yield) to the two-thirds power. This is a measure of the effectiveness of a given number (N) of nuclear weapons, compared with 1 Mt as a standard. Because of the nonlinear effects that occur with increases in warhead yield, a cluster of smaller yield weapons with a total megatonnage less than 1 large yield weapon could nevertheless have a similar or greater area of destruction than the single large yield weapon. For example, the destructive area of 4 1 Mt weapons is approximately the same as that of a single 8 Mt weapon.

b. An adjustment in the weapon requirements is given to account for the possibility of an effective antiballistic missile (ABM) system that is postulated for the Moscow area. The additional weapons required are those that would be necessary to overwhelm such a system, assuming that it is effective against a normal attack. The Moscow ABM system is here assumed to have 100 launchers for antiballistic missiles.

Source: Geoffrey Kemp, "Nuclear Forces for Medium Powers, Parts II and III. Strategic Requirements and Options," Adelphi Papers 107, (London, England: International Institute for Strategic Studies, 1974).

The damage was evaluated by criteria developed in the mid-1960s by former Secretary of Defense Robert McNamara. He defined the level of unacceptable damage for the Soviet Union as 20 to 25 percent of the population killed and 50 to 67 percent of its industrial capacity destroyed. He estimated that 400 megaton equivalents would be required to assure these damage levels, as shown in Table 10-3. Using these crude criteria as a rule of thumb for an effective "assured destruction" attack, apparently Attack D-4 and perhaps D-3 (see Figure 10-4) on the Soviet Union and Attacks A-1 and A-2 and, perhaps, A-3 (Figure 5-3) on the United States satisfy these criteria specifications.[12] More recently, the capacity to destroy a minimum of 200 major Soviet cities (Attack D-4) was proposed

Table 10-3. McNamara "Assured Destruction" Criteria for Soviet Population and Industry Destroyed—Assuming 1972 Total Population of 247,000,000 and Urban Population of 116,000,000.

1 Mt Equivalent Delivered Warheads	*Total Population Killed*		*Percent Industrial Capacity Destroyed*
	Number (millions)	*Percent*	
100	37	15	59
200	52	21	72
400	74	30	76
800	96	39	77
1,200	109	44	77
1,600	116	47	77

Source: Alain G. Enthoven and K. Wayne Smith, *How Much is Enough?* (New York: Harper & Row, 1971), p. 207.

as the level necessary to deter a Soviet nuclear attack.[13] Of interest is the fact that, for both the United States and the Soviet Union, the assured destruction levels are met with fewer than the 400 megaton equivalents McNamara postulated as necessary to deter the Soviet Union. Kemp's study thus reinforces the ACDA findings about the similarity of Soviet and U.S. vulnerability.

EFFECTIVE U.S. RETALIATION

The 1978 ACDA study also examined the effects of an attack on key Soviet industries. This study and one by the Congressional Budget Office, discussed below, address the second question posed at the beginning of this chapter: Whether the United States, in principle, has an effective retaliatory force after a surprise attack? ACDA presumed that a large scale retaliation by the United States occurred after a preemptive attack by the Soviet Union. The successful first strike by the Soviet Union results in the United States losing the bulk of its intercontinental ballistic missiles (ICBMs); all its nuclear weapon submarines in port (40 to 50 percent of its force); and its nonalert bombers (70 percent of the force). If, for example, 30 percent survival for ICBMs was assumed, more than 4,000 weapons would be available.[14] The United States then retaliates by attacking Soviet strategic forces, other Soviet military targets, and its industry.[15]

The effects on the Soviet Union are shown in Figures 10-5, 10-6, 10-7, and 10-8. The diagonal lines represent collateral damage to industries or facilities not directly attacked, damaged because of their physical proximity to the targets. As the four graphs reveal, the losses in primary metals (Figure 10-5), petroleum products (Figure 10-6), electric power industry (Figure 10-7) and other selected industries (Figure 10-8) are staggering—nearly 80 percent destruction in each category. Industry losses, in general, are heavy.

The implications of losses of this magnitude are illustrated by the potential results of extensive petroleum refinery destruction (shown in Figure 10-6). An Office of Technology Assessment (OTA) study[16] indicated that in contrast to the United States, the Soviet Union uses almost a third of its gasoline and diesel fuel for basic agricultural needs. Refinery losses of the magnitude of the ACDA report would therefore be devastating although the cruder state of Soviet agriculture might permit some production to continue. The OTA study also showed that about 75 percent of the Soviet Union's capacity is represented by twenty-four refineries and is vulnerable to an attack of ten missiles. Thus, even a considerably smaller selective attack than the ACDA scenario could still be quite effective against these targets. The ACDA study concluded[17] that the overall effect of their proposed attack would be:

1. Sixty-five to 70 percent of destruction of key Soviet production capacity from U.S. forces in normal day-to-day alert status;
2. Eighty-five percent destruction of key Soviet production capacity from a generated alert U.S. force status;
3. Sixty percent collateral damage to nontargeted Soviet production capacity from normal alert; and
4. Eighty percent collateral damage to nontargeted Soviet production capacity from generated alert.

The terms "generated" and "nongenerated" represent situations where there is a military alert before the attack (generated), and where military preparedness is at a normal level (nongenerated). In the generated case, there is a higher survival of nuclear weapon systems, particularly bombers.

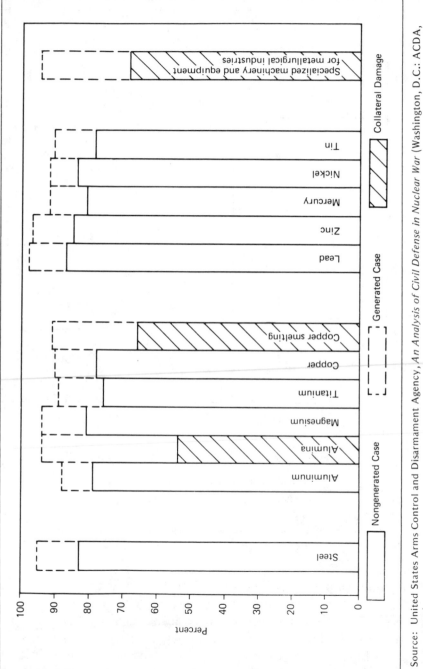

Figure 10-5. Damage Assessment—Primary Metals Production/Processing (percent of national capacity).

Source: United States Arms Control and Disarmament Agency, *An Analysis of Civil Defense in Nuclear War* (Washington, D.C.: ACDA, December 1978), p. 7.

Figure 10-6. Damage Assessment—Petroleum Products.

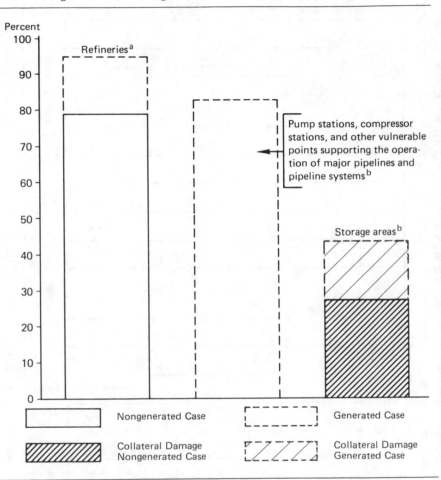

a. Percent of national capacity.

b. Percent of number of facilities.

Source: United States Arms Control and Disarmament Agency, *An Analysis of Civil Defense in Nuclear War* (Washington, D.C.: ACDA, December 1978), p. 8.

A study similar to ACDA's was done by the Congressional Budget Office (CBO).[18] It examined the ability of U.S. strategic forces surviving a Soviet preemptive attack to inflict military and economic damage on the Soviet Union. Present, mid–1980s, and 1990s strategic capabilities were examined. Surviving weapons capabilities are shown in Figure 10-9 and Table 10-4 for the three different time

Figure 10-7. Damage Assessment—Electric Power Generation, Transmission, and Equipment Manufacture (percent of national capacity[a]).

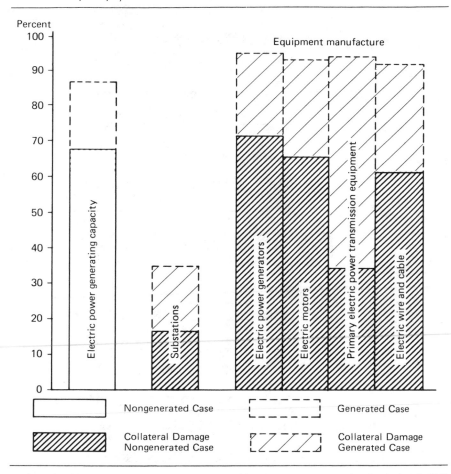

Source: United States Arms Control and Disarmament Agency, *An Analysis of Civil Defense in Nuclear War* (Washington, D.C.: ACDA, December 1978), p. 8.

a. Percent of installations, not capacity for sub stations.

periods as well as two levels of strategic readiness, normal (nongenerated) and increased alert (generated) status. In all cases, approximately 5,000 or more weapons are available. However, it should be noted as we proceed into the 1980s that the bomber and submarine forces assume an increasing share of the retaliatory responsibility, highlighting the assumed vulnerability of U.S. land-based missiles.

Figure 10-8.   Damage Assessment—Other Selected Targets (all damage is collateral).

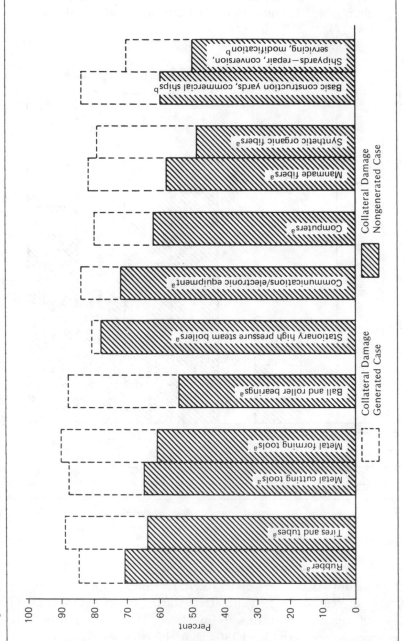

a. Percent of national capacity.
b. Percent of number of facilities.

Source: United States Arms Control and Disarmament Agency, *An Analysis of Civil Defense in Nuclear War* (Washington, D.C.: ACDA, December 1978), p. 8.

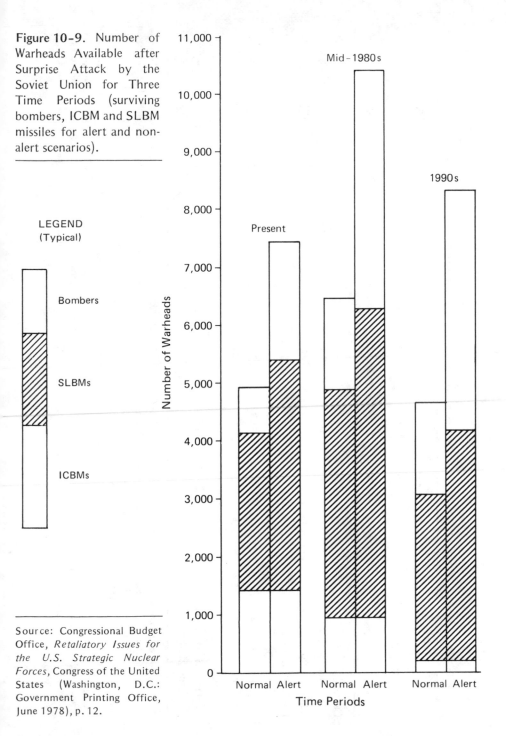

Figure 10-9. Number of Warheads Available after Surprise Attack by the Soviet Union for Three Time Periods (surviving bombers, ICBM and SLBM missiles for alert and non-alert scenarios).

LEGEND
(Typical)

Bombers

SLBMs

ICBMs

Number of Warheads

Mid-1980s

1990s

Present

Normal Alert   Normal Alert   Normal Alert

Time Periods

Source: Congressional Budget Office, *Retaliatory Issues for the U.S. Strategic Nuclear Forces*, Congress of the United States (Washington, D.C.: Government Printing Office, June 1978), p. 12.

Table 10-4. Estimated U.S. Strategic Forces Surviving a Hypothetical Soviet First Strike (warheads).

	a	b	c	d	e	f	g	h	i
		Minuteman						Cruise	
	Titan	II	III	Poseidon	Trident	SRAM	Bomb	Missile	Total
Current Forces									
Day-to-day alert	31	331	1,062	2,720	—	342	432	—	4,918
Generated alert	31	331	1,062	3,968	—	912	1,152	—	7,456
Finite Deterrence Force									
Mid–1980s									
Day-to-day alert	10	205	753	1,920	1,984	336	236	1,000	6,444
Generated alert	10	205	753	2,560	2,752	888	624	2,640	10,432
1990s									
Day-to-day alert	2	41	150	—	2,880	336	236	1,000	4,645
Generated alert	2	41	150	—	3,968	888	624	2,640	8,313

Source: Congressional Budget Office (CBO), *Retaliatory Issues for the U.S. Strategic Nuclear Forces*, Congress of the United States (Washington, D.C.: Government Printing Office, June 1978), p. 12. The number of surviving bombers and submarines was computed from Tables 1–3 based on a 30 percent bomber alert rate, 55 percent for Poseidon and 66 percent for Trident submarines for the day-to-day alert case. For generated alert conditions, 80 percent of the bombers and submarines were assumed to be on alert. (See Department of Defense, *Annual Report, Fiscal Year 1978*, p. 133; and *Fiscal Year 1978 Authorization for Military Procurement, Research and Development, and Active Duty, Selected Reserve, and Civilian Personnel Strengths*, Hearings before the Senate Committee on Armed Services, 95: 1 (April 1977), Part 10, p. 6621). The number of surviving ICBMs for current forces is based on calculations using 1,840 warheads on 310 Soviet MIRVed missiles, all accurate to 1,500 feet CEP with 0.75 reliability and 2,000 psi hardness for Minuteman silos. For the mid–1980's and 1990's ICBM forces, estimates are taken from Congressional Budget Office, *Counterforce Issues for the U.S. Strategic Nuclear Forces*, Background Paper (January 1978).

Table 10-5. Retaliatory Capabilities of the Finite Deterrence Force: Percent Damage to Soviet Target Base.

	Current	Mid–1980s	1990s
Total Force[a]			
Industrial target base	80	80	80
Military targets	90	90	90
Capability to Hedge against Soviet Developments[b]			
A. No ballistic missile warheads, only bombers attack			
Industrial target base only	75	80–85	75–85
Industrial and military targets	35	55–60	50–60
B. No surviving ICBMs, only bombers and submarines attack			
Industrial target base only	85	90	90
Industrial and military targets	65	80–85	75–85
C. No surviving submarines, only bombers and ICBMs attack			
Industrial target base only	90	85–90	80–85
Industrial and military targets	70	70–75	55–65
D. No bomber weapons, only submarines and ICBMs attack			
Industrial target base only	90	90	85–90
Industrial and military targets	75	75–80	60–70

a. Weapons expected to survive a first strike are allocated to achieve over 80 percent damage to the industrial target base, assuming half were hardened to 30 psi. One thousand submarine warheads are held in reserve. The remainder of the weapons are allocated to military targets other than silos (at least one ballistic missile weapon is allocated to each military airfield and 100 SRAMs are allocated to air defense sites). No Soviet ICBM silos are included in the military target base.

b. All surviving weapons of forces indicated are allocated; no weapons are held in reserve. For the mid-1980s column, the low end of the range assumes a 20 percent growth in industrial targets; the high end assumes no growth. For the 1990s column, the low end of the range assumes a 40 percent growth in industrial targets; the high end assumes no growth.

Source: Congressional Budget Office, *Retaliatory Issues for the U.S. Strategic Nuclear Forces*, Congress of the United States (Washington, D.C.: Government Printing Office, June 1978), p. xvi.

The effectiveness of these attacks are shown in Table 10–5 for the three time periods, and various combinations of weapon availability, for example, row D is an attack only with land and submarine missiles; no bombers. For the first category titled, Total Force, 80 percent of the Soviet industrial target base and 90 percent of military facilities other than missile silos would be destroyed by the full retaliation force (bombers, ICBMs, and SLBMs) even assuming the retention of 1,000 weapons (10 to 20 percent of surviving forces). Each element of the present U.S. strategic forces—bombers, ICBMs, and submarine-launched ballistic missiles (SLBMs)—independently, could destroy 75 percent or more of the Soviet industrial target base even after a first strike. In the future, it was assumed not to be true for the existing U.S. ICBM force, if no modifications were introduced, because of increasing losses in the 1980s (Figure 10–9). However, as Table 10–5 reveals, the expected improvements in U.S. strategic forces keep their destructive capabilities for retaliation high. All three studies indicate a high degree of industrial vulnerability, although Kemp's study provides a better basis for distinguishing minimum weapon needs.

SELECTED ATTACKS

The 1974 Metis study prepared for ACDA looked at the Soviet as well as the U.S. vulnerability question previously discussed in Chapter 5. It examined the question of whether low-level attacks could significantly damage warmaking capability, if targeted against critical industrial sectors. As the authors noted:

> The economic and social institutions which support a society's war-making capability are highly interactive. One industry or economic sector can critically affect many of the other sectors, even though that output is not immediately required to sustain the final demands of the war-making.
>
> The same considerations apply to the relationships between other sectors of the economy. Loss of output in one basic industry through nuclear damage can severely inhibit or cripple output in another, dependent but undamaged or partly damaged industry. These dependencies create a "ripple" effect throughout the entire national economic base and significantly retarding or preventing overall economic recovery.[19]

Using input–output tables[20] for the Soviet economy as they did for that of the United States, the authors of the Metis study concluded that, by creating bottlenecks in defense-related production, a general 10 percent reduction of industrial capacity in the Soviet Union would have economic effects far more serious than the numbers of weapons might suggest. The output from Table 10-6 illustrates the impact of a general 10 percent industrial loss on the Soviet economy. As the table shows, shortfalls (reductions in output) can be quite severe, implying serious disruptions of the economy. However, caution should be used in interpreting the input–output methodology. Substitution of other materials, products, or means of production such as labor may be possible. Therefore, the actual percent reductions shown are subject to considerable uncertainty.

This study provides an important insight. While ACDA, Kemp, and the CBO studies indicated that the general vulnerability of Soviet industry is significant, the Metis discussion reveals the potential of small sophisticated attacks. Thus the combination of the possible economic bottlenecking discussed in the Metis study, and the small number of key targets in critical industry discussed previously, makes a strategy of selected industrial destruction quite viable. The result is that the real impact of a well-designed small (few hundred weapons) attack on the Soviet Union's economy could be magnified by concentrating on basic industries, such as iron and steel works, forging and miscellaneous products, blast furnaces and basic steel products, petroleum products, electronic components, and chemical products. As the Metis study also indicated, (discussed in Chapter 5) the United States is in a similar predicament.

Table 10-6. Bottlenecking Effects—Soviet Union.

Bottleneck Sector	Number of Sectors Satisfied	Final Demand Shortfall (percent)
Machine tools	19	93.6
Forging-pressing M&E	20	93.5
Precision instruments	38	86.3
Nonferrous ores, pumps, and compressors, transportation M&E	38	84.1

Source: Modified from The Metis Corporation, "Data Base and Damage Criteria for Measurement of Arms Limitation Effects on War Supporting Industry," Contract no. ACDA/WEC-242 (Alexandria, Virginia: Metis Corporation, June 1974), p. 52.

Postattack Recovery

A final element in the discussion of Soviet vulnerability is the issue of the comparative resilience of the Soviet versus U.S. economies, that is, postattack recovery.

In Chapter 5, we described the difficulties for U.S. recovery based on a Stanford Research Institute model projection. In that study, an attempt was made to make a similar estimate of the Soviet Union's recovery capabilities. This included two attacks. The heavy attack assumed 65 percent urban population and 70 percent plant capacity losses (comparable to the Congressional Budget Office's and ACDA's attacks), and the medium attack resulted in 55 percent urban population and 60 percent plant capacity losses (similar to Kemp's Attack D-4). The model used a measurement of the Soviet economy called Net Material Product (NMP)[21] which is similar to the GNP. The analysis is shown in Table 10-7 and Figure 10-10. It indicates severe long term economic recovery difficulties similar to those found for the United States. While these results should be viewed with caution because of the preliminary nature of the calculations and the inadequacy of the Soviet data, it is interesting that the authors concluded, "the general characteristics of the U.S. and Soviet economies may not be as different as often asserted, and may lean to similar recovery capabilities."[22]

Taken together, the Kemp, Metis, and ACDA studies indicate that substantial damage can be achieved in the Soviet Union, as it was for the United States, by relatively low numbers of weapons aimed at crucial targets. The addition of the Stanford Research Institute recovery analysis reinforces the observation that the U.S. and Soviet economies have generally similar vulnerabilities. Tables 10-2 and 5-3 suggest that the Soviet Union may be even more vulnerable than the United States in numbers of warheads and megatonnage requirements. The United States is highly urbanized and has several massive urban centers, such as New York and Los Angeles, which are much larger than any Soviet cities. Soviet urban areas, however, are much more compact, owing partly to the absence of private automobiles in any significant numbers. Thus, while it requires the destruction of 204 Soviet cities to eliminate approximately the same portion of industrial capacity, 60 to 65 percent, found in the seventy-one standard metropolitan statistical areas (SMSAs), the compactness of these

Table 10-7. Illustrative Results: Analysis of the Relationship of Surviving Capacity versus Recovery Rate (*USSR 1972 Runs with 16 Sector Model*).

Run	Attack Level	Surviving Capacity GNP	Initial Noninvestment Demand	Postattack NMP-Year					Average Annual Growth
				One	Two	Three	Four	Five	
32-B	Medium	75%	38%	41.9%	39.2%	56.7%	58.9%	72.2%	14.6%
37-C	Heavy	71	30	32.7	30.6	44.8	46.1	62.4	17.5

Notes: Investment cost per ruble of incremental NMP was 2.0 for both runs.

The objective function used for optimization was the present value of the future stream of NMP. For definition of NMP see page II-11.

The stipulated lower level for noninvestment demand was increased at the rate of four percent per year from year two to year five.

The uniform growth rate from the fifth year on was set at four percent.

The depreciation rate was set at five percent.

For the heavy attack it was assumed that 29 percent of the population (65 percent of the urban population) and 70 percent of plant capacity in each sector was lost.

For the medium attack it was assumed that 25 percent of the population (55 percent of the urban population) and 60 percent of plant capacity in each sector was lost.

Source: F.W. Dresch, and S. Baum, *Analysis of the U.S. and USSR Potential for Economic Recovery Following A Nuclear Attack*, (Menlo Park, California: Stanford Research Institute, Strategic Studies Center, January 1973), p. II-9.

Figure 10-10. Postattack Recovery Measured by Net Material Product (NMP)[a] — USSR.

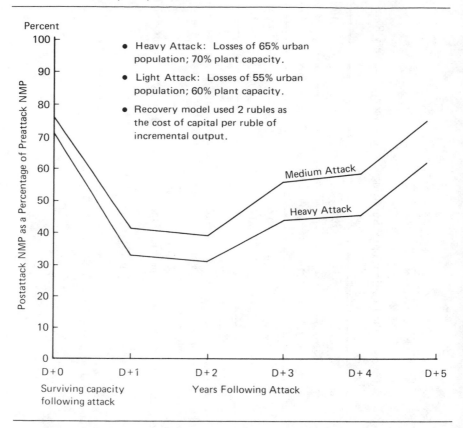

a. Net Material Product (NMP) — Goods and structures going to final demand.

Source: F.W. Dresch, and S. Baum, *Analysis of the U.S. and USSR Potential for Economic Recovery Following a Nuclear Attack*, Stanford Research Institute, Strategic Studies Center, (Menlo Park, California: January 1973), p. II-10.

Soviet cities substantially diminishes the weapon requirements per city.

To provide a comparison of strategic needs with strategic capabilities, Figure 10-11 shows American forces in relation to the requirements for Attacks D-1 and D-4 on the Soviet Union, while Figure 10-12 depicts current Soviet forces in relation to the weapon requirements for Attacks A-1 and A-4 on the United States.[23] It

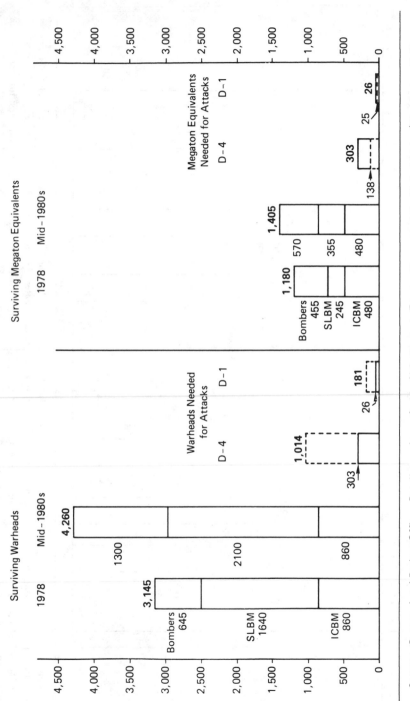

Figure 10-11. U.S. Weapon Capability versus Requirements for Hypothetical Attacks D–1 and D–4 on the Soviet Union. Requirements for Attacks D–1 and D–4 using 50 kt (– – – –) or 1 megaton (——) weapons are shown.

Source: Congressional Budget Office, *Retaliatory Issues for the U.S. Strategic Forces*, Congress of the United States (Washington, D.C.: Government Printing Office, June 1978), pp. 8–9. Basic strategic weapon estimates—U.S.

Figure 10–12. Surviving Soviet Weapon Capabilities Compared to Requirements for Hypothetical Attacks A–1 and A–4 on the United States.

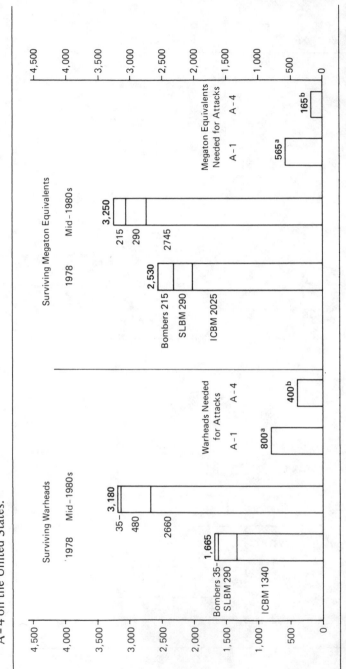

Sources: Congressional Budget Office, *Counterforce Issues for the U.S. Strategic Nuclear Forces*, Congress of the United States (Washington, D.C.: Government Printing Office, January 1978), p. 16. Basic strategic weapon estimates—USSR.

International Institute for Strategic Studies, *The Military Balance, 1978–1979* (London, England: The International Institute for Strategic Studies, 1978). Basic strategic weapon estimates—USSR.

a. 500 one megaton, 300 one hundred kiloton weapons.
b. 100 one megaton, 300 one hundred kiloton weapons.

should be evident that both countries possess substantially greater numbers of weapons and equivalent megatonnage than would be required for an extremely damaging retaliatory attack, even when only the immediate, direct, and easily quantified nuclear effects are considered.

Moreover, Figures 10–11 and 10–12 show actual weapons and megatonnage estimated to reach targets. For this purpose, it was assumed that one out of five missiles fired will malfunction, half of the submarine fleets will be out of firing position, and of those in firing position 20 percent wll be destroyed by antisubmarine weapons and half of the ICBMs will be fired, implying a more effective first strike against ICBMs than is considered feasible under existing conditions. It is also assumed that only a quarter of the total U.S. or Soviet bomber forces penetrates air defenses and reach targets.[24]

In the case of the small hypothetical attacks, the available weapons and megatonnage in each country exceed requirements by more than a factor of ten. Or, in cruder terms, each major type of delivery system or launch-vehicle (long-range bombers, ground-launched ballistic missiles, or submarine-launched ballistic missiles) has by itself, as noted in the Congressional Budget Office study, the numbers of nuclear weapons and equivalent megatonnage necessary to inflict very heavy damage, although each does not necessarily have the full targeting capability.

The discussion above illustrates two important points. The first is that the United States will have sufficient capability to retaliate against the Soviet Union (and vice versa) to achieve a level of destruction equal to the devastation wrought against the United States. Second, the Soviet economy offers the same selective opportunity for bottlenecking as the United States's—providing additional support for the first point.

CIVIL DEFENSE EFFECTIVENESS

While one focus of this chapter has been on describing Soviet vulnerability to nuclear attack, the question has been posed about whether these effects can be reduced. A substantial debate developed about the effectiveness of Soviet civil defense efforts in diminishing the vulnerability of populations (casualties) and industrial capacity.[25] The possibility of diminishing effects will be reviewed briefly, first for casualties, then for industrial damage.

Casualties

The casualties from an industrial attack on the Soviet Union can also be quite substantial. The CIA predicted a range from over 100 million for minimal civil defense preparation to the low tens of millions (50 percent being fatalities)[26] for a week of evacuation and preparation. A range of fatalities are indicated by Figure 10-13, produced by ACDA.[27] They are in general agreement with the CIA's estimates and those made by the Congressional Budget Office.[28]

The first bar represents no civil defense with 80 to 90 million fatalities; the second represents effective urban evacuation and shelter resulting in 25 to 35 million fatalities. The stripped portion of the seventh and final column shows the wide uncertainty associated with evacuation and shelter preparation. The maximum estimate assumed the attack begins in the first hours of evacuation and the lowest estimate is similar to the assumptions of column 2, best evacuation and shelter. The other columns refer to combinations of ground burst, evacuation time, and a direct attack on evacuated population. The latter possibility, attacking population directly, is an important counter strategy to minimize the effectiveness of a planned evacuation. As the CBO pointed out, the act of implementing civil defense would probably trigger an increased alert status of U.S. strategic force. This in turn would insure more surviving weapons available to use just this type of targeting strategy.

The low end of the range for ACDA casualty estimates is higher than the more optimistic survival projections made by critics of the present U.S. strategic policies. Nevertheless, the casualty levels, which will occur simultaneously, under the most optimistic assumptions would be unprecedented even for a nation such as the Soviet Union that has experienced massive numbers of injuries and deaths in wartime invasions. The Soviet Union did absorb 20 million casualties in World War II but they occurred over a six year period, 1940 to 1945, not within days or weeks.

Industrial

The ability of the Soviet Union (and the United States) to reduce industrial damage has also been identified by critics of the present

Figure 10-13. Sensitivity of Immediate Fatalities to Attack Assumptions (U.S. Forces Generated).

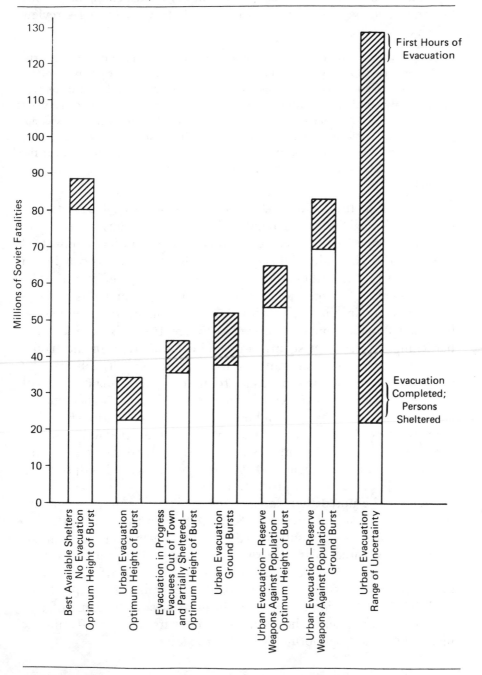

Source: United States Arms Control and Disarmament Agency, *An Analysis of Civil Defense in Nuclear War* (Washington, D.C.: ACDA, December 1978), p. 12.

U.S. civil defense posture. A number of possibilities from "hardening" machinery (by physically protecting it) to dispersing or placing factories underground has been discussed. However, a CIA review concluded:

> Soviet measures to protect the economy could not prevent massive industrial damage. The Soviet program for dispersal of industry appears to be offset by a contrary tendency for investments in new facilities to be inside or near previously existing installations. The Soviet measure for protecting the work force, critical equipment, and supplies and for limiting damage from secondary effects could contribute to maintaining and restoring production after an attack. We expect some improvements in the level of protection for the economy, but any radical change in its vulnerability to nuclear attack is unlikely.[29]

Moreover, as the 1978 ACDA study pointed out, effective targeting of individual industrial plants with single weapons, particularly with improving MIRV accuracy, would make significant industrial protection of key industrial sectors very difficult.[30] This conclusion is supported by the CBO study which examined the effects of hardening (increasing protection against blast) of Soviet industrial machinery. Only in the case of the relatively inaccurate submarine-launched Poseidon missiles shown in Figure 10–14 is the industrial hardening successful at significantly reducing damage. In the figure, the lower two lines represent extensive protection. The horizontal axis uses the number of submarines to indicate increasing numbers of weapons. However, accuracy becomes so critical at 50 percent destruction that increasing numbers of missiles (submarines) do not help significantly. For comparison, the effect on the ability of the new more accurate Trident missile to destroy hardened targets successfully is shown in Figure 10–15. The curve marked 80 psi represents a high level of target protection.

It should be noted that none of these analyses appear to account for multiple blast and thermal effects. Although the effect of neighboring detonations are substantially smaller in magnitude than the 30 or 80 psi direct blast pressure, their appearance before or after the main blast may serve to disrupt and degrade the effectiveness of defensive measures in critical ways. For example, ignitable debris could be created prior to the main blast to negate the value of firebreaks, or conversely, the main blast may itself create flammable material for the neighboring explosion to ignite.

Figure 10-14.   Effect of Industrial Hardening on Poseidon Effectiveness.

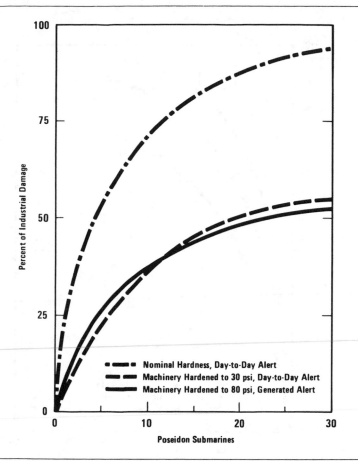

Source: Congressional Budget Office, *Retaliatory Issues for the U.S. Strategic Nuclear Forces*, Congress of the United States (Washington, D.C.: Government Printing Office, June 1978), p. 26.

In summary, while there do exist strategies that if unchallenged could reduce industrial damage and casualties, they do not appear to have been implemented by the Soviet Union on a massive scale. The closest to an effort in this direction is the unusually deep subways built in some cities.[31] More critically, with the availability of accurate multiple warhead (MIRV) weapons, the industrial protection possibilities are limited by the United States's ability to specifically target

Figure 10-15. Effect of Industrial Hardening on Trident Effectiveness.

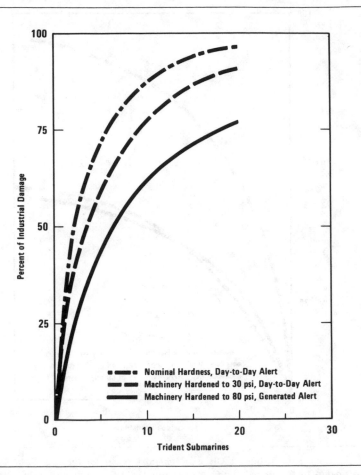

Legend:
- ■ ━ ■ ━ ■ Nominal Hardness, Day-to-Day Alert
- ━ ━ ━ Machinery Hardened to 30 psi, Day-to-Day Alert
- ━━━ Machinery Hardened to 80 psi, Generated Alert

Y-axis: Percent of Industrial Damage

X-axis: Trident Submarines

Source: Congressional Budget Office, *Retaliatory Issues for the U.S. Strategic Nuclear Forces*, Congress of the United States (Washington, D.C.: Government Printing Office, June 1978), p. 26.

key industries—promising disruption of even undamaged parts of the economy in a manner revealed by the 1974 Metis study. Direct population protection, while potentially more fruitful, could also be defeated by either early attacks or selected targeting of evacuation areas. This is a key point since the attacker has the option to choose the time, place, and circumstances (e.g., weather), and thus turn any civil defense strategy requiring three to seven days into a shambles.

Furthermore, the attacker has the option not to attack. In this case, the Soviet economy would be essentially closed down during evacuation, and the dilemma previously discussed for the United States, of continuing economic chaos or losing evacuation as a meaningful strategy, will have to be confronted by the Soviet Union. Finally, the studies by the Central Intelligence Agency, the Congressional Budget Office, and the Arms Control and Disarmament Agency cited above do not support the contention that passive defenses will significantly lessen the population and industrial damage from all-out attacks.

PERSPECTIVE

There is no indication that a well-planned nuclear attack on the Soviet Union's industrial base would fail to achieve its purpose—the simultaneous occurrence of unprecedented industrial damage and casualties throughout that nation, resulting in unacceptable damage to its economy and broader social structure. Moreover, given the accuracy, flexibility, and numbers of U.S. strategic weapons, particularly its missiles, it appears possible to checkmate successfully or undercut any strategy designed to reduce casualties and industrial destruction. Thus, Soviet economic vulnerability is similar to the United States's. It has smaller sized cities but higher urban economic and population concentrations. While the number of cities that the United States is required to attack is larger, their size permits fewer weapons per city to be used compared to metropolitan areas in the United States. The Soviet Union is also vulnerable to bottlenecking, since key industrial sectors are concentrated in relatively few targets. In fact, the Soviet economy appears to experience considerable bottlenecking because of its inefficiency, in the course of normal operation,[32] which could exacerbate the actual effects.

Therefore, discussion of U.S. vulnerabilities and problems, while perhaps differing in detail, still represents a good basis for estimating the common problems of industrialized societies in life after nuclear war.

NOTES TO CHAPTER 10

1. U.S. Arms Control and Disarmament Agency, *An Analysis of Civil Defense in Nuclear War* (Washington, D.C.: ACDA, December 1978).

2. The methodology used did not include nonpopulated urban areas such as commercial districts, rivers, lakes, or large parks. Thus, total land area used in this comparison is less than the computed area based on city limit dimensions.

3. While Soviet urban population represents a smaller proportion of the total population than the United States's, the absolute numbers are almost identical (United States: 131 million; Soviet Union: 126 million).

4. Nautical mile = 1.151 statute miles. One nautical mile squared (NM^2) is equal to 1.325 statute miles squared.

5. The overpressure for 40 Kt at 1.5 NM^2 is approximately 6 psi (pounds per square inch), while 200 Kt is 15 psi. This is above the 5 psi criteria used for virtual destruction. No specific weapon size was given in the report.

6. The physical dispersion of these targets, however, might force more missiles to be used against one nation or the other since the geographical area that warheads from a single MIRVed missile can accurately hit is physically limited.

7. One megaton (Mt) weapon would enclose within the 5 psi, eight or nine times the area of a 40 Kt weapon or three times the area of a 200 Kt weapon, thus larger weapons would reduce the actual numbers of bombs or warheads.

8. U.S. Arms Control and Disarmament Agency, p. 6.

9. Ibid., p. 5.

10. See H.W. Kendall, *The Bulletin of the Atomic Scientists* 35, No. 7 (September 1979): 34; and Gary L. Guertiner, "SALT and Carter's Dilemma," *World View* (September 1979): 11.

11. Geoffrey Kemp, "Nuclear Forces for Medium Powers. Part I. Targets and Weapons Systems, Parts II and III. Strategic Requirements and Options." *Adelphi Papers* 106 and 107 (London: International Institute for Strategic Studies, 1974).

12. Kemp, Part I, p. 25.

13. U.S. Department of Defense, *Annual Report, Fiscal Year 1979*, (Washington, D.C.: Government Printing Office), p. 55.

14. The ACDA study stated that the bulk of the U.S. ICBMs were destroyed but gave no specific levels—the level above 30 percent is just for illustrative purposes.

15. A force of 10 to 15 percent of the United States's surviving warheads was assumed held in reserve for future retaliation.

16. Office of Technology Assessment, *The Effects of Nuclear War* (Washington, D.C.: Government Printing Office, May 1979), p. 79.

17. U.S. Arms Control and Disarmament Agency, p. 8.

18. Congressional Budget Office, *Retaliatory Issues for the U.S. Strategic Nuclear Forces* (Washington, D.C.: Government Printing Office, June 1978).

19. The Metis Corporation, "Data Base and Damage Criteria for Measurement of Arms Limitation Effects on War Supporting Industry," contract no. ACDA/WEC-242 (Alexandria, Va.: June 1974), p. 3.

20. Input-output tables provide a way of seeing how one industry contributes to production in other industries and, conversely, how all other industries contribute to production in a single industry. Using a table (matrix) of this type, a picture of the interaction of industries and, more importantly, the identification of which industries play key roles in production by others can be developed.

21. Net Material Product (NMP) is approximately equal to the value of goods and structures going to final demand and differs from GNP only by excluding nonproductive services (services not contributing to the production of tangible product).

22. F.W. Dresch, and S. Baum, *Analysis of the U.S. and USSR Potential for Economic Recovery Following A Nuclear Attack*, Strategic Studies Center, (Menlo Park, California: Stanford Research Institute, January 1973), p. II-13.

23. Estimates of Soviet future strength vary widely: the numbers shown are indicative, not definitive. The reader is cautioned taking estimates of future Soviet capabilities too literally.

24. A reliability factor of 0.81 was assumed for all missiles on both sides. While some complex targeting and re-targeting factors are ignored, these are conservative estimates of available forces.

25. For examples, see T.K. Jones, "Soviet Civil Defense" in *Civil Defense Review*, Hearings by the Civil Defense Panel of the House Armed Services Committee, 94th Cong., 2nd sess. (Washington: Government Printing Office, 1976), pp. 206-267; "Industrial Survival and Recovery After Nuclear Attack" in *The Defense Industrial Base: Industrial Preparedness and Nuclear War Survival.* Hearings before the Joint Committee on Defense Production, 94th Cong., 2nd sess. (Washington: Government Printing Office, 1977); and Leon Goure, *Shelters in Soviet War Survival Strategy* (Washington: Advanced International Studies Institute, Inc., 1978).

26. Central Intelligence Agency, *Soviet Civil Defense*, NI 78-10003, (July 1978), p. 14.

27. U.S. Arms Control and Disarmament Agency, 1978, p. 12.

28. Congress Budget Office, pp. 22-24.

29. Central Intelligence Agency, p. 3.

30. U.S. Arms Control and Disarmament Agency, 1978, pp. 9-11.

31. However, it should be noted that the plans of most concern to civil defense advocates are those relying on evacuation.

32. Hedrick Smith, *The Russians* (New York: Ballantine Books, 1976), pp. pp. 285-320.

IV SUMMARY

11 EPILOGUE AS PROLOGUE
Some Observations

As I was writing this book, someone asked me to describe what life would be like after nuclear war. The individual thought it was important to confront people with the possibility of living in the world after a nuclear exchange. The question was posed in the starkest terms: Would the living envy the dead?

As startling and compelling as that question is, it is only the starting point. There are other very significant questions that must be examined as well. The most critical ones concern our ability to translate the consequences of nuclear war from an appropriately horrifying tale to the stuff that genuinely influences the sometimes arcane, contentious, and demanding process called strategic decisionmaking. Are we willing to face the implications of the domestic and international effects of nuclear war and decide: How much is enough? Will the apparent plausibility sophisticated technology gives to dangerously flawed nuclear strategies be recognized and resisted? Can national decisions about strategic nuclear policy achieve the proper balance—a combination of sensitivity to military needs and resistance to domination by the powerful imagery of the worst case? This is the territory that must be explored before our journey is complete.

It is important to make the observation that there will be many survivors in the world, and even in the nations directly involved in a nuclear war. Nuclear war may indeed have the appearance of Armageddon, but it is distinctly not the end of the world. However, for those nations involved in a nuclear exchange it may indeed be the end of *their* world. After an attack using weapons with the destructive power of only a few hundred megaton equivalents, the United States, Soviet Union, or other countries may resemble underdeveloped nations lurching from one economic and political crisis to another. The process of postattack economic recovery is like that of economic development or growth; it requires the production of surpluses to support expansion beyond the limited, surviving economic base. In contrast to these needs, a postattack society will be confronted with extensive destruction of basic industries, damage to vital economic links such as transportation and communications, as well as the burden of major relief efforts that will tax surviving assets. Further, the factors that make rapid recovery from a small-scale disaster possible—limited damage, modest casualties, surviving leadership and technical skills, and the availability of external, easily mobilized human and material resources—will almost certainly be absent following a nuclear attack involving several hundred weapons targeted at a nation's industrial base.

Under these circumstances it is unlikely that a nation will be able to generate the surpluses necessary for rapid economic growth or recovery for ten years, more likely longer. This should be true even if hostilities are terminated immediately after these attacks. If a state of war or near-war continues, the demands of defense will divert even more of the limited stock of usable industrial facilities away from economic recovery.

More critically, from our smallest 100 1-megaton weapon attack or counterforce attacks to the largest conceived—even beyond those discussed in this book—the world around these damaged nations will change. World politics after nuclear war has not been the subject of much study, yet it is pivotal. The realignment of power relationships among nations, the control of resources, and the political price demanded by noncombatant nations for recovery assistance are rarely, if ever, the topic of public discussion. The debate normally ends as the bombs fall and the dead are counted. This is a dangerously narrow viewpoint. In fact, if world politics has already passed beyond the reach of simple political and military control of the superpowers, what will the world be like when these surviving powers are reeling from each others' nuclear blows—even those considered modest and restrained by many strategic planners? Worldwide turmoil will exist even for a limited war scenario. World politics and economics will be thrown into chaos by a potential combination of paralysis (trade frozen by fear of retaliation against a nation dealing with a superpower or its close allies), aggressive opportunism (battles for regional hegemony among smaller nations), and general economic instability (international monetary disruptions).

The unpleasant reality is that the "winners" of nuclear war may be nations that are rarely, if ever, publicly acknowledged by strategic planners and public officials; for example, potential regional powers such as India, Mexico, Brazil, Nigeria, and Indonesia. Those powers that one might expect to dominate because of their present political, economic, and military strength—Japan, China, Western Europe—may fare no better than the United States and Soviet Union, particularly in any major nuclear war. Indeed, they are unlikely to escape without substantial direct or indirect damage. Thus, the substance of national and individual life after nuclear war may be the subject of the agendas of nations not particularly disposed to allow the damaged nations the power, prestige, and material comforts they previously assumed as their own. Even if disposed to provide aid altruistically, or at least from perceived self-interest, these nations will be without the economic resources the United States had after World War II, when it supported the remarkable recovery of its European allies, as well as its former adversaries, Japan, and Germany.[1]

An even less comforting alternative view is that world political and economic life may degenerate into factionalism and chaos, with nations unwittingly or indifferently undercutting the recovery of the damaged nations. The chaos will be triggered, as it was in the depression of the 1930s, by the collapse of the economies of the major powers. This scenario is in contrast to those optimistic scenarios of the "winning" nation forcing other undamaged or partially damaged nations to do its bidding, that is, provide their resources and products.[2] While these war winning scenarios are plausible sounding possibilities, plausibility is hardly the basis for risking national life, particularly if the viability of national power may be at stake. In this war winning case, miscalculation is of particular concern, for despite the likelihood of an extensive base of remaining military weapon technology, there is no guarantee the United States, the Soviet Union, or any other nation will have the critical supporting economic and social structure to ensure that its military capabilities are of any real value.

Ironically, it should be evident that under these circumstances the rest of the world cannot view itself as concerned but distant spectators to any strategy of limited or full-scale nuclear war. As we have seen, even with a limited nuclear war, the world economic system, particularly the food production system, will be in varying degrees of chaos, and defense alliances will be in total confusion or collapse. The other end of the spectrum, full scale war, is even less comforting for all nations, even for those possible "winners." This perception of the postattack world is by no means unique, as a recent United Nations report made clear:

> Even more serious than radioactive fallout, however, would be the global consequences of a large nuclear war on the world economy and on vital functions of the international community. The sudden collapse of many of the world's leading trading nations as well as of established mechanisms for international transactions would lead to profound disorganization in world affairs and leave most other nations, even if physically intact, in desperate circumstances. Widespread famines could occur, both in poor developing countries and in industrialized nations. Those starving to death might eventually outnumber the direct fatalities in the belligerent countries. Even non-belligerent States might enter a downward spiral leading to utter misery for their populations, and almost all would suffer a loss of standards corresponding to many decades of progress. Economic conditions such as these might trigger latent political instabilities, causing upheavals and civil and local wars.[3]

To be relatively powerful in a world of economic and political collapse and hostile military competition is hardly a desirable goal. In sum, life after nuclear war may not have the living envy the dead, but it will have most nations and individuals envying with a passion the *status quo ante.*

Thus, despite all the brave talk about surviving or winning a nuclear exchange, one of the key lessons of this inquiry is that the effect of nuclear weapons on society and international standing is far more damaging than we have been ready to admit. Therefore, the weapons requirements necessary to create unacceptable damage are significantly smaller than we have been willing to acknowledge (Figures 10–11 and 10–12). They are indeed a small fraction of *surviving* strategic forces (20 percent) even if high losses of weapons are assumed. The consequence of understating the effects of nuclear war is that strategic policy decisions are driven by inflated weapons requirements and, equally important, overstatements of the potential political flexibility for fighting certain types of nuclear war created by sophisticated weapons technology. This illusion of flexibility is likely to be a key issue of the 1980s.

This last conclusion leads to a second critical point. The introduction by the United States and Soviet Union in the 1970s of large numbers of MIRVed missiles with highly accurate nuclear warheads foreshadowed an era of continually expanding strategic military options. These nuclear options, built upon a dynamic, highly sophisticated technological base, have become increasingly subtle in their design, and thus difficult to manage, and more importantly, to reject. The sophistication of the technology itself has become a critical factor in shaping strategy. Part of the compelling character of present strategic proposals is that technological advances allow them to be portrayed as having such limited destructiveness that they begin to have the appearance of a well-planned but extremely restrained conventional war. Therefore, weapons technology and the goal of a controlled nuclear conflict leading to strategic military advantage reinforce each other. In contrast, when examined in depth, the destructiveness of limited nuclear war is clearly not restricted, but instead highly threatening. This contrast between actual or perceived damage created in a limited nuclear war and the military ideal makes the risks involved in its initiation very high, and consequently, the margin of success very thin. The consequences of a miscalculation are so great that they should give pause to the most confident and daring military planner on either side—Soviet as well as American. This conclusion points to an important observation. Despite our primary focus on the United States, the problems described are not unique to this country and should serve as a compelling warning to anyone attracted to the illusion of nuclear war winning.

Nevertheless, despite these warnings, weapons technology will improve, accuracy and flexibility will grow, and controllable nuclear war will appear within grasp. This in turn will spawn a plethora of countermeasures, equally sophisticated and expensive. The proposed MX missile system is a case in point. Therefore, effective political grasp of the controllability issue will be of great importance, since the concept of rationally controlled nuclear assaults is likely to appear explicitly or implicitly in many future strategic policy and technology decisions. One of the objectives of this book is to provide some tools to draw out and fully expose the implications of these types of decisions—to "disrobe" these options and expose their critical inadequacies. There is no magic formula to deal with these issues, just a steady, tough-minded approach to the problem. In fact, part of successfully utilizing the observations and conclusions found in this book is recognizing that they will only affect a decisionmaking process already sensitive to these issues—they have no life of their own.

With this in mind, a central question arises: How does the decisionmaking process respond to these issues? In order to discuss this question usefully, a distinction should be made between the way the political decisionmaker and the military planner approach strategic problems. (The term "political" is used in the broadest sense of the word—the integration of domestic, economic, social, political as well as international strategic and general foreign policy considerations).

For the strategic military planner, a key goal is to minimize "regret"—the regret being the results of a miscalculation. This predisposition is strongly reinforced by the fact that deterrence is fundamentally psychological, a strategy based on your adversary's perception of your own nuclear strength. The object of this strategy is to intimidate the adversary, confronting that nation with the *certainty* that you possess a devastating nuclear capability under any circumstances. Thus, the planner's logic is driven to examine the worst case. In terms of destruction, this means assuring an effective surviving nuclear weapons capability. The planner in this case will assume that the attack attains the highest level of effectiveness against U.S. military targets, while the U.S. nuclear response will encounter the greatest failure. The outcome of this approach is that the planner assumes an extremely low survival rate for U.S. nuclear capabilities and understates the effectiveness of the U.S. weapons that respond. This combination drives the planner to incorporate massive overkill into the system to minimize regret. In contrast, the worst case for a first strike or counterforce capability by the United States would have the United States's missiles and bombers being subject to a high degree of failure, while damage to Soviet civilian targets would be estimated as high as possible, creating the greatest potential for escalation and effective retaliation by the Soviet Union. This again drives the planner to develop more accurate missiles and the largest numbers of weapons to increase effectiveness.

This approach in its proper context is useful, since it represents an extremely cautious perspective for military planning. It is a perspective in which the underlying objective is to have a level of military capability (best weapons) in peacetime that insures that no one will regret the military outcome of any conceivable war. In contrast, the political leader must attempt to avoid wars that would be regretted politically because they are lost, or inconclusive and "unworthy." For an example of the latter, compare Vietnam and World War II in their public acceptability and political impacts. Nuclear war will be regretted in almost any conceivable context, and thus the imperative for political leaders is to avoid war—otherwise they have failed. Given these different perspectives and values, the problem arises when the analyses generated by the military approach begin to be used as the centerpiece for the political decisionmaking process, which must balance broader foreign and domestic policy demands. Perhaps part of the explanation for this emphasis on the worst-case military perspective is that it may appear technically more precise; that is, it can be supported by quantitative analysis. In contrast, the overall political evaluation, particularly one which lacks the support of systematic consequence assessments, can appear too soft, unable to present forcefully its own concept of regret. Instead of creating a balanced, realistic view of the opportunities and uncertainties embedded in any strategic policy, the military planners' limited view dominates the discussion.

The values of the civilian decisionmaker (in congress or the presidential or cabinet level) do of course enter the process, particularly at budget time, but it appears to be generally intuitive—the result of cabinet level or presidential decisions, or perhaps congressional resistance. In short, those values lack the credibility of a systematic policy.

An example of this problem evolved from the 1974 presentation of the concept of limited war.[4] The capabilities attributed to the Soviet Union's counterforce for damaging U.S. land-based missiles were used as a justification for requesting the development of U.S. missiles with higher accuracy, ICBM systems with better retargeting capabilities, and ultimately, for a more secure land-based missile system—at present the MX. In terms of deterrence (assuring missile survival for retaliation), the presentation of the most effective attack on U.S. missiles coupled with the least amount of damage to U.S. civilian targets was understandable. It provided a graphic illustration of the problem. But the limited war concept included more. It assumed retaliation against the Soviet Union's strategic military forces and implicitly supported, even if not consciously intended at that point, the emerging concept of offensive war fighting capabilities. In contrast, the type of information that should have been presented for supporting this type of U.S. strategy would depict the poorest possible U.S. missile performance against Soviet targets, resulting in the worst civilian damage for the Soviets.

Of equal significance, the controllability issue—the potential for restraining escalation—was not satisfactorily raised or addressed initially, nor was the possible reaction of the Soviet Union to an emerging, clearly defined U.S. first strike capability. These types of questions did not begin to emerge fully as critical factors until the Office of Technology Assessment (OTA) review group, discussed in Chapter 3, postulated a substantially worse case than originally presented. Essentially, the congressional decisionmaker only saw a narrow perception of the problem.

To correct these deficiencies and create the basis for a satisfactory political decision, strategic decisions must evolve out of a process in which all the complex ramifications of a policy are stated explicitly. This process should be public, and for effectiveness, adversarial. Further, the substance of the discussion must be enlarged in at least two dimensions. The first is the appropriate range of consequences and effects from nuclear war—the inclusion of social, political, and institutional changes, as well as a discussion of international economic and political relationships. This would require a variety of perspectives and skills, such as policy analysts, and political scientists to be utilized in this process. The other dimension is the need to contrast or incorporate the worst case in a wider range of possible alternative outcomes, defining the uncertainty and, explicitly, the nature of the price of being wrong. Again, political debate, as opposed to the military planning process, needs a much broader framework within which to work. Unacceptable damage in many instances has a different set of meanings for the two groups, and without this distinction made explicit, the ultimate political decisions shaping strategic policy will be seriously flawed. Therefore, the public review process, even more critically than the one used internally in the executive branch, requires strategic policymakers to display the appropriate information comprehensively and understandably. Above all, what is required of all actors is realism—a sober consideration of all relevant information.

PROLOGUE

Despite the importance of creating a more realistic understanding of the effects of nuclear war and assuring its place in strategic planning, there are larger issues about the future of nuclear weapons policy that need to be addressed. It is clear that the early 1980s may be a difficult time in which to resolve strategic weapon issues, given the current atmosphere of hostility between the United States and Soviet Union. However, the consequence of nuclear war is so fearsome that eliminating or reducing its possibility is an imperative. The critical requirement in the short term is to regain a sense of effective direction and believable goals. Part of successfully meeting this objective is to restructure a credible arms control process.

The first element is an honest appraisal of why strategic arms limitation objectives appear to have been derailed. One reason for this problem is that arms control agreements of limited scope had been given the aura of disarmament agreements, or at least indicators of a general movement in that direction. In this manner these agreements became tied to and, more importantly, became themselves, the litmus test for the relaxation of tension between the United States and the Soviet Union—detenté.

However, arms control and disarmament are very different in concept. Arms control has a primary objective—slowing or stopping the nuclear weapons development process.[5] What it has actually achieved is the slowing down or diverting of the development and deployment process under limited circumstances. The antiballistic missile (ABM) restraints under SALT I are an example of minimizing the potential of weapon systems for creating unstable and highly dangerous military possibilities. Disarmament, on the other hand, has much broader and loftier goals with regard to relationships among adversaries. It seeks to reduce weapons levels and constrain weapons development, thus requiring considerable underlying trust. It cannot be separated from national confidence and perceptions of an adversary's intentions. The confusion between limited arms control objectives and the more demanding disarmament criteria of mutual trust and identifiable arms reduction certainly contributed to the disillusionment that finally disrupted the strategic arms limitations process in the late 1970s. Yet the primary reason for this failure is that the Strategic Arms Limitation Treaty (SALT) process in the latter part of the

1970s could not realistically be detached or insulated from the larger international foreign policy issues. At some point a process such as SALT has only a limited life apart from the general relationship with an adversary (in this case the Soviet Union) and the even more general international process.

Understandably, therefore, when neither the United States nor the Soviet Union could or would separate SALT II from other international or domestic considerations, the process began to collapse. The Soviet Union, particularly in Afghanistan, demonstrated its unwillingness to create the atmosphere needed to assure a SALT–type agreement when it interfered with its perceived global interests. The United States did not appear to be any more willing or able to create an appropriate political atmosphere. The administration of President Carter tried to change SALT II in 1977 when it should have been insuring that the process was stabilized. It lost the power of a newly elected administration to overcome a growing unease about Soviet international actions (for example, the Cuban surrogate role in Angola). It played a China card, declaring its intention in December 1978 to normalize relations with The People's Republic—a critical moment that delayed a Soviet signing and pushed the treaty further into 1980 election year politics. The Carter administration seemed to act as if this arms control agreement could be insulated indefinitely from political change. Clearly that was not the case.

While the United States's relations with the Soviet Union and the character of SALT are significant contributors to the present atmosphere of dissatisfaction, other potent forces were also working to undercut SALT. It is critical to understand them. One indication of the dominance of more fundamental issues was the speed with which national discussion of specific technical issues, such as verification and comparative strategic strength under the SALT II treaty, was transformed into a more general debate about U.S. military power. SALT II became a focal point for these deeper concerns. These concerns revolved around the growing public sense of national impotence not solely confined to the military balance with the Soviet Union. The American people perceived themselves as being manipulated by other nations—unable to control the direction of international events that created domestic changes and problems (inflation, energy availability) directly touching their lives.

These external changes even reshaped domestic social and economic goals. The most dramatic element in creating this atmosphere was the emergence of OPEC (Organization of the Petroleum Exporting Countries), and the domestic and international effects of the foreign dominance of oil supplies. This clearly demonstrated to Americans the consequences of a changing balance of world economic and political power. OPEC, the Iranian revolution and its aftermath, the results of the Vietnam War, and the weakness of our steel industry and dollar on international markets have had much more to do with the collapse of the SALT process than we have recognized however genuine the fear of Soviet intentions.[6] Therefore, in many subtle ways one of our real adversaries is the seemingly incomprehensible and particularly uncontrollable international changes and their attendant frustrations. The SALT process came to symbolize these frustrations and thus was the recipient of a huge reservoir of anger (as the Panama Canal Treaty, to a less dramatic degree, had been before it).

Unless these other issues are identified and directly addressed, the arms control process will remain burdened with concerns that, while not wholly irrelevant, substantially confuse the importance of the benefits of arms limitation initiatives. Everyone has to face the facts and deal with these issues. While the avoidance of nuclear war is a transcending imperative that can and must be pursued in its own right, the issues of the economy (inflation, unemployment, and industrial development strategies), dependence on foreign resources (energy and resource policies), and conventional military development, as well as a measured restrained response to strategic needs, have to be dealt with in a satisfactory manner to assure that the United States will be willing to sustain a step by step arms control, and eventually, a disarmament process.

However, this challenge should be put in proper perspective. The United States is far from being at any disadvantage with regard to a capable deterrence; a flexible, sophisticated, limited type of retaliation attack will not be out of reach in the 1980s. Accurate Trident missiles and the small number of surviving ICBMs projected under the worst case could do a credible job, given what this book has identified as the possible magnitude of the effects of even a small attack. Heavy losses of ICBMs would make a controlled, sophisticated response more uncertain, but it would be far from unattainable. Thus, it is not simply the survival of a credible deterrence capability that is the question for the next decade but the restoration of U.S. confidence in its existing power.

If this is the case, in which directions should we proceed? An attempt should be made to negotiate some type of arms control agreement, even if limited, in order to keep the SALT process alive. At the same time, a debate about acceptable terms for a SALT agreement should be initiated. There are several reasons to explore these possibilities. First, it is to neither side's advantage to have a completely unfettered strategic arms race. The weaknesses of both the U.S. and Soviet economies in the next decade are likely to make this apparent. Another reason is that an educational debate, especially after the election year politics of 1980, may be possible, and would be desirable for rebuilding arms control and eventually the disarmament process. If the debate is correctly constructed it will force a clarification of the direction this policy should take. The control of nuclear weapons is too important a concern to be allowed to drift aimlessly. Thus, initiatives such as a comprehensive test ban treaty and an antisatellite treaty might be useful starting points, even if not immediately attainable. For its part, the Soviet Union has to show some interest in reducing tensions. Its international behavior (particularly at this time toward Poland and the Middle East) will be crucial harbingers of future relations.

There is one area of nuclear policy in which U.S. and Soviet interests do dovetail, and that is nonproliferation. While the developing nations are unlikely to be in the position to deliver even a small nuclear attack against any of the present nuclear powers in this century, they do present crucial threats to their neighbors. The promise of serious local instability that can propagate into a worldwide conflict is the greatest concern. Pakistan versus India, Iraq versus Iran, and Brazil versus Argentina are just examples of a few possibilities. The crucial problem is that small nations with few weapons and no worldwide responsibilities may be less constrained in their use of nuclear weapons—particularly unstable societies. It is in U.S. and Soviet interest to cooperate on the issue of nonproliferation, no matter what their other differences, and this mutual interest should be exploited.[7]

Despite areas of possible cooperation and agreement, it seems, that the details of an arms control proposal and process between the United States and Soviet Union is less important than the following two elements. The first is the United States's perception of its own power. It must have confidence in its ability to handle both Soviet threats and the more complex international demands, particularly foreign resource manipulations. As already outlined, this will require a strong transitional energy policy to minimize overdependence on foreign sources, short-term emergency energy management for the United States and its allies to reduce foreign political manipulation, and a mastery of the economy in the 1980s. Moreover, regaining the confidence of our allies in the manner we conduct foreign policy will also be crucial, for it affects critically the respect the Soviet Union will accord our military power. The second element is keeping the arms control agenda on the political table. This will be a matter of political will and educational skill.

This second goal is less difficult to achieve than it might appear. While this discussion has identified a variety of issues that might or have disrupted an arms control process, there is ample evidence that agreements can be achieved under adverse conditions such as the increasing international conflicts of the late 1970s and early 1980s. Examples are the sudden disappearance of the "missile gap" of the 1960 election, and the emergence of a partial test ban treaty signed in the atmosphere of confrontation (such as the Berlin and Cuban missile crises) of the early 1960s. In fact, the Cuban missile crisis may have sharpened the reality and fearsomeness of nuclear war for both sides, providing motivation for a limited nuclear accommodation.

While the 1980 U.S. election appeared to have negative short-term connotations for arms control, it was in some ways cathartic. The incumbents were the object of a great deal of displaced anger and frustration about the state of the world. However, after expressing this anger, the public might be less hostile to arms control initiatives. In fact, they might be ready for a dramatic new initiative such as substantial *mutual* reductions in strategic weapon levels. As I have tried to show, the requirements for effective deterrence are so small compared to present strategic forces that these reductions can be militarily acceptable. Whether the Soviet Union would be receptive to this type of initiative is an entirely different question. Moreover, negotiating an agreement of this type would be extremely difficult, particularly in an atmosphere of mutual distrust. Thus, renewing this process will not be easy. Initially it may require lower expectations about what will be achieved in an arms limitation agreement. Frustrations over a lack of progress in real disarmament on one side of the political spectrum, and the feeling on the other side that complex and limited agreements are smokescreens behind which sinister changes in the strategic balance occur, will make this difficult. Therefore, the road ahead will be difficult but not impossible, and, as noted, it may provide some dramatic opportunities.

This chapter is entitled "Epilogue as Prologue" because this book is a starting point. It is not a new beginning—that would fail to recognize the vast efforts by groups and individuals to nurture and develop the arms control process. But we have reached a watershed, a crucial low point in a process filled with uncertainty and low points. It is time to reconstruct the process patiently and to reexamine the goal of arms control and disarmament policy.

What rough beast slouches toward Bethlehem to be born? It is a question for the leaders of the 1980s.

NOTES TO CHAPTER 11

1. The saga of post World War II Japan and Germany would have been quite different if these nations had been treated with malignant indifference or the same hostility expressed to the losers of World War I. Significantly, the price for aid for the two losers was, of course, to become temporary client states of the United States.
2. C.S. Gray, and K. Payne, "Victory Is Possible," *Foreign Policy*, (Summer 1980): 14–17.
3. United Nations General Assembly, "General and Complete Disarmament, Comprehensive Study on Nuclear Weapons," Report of the Secretary General, A/35/392, English Annex, (New York: U.N. General Assembly, September 12, 1980), p. 151.
4. Subcommittee on Arms Control, International Organizations and Security Agreements, *Analysis of Effects of Limited Nuclear Warfare*, Committee on Foreign Relations, United States Senate, (Washington, D.C.: Government Printing Office, September 1975), p. 101.
5. An expanded discussion of one view of "arms control" theory can be found in Barry M. Blechman's, "Do Negotiated Arms Limitations Have a Future?" *Foreign Affairs*, 59, no. 1 (Fall): 112–118.
6. Arthur Katz, "SALT and International Reconciliation," *The Bulletin of the Atomic Scientists*, 36, no. 5, (May 1980): 3.
7. An emerging power may view this as patently unfair. Clearly the policy must be designed not to alienate these nations so that they create a network of nuclear supports that circumvents the intended restrictions of a nonproliferation agreement, but both major powers have a stake in applying their political, economic, and in extreme circumstances, even military power to constrain these developments.

APPENDIXES

THREE MILE ISLAND
A Contemporary Case Study

On Wednesday, March 28, 1979, 36 seconds after the hour of 4:00 a.m., several water pumps stopped working in the Unit 2 nuclear power plant on Three Mile Island, 10 miles southeast of Harrisburg, Pennsylvania. Thus began the accident at Three Mile Island. In the minutes, hours, and days that followed, a series of events—compounded by equipment failures, inappropriate procedures, and human errors and ignorance—escalated into the worst crisis yet experienced by the nation's nuclear power industry.

The accident focused national and international attention on the nuclear facility at Three Mile Island and raised it to a place of prominence in the minds of hundreds of millions. For the people living in such communities as Royalton, Goldsboro, Middletown, Hummelstown, Hershey, and Harrisburg, the rumors, conflicting official statements, a lack of knowledge about radiation releases, the continuing possibility of mass evacuation, and the fear that a hydrogen bubble trapped inside a nuclear reactor might explode were real and immediate. Later, Theodore Gross, provost of the Capitol Campus of Pennsylvania State University located in Middletown a few miles from TMI, would tell the Commission [on the Accident at Three Mile Island]:

> Never before have people been asked to live with such ambiguity. The TMI accident—an accident we cannot see or taste or smell . . . is an accident that is invisible. I think the fact that it is invisible creates a sense of uncertainty and fright on the part of people that may well go beyond the reality of the accident itself.

The reality of the accident, the realization that such an accident could actually occur, renewed and deepened the national debate over nuclear safety and the national policy of using nuclear reactors to generate electricity.[1]

The accident at Three Mile Island (TMI) nuclear power plant was, as the report of the President's Commission described, a major event, a watershed for U.S. civilian nuclear power policy. For the purposes of this book, however, it is more than that; it represents a unique opportunity to observe the impacts on a segment of the U.S. population of the real and, more importantly, the perceived threat of sudden widespread public radiation exposures. The perceived threat is important in this case since the actual short- and long-term health effects appear to be comparatively small. There may actually have been more generally threatening situations, such as fallout contamination from individual domestic nuclear tests in the 1950s, but none drew the attention or generated the powerful concerns that this accident did. Threat, uncertainty, and, finally, evacuation all occurred in ample measure—providing a rare opportunity to test the validity, however inadequately, of some of the findings of this book. Most importantly, it is a unique opportunity to look at the effects of nuclear imagery on behavior in society where a strong external support system (an intact nation) still exists.

THE SETTING

As the Nuclear Regulatory Commission (NRC) study noted, it is significant that the accident occurred in a region familiar with civil defense, evacuation, and the threats posed by major disasters.[2] The residents of this area were particularly hard hit by Hurricane Agnes in 1972 and another hurricane in 1975, when 20,000 were reported to have been forced to flee their homes. Thus, they were more experienced than many areas in the United States in the demands of disasters.

In the discussion below, the institutional demands created by the TMI accident will be evaluated and the behavioral and social impacts discussed. The basic source for this discussion is the *Report of The President's Commission on the Accident at Three Mile Island* (the Kemeny Commission) and the Nuclear Regulatory Commission's parallel studies.[3]

EVACUATION

Approximately 40 percent of the population (145,000) within fifteen miles of the damaged reactor were evacuated for an average of five days. The highest percentage (60 percent)[4] was closest, within five miles, as would be expected. Except for pregnant women and small children within five miles of the power plant, the other departures were not recommended by public authorities—they were made voluntarily. Among the reasons given for leaving were the dangers of the situation (90 percent); to protect children (61 percent); because information was confusing (83 percent); and to avoid the confusion or danger of a forced evacuation (76 percent). When asked what reasons had a decisive—namely, critical—impact on the decision to evacuate, confusing information and avoidance of forced evacuation ranked second (19 percent) and third (14 percent), respectively; first (30 percent) was the danger signaled by the appearance of a hydrogen bubble.[5] The desire to avoid forced evacuation is particularly interesting, since it appears to imply that there was a high distrust of the government's ability to provide satisfactory evacuation planning. The distrust of government in this instance appeared to focus on the possibility of panic and clogged highways, trapping those close to the accident.[6] The second problem—confused information—was in large measure caused by individuals having too much responsibility to make decisions with too little information. Many realized that they did not have the proper information and were unlikely to get it—so they left the area, assuming it was better to be safe than sorry.[7] In fact, this was a very rational response, particularly since in contrast to other familiar disasters, they had no way to assess the information personally and appeared to be highly distrustful of government officials.[8]

Under these circumstances, the drive to avoid a poorly planned evacuation, coupled with a highly confused situation where precise information about the type of dangers that exist was lacking and the desire to be with one's own during crises (78 percent stayed with relatives or friends), combined to control the decisions of the evacuees. Reproducing these circumstances under the conditions of actual or impending nuclear war would not be difficult and thus could easily make a massive preattack evaluation plan quickly crumble into chaos or at best make it difficult to control the situation effectively.

In contrast, of those who stayed, one-third gave concerns about looters as a reason. While fear of looting did not appear to be the primary reason for staying, it nevertheless appeared to be a possible factor contributing to resistance to leaving. In fact, this was a very rational response to uncertainty, since considerable looting had occurred previously (e.g., after the 1972 hurricane);[9] curiously, none occurred this time—which may be a tribute to both the confused information and the powerful threat that the accident represented. Looting might also be a strong factor in motivating a return to evacuated areas. These fears plus a fatalistic attitude among the older segment of the population—"Whatever happens is in God's hands"—could undercut evacuation in an imminent nuclear war situation.[10] The above discussion points to potentially highly destructive forces at work on controlled evacuation pulling in two directions—one part of the population outward and a different segment inward. The centrifugal forces are likely to grow in a stalemated crisis that includes preattack evacuation.

DISTRUST

One factor that emerged from the President's Commission surveys was that there was a high level of distrust of federal and state authorities as well as of the utility itself.[11] This distrust decreased over four months but nevertheless remained above the expected national average (Figure A-1). In evaluating the actual survey results it was clear that while the utility company fared worse in these surveys, the federal officials were also perceived negatively. Interestingly, a matched group of young mothers with children from the TMI area and from outside the immediate area (Wilkes-Barre) showed similar negative perceptions. Apparently, at least to some degree, experiencing this event through the media was as traumatic as experiencing the threat more directly. Part of the basis of distrust can be clearly attributed to the confused, indecisive way federal officials handled the initial period of four or five days after the accident. In fact, the inability to act decisively may have in large part created the psychological trauma of this accident.

In contrast, the NRC survey found that the governor of Pennsylvania and the NRC were cited as the most helpful sources of information.[12] The overall NRC sample was split evenly, however, between those dissatisfied and those satisfied with the way information was given. The closer to TMI a person lived, the less likely he or she was to be satisfied. Reinforcing the dissatisfaction was the general response, even among those that remained pronuclear, that they were never truly made aware of the dangers of a nuclear power plant.

Figure A-1. Change of Distrust of Authorities from April to August 1979 in General Population Area of Three Mile Island.

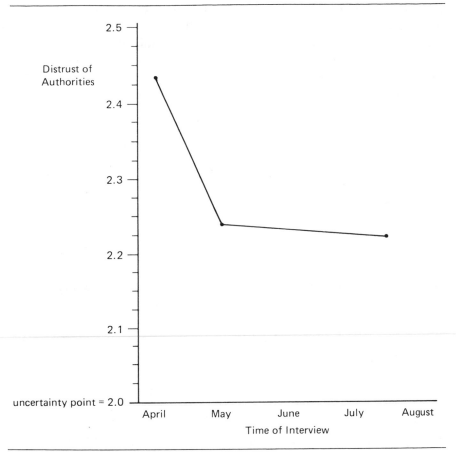

Source: Bruce Dohrenwend, Barbara Dohrenwend, Stanislav Kael, and George Worheit, *Technical Staff Analysis Report on Behavioral Effects to President's Commission on the Accident at Three Mile Island*. (Washington, D.C.: President's Commission on Three Mile Island, October 1979), p. 34.

While there appear to be some differences between the two surveys, the type of questions may be responsible for most of the ambiguity. The questions asked on three different occasions by the President's Commission were much more direct (and perhaps biasing)—for example, "Do you feel the information you were getting from state and federal officials during the TMI crisis was truthful?".

Actually, the hostile attitude toward Metropolitan Edison, the utility, since it was the operator and responsible party for the accident, might be more indicative of the attitude toward the government in the postattack or no attack evacuation period, as the government would be the responsible party in a nuclear war situation. Assuming the TMI Commission survey is correct, it would indicate how tenuous a base the political leadership might have if it was perceived as being unable to resolve and clarify the threatening ambiguity of a truly "foreign" experience.

There were other indicators of continuing distrust and uncertainty. In one case, they took the form of persistent rumors about events occurring at TMI. For example, Metropolitan Edison was supposed to be burning off the fuel remaining in TMI-1 (the sister reactor)[13] at night so as not to alarm the local populace.

These suspicions were increased by continuing contradictory statements in the press, such as differences of opinion about how much radiation was received by local population—a "continuing lack of clear, unambiguous information."[14] Another indication of a loss in confidence is the apparently permanent negative shift in the perception of TMI. Only 20 percent thought its advantages outweighed its disadvantages.[15] Before the accident, 50 percent felt that way. The importance of this shift is that it indicates a growing disillusionment. As previously noted, a general loss of trust in authority after a traumatic experience could compromise the leadership's flexibility for action or destroy its credibility to direct recovery.

Interestingly, an unusually large number of individuals said they were politically active in the TMI dispute even nine months after the accident.[16] This could indicate that there is a basis to believe the traumatic effects leading to a loss of trust would indeed be translated into concrete political actions. This conclusion, however, should be interpreted cautiously.

DEMANDS ON SOCIETY

One of the areas of greatest concern previously identified as a consequence of nuclear war was the demands on society, particularly its institutions, to respond adequately to postattack and even preattack needs. The TMI accident provides some insights with regard to these issues, however, because of the limited and unique nature of the accident, conclusions should again be carefully interpreted.

Emergency Response

According to the NRC study, "the accident at Three Mile Island strained existing emergency plans at all levels of government."[17] One of the key problems was "inadequate communication networks" between the various levels of government (federal, state, county, municipal).[18] Because no emergency was actually declared, additional confusion was created since local officials were legally responsible for public safety, not civil defense coordinators. According to the NRC, the Penn Emergency Preparedness Agency did play a key role. However, some municipalities had no designated civil defense coordinator and thus were never formally notified about the accident. There were numerous instances of poor coordination or confused ad hoc planning. For example, when a larger area around TMI was designated for possible evacuation, the buses that had been lined up for evacuating the communities inside the five mile zone disappeared.[19] Problems similar to those associated with TMI, but more serious in effect, could easily occur during a confused period before and immediately after a decision to initiate a preattack evacuation.

Schools

One of the more frightening aspects of this emergency situation was the fate of children in schools. In some instances children were frightened by seeing other children being removed by parents and also by teachers in tears. Children were dropped off at locked houses, left to fend for themselves.[20] In other areas, the school was evacuated as a whole, leaving uninformed parents in panic. In general, what is most disconcerting is the potential for separating children from parents in the midst of a surprise attack—leaving all parties frightened and demoralized. The separation of parents and children was reiterated by residents concerned with deficiencies in evacuation plans. It is not hard to appreciate the trauma of realizing that in the chaos of a postnuclear attack world parents and children might not be reunited.

Medical and Other Institutions

The key problem associated with hospitals was that they are "normally the destinations for victims of a disaster" and thus not prepared for evacuation themselves.[21] The President's Commission noted that while officials talked about a "few hours" of lead time, substantially more time would be needed.[22]

In particular, the NRC study identified four key problems. The first was that all hospitals were not capable of providing specialized care, and therefore placing patients with these problems required significant transportation coordination. For instance, during TMI, incubator babies would have required transportation to Philadelphia, more than fifty miles away. It takes little imagination, as noted previously, to understand the implications of this problem for vulnerable patients during a full-scale urban pre- or postattack evacuation—particularly since urban target areas generally contain the major receiving medical facilities (e.g., university hospitals) for the surrounding area. The second problem was identifying and removing key public medical records, a problem certain to be shared by individuals, businesses, and government. The third was to find support personnel, in this instance ambulance drivers, willing to go with patients and be separated from their own families during this crisis (role conflict). Finally, psychiatric patients were to be released early on medication or sedated for removal. These procedures represented some dangers to the community but more to disoriented and confused patients.

The mentally retarded and elderly also would have to be supported during this evacuation period. Complex problems would also arise with regard to prisoners. One strategy proposed during TMI was to release some (convicted of minor crimes) and transport others to appropriate host facilities. In the postattack period the situation in even remotely sited prisons—particularly maximum security ones—could deteriorate quickly for both society and prisoners if guards and other personnel decided to protect their families instead of assuming their job responsibilities.

In general, the problems cited above reinforce the concerns discussed previously about the enormous and complex demands that will have to be met in order to develop successfully a preattack evacuation strategy that will not be fraught with potential personal and social dangers. The postattack situation would be even less forgiving, since, even the possibility of short-term expedient measures will collapse as key support facilities (e.g., hospitals) will be destroyed.

PSYCHOLOGICAL IMPACTS

The President's Commission on TMI noted that "the major health effect of the accident appears to have been on the mental health of the people being in the regions of TMI and of the workers at TMI. . . . The highest level of mental distress were found among adults (a) living within 5 miles of TMI, or (b) with preschool children; and among teenagers (a) within 5 miles of TMI, (b) with preschool siblings, or (c) whose families left the area."[23]

The strongest effect was demoralization. The Kemeny Commission, using the definition of J.W. Foouk, described it as "a common distress response when people find themselves in a serious predicament and can see no way out."[24] Demoralization took the form of feelings of helplessness and depression. It was described by one responsible mental health professional as an emotional reaction to the inability to act. Thus individuals capable of appropriate actions were reduced to feelings of helplessness and dependency because the problem was beyond their realm of experience and no adequate information was available to guide them.[25]

At the time of the accident, an additional 10 percent of the household heads (male and female) suffered levels of demoralization similar in severity to clients of community mental health centers. The total observed level was approximately 25 percent, the ordinary level was indicated to be 15 percent. The average level of demoralization in the whole population, as indicated by Figure A-2, was increased, returning to normal over time.[26] The NRC study found while psychosomatic problems (loss of appetite, difficulty in sleeping, and irritability) disappeared, actual somatic ones (stomach trouble, diarrhea, constipation, etc.) continued to affect a small percentage of the population four months later.[27]

Also, about 25 percent of the respondents in July still felt TMI represented a very serious threat to their family.[28] This continuing stress was also identified in the increase from 12 percent before the accident to 41 percent in July of those still very concerned about radioactive emissions from TMI.[29] The Pennsylvania Health Department study (Houts et al.) in January 1980 supported these findings.

Figure A-2.   Relation of Time of Interview to Level of Demoralization.

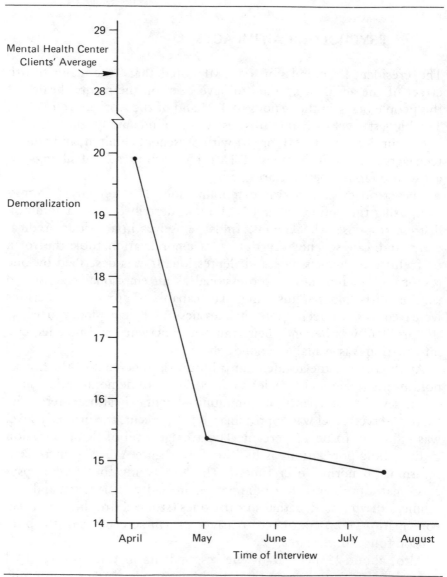

Source: Bruce Dohrenwend, Barbara Dohrenwend, Stanislav Kael, and George Worheit, *Technical Staff Analysis Report on Behavioral Effects to President's Commission on the Accident at Three Mile Island.* (Washington, D.C.: President's Commission on Three Mile Island, October 1979), p. 34.

It found symptoms of distress and concern even nine months later among 10 to 20 percent of the population within fifteen miles of TMI. This distress took the form of statements of being upset about TMI, concern about safety for themselves and their families, and reporting of symptoms frequently associated with stress.[30] The stress, however, appeared to be related to continuing distrust of public officials and the utility rather than demoralization.

Bromet found that TMI mothers had an excess risk of experiencing clinical episodes of anxiety and depression during the year after the accident. They also reported more symptoms of anxiety and depression than did the control group of mothers.[31] One interesting apparent effect of the stress experienced by inhabitants of the TMI area, was an increase in physician's visits during the accident period and the four months following. Those visits were considered to be significantly related to the measures of stress (behavioral and psychosomatic symptoms) used in that study.[32]

There are some indications that the effect of evacuation played a role in intensifying emotions for 7th, 9th, and 11th graders surveyed; "Those who stayed in a potentially hazardous area showed significantly lower levels of psychological distress both during the accident and in the two months following the accident, compared with those who left the area."[33] Since they were children that had no choice in leaving, the interpretation of the finding could indicate evacuation was a traumatic experience, or alternately, that the child's family was generally more prone to be emotionally upset.

All these emotional effects point toward similar postdisaster psychological disorientation discussed by Janis.[34] One can only speculate on the extent that the emotional disruption would be intensified under the continuing threats posed in a preattack evacuation situation, with little external support for returning life to normal quickly.

NUCLEAR IMAGERY

If the power of nuclear imagery among the U.S. population was ever in doubt the reaction of those around the Three Mile Island plant should dispel any further questions. The quotation at the beginning of this Appendix seems indicative of the almost obsessive fear created by the mention of radiation. A housewife's reaction reinforces this observation:

On Friday a very frightening thing occurred in our area. A state policeman went door-to-door telling residents to stay indoors, close all windows, and turn all air conditioners off. I was alone, as were many other homemakers, and my thoughts were focused on how long I would remain a prisoner in my own home and whether my husband would be able to come home after teaching school that day.

Suddenly, I was scared, real scared. I decided to get out of there while I could. I ran to the car not knowing if I should breath the air or not, and I threw the suitcases in the trunk and was on my way within one hour. If anything dreadful happened, I thought that I'd at least be with my girls. Although it was very hot in the car, I didn't trust myself to turn the air conditioners on. It felt good as my tense muscles relaxed the farther I drove.[35]

Finally, the NRC noted that those in the TMI area who resented the accident had these feelings exacerbated by the fact that radiation is invisible. This means that when an accident does happen, the true extent of the threat is not obvious to the layperson. For example, a continuing concern in the area is that "no one is perceived as being sure about how serious the accident was."[36] It therefore is not difficult to understand why there had been a strong desire to flee, not just to evacuate the area temporarily. This reaction was noted by the Kemeny Commission: "Feelings in the population within 20 miles of TMI about *continuing to live in the area* were mixed and uncertain. Relatively unfavorable attitudes, though still generally uncertain rather than negative, were expressed by people living within five miles of TMI, and by mothers of pre-school children."[37] This was supported by the NRC, which found that 30 percent of those surveyed within five miles of TMI indicated they considered moving. Overall, 19 percent considered this option for all distances. Of this 19 percent, 22 percent of this group (4 percent of the total) said they definitely will move.[38] Another measure of the trauma of this experience is that a small group (3 percent) have considered changing jobs—about half had taken definite steps.

PERSPECTIVE

There is something unique and relevant about Three Mile Island, which was noted by investigators, some of whom were in the area during the accident. It was the deeply disturbing feeling that what people were being asked to deal with was an event beyond their experience, an event that confronted them with a danger they could not see, or hear, or feel—radiation. (This was a phrase repeatedly used by investigators both in their reports and phone conversations.) It was an event that left them helpless because they did not know what to do. More disturbing, even those who should have known (public officials) did not or at least were perceived as not knowing. Clearly, the imagery of radiation appeared as strong and threatening, in some ways as it was to the survivors of Hiroshima and Nagasaki. Intensifying the strength of the nuclear imagery, to that sense of vulnerability, was the lack of decisive action and the resulting uncertainty and ambiguity that pervaded the event. The ease with which a general lack of trust for public and utility officials, and for official policies (nuclear power development) could be generated by inept (or the perception of inept) leadership illustrates the vulnerability of leaders to a precipitous loss of confidence in highly emotional and threatening crises, at least in the short run—even if little dangerous actually happens. This indicates that the conduct of the crisis can be as important as the actual resolution. Interestingly, at least one group of academic researchers[39] came to the conclusion that controlling evacuation behavior during a nuclear disaster situation (peacetime or wartime) would be extremely difficult even if the evacuation orders were not confused and indecisive, as they were for TMI. They felt that unlike natural disasters, the nuclear (radiation) event was so extraordinary that many were and would be unwilling to rely on the federal government to effectively guide them. The implications for postattack control or, particularly, orderly evacuation would be very serious if this conclusion turned out to be accurate.

The accident pointed to many problems predicted by past events. One is the complex social and economic demands on society: children separated from parents; institutions (hospitals, nursing homes, prisons) required to reverse their normal roles, dispersing the ill, the elderly, and the criminal to marginal care or perhaps none at all; and financial institutions and businesses forced to dispense monies or close their productive activities in a manner that could be damaging to the institution and detrimental to society. Role conflict was also seen between officials' duties and personal responsibilities. For example, in one hospital half the nuclear medicine staff (radiology) evacuated.[40]

As noted, the emotional reactions to the confusion and fear was severe in a substantial portion of the population—10 percent. Whatever the exact psychological reasons, an emotional response of that kind is likely to be much more prolonged and debilitating if the stress of nuclear destruction and possibly continuing war remains unrelieved.

In the final analysis, the key finding of TMI was, directly or through the media, in a very real sense, that the U.S. generated its first nuclear "survivors." The result was that while the highly emotional initial reaction faded, the experience was serious enough to shake the trust of even staunch supporters of nuclear power, and by implication, the trust of individuals in the federal officials that controlled and supported it. While some claimed part of their reaction was related to the perception that they were not properly informed about the dangers of nuclear energy, it is more likely that this kind of "informational innoculation" would have been of little use, the sense of foreignness and threat appeared to be too great. The powerful nationwide effect of this accident was summarized by a supporter of nuclear energy. "It's not true that nobody died at Three Mile Island. The nuclear industry may have died."[41]

Translating these findings into the context of nuclear war, one can easily foresee two to three hundred potential situations similar to TMI occurring around U.S. urban centers. The evacuation responsibility will be clearer, under these circumstances, but the ambiguity and confusion may be just as real. The most severe uncertainty is likely to occur in a preattack evacuation, while organizational confusion is more likely to be dominant after an attack. The social and economic disruption will be much greater under any circumstances since there will be no relatives, nearby hospitals, or other institutions to support the evacuees or survivors. The demoralization and mistrust is also likely to be severe, particularly in a prolonged preattack period of uncertainty, or after the overpowering experiences of an actual attack.

In conclusion, TMI, while far from a perfect analogy for a preattack nuclear evacuation or nuclear war itself, should be a sobering reminder of the vulnerability of leaders, institutions, and the social and economic organizations of contemporary industrial society. It supports the conclusions drawn here from the historical record, and points to a consistent and sobering picture of life after nuclear war.

NOTES TO APPENDIX A

1. *Report of the President's Commission on the Accident at Three Mile Island* (Washington, D.C., October 1979), p. 81.

2. Cynthia B. Flynn and J.A. Chalmers, *The Social and Economic Effects of the Accident at Three Mile Island: Findings to Date* NUREG-CR-1215, (Washington, D.C.: Government Printing Office, January 1980), pp. 17–18.

3. Ibid.; and Cynthia B. Flynn, *Three Mile Island Telephone Survey, Preliminary Report on Procedure and Findings* (Mountain West Research Inc. with Social Impact Research Inc., NUREG/CR-1093, September 24, 1979).

4. Flynn, pp. 14–16.

5. Ibid., p. 22.

6. Flynn, p. 25.

7. Cynthia B. Flynn, Investigator, NRC Telephone Survey, private communication.

8. Raymond Goldstein, coauthor of President's Commission on Behavioral Effects Study, private communication.

9. Cynthia B. Flynn, private communication.

10. Flynn, p. 21.

11. *Report of the President's Commission*, p. 7.

12. Flynn and Chalmers: this may be less an expression of confidence than it appears, since it was based on personalities (NRC representatives) and their willingness to admit that they did not know the answers.

13. Flynn and Chalmers, p. 66.

14. Ibid., p. 67.

15. Flynn, p. 41.

16. P.S. Houts, R.W. Miller, G.K. Tokuhata, and K.S. Ham, *Health-Related Behavioral Impact of the Three Mile Island Nuclear Incident* (TMI Advisory Panel on Health Research Studies of the Pennsylvania Department of Health, April 8, 1980), p. 19.

17. Flynn and Chalmers, p. 28.

18. Ibid., p. 31.

19. Ibid., p. 34.

20. Ibid., pp. 37, 38.

21. Ibid., p. 39.

22. *Report of the President's Commission*, p. 40.

23. Ibid., p. 35.

24. J.W. Foouk, *Persuasion and Healing* (Baltimore, Maryland: Johns Hopkins University Press, 1973).

25. Janet Kelley, health official in Pennsylvania. Private communication.

26. *Technical Staff Analysis Report on Behavioral Effects to President's Commission on the Accident at Three Mile Island*, (Washington, D.C.: President's Commission on the Accident at Three Mile Island, October 1979), p. 26.

27. Flynn and Chalmers, p. 65.

28. Flynn, p. 34.

29. Ibid., p. 35.

30. Houts, et al., chapter 5, p. 20. These findings were also discussed in Peter Houts, R.W. Miller, G.K. Tokuhata, and K.S. Ham, *Health-Related Behavioral Impact of the Three Mile Island Nuclear Incident*, Part II. (TMI Advisory Panel on Health Research Studies of the Pennsylvania Department of Health, November 21, 1980).

31. Evelyn Bromet, "Three Mile Island: Mental Health Findings" (Pittsburgh, Pennsylvania: Western Psychiatric Institute and Clinic, University of Pittsburgh, October 1980).

32. Teh–wei Hu, Kenneth S. Slaysman, Kum S. Ham, and Marion Yoder, *Health-Related Economic Costs of the Three Mile Island Accident*, Institute for Policy Research and Evaluation, Pennsylvania State University (University Park, Pennsylvania: Center for Research on Human Resources, May 1980), p. 48.

33. *Technical Staff Analysis Report on Behavior Effects*, p. 43.

34. See Irving Janis, *Air War and Emotional Stress* (New York: McGraw–Hill, 1951).

35. Flynn and Chalmers, p. 21.

36. Ibid., p. 68.

37. Jacob Fabricant, "Summary of the Public Health and Safety Task Force on the Accident at Three Mile Island" (Washington, D.C.: President's Commission on the Accident at Three Mile Island, October 1979), p. 18.

38. Flynn, p. 39.

39. Raymond Goldstein, private communication.

40. Ibid.

41. U.S. Representative Mickey Edwards as quoted in *Congressional Quarterly Weekly Reports*, November 14, 1977, p. 2665.

U.S. URBAN POPULATION VULNERABILITY

The tables in Sections 1 and 2 of this appendix have been adapted from a recent study, *U.S. Urban Population Vulnerability*, published by the U.S. Arms Control and Disarmament Agency.[1] Section 1 illustrates the number of casualties (dead and injured) expected as a result of urban attacks producing the maximum number of deaths. Casualties from weapons with yields from 50 kilotons to 20 megatons are shown for the 200 largest U.S. cities. Section 2 illustrates the total nationwide fatalities expected from attacks with different numbers of weapons (100 to 4000) and explosive yields (50 kilotons to 1 megaton).

This information is provided to demonstrate some of the effects of a wider spectrum of attacks than those discussed in the body of this book.

SECTION 1: VULNERABILITY OF URBAN AREAS TO NUCLEAR ATTACK

Listed below are the total casualties (dead and injured) and fatalities for the 200 largest U.S. urban areas. As Figure B–1 illustrates, first each urban area is identified, its number of concentrated population centers is given, and its population (as of the 1970 census) is noted.

377

Figure B-1. Key to Section 1.

Yield of Weapons in Kilotons

City Name	POP	F/C	50	100	200	500	750	1000	5000	20000
Aberdeen, SD	27	F	21	24	26	27	27	27	27	27
2		C	26	27	27	27	27	27	27	27
	No. Whs.		1	1	1	1	1	1	1	1

Number of warheads

Number of casualties (injured and dead, in thousands)

Number of fatalities (thousands)

Population of urban area (thousands)

Number of concentrated areas within the urban area

The dominant corporate city within the urban area

The fatalities (F), casualties (C) and number of weapons (No. Whs.) are given for weapons yields ranging from 50 kilotons to 20 megatons.

It is important to note that the weapons are targeted specifically to produce the highest fatalities, not directed toward producing the maximum economic damage, as was the intention in Scenarios A-1 through A-4 of this book.

SECTION 2: NATIONWIDE URBAN FATALITIES FROM DIFFERENT NUCLEAR ATTACKS

The percentages of urban population killed in attacks using different numbers and sizes of weapons are shown in the table below. It is assumed that the weapons system is 85 percent reliable; that is, 15 percent of the warheads do not reach their targets. Another assumption is that the accuracy of the missiles or bombs is not perfect, but has what is called a "circular error probable" (CEP) of 0.2 nautical miles (NM); this means that 50 percent of the warheads will fall within two-tenths of a nautical mile of the target, while the other fifty percent will miss the target by a larger distance. This error is less crucial for population attacks than for attacks against strategic targets such as ICBMs, because the target is a large area rather than a specific point. The object of the attacks is to produce maximum fatalities.

If the urban fatalities for 100 (first row) and 500 (fifth row) one-megaton weapons (last column) in this table are compared with attacks A-4 and A-1 respectively (keeping in mind the economic orientation of the A-4 and A-1 attacks), the overall urban fatality estimates appear to be consistent with the projections in this book.

NOTE TO APPENDIX B

1. United States Arms Control and Disarmament Agency, *U.S. Urban Population Vulnerability*, (Washington, D.C.: USACDA, August 1979).

Table B-1. Vulnerability of Urban Areas to Nuclear Attack.

City Name	POP	F/C	50	100	200	500	750	1000	5000	20000
Abilene	94	F	39	63	72	82	87	87	93	94
4		C	71	82	87	92	93	93	94	94
		No. Whs.	1	1	1	1	1	1	1	1
Akron	463	F	54	70	123	195	230	261	398	452
38		C	131	175	247	331	362	381	447	462
		No. Whs.	1	1	1	1	1	1	1	1
Albany, GA	83	F	26	42	52	67	72	76	83	83
7		C	50	63	73	80	80	83	83	83
		No. Whs.	1	1	1	1	1	1	1	1
Albany, NY	457	F	53	78	103	140	158	177	315	419
51		C	114	134	174	230	254	286	410	451
		No. Whs.	1	1	1	1	1	1	1	1
Albuquerque	367	F	49	101	145	189	214	240	337	364
22		C	140	184	231	288	307	319	359	367
		No. Whs.	1	1	1	1	1	1	1	1
Allentown	267	F	54	75	100	152	172	191	261	276
35		C	107	137	173	224	241	250	275	276
		No. Whs.	1	1	1	1	1	1	1	1

Alton	98	F	22	32	41	59	68	75	95	98
12		C	40	57	68	85	91	93	98	98
		No. Whs.	1	1	1	1	1	1	1	1
Altoona	87	F	35	46	57	70	74	78	86	87
11		C	58	68	73	81	83	85	87	87
		No. Whs.	1	1	1	1	1	1	1	1
Amarillo	129	F	38	55	68	93	102	108	128	129
12		C	75	89	104	120	123	124	129	129
		No. Whs.	1	1	1	1	1	1	1	1
Anchorage	132	F	29	42	60	96	106	116	130	132
15		C	60	84	102	123	126	130	132	132
		No. Whs.	1	1	1	1	1	1	1	1
Ann Arbor	188	F	41	61	80	102	109	118	176	188
15		C	87	103	120	140	152	159	187	188
		No. Whs.	1	1	1	1	1	1	1	1
Appleton	136	F	46	55	63	77	85	92	125	135
11		C	65	78	86	109	116	121	133	136
		No. Whs.	1	1	1	1	1	1	1	1
Atlanta	1298	F	44	57	97	190	250	363	720	1037
104		C	115	186	275	510	614	713	1061	1224
		No. Whs.	1	1	1	1	1	1	1	1

Table B–1. continued.

City Name	POP	F/C	50	100	200	500	750	1000	5000	20000
Augusta	162	F	29	48	66	94	112	122	157	162
		C	74	97	118	136	146	152	162	162
19		No. Whs.	1	1	1	1	1	1	1	1
Aurora	153	F	49	70	83	102	108	112	138	151
		C	86	98	109	122	129	131	149	153
12		No. Whs.	1	1	1	1	1	1	1	1
Austin, TX	334	F	41	52	129	194	221	240	315	333
		C	95	140	227	282	294	304	331	334
11		No. Whs.	1	1	1	1	1	1	1	1
Bakersfield	186	F	35	61	79	124	142	154	182	186
		C	74	108	145	167	176	178	186	186
9		No. Whs.	1	1	1	1	1	1	1	1
Baltimore	1484	F	58	264	186	494	636	704	1151	1393
		C	181	573	527	956	1041	1105	1381	1468
59		No. Whs.	1	1	1	1	1	1	1	1
Baton Rouge	278	F	58	75	93	143	170	188	261	278
		C	112	133	165	226	242	250	276	278
18		No. Whs.	1	1	1	1	1	1	1	1
Beaumont	110	F	20	39	57	83	91	96	110	110
		C	54	79	92	103	105	107	110	110
7		No. Whs.	1	1	1	1	1	1	1	1

City										
Billings	82	F	34	51	63	73	76	78	82	82
5		C	65	71	76	80	81	81	82	82
		No. Whs.	1	1	1	1	1	1	1	1
Biloxi	122	F	26	31	40	50	54	56	95	116
16		C	41	47	54	66	76	79	113	122
		No. Whs.	1	1	1	1	1	1	1	1
Binghamton	163	F	35	51	68	90	104	111	150	163
19		C	72	89	106	131	141	143	163	163
		No. Whs.	1	1	1	1	1	1	1	1
Birmingham	549	F	43	65	87	154	193	224	403	503
55		C	105	146	227	316	359	390	500	539
		No. Whs.	1	1	1	1	1	1	1	1
Boise City	115	F	31	63	85	104	109	111	115	115
3		C	76	98	108	113	114	115	115	115
		No. Whs.	1	1	1	1	1	1	1	1
Boston	2884	F	88	133	242	456	585	695	1428	2018
242		C	346	444	727	1116	1304	1430	2132	2550
		No. Whs.	1	1	1	1	1	1	1	1
Boulder	99	F	42	59	76	91	95	97	99	99
4		C	81	89	94	98	98	99	99	99
		No. Whs.	1	1	1	1	1	1	1	1

Table B-1. continued.

City Name	POP	F/C	50	100	200	500	750	1000	5000	20000
Buffalo	939	F	151	82	250	403	460	516	793	910
69		C	331	297	511	665	727	766	899	938
		No. Whs.	1	1	1	1	1	1	1	1
Canton	237	F	47	67	97	135	153	168	218	234
29		C	99	130	159	190	205	212	233	237
		No. Whs.	1	1	1	1	1	1	1	1
Cedar Rapids	129	F	33	45	65	92	100	108	127	129
10		C	68	85	103	119	121	126	129	129
		No. Whs.	1	1	1	1	1	1	1	1
Charleston, SC	219	F	34	41	54	98	117	132	200	214
25		C	60	81	110	157	177	188	214	219
		No. Whs.	1	1	1	1	1	1	1	1
Charleston, WV	145	F	29	40	54	71	79	83	116	136
20		C	60	68	83	100	107	112	135	144
		No. Whs.	1	1	1	1	1	1	1	1
Charlotte	313	F	46	61	89	156	190	210	297	313
26		C	108	141	196	255	276	284	312	313
		No. Whs.	1	1	1	1	1	1	1	1

City										
Chattanooga 26	216	F	22	50	68	106	124	138	196	215
		C	69	101	136	170	181	191	215	216
		No. Whs.	1	1	1	1	1	1	1	1
Chicago 290	6659	F	121	114	570	923	969	1165	2251	3824
		C	587	549	1377	1931	2236	2519	3981	5366
		No. Whs.	1	1	1	1	1	1	1	1
Cincinnati 88	1145	F	37	119	182	279	345	396	763	979
		C	163	281	392	579	676	726	986	1095
		No. Whs.	1	1	1	1	1	1	1	1
Cleveland, OH 105	1890	F	75	97	148	450	520	572	985	1369
		C	183	268	422	776	869	952	1403	1651
		No. Whs.	1	1	1	1	1	1	1	1
Colorado Springs 17	254	F	26	67	98	138	159	173	233	253
		C	82	132	166	202	213	222	251	254
		No. Whs.	1	1	1	1	1	1	1	1
Columbia, SC 23	245	F	27	58	85	131	156	170	232	244
		C	58	130	165	207	219	224	244	245
		No. Whs.	1	1	1	1	1	1	1	1
Columbus, GA 14	186	F	21	46	55	106	126	138	176	185
		C	50	99	118	156	164	168	184	186
		No. Whs.	1	1	1	1	1	1	1	1

Table B–1. continued.

City Name	POP	F/C	50	100	200	500	750	1000	5000	20000
Columbus, OH	801	F	53	70	121	298	360	403	657	770
41		C	107	243	334	535	600	633	763	798
		No. Whs.	1	1	1	1	1	1	1	1
Concord, CA	302	F	31	51	78	133	157	172	261	295
34		C	96	130	171	216	232	247	295	302
		No. Whs.	1	1	1	1	1	1	1	1
Corpus Christi	189	F	46	69	95	134	151	161	185	189
10		C	85	125	146	173	180	182	189	189
		No. Whs.	1	1	1	1	1	1	1	1
Dallas	2087	F	47	92	147	214	286	345	803	1211
161		C	156	254	372	473	671	760	1246	1571
		No. Whs.	1	1	1	1	1	1	1	1
Davenport	250	F	52	65	94	146	169	186	240	250
22		C	102	123	164	208	223	230	249	250
		No. Whs.	1	1	1	1	1	1	1	1
Dayton	702	F	56	93	120	186	245	287	479	592
62		C	142	184	258	369	433	461	603	660
		No. Whs.	1	1	1	1	1	1	1	1

City			1	2	3	4	5	6	7	8
Daytona Beach 13	126	F	39	52	68	89	95	101	120	126
		C	72	82	99	112	116	118	125	126
		No. Whs.	1	1	1	1	1	1	1	1
Decatur, IL 8	96	F	29	52	64	81	86	91	96	96
		C	61	77	86	93	96	96	96	96
		No. Whs.	1	1	1	1	1	1	1	1
Denver 56	1162	F	35	59	95	219	313	437	821	1061
		C	130	212	340	584	706	804	1055	1145
		No. Whs.	1	1	1	1	1	1	1	1
Des Moines 12	269	F	47	70	94	140	167	187	255	269
		C	101	130	169	223	237	246	268	269
		No. Whs.	1	1	1	1	1	1	1	1
Detroit 205	3858	F	43	117	161	520	624	783	1691	2730
		C	183	371	703	1260	1479	1737	2857	3466
		No. Whs.	1	1	1	1	1	1	1	1
Duluth 16	116	F	25	32	43	62	72	81	110	116
		C	49	61	74	93	101	104	116	116
		No. Whs.	1	1	1	1	1	1	1	1
Durham 9	103	F	37	54	68	85	91	96	102	103
		C	69	81	91	99	102	102	103	103
		No. Whs.	1	1	1	1	1	1	1	1

Table B-1. continued.

City Name	POP	F/C	50	100	200	500	750	1000	5000	20000
Easton	87	F	32	44	58	75	79	81	87	87
		C	62	69	77	85	86	87	87	87
11		No. Whs.	1	1	1	1	1	1	1	1
El Paso	385	F	45	75	101	154	181	208	339	379
		C	99	163	210	267	298	316	374	385
31		No. Whs.	1	1	1	1	1	1	1	1
Erie	174	F	68	86	107	136	144	150	171	174
		C	114	130	147	162	168	170	174	174
14		No. Whs.	1	1	1	1	1	1	1	1
Eugene	154	F	31	49	66	99	112	123	152	154
		C	68	92	113	139	143	146	154	154
12		No. Whs.	1	1	1	1	1	1	1	1
Evansville	138	F	46	65	81	106	115	122	138	138
		C	89	103	117	132	133	135	138	138
11		No. Whs.	1	1	1	1	1	1	1	1
Fargo	92	F	38	58	73	85	88	91	92	92
		C	73	83	87	91	92	92	92	92
6		No. Whs.	1	1	1	1	1	1	1	1

City		F/C/No. Whs.								
Fayetteville, NC 21	174	F	26	40	49	71	85	96	159	173
		C	56	63	88	117	129	137	172	174
		No. Whs.	1	1	1	1	1	1	1	1
Flint 18	295	F	42	57	132	180	208	224	282	294
		C	119	145	215	256	267	272	293	295
		No. Whs.	1	1	1	1	1	1	1	1
Fort Smith 8	83	F	29	40	51	64	68	70	81	83
		C	53	60	69	76	78	80	83	83
		No. Whs.	1	1	1	1	1	1	1	1
Fort Wayne 17	228	F	54	88	112	149	166	180	221	228
		C	120	148	174	203	209	215	228	228
		No. Whs.	1	1	1	1	1	1	1	1
Fresno 15	289	F	34	60	94	177	206	227	281	289
		C	102	151	199	254	266	272	289	289
		No. Whs.	1	1	1	1	1	1	1	1
Gainesville, FL 7	88	F	34	47	63	78	83	85	88	88
		C	62	73	82	87	87	88	88	88
		No. Whs.	1	1	1	1	1	1	1	1
Gastonia 11	102	F	28	32	41	55	62	68	94	101
		C	46	55	66	78	83	85	101	102
		No. Whs.	1	1	1	1	1	1	1	1

Table B-1. continued.

City Name	POP	F/C	50	100	200	500	750	1000	5000	20000
Grand Rapids	359	F	57	63	118	178	212	236	328	354
31		C	130	166	220	280	302	317	353	359
		No. Whs.	1	1	1	1	1	1	1	1
Green Bay	144	F	50	54	81	113	123	130	143	144
6		C	80	108	122	137	139	140	144	144
		No. Whs.	1	1	1	1	1	1	1	1
Greensboro	155	F	29	47	69	106	121	131	154	155
18		C	77	101	122	143	149	151	155	155
		No. Whs.	1	1	1	1	1	1	1	1
Greenville, SC	185	F	21	54	88	115	132	141	179	184
14		C	74	111	139	161	166	173	184	185
		No. Whs.	1	1	1	1	1	1	1	1
Harrisburg	253	F	42	55	88	132	155	167	229	249
33		C	96	130	160	201	212	222	248	253
		No. Whs.	1	1	1	1	1	1	1	1
Hartford	651	F	56	69	162	216	252	278	453	570
52		C	97	123	272	358	408	435	573	626
		No. Whs.	1	1	1	1	1	1	1	1

Honolulu 37	483	F	79	102	134	200	234	257	381	452
		C	159	203	253	308	343	362	449	478
		No. Whs.	1	1	1	1	1	1	1	1
Houston 73	1807	F	40	49	167	288	353	448	1060	1523
		C	160	289	404	675	867	953	1521	1726
		No. Whs.	1	1	1	1	1	1	1	1
Huntington 16	161	F	37	45	53	65	70	73	101	144
		C	55	62	68	82	85	94	140	159
		No. Whs.	1	1	1	1	1	1	1	1
Huntsville 18	143	F	26	40	64	91	106	112	137	143
		C	61	88	106	126	132	136	142	143
		No. Whs.	1	1	1	1	1	1	1	1
Indianapolis 47	780	F	30	55	94	260	266	358	598	724
		C	71	136	281	472	521	566	724	773
		No. Whs.	1	1	1	1	1	1	1	1
Jackson, MS 14	191	F	45	59	81	120	136	146	183	191
		C	85	114	139	165	175	180	191	191
		No. Whs.	1	1	1	1	1	1	1	1
Jacksonville, FL 50	547	F	37	79	111	186	232	266	463	534
		C	91	187	267	351	398	434	527	547
		No. Whs.	1	1	1	1	1	1	1	1

Table B-1. continued.

City Name	POP	F/C	50	100	200	500	750	1000	5000	20000
Johnstown	90	F	29	40	57	74	80	83	90	90
13		C	57	69	79	87	89	89	90	90
		No. Whs.	1	1	1	1	1	1	1	1
Joliet	166	F	51	73	98	127	142	150	165	166
14		C	105	128	142	158	161	163	166	166
		No. Whs.	1	1	1	1	1	1	1	1
Kailua	94	F	28	37	46	74	80	86	94	94
9		C	50	63	80	90	91	94	94	94
		No. Whs.	1	1	1	1	1	1	1	1
Kalamazoo	134	F	42	56	75	103	110	117	131	134
12		C	80	100	109	125	129	130	134	134
		No. Whs.	1	1	1	1	1	1	1	1
Kansas City	1027	F	59	92	121	255	307	352	688	912
73		C	138	197	321	506	592	670	908	1005
		No. Whs.	1	1	1	1	1	1	1	1
Kenosha	83	F	61	70	77	81	83	83	83	83
2		C	76	80	81	83	83	83	83	83
		No. Whs.	1	1	1	1	1	1	1	1

City											
Killeen 4	93	F	52	64	75	86	89	91	93	93	
		C	77	85	89	91	93	93	93	93	
		No. Whs.	1	1	1	1	1	1	1	1	
Knoxville 23	209	F	28	54	77	119	140	149	198	208	
		C	78	114	147	175	188	191	208	209	
		No. Whs.	1	1	1	1	1	1	1	1	
Lafayette, LA 11	102	F	34	50	69	89	93	98	102	102	
		C	72	84	93	101	101	102	102	102	
		No. Whs.	1	1	1	1	1	1	1	1	
Lake Charles 7	96	F	23	43	56	73	80	86	95	96	
		C	54	71	81	90	92	93	96	96	
		No. Whs.	1	1	1	1	1	1	1	1	
Lakeland 8	84	F	29	42	57	73	78	81	84	84	
		C	56	69	77	83	83	84	84	84	
		No. Whs.	1	1	1	1	1	1	1	1	
Lancaster, PA 9	110	F	58	70	81	96	102	103	110	110	
		C	84	91	101	108	109	109	110	110	
		No. Whs.	1	1	1	1	1	1	1	1	
Lansing 15	245	F	44	59	94	143	169	184	237	245	
		C	97	117	178	211	222	228	245	245	
		No. Whs.	1	1	1	1	1	1	1	1	

Table B-1. continued.

City Name	POP	F/C	50	100	200	500	750	1000	5000	20000
Las Vegas	292	F	33	59	102	162	187	205	280	292
23		C	94	147	202	247	262	270	291	292
		No. Whs.	1	1	1	1	1	1	1	1
Lawrence, MA	117	F	51	70	88	105	110	113	117	117
9		C	89	101	110	116	116	117	117	117
		No. Whs.	1	1	1	1	1	1	1	1
Lawton	93	F	32	49	61	77	82	86	93	93
7		C	64	75	82	90	90	92	93	93
		No. Whs.	1	1	1	1	1	1	1	1
Lexington	178	F	54	78	102	138	152	158	178	178
13		C	104	127	154	168	173	176	178	178
		No. Whs.	1	1	1	1	1	1	1	1
Lincoln	168	F	35	81	110	140	151	156	168	168
7		C	101	136	150	162	165	166	168	168
		No. Whs.	1	1	1	1	1	1	1	1
Little Rock	246	F	30	41	68	116	140	155	224	245
21		C	72	112	149	193	205	216	243	246
		No. Whs.	1	1	1	1	1	1	1	1

Los Angeles 450	F	90	121	155	369	671	816	2033	3828
	C	231	375	815	1149	1793	2010	4205	6275
8664	No. Whs.	1	1	1	1	1	1	1	1
Louisville 60	F	70	89	134	229	282	323	561	679
	C	144	200	301	443	499	542	674	712
717	No. Whs.	1	1	1	1	1	1	1	1
Lubbock 7	F	22	73	107	131	142	146	162	163
	C	72	123	143	153	157	161	163	163
163	No. Whs.	1	1	1	1	1	1	1	1
Macon 8	F	35	40	73	93	102	107	124	125
	C	74	83	104	115	120	121	125	125
125	No. Whs.	1	1	1	1	1	1	1	1
Madison 19	F	39	49	73	115	133	147	200	209
	C	85	111	137	175	187	192	209	209
209	No. Whs.	1	1	1	1	1	1	1	1
Manchester 4	F	42	67	79	90	95	95	99	99
	C	75	89	95	99	99	99	99	99
99	No. Whs.	1	1	1	1	1	1	1	1
Memphis 34	F	35	130	104	293	339	372	575	672
	C	146	284	287	479	521	555	664	695
698	No. Whs.	1	1	1	1	1	1	1	1

Table B–1. continued.

City Name	POP	F/C	50	100	200	500	750	1000	5000	20000
Miami	2320	F	75	121	201	307	366	469	944	1420
111		C	225	321	444	725	762	965	1472	1878
		No. Whs.	1	1	1	1	1	1	1	1
Milwaukee	1137	F	76	198	234	299	462	521	885	1056
48		C	233	402	504	669	755	849	1050	1120
		No. Whs.	1	1	1	1	1	1	1	1
Minneapolis	1577	F	49	67	88	315	299	443	940	1321
67		C	133	216	369	647	739	835	1331	1504
		No. Whs.	1	1	1	1	1	1	1	1
Mobile	276	F	43	56	85	133	160	179	252	271
20		C	85	104	157	211	230	240	270	276
		No. Whs.	1	1	1	1	1	1	1	1
Modesto	128	F	50	62	77	103	110	117	127	128
9		C	80	96	112	121	125	126	128	128
		No. Whs.	1	1	1	1	1	1	1	1
Monroe, LA	107	F	22	40	56	81	90	93	107	107
10		C	59	76	89	100	103	106	107	107
		No. Whs.	1	1	1	1	1	1	1	1

City										
Montgomery	158	F	32	65	96	126	138	143	158	158
8		C	84	119	135	149	154	155	158	158
		No. Whs.	1	1	1	1	1	1	1	1
Muncie	87	F	41	57	67	79	83	84	87	87
5		C	68	76	81	87	87	87	87	87
		No. Whs.	1	1	1	1	1	1	1	1
Muskegon	101	F	32	45	60	81	88	93	101	101
12		C	64	79	90	96	99	101	101	101
		No. Whs.	1	1	1	1	1	1	1	1
Nashville	398	F	43	69	93	147	181	208	332	385
44		C	108	146	197	265	291	315	383	397
		No. Whs.	1	1	1	1	1	1	1	1
New Bedford	136	F	43	63	84	116	120	128	136	136
14		C	86	104	121	131	134	136	136	136
		No. Whs.	1	1	1	1	1	1	1	1
New Orleans	1015	F	83	109	170	359	443	503	822	971
53		C	227	327	483	678	750	795	963	1009
		No. Whs.	1	1	1	1	1	1	1	1
New York	16323	F	322	518	746	1208	1454	1667	4524	7698
714		C	999	1425	2044	3265	3881	4505	8750	11572
		No. Whs.	1	1	1	1	1	1	1	1

Table B-1. continued.

City Name	POP	F/C	50	100	200	500	750	1000	5000	20000
Newburgh	81	F	33	40	49	65	70	72	80	81
9		C	52	59	69	76	79	80	81	81
		No. Whs.	1	1	1	1	1	1	1	1
Newport News	267	F	42	54	74	122	147	162	225	250
32		C	78	102	143	194	209	217	253	263
		No. Whs.	1	1	1	1	1	1	1	1
Niagara Falls	110	F	44	53	62	82	90	95	109	110
12		C	67	76	87	102	105	106	110	110
		No. Whs.	1	1	1	1	1	1	1	1
Norfolk	688	F	48	58	97	180	236	273	497	627
64		C	131	162	266	376	451	485	625	674
		No. Whs.	1	1	1	1	1	1	1	1
Odessa	87	F	30	54	70	81	85	86	87	87
4		C	62	79	83	87	87	87	87	87
		No. Whs.	1	1	1	1	1	1	1	1
Ogden	96	F	24	55	65	82	88	89	96	96
6		C	58	79	85	93	95	96	96	96
		No. Whs.	1	1	1	1	1	1	1	1

City			1	2	3	4	5	6	7	8
Oklahoma City 46	499	F	37	60	83	138	184	221	399	479
		C	88	131	190	306	354	378	472	498
		No. Whs.	1	1	1	1	1	1	1	1
Omaha 34	524	F	33	46	140	224	269	295	454	510
		C	90	175	291	363	406	430	508	524
		No. Whs.	1	1	1	1	1	1	1	1
Orlando 43	407	F	28	42	85	143	181	208	342	396
		C	77	131	206	280	306	330	394	406
		No. Whs.	1	1	1	1	1	1	1	1
Oxnard 20	202	F	45	58	78	99	113	121	186	201
		C	76	92	114	141	154	165	200	202
		No. Whs.	1	1	1	1	1	1	1	1
Pensacola 17	182	F	41	58	82	115	131	139	175	182
		C	90	108	131	158	163	171	182	182
		No. Whs.	1	1	1	1	1	1	1	1
Peoria 20	208	F	41	61	89	128	143	155	200	208
		C	93	118	149	175	187	190	207	208
		No. Whs.	1	1	1	1	1	1	1	1
Petersburg 14	104	F	28	39	49	64	71	74	98	104
		C	53	63	74	86	90	92	103	104
		No. Whs.	1	1	1	1	1	1	1	1

Table B-1. continued.

City Name	POP	F/C	50	100	200	500	750	1000	5000	20000
Philadelphia	4557	F	98	159	279	406	533	641	1899	2906
		C	304	450	790	1381	1669	1753	3070	3786
204		No. Whs.	1	1	1	1	1	1	1	1
Phoenix	996	F	36	54	88	276	318	380	670	884
		C	123	164	276	531	584	650	876	967
46		No. Whs.	1	1	1	1	1	1	1	1
Pittsburgh	1716	F	76	161	212	320	385	467	981	1327
		C	234	344	476	727	854	940	1349	1559
151		No. Whs.	1	1	1	1	1	1	1	1
Portland, ME	115	F	38	51	65	88	98	102	114	115
		C	70	83	94	107	112	113	115	115
12		No. Whs.	1	1	1	1	1	1	1	1
Portland, OR	782	F	25	142	113	264	292	388	619	744
		C	133	307	326	477	547	594	736	777
25		No. Whs.	1	1	1	1	1	1	1	1
Providence	892	F	52	69	167	246	290	328	532	704
		C	93	108	316	433	488	519	719	835
69		No. Whs.	1	1	1	1	1	1	1	1

City	No.	Code									
Provo	8	103	F	51	57	69	83	90	94	103	103
			C	72	82	88	98	101	101	103	103
			No. Whs.	1	1	1	1	1	1	1	1
Pueblo	8	109	F	36	46	65	88	97	101	109	109
			C	67	84	98	105	108	109	109	109
			No. Whs.	1	1	1	1	1	1	1	1
Racine	5	121	F	52	65	87	107	111	116	121	121
			C	80	101	111	117	121	121	121	121
			No. Whs.	1	1	1	1	1	1	1	1
Raleigh	17	183	F	39	60	78	110	127	137	175	183
			C	86	109	131	156	166	171	181	183
			No. Whs.	1	1	1	1	1	1	1	1
Reading	22	178	F	61	83	104	133	147	151	177	178
			C	107	127	147	164	167	174	178	178
			No. Whs.	1	1	1	1	1	1	1	1
Reno	9	123	F	28	51	68	95	105	111	123	123
			C	64	91	106	116	119	121	123	123
			No. Whs.	1	1	1	1	1	1	1	1
Richmond, VA	40	477	F	29	78	111	191	231	258	411	467
			C	107	188	228	340	371	393	461	477
			No. Whs.	1	1	1	1	1	1	1	1

Table B-1. continued.

City Name	POP	F/C	50	100	200	500	750	1000	5000	20000
Riverside	541	F	29	65	92	134	159	175	306	445
49		C	49	128	161	227	259	280	435	512
		No. Whs.	1	1	1	1	1	1	1	1
Roanoke	168	F	20	42	62	96	114	124	162	168
18		C	56	89	118	142	151	156	168	168
		No. Whs.	1	1	1	1	1	1	1	1
Rochester, NY	599	F	123	144	212	300	340	366	521	587
48		C	243	292	361	450	482	506	583	599
		No. Whs.	1	1	1	1	1	1	1	1
Rockford	198	F	26	68	108	146	158	169	195	198
11		C	79	134	160	181	188	191	198	198
		No. Whs.	1	1	1	1	1	1	1	1
Sacramento	745	F	50	80	106	182	225	269	526	677
38		C	133	187	268	384	457	497	674	732
		No. Whs.	1	1	1	1	1	1	1	1
Saginaw	147	F	39	56	86	120	132	136	147	147
8		C	78	114	129	143	145	145	147	147
		No. Whs.	1	1	1	1	1	1	1	1

City											
Saint Louis 131	1800	F	57	159	205	359	463	543	1083	1492
		C	214	386	524	839	973	1065	1508	1712
		No. Whs.	1	1	1	1	1	1	1	1
Saint Petersburg 42	651	F	25	63	90	227	257	278	445	592
		C	94	134	178	351	390	410	585	638
		No. Whs.	1	1	1	1	1	1	1	1
Salem 9	113	F	33	45	64	88	97	101	113	113
		C	69	86	98	108	110	110	113	113
		No. Whs.	1	1	1	1	1	1	1	1
Salt Lake City 28	483	F	34	73	103	188	230	264	424	476
		C	120	175	241	337	369	399	471	483
		No. Whs.	1	1	1	1	1	1	1	1
San Antonio 32	865	F	41	54	106	359	421	464	709	836
		C	76	105	340	602	656	691	825	862
		No. Whs.	1	1	1	1	1	1	1	1
San Diego 65	1347	F	66	92	127	271	339	399	871	1192
		C	132	218	302	677	789	850	1191	1311
		No. Whs.	1	1	1	1	1	1	1	1
San Francisco 147	3613	F	96	119	183	511	580	624	895	1538
		C	176	235	538	779	861	930	1490	2276
		No. Whs.	1	1	1	1	1	1	1	1

Table B-1. continued.

City Name	POP	F/C	50	100	200	500	750	1000	5000	20000
San Rafael	207	F	28	43	59	90	105	115	168	196
27		C	65	90	115	145	154	166	197	206
		No. Whs.	1	1	1	1	1	1	1	1
Santa Barbara	151	F	32	54	69	86	95	103	139	150
16		C	65	83	94	117	126	129	149	151
		No. Whs.	1	1	1	1	1	1	1	1
Santa Cruz	98	F	30	41	53	71	77	81	96	98
8		C	53	61	77	87	90	93	98	98
		No. Whs.	1	1	1	1	1	1	1	1
Santa Rosa	84	F	40	51	62	76	79	81	84	84
6		C	63	72	78	83	84	84	84	84
		No. Whs.	1	1	1	1	1	1	1	1
Sarasota	224	F	32	44	61	86	94	102	160	208
22		C	67	84	100	125	138	141	206	222
		No. Whs.	1	1	1	1	1	1	1	1
Savannah	152	F	46	76	90	111	123	129	149	152
12		C	91	112	125	139	143	145	152	152
		No. Whs.	1	1	1	1	1	1	1	1

City		1	2	3	4	5	6	7	8
Scranton 374	F	47	65	95	123	137	142	201	299
46	C	97	114	136	166	182	194	282	358
	No. Whs.	1	1	1	1	1	1	1	1
Seaside 135	F	31	36	47	73	86	95	129	135
13	C	53	67	86	112	120	123	134	135
	No. Whs.	1	1	1	1	1	1	1	1
Seattle 1213	F	36	90	124	239	293	332	622	908
88	C	154	204	321	460	547	604	931	1102
	No. Whs.	1	1	1	1	1	1	1	1
Shreveport 226	F	21	73	114	149	168	177	219	226
13	C	82	141	172	197	208	213	226	226
	No. Whs.	1	1	1	1	1	1	1	1
Sioux City 90	F	33	40	54	74	81	83	90	90
8	C	58	66	80	88	88	89	90	90
	No. Whs.	1	1	1	1	1	1	1	1
South Bend 282	F	40	54	79	127	145	157	207	255
23	C	78	114	153	181	193	201	246	274
	No. Whs.	1	1	1	1	1	1	1	1
Spokane 254	F	28	48	92	137	157	170	230	250
12	C	87	127	168	199	212	222	249	254
	No. Whs.	1	1	1	1	1	1	1	1

Table B-1. continued.

City Name	POP	F/C	50	100	200	500	750	1000	5000	20000
Springfield, IL	131	F	48	69	88	113	120	121	131	131
10		C	91	107	119	129	131	131	131	131
		No. Whs.	1	1	1	1	1	1	1	1
Springfield, MA	415	F	62	80	108	173	207	233	355	403
42		C	126	171	223	299	322	340	400	414
		No. Whs.	1	1	1	1	1	1	1	1
Springfield, MO	127	F	37	58	79	105	113	119	127	127
9		C	85	100	112	123	125	127	127	127
		No. Whs.	1	1	1	1	1	1	1	1
Springfield, OH	95	F	39	54	70	83	87	89	94	95
7		C	66	80	88	93	93	94	95	95
		No. Whs.	1	1	1	1	1	1	1	1
Stockton	164	F	44	71	88	121	134	141	163	164
9		C	93	118	134	151	158	159	164	164
		No. Whs.	1	1	1	1	1	1	1	1
Syracuse	355	F	53	101	142	199	227	246	327	351
35		C	136	194	239	386	306	314	351	355
		No. Whs.	1	1	1	1	1	1	1	1

City											
Tacoma	33	299	F	42	52	70	122	145	166	257	292
			C	83	107	132	205	221	242	290	299
			No. Whs.	1	1	1	1	1	1	1	1
Tallahassee	8	95	F	45	58	72	86	91	93	95	95
			C	73	82	90	94	95	95	95	95
			No. Whs.	1	1	1	1	1	1	1	1
Tampa	18	396	F	42	55	80	178	207	233	346	390
			C	76	131	194	294	318	331	385	395
			No. Whs.	1	1	1	1	1	1	1	1
Toledo	44	470	F	64	94	139	223	260	295	426	466
			C	159	222	287	361	388	409	461	470
			No. Whs.	1	1	1	1	1	1	1	1
Topeka	5	118	F	19	54	81	100	106	110	118	118
			C	55	94	106	113	116	118	118	118
			No. Whs.	1	1	1	1	1	1	1	1
Tucson	9	379	F	51	75	96	181	215	241	346	376
			C	106	145	202	285	320	333	371	379
			No. Whs.	1	1	1	1	1	1	1	1
Tulsa	27	369	F	31	69	98	174	205	228	330	363
			C	92	170	209	277	307	315	361	369
			No. Whs.	1	1	1	1	1	1	1	1

Table B-1. continued.

City Name	POP	F/C	50	100	200	500	750	1000	5000	20000
Tuscaloosa	88	F	34	42	54	71	78	80	88	88
10		C	59	69	74	85	86	87	88	88
		No. Whs.	1	1	1	1	1	1	1	1
Utica	130	F	49	64	81	107	115	120	130	130
13		C	87	98	112	125	128	129	130	130
		No. Whs.	1	1	1	1	1	1	1	1
Vallejo	85	F	38	50	62	74	80	82	85	85
6		C	63	71	78	83	84	85	85	85
		No. Whs.	1	1	1	1	1	1	1	1
Vancouver	85	F	26	39	53	69	75	79	85	85
5		C	51	61	75	82	83	84	85	85
		No. Whs.	1	1	1	1	1	1	1	1
Waco	113	F	26	45	64	89	95	102	113	113
10		C	65	84	94	108	110	111	113	113
		No. Whs.	1	1	1	1	1	1	1	1
Washington, D.C.	2554	F	112	150	226	411	526	624	1441	2114
208		C	307	461	677	1080	1280	1419	2115	2447
		No. Whs.	1	1	1	1	1	1	1	1

Waterbury 12	138	F	57	70	87	106	114	119	136	138
		C	90	102	116	128	130	132	138	138
		No. Whs.	1	1	1	1	1	1	1	1
Waterloo 12	107	F	31	42	55	74	80	86	104	107
		C	59	69	82	93	98	103	107	107
		No. Whs.	1	1	1	1	1	1	1	1
West Palm Beach 33	358	F	34	50	59	103	123	133	244	307
		C	64	89	113	186	210	224	308	341
		No. Whs.	1	1	1	1	1	1	1	1
Wheeling 18	114	F	20	31	44	62	69	71	102	112
		C	48	59	70	87	92	93	112	114
		No. Whs.	1	1	1	1	1	1	1	1
Wichita 15	290	F	32	50	109	185	207	219	273	289
		C	100	136	201	250	257	263	288	290
		No. Whs.	1	1	1	1	1	1	1	1
Wichita Falls 12	98	F	18	35	45	64	72	77	96	98
		C	44	62	73	86	90	94	98	98
		No. Whs.	1	1	1	1	1	1	1	1
Winston–Salem 19	152	F	34	48	69	100	114	124	151	152
		C	79	100	119	138	144	147	152	152
		No. Whs.	1	1	1	1	1	1	1	1

Table B-1. continued.

City Name	POP	F/C	50	100	200	500	750	1000	5000	20000
Worcester	231	F	62	93	117	159	174	190	225	231
20		C	125	154	181	203	214	220	231	231
		No. Whs.	1	1	1	1	1	1	1	1
York	112	F	49	63	78	95	99	103	111	112
11		C	81	90	101	107	108	109	112	112
		No. Whs.	1	1	1	1	1	1	1	1
Youngstown	387	F	30	63	91	149	178	196	285	352
37		C	63	151	188	239	263	270	341	380
		No. Whs.	1	1	1	1	1	1	1	1

Table B-2. U.S. Urban Fatalities as a Function of the Number of Attacking Weapons and Warhead Yield (*results expressed as percentage of U.S. urban population of 132 million*).

Number of Weapons (0.2 NM CEP, .85 Reliability)	Warhead Yield (Kilotons)					
	50	100	200	500	750	1,000
100	6	8	11	19	23	27
200	9	13	18	29	35	40
300	12	17	24	38	45	50
400	15	21	29	45	52	58
500	17	24	34	51	59	64
1,000	28	39	52	72	79	84
1,500	37	50	65	84	90	94
2,000	44	59	75	92	96	98
2,500	51	67	82	96	99	100
3,000	57	73	87	98	100	
3,500	63	78	91	100		
4,000	67	83	94			

INDEX

413

ABOUT THE AUTHOR

Arthur M. Katz received a Ph.D. in chemistry from the University of Rochester and an M.S. in meteorology from MIT. He has spent the last ten years involved with a broad range of issues related to science, technology, and public policy, including urban transportation, the environment, and energy. During the past five years, he has concentrated on nuclear energy policy and energy-related environmental problems. Dr. Katz has authored or co-authored numerous papers and articles on science and public policy, most recently a report entitled "Economic and Social Consequences of Nuclear Attacks on the U.S." for the Joint Committee on Defense Production of the U.S. Congress.